THE ECONOMIST
BOOK OF OBITUARIES

The Economist

BOOK OF OBITUARIES

Keith Colquhoun and Ann Wroe

Bloomberg Press
New York

THE ECONOMIST IN ASSOCIATION WITH PROFILE BOOKS LTD

Published in the United States and Canada by Bloomberg Press
Published in the U.K. by Profile Books Ltd, 2008
Copyright © The Economist Newspaper Ltd, 2008

Printed in Canada
1 3 5 7 9 10 8 6 4 2
Library of Congress Cataloging-in-Publication Data on file

ISBN 978-1-57660-326-0

Contents

Introduction

F OR MORE than 150 years after its founding in 1843, *The Economist* had no Obituary page. Why this was so can only be a matter of conjecture. Perhaps, in a paper proudly founded on anonymity and chary of all cults of personality, it seemed improper to give so much attention to individuals. Perhaps, in a paper that boldly promoted progress, there was no natural place for valedictories. When I joined the paper (always "the paper") in 1976, the cult of optimism was so rampant that I was discouraged from travelling anywhere that might produce downbeat stories. The grave, one imagines, is the *ne plus ultra* of that genre.

Yet not necessarily. And besides, by the late 1980s and early 1990s, the British way with obituaries was becoming lively, literary and irreverent. The rivalries of Hugh Montgomery-Massingberd and James Fergusson, the clever and relatively young obituary editors of the *Daily Telegraph* and the *Independent* respectively, had turned their obituary sections into some of the best read and most discussed pages of their respective newspapers. And it was from the *Independent* that Robert Cottrell came to *The Economist* in 1993.

Robert – one of our most stylish writers, and a man addicted to large dogs and satin waistcoats – suggested to *The Economist*'s then editor, Bill Emmott, that a single obituary each week could add zest to the paper's back pages, and provide a way of looking at issues and achievements outside the usual scope of current events. He helped his case by commissioning a piece on the more striking and funny newspaper obituaries of recent years from Martin Weyer, a *Telegraph* contributor, for the Christmas issue in 1994. Delighted by Mr Weyer's piece, and persuaded that obituaries would "add a sense of history and humanity to a paper often rather lacking in both", Bill gave Robert the job of launching the new page.

Once it was launched, however, no one seemed particularly keen to take on the full-time job of being the paper's undertaker – until Bill, by happy chance, asked Robert's near-neighbour on the 13th floor, Keith Colquhoun. Keith was a writer of novels as well as a journalist; and his pen, apparently smooth as silk but in fact as sharp as a stiletto, took command of the page in 1995 and went on for eight years. I succeeded him – a hard act to follow – in November 2003.

When I took over, Keith and I had lunch in the local Italian dive. He had kept an enormous list of his subjects, collated by geography and gender, and told me that it was important to keep down the number of Americans (who would otherwise take over), to give a fair whack to the Asians, and to try my damnedest to get more women in. I've found all these precepts good advice, but hard to keep. Not many women feature in this book: a sobering reflection of the struggle they have had, even in the 20th century, to lead lives half as interesting as men's. And there are an awful lot of Americans; but when a country is Top Nation, that becomes rather hard to avoid.

A ration of one candidate a week certainly concentrates the mind: the more so because the Obituaries Editor usually has no more than two days to research and write the piece. Speed reading becomes essential and the London Library, conveniently round the corner, a godsend. Google, of course, helps too; but there is no substitute, I still find, for books. They allow the total immersion in a character that is necessary.

The Economist's stock of obituaries (sometimes irreverently called the "morgue") is pitifully small. Some newspapers, I'm told, have hundreds of obituaries ready. There are ten obituaries in ours as I write, and I have never yet been able to pluck one out and use it. It is an unwritten law that the people in the morgue will never die. They achieve a kind of eternal life, getting wirier and stronger by the day.

The candidates' criteria have, I think, stayed unchanged since the page was started. They must have led interesting and thought-provoking lives. Whether they have led good lives, in the usual meaning of "good", couldn't matter less. We are not in the business of eulogies, or even of appreciations. The bad, the immoral, or the flighty sometimes make the best copy. I took a good deal of flak for obituarising Anna Nicole Smith; but hers was a wonderful and poignant story of a doomed search for celebrity. We've obituarised monopolists and petty tyrants as well as modern-day saints. Keith always had a soft spot for the minor players, even if – perhaps especially if – a major player had died in the same week; he taught me that there is a story worth hearing in almost every life.

What makes an *Economist* obituary? No rules are laid down except the length, 132 lines or around 1,000 words, and the shape of the illustration (which, most perversely, in recent years has been not portrait, but landscape). The rest is left to the writer, a glorious freedom which the obituaries editor traditionally hogs almost entirely to himself. Colleagues often try to muscle in (and sometimes succeed, always to good effect); families of the dead, or their friends, often lobby us. But the editor refuses almost all outside petitions, because he (or she) wants no one interfering with the sheer joy of the job.

Perhaps joy and death seem strange bedfellows. Not to me. Speaking now purely for myself, I see my obituaries as progress reports on a life that continues, somehow, elsewhere. My purpose is to try to distil the essence of that life as it passes, and to try to describe it as far as possible from the point of view of the subject. For what has gone away from the world, for better or worse, is that particular perspective and that particular voice.

When we were first discussing this book, Keith said that a good title for it might be "A Sparrow's Flight". The allusion, of course, is to Bede's metaphor of human life as a sparrow flying through a banqueting hall, from darkness and out again to darkness, with one brightly lit moment in between. Of course, it is also possible that the banqueting hall is murkier than the before and after. But whichever is true, that moment of passage – that flickering of wings amid the hubbub of the Earth – is what we have to catch.

Ann Wroe
July 2008

THE OBITUARIES

Red Adair

Paul Neal ("Red") Adair, firefighter, died on August 7th 2004, aged 89

A S HE flew into Kuwait in March 1991, Red Adair could see nothing. The sky was filled with black smoke to a height of 15,000 feet, and it was impossible to tell what was north, south, east or west. The smoke came from burning oilfields, sabotaged by Saddam Hussein as his troops retreated. Each day, 5m barrels, worth $150m, were going up in flames.

From the crater that was Kuwait City's airport, Mr Adair surveyed the scene. The horizon was filled with one continuous fire. At the core of the wells the temperature was 3,000°F, or about the heat needed to melt steel. On the ground, 50 feet away, it was still close to 1,000°. The fires were often not shooting up straight from the wellhead, but spewing out in all directions. Mr Adair and his men donned their overalls, discarded their plastic hats in favour of aluminium, and set about doing their job. "Red", by the way, was then 75.

In retrospect, Mr Adair – never wanting in confidence or cockiness where fires were concerned – thought Kuwait had been easy. "We put all the fires out with water, just went from one to the next." In fact, he reversed the flow in the oil pipes, pumping the nearest sea ("the Adriatic" as he blithely supposed) into the oilfields and saturating the ground with water before capping the wells. His 76th birthday found him joyfully moving the giant valves into position with a crane. In the end, he put out in nine months a conflagration that was expected to burn uncontrollably for three to five years.

The hard part for Mr Adair was getting the equipment he wanted, and at once, out of the relevant governments. Only a personal chat with President Bush senior at the White House got him his bulldozers, piping and cement in a time he thought reasonable, cutting through the red tape. The Kuwaiti government played up over his demand for an aircraft full of whiskey ("Do they want their fires out, or not?"), and he never got the 4,000 pigs he had requested to detonate the mines which Saddam was supposed to have strewn across the oilfields.

If Kuwait was an easy sort of fire, by his standards, what was a tricky one? Perhaps the first with which he seized the world's attention, in 1962. The "Devil's Cigarette Lighter" had been burning for six months in the desert sands of Algeria, fuelled by a daily diet of 550m cubic feet of gas; the flames were seen by John Glenn from space as he orbited the Earth. Mr Adair used underground water to soak the area for miles around and then laid explosives, with which he blew out the fire. This technique, starving fires of oxygen and then instantly capping the well with mud and cement, remained his favourite.

More hazardous still were fires out on oil platforms, such as the Bravo blowout in the North Sea in 1977 and the Piper Alpha disaster, off Aberdeen, in 1988, where the capping of the well had to be done in the face of mountainous seas. For these jobs, Mr Adair used support-and-rescue ships and semi-submersible fire-boats all of his own design. At Piper Alpha, where 167 men had died, huge

Appropriately enough, he was called "Red" because of his flaming hair. Exposed early on to the roar of the forge and the flying sparks from the anvil, he had no fear of fire. When others fled, he would walk straight up to the blaze. He saw fires as individual creatures; none could be treated like another. All the same, "I haven't met one yet you can't lick in around six weeks."

pieces of debris had to be moved from the wellhead by cranes tossing like flotsam amid the wind and the waves.

Mr Adair was proud of his equipment and, to prove it, made sure most of it was red. Red cranes, red overalls, red bulldozers and red boots announced to the world that his team had been called to the scene. From the first days of the founding of his firefighting company, in 1959, his men tooled round the dry scrub of the Texas oilfields in red Lincolns, easy to spot when needed. Off the job, Mr Adair sported red long-johns and drove a red Bentley. Short and stocky he might be, but he was full to the brim with Texas swagger. He was never more thrilled than when John Wayne played him in "Hellfighters" and he, Red Adair, was called in to give the Duke technical advice.

The blacksmith's boy

He was born in Houston in 1915, one of eight children in a blacksmith's family.

Yet only chance got him into his dangerous trade. After dropping out of school, he worked on the railroad, in a drug store and as an itinerant labourer. One day in 1938 he was taking equipment to an oilfield near Alice, Texas, when a well blew. The crew fled; the firefighters, though trained in oilfield work, could not control the blaze. "Boy, do you want to work and make some money?" he was asked.

In more than 50 years of firefighting, he dealt with almost 3,000 fires. Remarkably, he was never much hurt. A crane crushed him once, and he suffered a few days of smoke-blindness. Exploding gas threw him in the air, but he seemed to bounce. In his later years he was deaf, not surprisingly, for much of his life had been spent amid the roar of flames or explosions. He perfected the art of snoozing while conflagrations raged around him.

Although he anticipated Heaven, he rather hoped for a sighting of Hell. ∎

Alex the African Grey

Science's best known parrot died on September 6th 2007, aged 31

THE LAST time Irene Pepperberg saw Alex she said goodnight as usual. "You be good," said Alex. "I love you." "I love you, too." "You'll be in tomorrow?" "Yes, I'll be in tomorrow." But Alex (his name supposedly an acronym of Avian Learning Experiment) died in his cage that night, bringing to an end a life spent learning complex tasks that, it had been originally thought, only primates could master.

In science as in most fields of endeavour, it is important to have the right tool for the job. Early studies of linguistic ability in apes concluded it was virtually non-existent. But researchers had made the elementary error of trying to teach their anthropoid subjects to speak. Chimpanzee vocal cords are simply not up to this – and it was not until someone had the idea of teaching chimps sign language that any progress was made.

Even then, the researchers remained human-centric. Their assumption was that chimps might be able to understand and use human sign language because they are humanity's nearest living relatives. It took a brilliant insight to turn this human-centricity on its head and look at the capabilities of a species only distantly related to humanity, but which can, nevertheless, speak the words people speak: a parrot.

The insight in question came to Dr Pepperberg, then a 28-year-old theoretical chemist, in 1977. To follow it up, she bought a one-year-old African Grey parrot at random from a pet shop. Thus began one of the best-known double acts in the field of animal-behaviour science.

Dr Pepperberg and Alex last shared a common ancestor more than 300m years ago. But Alex, unlike any chimpanzee (with whom Dr Pepperberg's most recent common ancestor lived a mere 4m years ago), learned to speak words easily. The question was, was Alex merely parroting Dr Pepperberg? Or would that pejorative term have to be redefined? Do parrots actually understand what they are saying?

Bird brained

Dr Pepperberg's reason for suspecting that they might – and thus her second reason for picking a parrot – was that in the mid-1970s evolutionary explanations for behaviour were coming back into vogue. A British researcher called Nicholas Humphrey had proposed that intelligence evolves in response to the social environment rather than the natural one. The more complex the society an animal lives in, the more wits it needs to prosper.

The reason why primates are intelligent, according to Dr Humphrey, is that they generally live in groups. And, just as group living promotes intelligence, so intelligence allows larger groups to function, providing a spur for the evolution of yet more intelligence. If Dr Humphrey is right, only social animals can be intelligent – and so far he has been borne out.

Flocks of, say, starlings or herds of wildebeest do not count as real societies. They are just protective agglomerations in which individuals do not have complex social relations with each other. But parrots such as Alex live in societies in the wild, in the way that monkeys and apes do, and thus Dr Pepperberg reasoned, Alex might have evolved advanced cognitive abilities. Also like primates, parrots live long enough to make the time-consuming process of learning worthwhile. Combined with his ability to speak (or at least "vocalise") words, Alex looked a promising experimental subject.

And so it proved. Using a training technique now employed on children with learning difficulties, in which two adults handle and discuss an object, sometimes making deliberate mistakes, Dr Pepperberg and her collaborators at the University of Arizona began teaching Alex how to describe things, how to make his desires known and even how to ask questions.

By the end, said Dr Pepperberg, Alex had the intelligence of a five-year-old child and had not reached his full potential. He had a vocabulary of 150 words. He knew the names of 50 objects and could, in addition, describe their colours, shapes and the materials they were made from. He could answer questions about objects' properties, even when he had not seen that particular combination of properties before. He could ask for things – and would reject a proffered item and ask again if it was not what he wanted. He understood, and could discuss, the concepts of "bigger", "smaller", "same" and "different". And he could count up to six, including the number zero (and was grappling with the concept of "seven" when he died). He even knew when and how to apologise if he annoyed Dr Pepperberg or her collaborators.

And the fact that there were a lot of collaborators, even strangers, involved in the project was crucial. Researchers in this area live in perpetual fear of the "Clever Hans" effect. This is named after a horse that seemed to count, but was actually reacting to unconscious cues from his trainer. Alex would talk to and perform for anyone, not just Dr Pepperberg.

There are still a few researchers who think Alex's skills were the result of rote learning rather than abstract thought. Alex, though, convinced most in the field that birds as well as mammals can evolve complex and sophisticated cognition, and communicate the results to others. A shame, then, that he is now, in the words of Monty Python, an ex-parrot. ∎

Momofuku Ando

Momofuku Ando, inventor of instant noodles, died on January 5th 2007, aged 96

FOR CENTURIES men and women have turned to the east for the secret of life, health and happiness. But Momofuku Ando taught that there is no need to climb half-naked up a mountain peak, or meditate for hours on a prayer-mat, or knot one's legs round one's neck while intoning "Om" through the higher nasal passages. One should simply

Peel off lid.
Pour boiling water.
Steep for three minutes.
Stir well and serve.

Nothing was easier. Of course, the unenlightened could stumble sometimes, burning their tongues, or jabbing in a fork after only one minute of silent contemplation, which bent the prongs and sprayed the soup over the keyboard. But the patient disciple achieved fulfilment: mouthful upon mouthful of warming, strangely angular noodles, in flavours such as "Hearty Chicken" or "Shrimp Picante".

Most devotees of Cup Noodle did not investigate the mystery further. Giddily grateful as they were to be relieved of cooking, it might have been electrical wire they were eating, or sauteed rubber bands. But some, after many portions, could make an unthinking mantra of the list of ingredients: Wheat Flour, Palm Oil (Tocopherols), Tapioca Starch, Salt, Dehydrated Vegetables (Cabbage, Green Onion, Carrot), Disodium Guanylate, Disodium Inosinate. And at the highest level one follower succeeded in straightening the noodles out, discovering in his cup eight strands 2mm in diameter and measuring 40cm (16

inches), evidently extruded with perfect uniformity, and cut into perfect lengths.

The cult was global. In 2005, 86 billion servings of instant noodles were eaten around the world. And all this began with a vision, as such things do. One cold night in 1957, walking home from his salt-making factory in Osaka, in Japan, Mr Ando saw white clouds of steam in the street, and a crowd of people gathering. They were waiting for noodles to be cooked to order in vats of boiling water, and were prepared to wait a long time. Why not make it easier? thought Mr Ando. And why not try to do it himself?

His life until then had been a bit of a mess. He had sold dress fabrics, following in the footsteps of the grandparents who had brought him up. He had sold engine-parts, prefabricated houses, magic-lantern projectors, socks. He had presided over a credit association, which had gone bust, and tried to launch a scholarship scheme for poor students, which had landed him in jail for tax evasion. But now the "steadily rising" clouds (or possibly, as in the cartoon on the homepage of his Instant Noodle Museum in Osaka, one fluffy white cloud with a kettle dangling from it) had shown him the Way.

Nights in the shed

The road was long. It took a year, working night and day in a shed in his back garden, to find the secret of bringing noodles back to life. Mr Ando cooked quantities, but had trouble getting the moisture out and keeping any flavouring in. He sprayed them with chicken soup from a watering can, and festooned the shed with them. The secret, picked up from his wife as she cooked vegetable tempura, was to flash-fry the cooked noodles in palm oil. This made them "magic".

In 1958 instant noodles went on the market, yellowish wormy bricks in cellophane bags, and were laughed at by fresh-noodle makers all over Japan. They were just a high-tech craze, costing six times as much as the fresh stuff; they would never catch on. By the end of the first year Mr Ando had sold 13m bags and had attracted a dozen competitors. He never looked back. In 1971 came noodles in heat-proof polystyrene cups, so that the hungry did not even need to get their bowls out of the cupboard. The Japanese voted instant noodles their most important 20th-century invention, Sony Walkmans notwithstanding. Mr Ando's firm, Nissin, became a $3 billion global enterprise.

But it was never just a company, and instant-noodlemaking never just an industry. The three sayings of Mr Ando became a philosophy of life:

> Peace will come when people have food. Eating wisely will enhance beauty and health. The creation of food will serve society.

Mr Ando practised what he preached. He ate *Chikin Ramen*, his original flavour of noodles, almost every day until he died. Though sceptics pointed out that they were loaded with fat, salt and monosodium glutamate, he looked bonny and spry. Seabeds across Asia were littered with plastic noodle cups; but that was not his fault.

His TV advertising, meanwhile, showed what instant noodles were really all about. When the world turned to eating them, barriers fell, children laughed and people loved each other. All liberating revolutions sprang from humanity's desire to gulp down steaming Cup Noodles whenever there was a chance. In 2006 a Japanese astronaut, on board the space shuttle *Discovery*, supped Mr Ando's noodles from a handy vacuum pack. He appeared on the TV ads weightless and smiling, his enlightenment complete. ∎

Brooke Astor and Leona Helmsley

Brooke Astor and Leona Helmsley, grandes dames of New York, died on August 13th and 20th 2007 respectively, aged 105 and 87

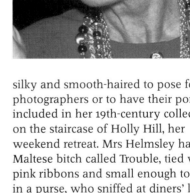

THE CONCEPT of *richesse oblige* has various dimensions. The bottom line is that those who have come into oodles of money should give some of it back; the second-to-bottom line is that they should cut a certain style while doing so. Both Brooke Astor and Leona Helmsley, who died within a few days of each other, gave millions of dollars away. And their similarities ended there.

Mrs Astor was as small, delicate and fine as a Meissen cup, her tailoring exquisite and her jewels unobtrusive. Mrs Helmsley, though not large, favoured loud trouser suits and chunky diamond clips, with her mouth made big and cruel by scarlet lipstick. Mrs Astor set great store by good manners, civility, kind remarks and the careful handling of umbrellas; Mrs Helmsley believed in loud words and elbows. Mrs Astor had dogs as well-behaved as herself,

silky and smooth-haired to pose for photographers or to have their portraits included in her 19th-century collection on the staircase of Holly Hill, her weekend retreat. Mrs Helmsley had a Maltese bitch called Trouble, tied with pink ribbons and small enough to stuff in a purse, who sniffed at diners' legs in her restaurants and nipped their heels until they bled.

The Astor money, more than $120m by the time it was Brooke's to disburse, was old, from New York land and the fur trade. The Helmsley money, $5 billion by the time Leona got her hands on it, was pretty new, from property speculation. Both fortunes came from late third marriages to cunning husbands. But whereas Mrs Astor, aside from writing features for *House & Garden*, merely let the markets increase her pile and relished spending the capital (something, she admitted, that John Jacob Astor would have thought as outrageous as dancing naked in the street), Mrs Helmsley worked like a dragon to build up and expand her husband Harry's hotel empire. As a Manhattan hatter's daughter with several competitive siblings, she was used to graft and struggle. Mrs Astor, a solitary and dreamy child who had come by money almost magically, treated it like fairy dust to the end of her days.

Both, in their wildly different ways, were peremptory. Well into old age, Mrs Astor wore out the staffers of the Astor Foundation with her insistence on seeing every group and project that was asking her for money, and visiting them frequently to check that things were done as required. A run-down section of 130th Street in Harlem, Astor Row, had to have its porches and decorative brackets immaculately restored; a start-up furniture service for the poor had to include tea-cups and saucers. Meanwhile, at Helmsley hotels across Manhattan, underneath giant portraits of the "Queen" herself, quaking bellhops with huge armloads of laundry submitted to the scarlet, pecking fingernails and the icy tiara smile. "I won't stand for skimpy towels; why should you?" cried Mrs Helmsley's adverts in the *New York Times*.

Gloves and paper cups

The arrogance of big money, Mrs Astor wrote once, "is one of the most unappealing of characteristics". Mrs Helmsley, though fun to her friends, was arrogance personified: "Rhymes with rich", was *Newsweek*'s caption for her portrait on its cover. "We don't pay taxes," she was said to have told a housekeeper once; "only the little people pay taxes." Mrs Astor, a gentle soul, was upset when her first father-in-law, a colonel, yelled at his secretaries.

Mrs Helmsley believed staff existed to be barked at, slapped and called fags if appropriate; two of them sued her for firing them because they were gay. On visits to underprivileged areas Mrs Astor, gloved and immaculate because this was what the ordinary person expected of the rich, would happily sip from a paper cup and praise the hot-dog mustard on her paper plate. At the sight of a paper-cup-carrier in any of her reception areas, Mrs Helmsley would get her doormen to throw the offender out.

Vulgar showiness was also seldom seen in the Astor household. True, the glasses, silver and finger bowls bore the Astor initials or the Astor crest, but it was not half as obvious as the "H" on Leona's plastic soap-compacts. Mrs Astor could sport massed sapphires if one-upmanship seemed called for; but she owned only two country houses, not several, and her birthday was never marked, as Leona's once was, by a display of red, white and blue lights on the Helmsley-owned Empire State Building. Vulgarity led to trouble; which was why Leona, accused of "naked greed" by the judge, spent 18 months in Camp Fed in 1992–94 for tax evasion, when it was fairly clear that her real crime was to be both abrasive and rich.

New York gained hugely from both women. Mrs Astor gave to the Metropolitan Museum of Art, Rockefeller University, the Bronx Zoo and, her special favourite, the New York Public Library; Mrs Helmsley gave to New York-Presbyterian Hospital, the Weill Cornell Medical College and, her spell in prison evidently softening her, to poor children and hurricane victims. Both ended sadly, left alone with their dogs and the ghosts of their husbands in dust-draped city apartments or empty summer homes. But in the memory of most New Yorkers one was a saint and the other a sinner. *Richesse oblige.* ■

Oscar Auerbach

Oscar Auerbach, a doctor who stubbed out cigarettes, died on January 15th 1997, aged 92

WHEN OSCAR Auerbach established a link between smoking and cancer the everyday world of millions of people started to change. The companionable cigarette, the antidote to the pains of civilisation, the soldier's solace, the lovers' token, was now to be shunned. The cigarette that bears the lipstick's traces no longer seemed so romantic, now that it offered the prospect of premature death. Those who continued to smoke came to feel persecuted, snatching a guilty puff in the street away from the frowns of their abstemious workmates.

Dr Auerbach almost certainly had no idea of the impact his research was going to make. He was the single-minded scientist sometimes depicted in fiction, buried in his work, emerging from his laboratory only to lecture to students at New Jersey Medical School. He did not enter into the so-called "tobacco wars" waged between anti-smoking campaigners and the cigarette firms that fought hard to defend their markets. Indeed, the publicity given to some of his early findings greatly upset him. The *New England Journal of Medicine* declined to publish them because of its policy of using only previously unpublished results.

The doctor's findings were published later in other journals, but some tobacco companies pounced on their earlier technical rejection to claim that they were faulty. Sowing doubts about research into the effects of smoking has been a powerful tactic in the industry's slow and artfully managed retreat. Even now, many years after Dr Auerbach's work was made public, the tobacco people are far from conceding defeat. In the rich countries it is generally accepted that the tar and carbon monoxide in cigarettes do no good at all to the lungs (or the heart), and sales of cigarettes have fallen dramatically (although Americans alone still smoke more than a billion a day). In developing countries, in China for example, tobacco consumption is increasing. Deaths from diseases linked to smoking, at present estimated at 3m a year, are rising. On the other hand, an incalculable number of lives have been prolonged as a result of the publicity given to Dr Auerbach's work. It is not a bad memorial.

Under the microscope

As often happens when a discovery's time has come, the idea of a link between smoking and illness was mooted by a number of scientists. In Britain in 1951 Sir Richard Doll and Sir Austin Bradford Hill began a survey of smoking among some 34,000 male doctors which continued until the 1990s. In America there were similar large-scale studies. Dr Auerbach had studied diseases linked to social conditions since he had become a doctor in 1929 after studying in Vienna and New York. In the 1930s he was among those who sought the best treatment for tuberculosis. In the 1950s, while tuberculosis seemed to have yielded to drugs, cancer was unconquered. Dr Auerbach was a practical man. While, statistically, smoking seemed to be a culprit – the more you smoked the greater the chance of getting cancer – he

set out to seek medical evidence of the link. In his research, much of it financed by the American Cancer Society, he looked at tissue changes wrought by cigarette smoking in the lungs of people with cancer. A colleague of his recalled that the doctor might look at 2,000 slides a day. He offered direct, visual proof that cigarette smoke altered cells and that the damage intensified with every puff. Correlation had moved to causation.

In 1964 an increasingly health-conscious American government felt it had enough convincing evidence to take on the cigarette manufacturers. After a report by the surgeon-general on the dangers of smoking, cigarette packets were made to carry a health warning. At first this was the gentle advice, "Smoking may be harmful to your health". Now it is the no-nonsense "Smoking kills", in large type. In Britain and some other countries cigarette packets and advertisements have to carry similar labels.

Many of the subsequent findings about smoking came from Dr Auerbach's research: the possible danger of breathing in someone else's smoke, the so-called passive smoking; and the good news that if you give up smoking a damaged lung may heal. He trained a pack of dogs to smoke. Of the 86 beagles in the pack, 12 developed cancer. After the *New York Times* published the story in 1970, every television network in America carried a report of the smoking beagles. The tobacco industry was caught off guard. This story publicised the danger of smoking as nothing else had. The industry rushed to defend itself. Dogs were not the same as humans, its spokesmen said. This was nothing but a "scientific hoax".

However, there was a public reaction against the use of dogs in the experiment. The sorrowful beagles puffing away touched many a heart. Snoopy, the dog in the "Peanuts" cartoon, was a beagle, for goodness sake. But if Oscar Auerbach has sometimes been remembered as "the beagle man" he hardly noticed. His life was ordered in the laboratory and the lecture room, not in the irrational world outside. ■

Digby Baltzell

Edward Digby Baltzell, a WASP among the WASPS, died on August 17th 1996, aged 80

THE ACRONYM WASP, standing for White Anglo-Saxon Protestant, was probably invented by Digby Baltzell. He disclaimed its authorship, but dictionaries insist on dating it from 1964, when a book by Mr Baltzell, *The Protestant Establishment: Aristocracy and Caste in America*, was first published. His disclaimer may have been due less to modesty than irritation. Here was a distinguished academic, a fellow of Harvard and Princeton and goodness knows where else, but famous for his association with a single word. "You must meet the WASP man," a well-meaning hostess would say at a party.

The lifting of the word from a sociological tome and its liberation into popular use happened because, until then, there had been no instantly recognisable way of describing the ethnic ruling elite of America. "Gentry", "aristocracy" were European terms. WASP, too, had a pleasantly pejorative sound for non-WASPs. Wasps were parasites, stealing from the hard-working bees.

Mr Baltzell was in two minds, or possibly three, about WASPs. He was himself very much a WASP, and looked the part in his tweed jacket and striped shirt. He played tennis which, he complained, was a gentleman's game before it became professional. The WASP culture, based on honour, hard work and respect for others, was a model that everyone could emulate. That said, not all WASPs deserved admiration. Mr Baltzell was not at all keen on those of Philadelphia, although he was born there. He felt they had a tradition of weak leadership inherited from their egalitarian Quaker founders. The Boston WASPs, whose Puritan forebears had contributed much to modern democracy, were far superior. But Mr Baltzell's chief concern about the American elite was that it maintained barriers against minorities and was often racially prejudiced against talented outsiders. The authority of the white race, largely built up in England between the ages of Drake and Gladstone, was now being called into question around the world. America had become the world's most racially heterogeneous nation. To maintain its power in "an opportunitarian and mobile society" the elite had to be representative of the composition of society as a whole.

The example of Scarface
An unexpected hero of Mr Baltzell was Al Capone, whom he called "one of the organising geniuses of his generation". A poor boy from Brooklyn, Capone made millions by exploiting the market created by prohibition (a law passed by traditional Protestants largely to curb the drinking habits of the ethnic masses). He hated being called Scarface and instead took the name Anthony Brown. He showed his *noblesse oblige* by feeding thousands of poor Chicago citizens at his own expense. Those who worked for him had to be well dressed and speak respectfully. His son went to a private school and to Yale and married a well-connected girl. Capone, Mr Baltzell said, followed in the tradition of the American dream of the self-made man,

and was not much different from the self-made Protestant "robber barons" of an earlier era.

Capone, dismissed as a hoodlum in Hollywood films, could never have had his reputation salvaged even by a clever academic, but Mr Baltzell's endorsement of other talented Americans gained attention. "People talk about what Episcopalians [Anglicans] have accomplished and their power," Mr Baltzell said, "but what Jews have done in the United States since the second world war is now the great untold story."

Towards the end of his life Mr Baltzell was working on a book that would have recorded the collapse of an elite based on Protestant power, and its gradual replacement by a meritocracy. The end of WASP power? Formally, yes. But the reality is that WASP has come simply to mean affluent white. Back in the 1960s, when Mr Baltzell first predicted the eventual end of the Protestant grip, the election of John Kennedy, a Roman Catholic, as American president seemed to offer evidence of the demise of the WASPs. Like Kennedy, Ronald Reagan proudly pointed to his Irish (Celtic) background.

But to most ordinary people the wealthy Kennedys and the outgoing Reagans seemed no different to earlier presidents: they were white and privileged, as are Bill Clinton and his once rival Bob Dole, an obvious WASP. Only Colin Powell, a black, would have broken the mould had he gone for the Republican nomination and won it, but he may have feared a white backlash.

The Hispanics, the American Chinese and Japanese and dozens of other minorities are still locked out of the highest levels of power (as indeed are women, some of whose representatives are so indignant about white supremacy that they have rejected most of the world's literature from Shakespeare onward as being by "dead white males"). Feminism never seems to have caught Mr Baltzell's attention, but the danger of racism is a theme throughout his writings. His melancholy conclusion was that "complete chaos and violence" will ensue if the world becomes divided into two opposing racial camps. ■

Sirimavo Bandaranaike

Sirimavo Bandaranaike, a "first" among women, died on October 10th 2000, aged 84

FAME CAME suddenly to Sirimavo Bandaranaike of Sri Lanka in 1960 when she was made the world's first female prime minister. Newspapers around the world had gentle fun speculating about the auguries of this event. No one predicted that her reign would be remembered by many with loathing. The continuing conflict between the Tamils and the majority Sinhalese, which so far has claimed more than 60,000 lives, had its origin in policies Mrs Bandaranaike pursued.

Historians may decide that Mrs Bandaranaike was an innocent, inheriting policies whose consequences she did not at first understand. That could be true. When she took over, Sri Lanka had been independent for 12 years, but the Buddhist Sinhalese felt that not enough had been done to restore the ascendancy of their pre-colonial "golden age". Mrs Bandaranaike's husband, Solomon, had become prime minister in 1956 promising to end privileges said to be enjoyed by the Tamils.

Whether the mainly-Hindu Tamils had more privileges than the Sinhalese under the British, or were simply more enterprising, is open to question. But the Sinhalese believed they had and were resentful that many Tamils had prospered in government and the professions under colonial rule, and had held on to their jobs after independence. Solomon Bandaranaike was murdered in 1959 by a Buddhist monk who wanted Sinhala rule speeded up. Mrs Bandaranaike became leader of Solomon's party. In a general election, the "weeping widow", as she was known, was swept to victory.

It does indeed seem that she may have started as a political innocent.

Solomon was a male chauvinist. Whenever he invited some friends to their home to discuss political affairs, her only role was to serve tea. All the same, Mrs Bandaranaike had a sharp mind. She had received a solid education at a local Roman Catholic school and had done social work among the rural poor. And, once in office, she quickly learnt the power of racial politics.

The favoured majority

Sirimavo Bandaranaike headed two administrations, in 1960–65 and 1970–77. William McGowan, in his book *Only Man Is Vile*, quotes her as saying, "The Tamil people must accept the fact that the Sinhala majority will no longer permit themselves to be cheated of their rights." She made Sinhala the sole official language, replacing English and ignoring Tamil. Sinhalese were favoured for university places and government jobs. School history books were rewritten to give prominence only to Sinhalese heroes.

Her government nationalised the country's main industries, and placed Sinhalese in charge. Even the tea estates, which were well run by Tamils, were turned over to Sinhalese control. The number of parliamentary seats Tamils could win was cut.

It took a long time for the Tamils' resentment to turn into civil war, and to a demand for their own state in the north-east of the island. It wasn't just the racism; the government was a bad manager. There was high unemployment and soaring inflation. At one stage clothing and sugar were rationed. An insurrection, stirred by Marxist slogans and manned by the unemployed, was put down with great brutality.

State-controlled newspapers sought to prop up Mrs Bandaranaike's declining popularity with pictures of her with Tito, Nehru and others in the "non-aligned movement", and she won their praises by expelling the American "peace corps" and closing the Israeli embassy. American aid was cut off; Soviet aid came in. Eventually she lost power to Junius Jayewardene (see page 164), who reshaped Sri Lankan politics, transferring most power to the presidency. Mrs Bandaranaike was expelled from parliament and deprived of her civil rights for six years for abuse of office.

These days, Sri Lanka is in some ways a different place. Many of the state industries have been privatised. But a Bandaranaike is back in power. The former prime minister's daughter, Chandrika Kumaratunga, is president. For the past six years she has been trying to end the conflict between Sinhalese and Tamils ignited back in those reckless times nearly half a century ago; and now kept going by Velupillai Prabhakaran, the leader of the Tamil Tigers guerrilla group, who, says Mrs Kumaratunga, probably correctly, is mentally ill. Why so many Tamils are willing to be led by an apparent madman may perhaps be explained by their deep and unshifting suspicion of the Sinhalese, even though Mrs Kumaratunga has long rejected Sinhala nationalism.

Mrs Kumaratunga was blinded in one eye last December when she was caught in the blast from a Tiger suicide bomber. Any time she leaves her presidential palace in Colombo, she takes the risk of another bomb attack. She has never publicly criticised her mother for her part in fomenting the Tamils' grievances. She has always been the fond daughter, and made her mother prime minister, a position that became a ceremonial one under her presidency. Sirimavo Bandaranaike did undoubtedly believe that she was doing good. She gave the country its present Sinhalese name, changing it from Ceylon. It means "resplendent island". ∎

Christiaan Barnard

Christiaan Barnard, heart surgeon and celebrity, died on September 2nd 2001, aged 78

IT WAS a decent enough lifespan, 78 years, but Christiaan Barnard had, it seems, planned to live much longer. In his search for an elixir he injected himself with cells taken from the fetuses of animals. "It's worth a try," he said. Ageing, he maintained, was abnormal. He was involved with a clinic in Austria that offered "rejuvenation therapy". He endorsed a skin cream that contained an ingredient said to have prolonged the lives of fruit flies but which was withdrawn from sale after customers complained that it was not working for them.

At Dr Barnard's lectures, for which he charged up to $10,000 a time, his listeners would sometimes become a little impatient when he dwelt at length on his experiences as a heart surgeon; they were keen to know what progress he was making on longevity. Heart transplants are no one's idea of fun, but most people are interested in a few tips about how to put off the trip to heaven.

Relax, take a holiday, put away your mobile phone, drink red wine. But that was not all, said the doctor, in case his listeners felt they were not getting their money's worth. Sex, he said, was the magic ingredient, preferably with romance, "the most beautiful, healthiest and most pleasurable way" to keep fit. It cheered up the audience, even though the advice was not new. Dr Barnard had practised romantic sex ever since he had become famous after performing the world's first human heart transplant in 1967.

To the delight of newspapers, especially in America and Europe, the wonder surgeon was wonderfully photogenic, and had kept his boyish good looks into his 40s. He had a good line in chat too and seemed to love publicity. In the entertainment business women especially, Sophia Loren, Gina Lollabrigida and others, recognised a soulmate. *Paris Match* said he was one of the world's great lovers. Our picture is of him with Grace Kelly in 1968. At the age of 42 he dumped his wife of 22 years and married a teenager. He was married once more. He had six children. "I have a woman in my life at all times," he said. But although immortality by way of sex eluded Dr Barnard, there were compensations. As a heart surgeon he did memorable work, although even here there are reservations to be made.

American restraints
Christiaan Barnard learnt about heart surgery in the United States, chiefly at the University of Minnesota, after working for ten years mainly in general practice in his native South Africa. Whatever ambitions American surgeons may have had to replace a failing heart with a healthy one, the medical ethics prevailing at the time were against using the heart of someone who was brain dead while the heart was still functioning, albeit artificially. Back in South Africa Dr Barnard joined the heart department of Groote Schuur Hospital in Cape Town and eventually headed a team of 30. "We didn't have the legal restraints that existed in the United States," he recalled. In 1967, after nine years of experiments, mainly on dogs, Dr Barnard and his team removed the heart

from a young woman brain dead after a car accident and used it to replace the wonky heart of a 55-year-old grocer. The substitute heart started to beat vigorously and the operation was deemed a success. The patient died 18 days later of pneumonia. Large doses of drugs designed to prevent the heart being rejected had left him open to infection. Dr Barnard's second transplant patient lived for 18 months after the operation. His longest-surviving patient lived with a substituted heart for 23 years.

Dr Barnard carried out 75 transplants before giving up surgery in the 1980s because of arthritis. An estimated 100,000 heart transplant operations have so far been carried out in various countries. In the United States it is claimed that 75% of patients can expect to live for at least five years after the operation. What Dr Barnard did was to show the way. Other heart surgeons, suppressing their irritation about his love of fame, have been generous in their praise for his courage in confronting the question of brain death. Today it is accepted in many countries that brain dead means dead, although in Japan there were no heart transplant operations for 31 years after a surgeon who carried out the operation in 1968 was accused of murder. Many Japanese take the view that a person is alive while the heart is beating, and the country's law on the subject of brain death remains cloudy.

Dr Barnard dismissed what he called the mystique of the heart. The object of desire in poetry since humans acquired words was simply a primitive pump. One of the doctor's charms was his simple directness, perhaps acquired from his father, a missionary who drew big crowds as a preacher. Dr Barnard's openness amused the glamorous, but it also made him respected in his own world in racial South Africa, where he had to make choices. They tended to be good ones. He campaigned for black doctors to have equal pay with whites. He employed non-white nurses to treat white patients. He operated on blacks and whites according to their needs. An American he operated on said he hoped he had been given a white heart. Dr Barnard said he could not say. You couldn't tell the difference. ∎

Doak Barnett

Arthur Doak Barnett, an American mandarin, died on March 17th 1999, aged 77

IN 1972 Richard Nixon sought to bring China back into the family of nations, as he put it. He went to Beijing, had a chat with Mao, and rekindled the difficult, but indispensable, relationship between America and China which is still evolving. Many people were surprised that Nixon of all people, an implacable opponent of communism, had broken the ice with China, which since its communist takeover in 1949 had been regarded as virtually an enemy of America. Doak Barnett was not at all surprised. For years he had sought to convince American politicians that eventually they would have to find a way to get on with the Chinese.

He saw himself as an educator. Some pupils he dismissed as too thick to consider new ideas. Some, such as William Fulbright, chairman of the Senate Relations Committee, were receptive, and the committee gave Mr Barnett a hearing when it reviewed the government's China policy in 1966. Some, such as Lyndon Johnson, president of the United States from 1963 to 1969, had the power to reach out to China, but as a Democrat Johnson feared he would be seen as soft on a country that was helping North Vietnam in its war against the American-supported South.

Richard Nixon, Johnson's Republican successor as president, was never likely to be thought of as soft. "I always felt that Nixon was the guy, because of his background," Doak Barnett recalled recently. In talks between Mr Barnett and his most promising pupil, Nixon responded enthusiastically to his idea of an American policy towards China "of containment but not isolation", which he had first put to the Fulbright committee. Containment was America's firm policy towards the Soviet Union; this new twist would demonstrate that America could be flexible, while remaining strong. Having protected his back in Washington, Nixon went off to Beijing, where, *Time* reported, he had a "glittering technical success". It was Nixon's finest hour, undiminished by his later fall. Mr Barnett was to whisper in the ears of the powerful for many years to come, but guiding America's long march to China he regarded as his life's main work.

When the communists arrived

Doak Barnett was an American who seemed to have a touch of Scottish stubbornness: his unusual middle name, which he used as his first name, was a nod to his Scottish ancestry. China he thought of as a second home. He was born in Shanghai. His parents were Christian missionaries. When the family eventually returned to the United States Doak was 15. He went to Yale and during the second world war was in the Marines. He returned to China in 1949 as a newspaper correspondent and was in Beijing when the communists took over. Along with most Americans he was expelled in 1950 at the start of the Korean war. He got a job with the United States consulate in Hong Kong and was given grants by American universities for research. This was the start of a long career in which Mr Barnett became acknowledged as a leading authority on

China. He stayed close to government, but kept his independence, most recently as a teacher at Johns Hopkins University.

In one of his books, *Uncertain Passage*, Mr Barnett noted that Americans tended to shape their views of China "to fit their own preconceptions and mood of the moment, with minimal understanding of the realities of the situation". Such views, he said in an earlier book, *Communist China and Asia*, partly arose from the "innumerable friendly ties, unique in their character, developed between the American and Chinese peoples" over a long period and ended by the communist takeover.

Who lost China? The debate was conducted in America with some ferocity, with the Democrats, then in government, especially being blamed for not giving enough help to Chiang Kai-shek and his Nationalists. Owen Lattimore, a China specialist who, like Mr Barnett, was a little in love with the country, was accused absurdly of masterminding American policy in favour of the communists. So getting

Richard Nixon to Beijing was the most delicate of operations.

The briefing that Nixon had before he set out was not all that different from the one given to Bill Clinton for his trip in 1998. America's protection of Taiwan was China's big worry, Nixon was told. Next was the threat of a resurgence of Japanese military power. The problem of a divided Korea was bound to arise. Nixon should assure the Chinese that America did not seek hegemony in Asia, and no doubt the Chinese would say the same.

Add to the list human rights and trade worries, neither subject then deemed important, and what has changed? Isolation has long been over (although China believes it is still being contained). Most important, China is these days dealt with by America as a normally awkward country. A Clinton adviser recently popped into the hospital where Mr Barnett was receiving treatment. What should be done about China's theft of America's nuclear secrets? China's overall policy, Doak Barnett reflected, was not to be a troublemaker. "Stay cool." ■

Syd Barrett

Roger "Syd" Barrett, leader of Pink Floyd, died on July 7th 2006, aged 60

TO THOSE who were young then, the late 1960s were the best thing since 1789. All that followed paled by comparison. This was the time of the Paris riots, with students hurling cobbles and the *flics* hurling tear-gas back; the first convulsions over the war in Vietnam; the Prague spring, quickly crushed by Soviet tanks; and everywhere the sense that the young, by sheer numbers, could overthrow the established order and make the world again.

If they failed to remake it, this was largely because they were out of it on one illegal substance or another. For many of them, the drug scene was a quick, soggy spliff behind the bike sheds, or a reverential division of a cake of greenish powder, washed down with a glass of Liebfraumilch and covered up with burning joss sticks. Yet at the highest levels of culture the new gods of rock music tripped on much more dangerous stuff, and sang about it. They did not find truth exactly, as much as yellow walruses, purple fields, kaleidoscopic skies and melting buildings, all of which were evoked in music and light shows so new and peculiar that the best way to appreciate them was by being prone and stoned yourself.

Syd Barrett was the very exemplar of this wild universe. As the leader of Pink Floyd, the highly successful psychedelic band that he christened in 1965, he wrote and sang of "lime and limpid green", of Dan Dare, of gingerbread men and, in the band's first hit, "Arnold Layne", of a transvestite who stole underwear from moonlit washing lines. His weird words and odd, simplistic melodies, sent through an echo-machine, seemed sometimes to be coming from outer space.

Yet there was also something quintessentially English and middle class about Mr Barrett. His songs contained the essence of Cambridge, his home town: bicycles, golden robes, meadows and the river. Startlingly, he sang his hallucinations in the perfect, almost prissy enunciation of the Home Counties. He made it possible to do rock in English rather than American, inspiring David Bowie among others. The band's first album, "The Piper at the Gates of Dawn" (1967), made Mr Barrett central, plaintively calling up the new age from some distant and precarious place.

Yet the songs were already tipping over into chaos, and by January 1968 Mr Barrett was unable to compose or, almost, to function. Dope, LSD and pills, consumed by the fistful, overwhelmed a psyche that was already fragile and could not bear the pressures of success. At concerts he would simply play the same note over and over, or stand still in a trance. If he played, no one knew where he was going, least of all himself. The band did not want to part with him, but could not cope with him; so he was left behind, or left them, enduring drug terrors in a cupboard under the stairs in his London flat. Casualties of "bad trips" usually recovered, with stark warnings for the unwary. Mr Barrett, famously, went on too many and never came back.

Friends, especially his Pink Floyd

painting for which he had trained at Camberwell School of Art. Ambushing journalists were told that his head was "irregular", and that he was "full of dust and guitars".

Mr Barrett was now the most famous recluse in British rock. Slight as his oeuvre had been, it proved impossible to forget. His death, from complications of diabetes, brought an outburst of regret from rock stars and fans who were still following him. Tom Stoppard's play "Rock 'n' Roll", which was playing at the Royal Court when he died, made him a metaphor for revolutionary music: in 1968 a Pan-figure piping liberation, in the 1990s a tired, grey man spotted in a supermarket.

colleagues, tried to encourage him to resurrect his career. Their attempts were heartbreaking. At various times in 1968 and 1969 microphones were put in front of him and he was persuaded to sing and play. Cruelly, the recordings of his solo efforts, "The Madcap Laughs" and "Barrett" (both 1970), caught everything: the nervous coughs, the desperate riffling of pages, the cries of frustration ("Again? I'll do it again now?"), the numbers of takes. The sleeve of "Madcap" showed a naked girl in attendance – there had been any number of those – but Mr Barrett oblivious to her, his face masked by long hair and mascara, crouched shivering on the floor.

Cambridge, where he had learned to play banjo and had proudly covered his first guitar with mirror-discs, seemed the best place to retreat to. He went back to live in his mother's cellar, boarding up the windows, and returned to the

Shining like the sun

His band last saw him in 1975 as they recorded, in "Shine on you Crazy Diamond", a tribute to him that sounded like yet more encouragement. ("Come on you raver, you seer of visions/Come on you painter, you piper, you prisoner, and shine.") Mr Barrett wandered in, fat and shaven-headed and hardly recognisable. As his friends sang "You shone like the sun", he seemed to laugh sarcastically. He stayed a while in the studio, and then went away.

On the recording, a guitar player drifting in space walks through a door and finds himself in a loud cocktail party. Managers and promoters come up and flatter him, cajole him into working for them, but at last he escapes again. This time, nobody can catch him. ■

Jean Baudrillard

Jean Baudrillard, philosopher of consumerism, died on March 6th 2007, aged 77

AT SOME point in his career – neither date nor time being important – Jean Baudrillard took a large red cloth, draped it over a chair in his apartment, and sat on it. He may have smoked or thought for a while, or scratched his nose; a large, doughlike nose, supporting glasses. He then got up, leaving an impression of his body behind. The image pleased him: so much so, that he took a photograph.

Since he made no comment on the event (beyond the fact that the chair was later broken), the exact details are conjectural. But by putting the cloth on the chair, and sitting on it, Mr Baudrillard added to the plethora of signs, objects and symbolic acts that made up, in his philosophical system, the whole woof and warp of the 20th century. By getting up, he left behind a "simulacrum" of himself: the truth, as he teasingly put it, that hid the fact that there was no truth there. And by photographing the chair

he made it "hyperreal": an image, which could be reproduced unendingly, of an object that claimed to have meaning and, in fact, had none.

Then he went to lunch.

Pourquoi pas? When a simulacrum is also a French *philosophe*, perhaps the most popular of recent decades, he needs a bottle of Merlot from time to time. And since he spent his days considering the seductive power of images and objects, it was fun to observe that he himself had such a power over the woman in the butcher's who wrapped up his *foie de veau*, just because she had seen him on television.

Whether Mr Baudrillard's world was utter nonsense, or whether it was a profound critique of a consumerist civilisation drowning in its own meaninglessness, was a matter for lively debate. Many of his French colleagues found him too much: noisy, mischievous, attached to no school (though he had sat at the feet of both Henri Lefebvre and Roland Barthes in his feverish years at Nanterre, when teaching had been interrupted by clouds of tear-gas and cobblestone-throwing). He said things that got him into trouble. His enthusiasm for the *événements* of 1968 painted him as a man of the Left, where *philosophes* belonged as naturally as fish in water; but Mr Baudrillard later broke with Marx, and called him a conservative. What he meant was that both communism and capitalism made human existence a matter of production and exchange, while he preferred to stress its symbolic side.

In any case, in his world, both the liberal and the communist narratives of history had collapsed. "The end of history" was no longer universal capitalism and democracy or the victory of the proletariat. It was summed up for Mr Baudrillard by a lone man jogging, oblivious to his surroundings, hearing only the music of his own sound-system and aware only of the statements he himself was making: health, fashion, endurance. He was running straight ahead, but with no end in view.

The desert of the real

Of all the people he offended, none took more umbrage than the Americans. This was interesting, for he was far more popular there than in France, lecturing on various campuses of the University of California and even appearing, at Whiskey Pete's outside Las Vegas, as some sort of lounge lizard in a gold lamé jacket. In 1986 he got in a car and drove across the country, both hating and adoring it. He had never been so fully in a land of hyperreality, cluttered with meaningless symbols or, as in Disneyland, with garish synthetic versions of ordinary life. He looked for America, he wrote, in "motels and mineral surfaces ... in the speed of the screenplay, in the indifferent reflex of television, in the film of days and nights projected across an empty space." There he found himself, playing a French philosopher, roaring through "the desert of the real".

Americans did not like his book. They did not care to be called "the only remaining primitive society". A few years later, they objected also to Mr Baudrillard's contention that the first Gulf war of 1991 had never taken place. But, in his view, it had not. The media had created a picture of conflict; but Saddam had deployed his troops, and America had dropped its bombs, as pure statements of power in a vacuum, and the two forces had never met. General Norman Schwarzkopf, the "victor" (though with no victory) had celebrated with a party in Disneyland: QED.

All this paled, however, beside Mr Baudrillard's musings on the terrorist attacks of September 11th 2001. This was the "absolute event", an inevitable reaction to "insufferable" American power. In the face of overweening globalisation, to destroy the twin towers was the only response. The symbol invited its destruction: "It was they who did it, but we who wished it."

Most Americans decided, at this point, that they did not understand Mr Baudrillard very well. But then few people did. Behind the panache of his ideas – often bunkum, yet sometimes catching acutely the media-dominated triviality of modern life – the man was hidden. "No background," he would growl, if you asked. Somewhere, there was German-speaking peasant stock and suspicious parents who wondered what on earth they had produced in this plump and bookish boy. Or perhaps there was really none of that at all: just a photograph of a suggestion of a human shape, on a red cloth on a chair. ■

Saul Bellow

Saul Bellow, an American novelist, died on April 5th 2005, aged 89

IN FORMAL pose, he was always fastidious. Long before Tom Wolfe, Saul Bellow's trouser creases were blade-sharp, his fingernails sheened, the brim of his fedora tipped just so. All of which was surprisingly fussy for a writer of such ebullient and Olympian reputation. Only when he broke into a grin did you realise that Mr Bellow was no mere dandy.

He did not speak so much as spill with words: colloquial and mandarin, lofty, streetwise and intimate, all at once. "Humboldt's Gift", the 1975 novel that won Mr Bellow a Pulitzer prize and the Nobel prize for literature, began thus:

> He was a wonderful talker, a non-stop monologuist and improvisator, a champion detractor. To be loused up by Humboldt was really a kind of privilege. It was like being the subject of a two-nosed portrait by Picasso, or an eviscerated chicken by Soutine.

Ten years before Mr Bellow was born, Henry James returned to New York and heard "the hard glitter of Israel" in the street-chatter of the Lower East Side. He was revolted at having "to share the sanctity of his American consciousness, the intimacy of his American patriotism with the inconceivable alien." Mr Bellow never pussyfooted about the sanctity of English; for him, the multiple ore of immigrant voices was there to be fired into a fiercer linguistic alloy. As Philip Roth wrote, his language alone closed the gap between Thomas Mann and Damon Runyon.

Character, rather than plot, animated Mr Bellow's novels and short stories. He disagreed with Virginia Woolf, who believed that, in the modern novel, character was dead. His works were dominated by "noticers" (hungry observers of the life around them), dreamers, seekers, men of the mind, not unlike Mr Bellow himself, who had grown up poor and were impatient to get out into the world.

Round them, beautifully chronicled, were the "daily monkeyshines", as well as "the cheapies, the stingies, the hypochondriacs, the family bores". Mr Bellow's heroes lived in a world of cranks, crooks and wide boys, about whom warnings were constantly issued by fearsome grandmothers. Yet they were filled with nobility of spirit and moral purpose. "What did Danton lose his head for," asks Augie of his brother Simon in "The Adventures of Augie March", "or why was there a Napoleon, if it wasn't to make a nobility of us all?" Neither of them amounted to much in the end, but the point of their lives was the quest. No one ever promised there would be gold at the end of their rainbows.

Robert Penn Warren said of "Augie March", which came out in 1953, that "from now on any discussion of fiction in America in our time will have to take account of it." Steering clear of fads and fashions, Mr Bellow made his mark by revivifying realism, even though he wrote mostly from the viewpoint of impression and memory rather than contemporaneous action. Almost single-handedly, he extended the life of the novel, holding its neck, another critic ventured, "from the blade of the postmodern".

Like Dickens, Mr Bellow made a

came wrapped in a sense of their own mortality. Steering clear of Northwestern University's tweedy English department, he graduated in 1937 in anthropology and sociology and later went to work for the Encyclopedia Britannica. He moved to New York and began writing, at first with little success. Only when he joined the merchant marine did he complete "Dangling Man", about a Chicagoan waiting to be drafted.

By the time "Augie" made his name, Mr Bellow was 38. Other great novels followed. "Henderson the Rain King", about an American millionaire who travels to Africa, had an even more ambitious canvas. "Humboldt's Gift" so impressed Samuel Beckett that it spurred him into arranging a meeting. He and Bellow shared a drink at the Pont Royal in Paris, but both men were shy and the encounter was awkward.

With success came a stern commitment to writing that contributed to Mr Bellow's four divorces. Term-time found him in Boston and Chicago, where he taught the European novel; summers took him to Vermont, where he lay in the bath and studied the stars through a skylight. In between he travelled – to Mexico, France and Israel – finding food for the business of writing.

Towards the end, the mortality that had lurked at the edges of the early novels moved to the fore. Mr Bellow's writing slowed, but the spring of words never failed him. Presented with a ridiculous dessert in a restaurant one night shortly before his last child was born, the 84-year-old Nobel laureate contemplated a circle of perfectly measured blobs of fruit coulis. "Ah," he remarked, impishly and instantly, "Euclidian pimples!" ∎

city his own: "clumsy, tender, stinking Chicago, dumped on its ancient lake bottom." Living in the Russian Baths district in "Humboldt's Gift" are "aged working stiffs, lone Ukrainian grandfathers, retired car-line employees, a pastry cook famous for his icings who had to quit because his hands became arthritic." "Chicago was a place that loved irregular people," Mr Bellow would say later.

The spring of words
He was born in 1915, the last of Abraham Belo's four children and the only one born in the New World. The family had come originally from Russia, via Quebec, with little Saul (then Solomon), smuggled across the American border. He learned both Hebrew and Yiddish, and his mother wanted him to be a Talmudic scholar or a rabbi. Often ill, he began to devour books – the Old Testament, Shakespeare, the great 19th-century Russians. This may be another reason why so many of his heroes

Ingmar Bergman

Ingmar Bergman, film and theatre director, died on July 30th 2007, aged 89

WHEN HE was filming "Winter Light", in 1961, Ingmar Bergman made a tour of the churches of northern Sweden. He and his cinematographer, Sven Nykvist, would sit in the hard pews from 11 in the morning till two in the afternoon, watching the light change. In the Swedish winter, there was no sun. A dim grey illumination came from the clouds, casting no shadows. The subtleties of the shifting light entranced Mr Bergman, who decided that his whole film should be lit that way.

Strong sunlight, in contrast, filled his nightmares. A sudden lurid glare in his films – from a naked light, from an empty street – usually marked the entry into psychosis. That was why he never considered going to Hollywood to make movies, though by the 1950s his reputation as a film-maker was already impressive. He needed clouds, trees and net curtains veiling the light, softening it and making it move. He needed light in small increments: flaring and fading in a paraffin lamp, or dimming with extraordinary slowness on a face (as it dimmed on Liv Ullmann's face in "Persona") until only a silhouette was left. From childhood, he had got up at six and noted the track of light on the wall opposite his window. After two months of darkness, a thread would reappear in January.

Lack of light was reinforced, for Mr Bergman, by the isolation of Swedish life: so few people scattered over a large country, in houses here and there in the forests and the fields where, round some dining table, decorous conversation hid the loneliness and tension that could not be expressed. In Mr Bergman's films, characters would often be silent, or scenes would unroll with no sound

but the whimper of wind, the drip of water or, especially, the tick and chime of watches and clocks. He saw people as puppets, controlled by some pitiless force much as he, in boyhood, had controlled his own marionettes in his toy theatre, making Mr Punch jibber and squawk in nonsense-language. Life decayed towards "a state of absolute nothingness", while his characters, clinging on, tried urgently and clumsily to communicate their feelings to each other.

He had been brought up with Lutheranism, a pastor's son subjected to sermons, beatings and high piety, and for all his protestations his films were full of it. His trilogy of the 1960s, "Through a Glass Darkly", "Winter Light" and "The Silence", were described by him as a "metaphysical reduction" in which God's absence was unmasked. Without God, he turned to self-examination. His characters saw themselves through windows and in mirrors, divided selves gazing on their darker aspects or their pasts. He let his camera rest unsparingly on faces until all masks dissolved, and the lips and the eyes seemed to express some unaffected truth.

Sex and wild strawberries

The man himself often lived up to his bleak dream-world: lean, intense, racked by stomach complaints, and with a special fondness for the rugged limestone island of Faro, off Sweden's east coast, where he built a low stone house on an empty sweep of rock. Though he adored film, and had done so ever since he had swapped half his tin soldiers for his big brother's magic lantern, film-making made him "bleed too much". Eight hours of waiting might be rewarded, he once said, with ten or 12 minutes of real creative work. He demanded total immersion both of his actors and of himself, and complete control of both the shoot and the script.

He was sparing both with budgets and with film, and compulsively private.

Lighter moments surfaced sometimes. His long, lesser-known career in theatre directing, in Gothenburg, Malmo and Stockholm, included comedies alongside his favourite Strindberg. Explosions of directorial frustration were followed by gales of laughter. Pretty women surrounded him, several of whom he married and two of whom (Ms Ullmann and Bibi Andersson) starred in "Persona", in 1966, as different aspects of the same self. He delighted in female subtlety, slyness and fecundity. Summer idylls in the woods featured milk and wild strawberries, as well as *al fresco* sex, to show the sweetness and brevity of passing time.

On the edge, in the corners, darkness waited. Death loitered in many films – as a stranger, a crone, a ballet-master and, most memorably, as a cloaked and white-faced figure in "The Seventh Seal" of 1957, with whom the hero-knight plays a drawn-out game of chess. Mr Bergman admitted that death terrified him. And short of that he had "the demons" to contend with, anxiety, rage, regret and shame, which kept him company like "flocks of black birds". Panic at his own dark aspects kept him alert and drove him on.

Critics wondered whether there was a general message in his films. Mr Bergman sometimes denied he had one. Yet he usually found a saving moment in the misery: a selfless communication, in word or gesture, between two human beings. At the end of "Wild Strawberries" the hero, an aged professor, is belatedly reconciled with his family and his past. As the scene was filmed, Mr Bergman noted, the old actor's face "shone with secretive light as if reflected from another reality". That secretive light, or hidden love, was just what the director had been searching for. ■

Bip

Bip, the world's quietest clown, died on September 22nd 2007, older than he seemed

WHEN THE spotlight faded on Bip last week, leaving not even a hand or a flower illuminated, it caused only a sigh of surprise. Bip had tried many times to put an end to himself. He would cut his wrists with a blade, nicking and wincing away from it, in case his copious blood gushed over his pure white sailor's trousers. He would shake out into his palm a handful of pills from a bottle, open his wide red mouth, and fail to swallow them. Stepping on a chair that wobbled under him, he would knot a noose round his scrawny neck, test it, yank it, gyrate his neck like a pigeon and step out into the void. Nothing worked. He went on living.

That he should wish to die was also not surprising. Often he was kept, crouching or standing, in a small cage on the stage. One by one he ran his hands along the bars until, with all his strength, he pushed two apart and jumped nimbly out; but then, right ahead of him, behind him, all round him, he found his palms flattening against a wall of glass. Each cage was contained in another. His hands often became birds, flickering and fluttering out of his sleeves, and he made them fly swiftly from their prisons, laughing as they flew. But the bars soon closed again round him.

Like all human beings, he dreamed; but his dreams were rarely successful. He hunted butterflies with a darting net, only to break their wings. He plucked flowers, then picked their petals out, and was surprised they died. When he tried to tame lions, they ate him, scorning the thin hoop he flourished in their direction. He walked against wind and made no progress. His black-ringed eyes and black-lined eyebrows registered sadness, wonder, perplexity and terror. But he did not know what malevolence was. He was, said the man who knew him best, a romantic, a Don Quixote tilting at windmills, and "alone in a fragile world filled with injustice and beauty".

To the naked eye Bip had only the clothes he stood up in: trousers, jacket, soft ballet shoes, striped jersey, and a crumpled opera-hat topped with a red flower. His lean limbs and white face were his only language. The spotlight played on him, and nothing else. Yet the silence around him was filled with chairs, tables, animals, trunks and escalators. It swarmed with lounging waiters, officious policemen, dog-walkers pulled to right and left of the path, old ladies knitting. Railway trains roared through, and Bip, bouncing and swaying in his seat, struggled to keep his suitcase from falling out of the rack. The sea flooded in, bringing a ship that could take Bip on his constant travels to America, to Japan and to Australia, and he staggered manfully up and down the pitching deck.

He was born, some said, in the Paris acting school in 1947, bred by Jean-Louis Barrault in "Les Enfants du Paradis" and raised at the tiny Théâtre de Poche in Montparnasse. Others made him far older, dating from the Athenian drama and the Japanese *noh* plays, via the *commedia dell'arte* and Charlie Chaplin. Parts of all this went into the making of him, as well as the imaginings of the young Marcel Marceau, in Strasbourg

in the 1930s, trying on his father's long trousers and contorting his body to make his friends laugh. His name, Bip, came loosely from Dickens's "Great Expectations". His hat, flower and sailor-costume solidified over time.

Becoming the tempest

He never spoke. Mr Marceau's father died in 1944 in Auschwitz, and Bip's silence was a tribute to all those who had been silenced in the camps. It was a recollection, too, of the necessary muteness of resistance fighters caught by the Nazis, or quietly leading children across the Swiss border to safety, as Mr Marceau had done. In one of his acts, "Bip Remembers", the sad-faced clown relived in mime the horrors of the war and stressed the necessity of love. In another, his hands became good and evil: evil clenched and jerky, good flowing and emollient, with good just winning.

His alter ego, who promoted him as Everyman all over the world, sometimes spoke for him. "Bip", said Mr Marceau, "is a hero of our time. His gaze is turned not only towards heaven, but into the hearts of men." Mr Marceau compiled his biography and painted his portrait, colouring him blue, rose and mauve as he walked through the city streets and sailed among the stars. He wrote a poem for him:

> A silent, fragile hand has drawn in space a white flower emptied of its blood.
> Soon it will open, blossom out.
> Soon, though faded, bloom again.

Mr Marceau was garrulous and gregarious where Bip was not. He ran his own mime company for almost 60 years, staging *mimodrames* when they were completely out of fashion, and started an international school in Paris to teach his skills to others. No mime artist could touch him. Hollywood loved him. Mr Marceau gave interviews frequently, sometimes in Bip's clothes, explaining him to the crowd: "If I do this, I feel that I am a bird. If I do this, I am a fish. And I feel that, if I do this, it's like a song ... To mime the wind, one becomes a tempest. Mime expresses ... the soul's most secret aspiration."

Bip simply moved on the stage, bird, fish, song, wind, tempestuously without a word, until he too became invisible. ∎

Vere Bird

Vere Cornwall Bird, who transformed Antigua, died on June 28th 1999, aged 89

PROUDLY, THE government of Antigua reports that its "offshore financial industry has grown by leaps and bounds". The American State Department agrees but its enthusiasm for the country's financial services is muted. Antigua, the department said in a report published in March, is "one of the most attractive centres in the Caribbean for money launderers".

Such comments were wounding to Vere Bird, who dominated Antiguan politics all his adult life. He considered himself pro-American, and allowed the United States to have military facilities on the island. What were the Americans grumbling about? Mr Bird's favourite topic was Antigua's transformation under his leadership from penury to relative prosperity. Antigua was a poor country with an economy based on an uncertain market in sugar. It now has a prosperous tourist industry and an even more prosperous financial industry, serviced by some 50 loosely regulated offshore banks. Mr Bird happily, and indeed truthfully, proclaimed that Antiguans have achieved the highest standard of living in the Caribbean. Life expectancy is about the same as western Europe's. Secondary education is free. Unemployment is below 5%. Mr Bird denied that the government tolerated money laundering, just as he dismissed reports that the island is a base for drug smuggling and arms running and has become a favoured meeting place for Russian, Italian and Colombian gangsters involved in these profitable trades.

The Antiguans believed him, or simply did not care where the money came from. Mr Bird won election after

election and, allowing for such niceties as unlimited campaign money and with radio and television biased to the government, the ballots were tolerably free. When Mr Bird stood down as prime minister in 1994, his son Lester took over. Lester was re-elected with a big majority at a general election in March.

Here comes the drummer-boy

When the British empire was being dismantled it was unsure what to do with its dozens of small islands like Antigua. Some in the Caribbean are so small that they have remained dependencies. But Antigua and its tiny sister island, Barbuda, with their combined population of 65,000, about that of a medium-sized town in Europe, were allowed to go it alone, bequeathed with a British-style parliament and a decent cricket ground. But whatever Britain's misgivings about granting independence to this sandcastle, with all the privileges and status of a sovereign state, it had no doubt that Vere Bird was its natural leader.

His towering height – getting on for seven feet – gave him a commanding presence in the Salvation Army, which he joined as a drummer-boy, rising to be a captain, and which provided him with the rudiments of education. The Sally Ann, with its street rallies, also taught him public speaking. Mr Bird's political speeches had the rhythm of forceful preaching, with frequent references to God. In 1951 he persuaded Antigua's sugar workers to strike for more pay. The story goes that when a white planter asked what the strikers would eat, Vere Bird said, "We will eat cockles and the widdy-widdy bush. We will drink pond water."

The widdy-widdy is a weed once used to feed slaves. Whether the strikers survived on it is unclear, but the planters eventually caved in and Mr Bird's reputation took wing. The same year, 1951, union representatives led by Mr Bird won all eight elected seats on the local legislature. The British nurtured him. He was made a minister in the colonial government, then chief minister. He became prime minister on independence in 1981 and his Antigua Labour Party won all subsequent general elections. The British declined to make Mr Bird a knight, an honour often handed out to successful people in former colonies. But Antigua made him a "sir" anyway.

"Papa" Bird's prestige as the man who gave Antiguans the dignity of independence to some extent protected him from criticism. At his funeral last week at the newly created National Heroes' Cemetery, the opposition leader, a long-standing critic of government corruption, said that "history cannot but be kind" to Vere Bird. History may be less kind to Mr Bird's family. As in Indonesia, where members of the Suharto family, rather than the former president, are getting most of the blame for corruption, in Antigua those under fire include some of Papa's relations. As with the Suhartos, the Birds and Papa's mistress, Cutie Francis, are sufficiently rich not to be too distressed if, as in Indonesia, the economy goes rotten. But ordinary Antiguans may not be spared. America is getting impatient with the dirty money of Latin American drug barons being laundered in the Caribbean. Since its warning shot in March, American banks have been told to apply "enhanced scrutiny" to their customers' dealings in Antigua. Partly as a result of pressure from Britain, nine of Antigua's offshore banks have been closed down. The mobsters, who value their privacy, are said to be leaving the Caribbean for more secluded Pacific islands. Papa's Antigua may have little that is permanent, save, perhaps, the widdy-widdy bush. ∎

Jean Bédel Bokassa

Jean Bédel Bokassa, a bad man in Africa, died on November 3rd 1996, aged 75

IT WAS impossible to caricature the African military dictator. He existed. There were two such dictators in the 1970s, ldi Amin Dada of Uganda, and Jean Bédel Bokassa of the Central African Republic, renamed by him the Central African Empire. They were half criminal, half clown. In their wakes they left tales of fantastic self-aggrandisement and casual butchery.

Both men were products of former imperial armies. They worshipped and they hated their colonial masters who had elevated them to command the "native" troops, but did not allow them to join the white officers for dinner. Mr Amin, who now lives quietly in Saudi Arabia, called himself Conqueror of the British Empire; Mr Bokassa believed he was Africa's Napoleon. They wore saucer-sized medals. Mr Bokassa's titles included that of Grand Master of Honour of the International Brotherhood of Knights of Stamp Collecting. The two men made a laughing stock of Africa when it needed understanding.

In Mr Bokassa's case the real scandal was that France backed him when he seized power in 1966 and indulged him for 14 years. Valéry Giscard d'Estaing, president of France from 1974 to 1981, was a hunting companion of Mr Bokassa and called him "France's best friend in Africa". In the end, though, Mr Giscard d'Estaing (like France itself) was humiliated when Mr Bokassa disclosed that he had given him a gift of diamonds (which the president said he had sold for charity).

On a golden throne

Jean Bédel Bokassa was one of 12 children of the chief of a village not far from Bangui, then the administrative centre of the French colony of Ubangi-Shari. While Jean was a child, his father was murdered and his mother committed suicide. Some have suggested this shock was at the root of his psychopathic tendencies. Mr Bokassa joined the French army and fought in the second world war and then in Vietnam. He lived through the French defeat of Dien Bien Phu and rose to the rank of captain, making him the most senior soldier in the Central African Republic when it became independent in 1960. In January 1966, almost certainly with French assistance, Mr Bokassa overthrew the president, his cousin, and took power.

In 1977 he crowned himself Bokassa the First in a ceremony of staggering opulence which mimicked the coronation of Napoleon. In the heat of the Bokassa stadium in Bangui, he wore ermine, diamonds and a golden olive wreath and, seated on a golden throne shaped like an eagle, placed a crown on his head.

No African heads of state attended the ceremony but it was packed with western diplomats, and France helped foot the bill. He once said, "Everything around here is financed by the French government. We ask the French for money, get it and waste it."

The capriciousness of his rule made execution and death by starvation in jail commonplace. It was said that he once discovered his lion-keeper feeding

with his picture on. The children protested and Mr Bokassa had 200 of them thrown into jail, where, according to witnesses, he beat some of them to death.

While he was visiting Libya in September 1979, 700 French paratroopers took over in Bangui and overthrew him, replacing him with the cousin he had deposed, David Dacko. Mr Bokassa was later to complain, "Every time we have a problem, the French have to come and meddle. Finally, you have to ask yourself, are we independent or are we not?"

Mr Bokassa tried to go to his chateau in France but he was turned away by an embarrassed French government and went to the Ivory Coast. Later, France relented and allowed him in, but restricted his movements. In 1986 Mr Bokassa suddenly left France and arrived in Bangui demanding that he be allowed to vindicate himself. He had been tried in his absence and sentenced to death but now he was given a fresh trial on 14 charges, including murder, theft and cannibalism. The cannibalism was never proved but he was sentenced to death for murder. The sentence was commuted, and after seven years in prison he was pardoned and emerged to live quietly in Bangui, seemingly a changed man. He said he had renounced alcohol and women (he acknowledged paternity of 54 children). Born a Christian, converting to Islam, Mr Bokassa now returned to Christianity, perhaps in a search for forgiveness. ∎

the lions' dinner to his own family. Mr Bokassa had him thrown to the lions but they, recognising their keeper, did not touch him. So Mr Bokassa fed the keeper to his crocodiles, which showed less discriminating taste.

Despite a series of spats with France, or at least with French ambassadors and ministers, Mr Bokassa remained broadly loyal to his old masters. He allowed France to retain its largest military base in Africa near Bangui, essential for protecting other Francophone territories in the region, including troublesome Chad from the Libyans. But in the end he became too much even for Paris. He began to flirt with Libya's Colonel Qadaffi and in 1979 he ruled that schoolchildren should wear uniforms

Joseph Bonanno

Joseph Bonanno, an American gangster, died on May 11th 2002, aged 97

A DISCOVERY made by Joseph Bonanno when he was quite young was that in a democracy it is possible to construct a criminal organisation largely immune from the law. The American constitution with its constraints designed to protect citizens from unfair prosecution could also be used to shield criminals providing there was enough money available to employ clever lawyers to manipulate the system. Confident of his protection, Mr Bonanno assembled an empire of crime with a turnover of billions of dollars. Despite the best efforts of the state, Mr Bonanno was never convicted of a serious crime. The state's successes were meagre. Mr Bonanno was once fined $450 on a minor charge and late in life was jailed for terms of eight and 14 months for refusing to answer questions, an offence deemed to be contempt of court. The

FBI tried to track his every move, even searching Mr Bonanno's dustbins for incriminating evidence. It ended up only looking foolish.

Al Capone, a gangster of America's prohibition era, seems to have been Joseph Bonanno's mentor, teaching him that, with money, you could get away with murder. Capone was jailed (for income tax evasion) in 1931, and Joseph Bonanno moved on. He had been born in Sicily and had links with the semi-feudal Sicilian families collectively known as the Mafia. When Benito Mussolini took power in Italy in 1922 he jailed many Mafia followers, accusing them, correctly, of gangsterism. Those that could get away fled to the United States. The Mafia flourished again in Italy only after the country surrendered in the second world war. By then Mr Bonanno's American branch of the

Mafia, consisting mainly of gangs run by Italian émigrés, was flourishing. Each had its speciality: drugs, prostitution, protection, gambling, whatever. Sometimes there were power struggles, and gangsters would murder each other, cheering up the FBI. Mr Bonanno rose in the 1960s to be the *capo di tutti i capi*, boss of bosses. He was said to have invented the "double coffin" in which the body of someone who had died naturally would conceal a murdered corpse. He was a careful man.

The tradition

If Joseph Bonanno had a weakness it was his desire for respectability. It was a difficult ambition, perhaps an impossible one. Mr Bonanno was a criminal. Everyone knew that, and criminals, even successful ones, are not respectable. Shakespeare, as always, put it rather well, noting that, however rich you were, the loss of a good name "makes me poor indeed". Mr Bonanno was not a literary man, although he did once get someone to help him write a book about himself called, seemingly without irony, *A Man of Honor*. In reviewing his career he says:

> The way of life I and my friends had chosen was but a means to attain social advancement and respectability. We didn't consider ourselves criminals.

In his campaign of denial Mr Bonanno relied on what he called "my tradition", a phrase often used by the mafiosi. He denied that he had dealt in drugs because "my tradition" outlawed them. He had nothing to do with prostitution because it was against "my honour". And so on. He sued the publishers of a paperback edition of *A Man of Honor* for depicting him on the cover as "a cheap gangster".

Pressed for a description of himself Mr Bonanno offered "venture capitalist": indeed, much money from his criminal activities was used to set up orthodox businesses such as hotels. He called his group of gangs "the commission" and he was "chairman". In another flight of fancy he said his work was like running a state. He had to maintain internal order and to conduct diplomatic relations with other leaders. Despite the self-flattery, there was an element of truth in it. Mr Bonanno was a dictator with absolute power over his subjects. Japan's tolerated gangsters, the Yakuza, have been compared to the Bonanno empire. But they have never gained the same sort of immunity, perhaps because Japan is a more rigid society.

The Mafia remains a sore in Italy. It has corrupted sections of Italian politics. Judges and priests, among others, brave enough to stand up to it have been murdered. That, however, is not how the Mafia has often been portrayed in books and films about its American branch. The most famous is Mario Puzo's romantic novel *The Godfather*, said to have been based on Mr Bonanno. Unlike its characters, real mafiosi are just as likely to be podgy and their women plain, and to have never uttered a witticism in their lives. *The Sopranos*, an American television series, continues the theme of fictional mafiosi.

Joseph Bonanno may have been the first Mafia godfather to die naturally. But he did not feel that he had been well treated by America. He said he resented being "hounded" by the FBI. Newspapers and television had been disrespectful. It was hurtful to be known as "Joe Bananas". Despite his dedicated work as chairman of the "commission", he had once had to disappear for two years for fear of ending up in a double coffin. Unlike other fathers he had been unable to enjoy watching his three children growing up in a quiet rural suburbia. He had had a precarious life. The heart bleeds. ∎

Habib Bourguiba

Habib Ben Ali Bourguiba, successor to Hannibal, died on April 6th 2000, aged 96

A T HIS palace in Tunis Habib Bourguiba liked to show visitors portraits of four men from North Africa he most admired. They were Hannibal, perhaps the greatest of military commanders, St Augustine, who was born in what is now Algeria, Jugurtha, a king who stood up to the Romans, and Ibn Khaldun, who changed the way of writing history. Above these portraits was a larger one, of Mr Bourguiba. Modesty was never his problem. And, indeed, if you put aside the more absurd, and nasty, aspects of his life, there remained great accomplishments. He may not be remembered as a saint, or even as "the mighty warrior" described in the Tunisian constitution, but he did things that were, in their own way, remarkable.

Soon after he had won independence from France, he abolished polygamy, legalised abortion, allowed women to contract their own marriages, sue for divorce, and marry non-Muslims, a liberation of women that today remains unmatched in the Arab world. Within a decade of independence, two thirds of Tunisians were literate, up from a third in colonial times. He created a modern, largely secular state, which attracted investors.

Tunisia remained formally Islamic, but with much of the dogma dumped. Mr Bourguiba sought to end fasting during Ramadan. His ransacking of religious trusts had echoes of Henry VIII's dissolution of the monasteries. Tunisia was the only Arab state without a minister for Islamic affairs. He was anti-colonial, but, he insisted, not anti-western; time has made his foreign policies look visionary. He advocated recognition of Israel at a time when most Arab nations still sought its extinction. Tunisia boycotted the Arab League. Yet, seemingly charitably, he gave Yasser Arafat and his Palestinians sanctuary when they were driven from Lebanon in 1982 and looked a spent force.

His way with opponents

Habib Bourguiba was a French-trained lawyer. Back in the 1930s he first became prominent in independence politics. The French knew a troublemaker when they saw one and Mr Bourguiba spent some 12 years in French jails, in the Sahara and on the Brittany island of Groix. Nevertheless, he said he admired the French, even while fighting them. During the second world war, when most Tunisian nationalists supported the German-Italian axis, Mr Bourguiba declined to reject the French, even when in 1942 the Germans let him out of his French prison. By then America had entered the war and the Germans were faltering in Russia. It looked likely that the French would be the future negotiators.

In 1956 Tunisia was granted independence, with the Bey of Tunis as head of state and Mr Bourguiba as his prime minister. But Mr Bourguiba, who styled himself as the first independent leader of his country since Hannibal, was disinclined to share power. One year after independence he abolished the monarchy and became president. His Tunisia was a one-party state. Opponents were cruelly swept aside. Rival independence leaders were either

hounded into exile or humiliated in show trials. Mr Bourguiba spat in public at ministers he sought to discipline. In 1961, Tunisian agents murdered a former comrade of Mr Bourguiba, Salah Ben Youssef, in Frankfurt.

Statues began popping up. His birthday, August 3rd, became Tunisia's national day. Streets were named after him. He had a mausoleum built of white marble and decorated with gold leaf. In 1975 he had parliament declare him president for life. Some people thought he was losing his mind. Tunisians were astonished when he said on television that he had only one testicle.

This fascinating disclosure was naturally much discussed by Tunisians. The mighty warrior had one son, by his first wife, Mathilde Lorrain, but other women were also important in his life. In 1961 he divorced Mathilde, after she had imbued him with her ideas of equality for women, apparently because Tunisians considered that a true patriot would not have a French spouse. His second wife, Wassila Ben Ammar, became a power behind the throne. Officials said she bugged cabinet meetings, and decided who should be

a minister. For the first time in the Arab world, a photo of the first lady began to appear alongside that of her husband. Mr Bourguiba divorced her in 1986, and he was looked after by his niece, Saida Sassi.

But by then Tunis's Camelot was unravelling. The judiciary, the press, the trade unions, which had all tasted freedom in the early years of the republic, had been shackled. Bread-riots were becoming frequent. Crushing Islamists was becoming an obsession. Mr Bourguiba was demanding mass executions after bombings in the tourist resorts of Sousse and Monastir.

In the end, Mr Bourguiba was better treated than he had treated his rivals. The coup was medical: on November 6th 1987, the prime minister, Zine el-Abidine Ben Ali, gathered a council of seven doctors who pronounced Mr Bourguiba senile and incompetent. For the next 13 years until his death he was under house arrest, his visitors mainly restricted to relations. If he sought a change of scenery he could visit his mausoleum, with the words engraved on the door, "Liberator of women, builder of modern Tunisia". ■

Donald Bradman

Sir Donald George Bradman, the greatest batsman, died on February 25th 2001, aged 92

L OOKING AT a picture of Donald Bradman in his heyday, perhaps the first thing you notice is that he is not wearing the armour that makes cricketers these days resemble Hannibal Lecter. Cricket seemed less brutal then; it still retained some of its flavour of a summer's game "invented by the English to give themselves some concept of eternity", as an anonymous wit put it. Would Sir Donald, as he subsequently became, have done so well in modern conditions, creating records that are unlikely ever to be beaten? No one knows, and to take sides can lead to a bar-room quarrel. But it is reasonable to say, under the journalist's protection of fair comment, that he would have had a tougher time of it, as indeed he did during the great bodyline bowling epic.

Cricket historians tend to hasten over this episode as being unworthy of the game. But it has persisted in public memory, if only because it is a drama easy to understand without needing to know the more arcane aspects of the game. Here was young Bradman, aged 24 and already a batting phenomenon feared wherever cricket was played, which in those days was at least all of the British empire. He was the weapon with which Australia looked forward to crushing the English team on its visit in 1932–33.

The English captain, Douglas Jardine, though, was equally determined to humiliate the Australians. Whether he called them "the convicts" has never been confirmed. It would have been in character. As the Australians sneeringly observed, he was a toff. Jardine decided to use a tactic called "leg theory". Despite its fancy name, in essence this amounted to sending down a very fast ball aimed at the batsman. Trying to avoid the missile, the batsman would fumble and deliver a catch to a nearby fielder.

The Australians were dismayed as their stars hobbled off the ground wounded. Even their Don was hit. Worse, he wasn't getting the huge scores he was used to. One time he managed only 13 runs against the English bowling tornado Harold Larwood. The dispute became political. Words were exchanged between the British and Australian cabinets. Eventually things calmed down. Bodyline bowling, it was seriously agreed, was not cricket.

The heroic years

Less serious people said it had been jolly exciting and welcomed home the victorious Jardine. But new rules ended bodyline. Jardine and Larwood were sacrificed from the English team. Donald Bradman resumed getting impossible scores. Australia won the next six encounters with England. A kind of awe developed around this self-taught batsman from the Australian outback whose very presence on the field depressed England's finest. Stories of his prowess reached the United States, which also has its favourite bat-and-ball game. An impressed observer on the *New York Times* wrote, "He simply keeps hitting and running until some sensible person in the stands suggests a spot of tea."

His more adulatory fans have

writer. John Howard, the Australian prime minister, simply thanked God for him and ordered a state memorial service. Sir Donald was Mr Howard's perfect Australian, anti-republican, admirer of royalty and politically a conservative. In every way except his mastery of the bat he seems to have been a fairly ordinary chap. As athletes do, he slowed down while quite young. In 1948, when he was 40, he was dismissed without scoring in his last game against England.

Sir Donald prospered as a stockbroker and for many years helped to select Australia's cricket team. He saw cricket developing into the gladiatorial game it is now, with fast bowlers challenging the restrictions brought in to end bodyline. Batsmen, in turn, were seeking more reliable protection than the rulebook. As well as leg pads and gloves, a player these days will wear a helmet with face guard, thigh pad and protection for chest, arms and abdomen. Running at all requires a special effort.

The game that in the 18th century had featured underarm bowling by players in lace shirts and knickerbockers has sought to keep its audience interested. As bowlers get ever faster, padded suits and strengthened helmets could make cricketers look like American footballers. Players may be wired up to get advice from their trainers. Cricket may move indoors to avoid the weather. Whether Sir Donald would have coped will be argued. The luxury of being remembered is his reward for being the best of his time. ■

suggested that not only was Sir Donald the greatest of cricketers but perhaps the greatest of all sportsmen, a claim that might be disputed by admirers of Pelé and Joe DiMaggio. It is said his exploits may have cheered up Australia in the 1930s, when the country was badly hit by the Great Depression. No one wanted its raw materials, and about a quarter of the workforce was jobless. But did families feel less hungry when word came over the radio that their hero had hit another couple of centuries?

Some who lived then have said this happened, and Sir Donald's beatification as an inspirational force in time of trouble has been much paraded since his death this week. "Australia's Churchill," declared a normally sober cricketing

Robert Brooks and Mickey Spillane

Robert Brooks and Mickey Spillane, suppliers of fantasies to American males, died on July 16th and July 17th 2006, aged 69 and 88

O N DAYS like this, the weather sat over Manhattan like a lid on a boiler. But the cab was cool. Mike Hammer jumped in, directed the driver to Midtown, and watched the city slide by.

He had heard of Mickey Spillane's death on the TV news as he took a shower. Sad, and hard to believe. Only weeks ago he had seen him in some fishing village in South Carolina, still looking like a street brawler from Elizabeth, New Jersey. Hammer could hear his voice now, a snarl of contempt for the writers who thought his books were repulsive and illiterate. What the hell, they sold. He was maybe the most popular fiction writer ever. A literary type once complained to him that seven of his books were among the ten top sellers of all time. "Lucky I only wrote seven books," growled Mr Spillane.

Good answer.

As the taxi revved and accelerated, Mike Hammer fingered the gun under his jacket. But the streets were quiet.

He and Spillane went back a long way, ever since Spillane had started banging out his adventures on the trusty Smith Corona. That was 1946, with "I, the Jury". Two dozen more had followed. The formula was no secret. Plenty of violence – guns, fistfights, gougings, torture, select amputations. Communist villains, just right for the 1950s. Oodles of sexual titillation, with luscious girls instinctively undressing as soon as Hammer appeared. So much sex and so much violence had never been seen before. Hammer was a private dick without hang-ups, as calm and laconically witty when staring down the barrel of a .45 as when urging a female DA to tie up her bathrobe. Every red-blooded American male could identify with him.

"Damn right," thought Mike Hammer.

Only an hour ago he had been tied to a chair, blood on his face, while some gonzo had forced a sodium pentothal injection into his resisting arm. Now he was on his way to meet a man who had information. He was taking no chances. They were meeting at a joint called Hooters, on the fairly good side of town. "Delightfully Tacky, Yet Unrefined", the billboard said. He could deal with that. And if things got hot, there were no rules of engagement for private cops like him.

The place was alive with frat boys. Bleached wood lined the walls, with college pennants. The Christmas lights were on, though it was July. And everywhere strolled the most amazing girls, with cantilevered breasts beneath their T-shirts and orange hot-pants as tight as dammit. They wore cowboy hats, wide smiles and tans that evidently went all over.

Wings with champagne

He found a table and, to calm himself down, read the promotional literature. The whole Hooters idea, he learned, had been an adolescent fantasy in which six men in 1983 had tried to recreate in Clearwater, Florida, the dream restaurants of their youth. The money ran out, and Robert Brooks had rescued them. Without him, this Paradise would never have reached New York.

Mr Brooks had been a self-made man, raised on a hardscrabble tobacco farm in

South Carolina. He had stacked up his fortune in the food business in Atlanta. After he took Hooters over, in the mid-1980s, the company boomed: 435 restaurants, soaring profits (of which Mr Brooks gave much to charity), a casino, a pro golf tour, a NASCAR racing series, an airline. Hell, thought Mike Hammer, he could have flown back to Newark on Hooters Air, with two beautiful Hooters girls attending to make sure his seatbelt was securely fastened. A crying shame it had stopped commercial flights after three years.

A man sat down at his table, cradling a beer. "Quite a place," he said.

"Damn right."

"You know Brooks was a Methodist? Didn't know what 'Hooters' meant?"

"You don't say."

"Used to bring ministers to his restaurants, to show them how wholesome it was. And how you could never go wrong with good food, cold beer and pretty girls."

Wholesomely, a waitress approached him. Her orange crotch was on a level with his chin, and her legs went on and on. "What'll you have?" she asked him.

"Anything you've got, honey."

The menu offered a Gourmet Chicken Wing Dinner: 20 wings and a bottle of Dom Perignon. Or an Oyster Roast: "Shuck at your own risk". He ordered the Chicken Wing Dinner with secret sauce.

"Breaded or naked?"

He liked this place.

When his beer came, in a cold, wet pitcher, he and his mystery companion drank a toast to Bob Brooks. All around them, happy jocks were doing the same. Mike Hammer smiled. Only yesterday he had kicked in a door at the top of a dark staircase, knocked an attacker to the floor, kicked him in the stomach, crunched his teeth one by one and then allowed a beautiful brunette, naked under an evening gown, to leave unmolested by the fire escape. Now he could almost forget that he was still on the job.

But he did not forget. As he left he slid into his newspaper a Hooters menu, damp but intact. Inside it, courtesy of his mystery companion, lay the recipe for the secret sauce. Adjusting his rod under his ice-cool armpit, he made for the door. ■

Rosemary Brown

Rosemary Isabel Brown, a musical psychic, died on November 16th 2001, aged 85

WRITERS ABOUT Rosemary Brown have tended to be cautious over her accomplishments. She claimed to have been in touch with Beethoven, Liszt, Chopin and some 20 other composers who had employed her as their contact on earth to receive their latest compositions.

Many people profess to be psychic, and some make great claims for their discipline. A debate is currently being conducted on the internet about whether globalisation is being driven by "psychic energy". But such matters, however intriguing, do not usually occupy the public stage. The psychic world tends to be a private one. What is particularly interesting about Mrs Brown is that she suddenly became famous in her native Britain and in the United States.

She made her public debut in a BBC television programme in April 1969. Her item was a short one, but it was noticed by several newspapers. Either Mrs Brown, a school dinner-lady from Balham, a London suburb, was a phenomenon, or, an equally promising story, the BBC had been taken in. It transpired that the BBC had not been taken in, but had been as baffled by the experience of Mrs Brown as were the reporters who increasingly came to knock at her door. How was it that a woman apparently of little musical ability had one day sat at a piano and had begun to play Chopin with ease, and Chopin music that no one had heard before?

As subsequently became clear, it wasn't quite like that. Rosemary Brown had been interested in music as long as she could remember. She had learnt the piano as a child and had hoped to be a dancer. She had long known she was psychic. She remembered having had

a chat with Franz Liszt when she was seven. He had always kept in touch and sometimes went shopping with her. It was true that when times were hard Mrs Brown had worked in a school kitchen, but she had had a more dignified job in the Post Office. Some musical friends had taken an interest in her contacts with dead composers and had recorded some of the music she had received. That was how she came to be taken up by the BBC.

All this helped to make Mrs Brown a more believable person, and created a public ever eager to know more about her.

No sex in heaven

"The undiscovered country, from whose bourn no traveller returns" is a worry for many people other than Hamlet. Members of the established faiths have been told what awaits them after death, but millions of others are unsure. They listened with interest to what Rosemary Brown had to say when she appeared regularly on television in Britain and the United States, including a spot on *The Johnny Carson Show*. In heaven, she said, there was no sex; "the earthy side of our being has been left behind". There was though, oddly, an interest in fashion. Clara Schumann was very dressy. Everyone was well. Beethoven was no longer deaf. There were no quarrels. Everything was in harmony. That didn't sound too bad. But was Mrs Brown making it all up? Was the music she said she was receiving any good? That had to be the test.

In the 1970s many music experts perused the scores that Mrs Brown had painstakingly taken down. Some were enthusiastic. Leonard Bernstein said he would "buy" the Rachmaninov. Peter Katin, an outstanding interpreter of Chopin, was happy to record many of the piano works. Most of the experts

were unsure. They were impressed by the sincerity of Mrs Brown, who seemed to have no interest in profiting materially from her fame. They liked much of the music but were bothered that it was not outstanding, not the work of genius.

On the other hand the music seemed too good to have been composed by an amateur, however enthusiastic. The compositions suggested a professional hand. Nor were the pieces pastiches. One critic noted the "advanced harmonies" of a Liszt piece. A Hungarian writer was particularly pleased that his country's most celebrated composer was still in form. Mrs Brown was not perturbed by the controversy. She said that her composer friends were simply demonstrating that there was life after death. In her book *Unfinished Symphonies* she sought to explain the mysterious nature of music by quoting a message she said she had received from Chopin.

> Great music is something that is really born in the spirit and is reproduced, perhaps very badly, in your world.

A heavenly helping hand has often been acknowledged by otherwise down-to-earth composers. Mozart, for one, was baffled where his marvellous music came from. However, psychiatrists who were asked for an opinion about Mrs Brown's music said that it had come from her own mind. They constructed a plausible picture of a talented woman who, through childhood poverty, had been deprived of a musical career and had returned to music after her husband had died. Her psychic experiences they ascribed to hysteria, using the term in its medical sense, of dissociation. Since the Enlightenment, religious visionaries of all kinds have often been called hysterics. Joan of Arc, Theresa of Avila: the list is long. Mrs Brown was in distinguished company. ■

John Cairncross

John Cairncross, scholar, and "fifth man" in the Cambridge group of Russian spies, died on October 8th 1995, aged 82

WHEN JOHN Cairncross was questioned about his work as a spy he insisted that he had never harmed his native Britain. He had passed information to the Soviet Union during the second world war only to help it in its fight against Germany, the common enemy at the time of the Russians and the British.

Mr Cairncross was one of five clever Britons known to have been recruited by the Soviet Union when they were at Cambridge and who later served their masters well. In a striking note of patriotism, all, in memoirs or interviews, have denied disloyalty to Britain. Spies they may have been, but, in their own minds, they remained decent. As far as is known, their interrogators do not appear to have seriously challenged this large claim. Whatever suspicions they may have had, it would perhaps have seemed impolite to offend these well-connected and intelligent men. After all, Anthony Blunt, the most senior of the five, had become Queen Elizabeth's adviser on art.

At any rate, all five were treated kindly. Anthony Blunt's only formal punishment was to be deprived of his knighthood. Kim Philby, Donald MacLean and Guy Burgess may have punished themselves by nipping off to Russia once they learnt that the game was up. But all died, as John Cairncross did, peacefully, in their own beds.

Defenders of Mr Cairncross say the Russians were entitled to the information he passed to them while he was working with a team which had broken a German method of coding known as Enigma. He acknowledged that he told the Russians about German battle plans before a decisive battle, at Kursk, in 1943. But, according to Yuri Modin, the Russian controller of the Cambridge five, Mr Cairncross also disclosed information about western nuclear plans, which may have been of use to Russia when it became an enemy.

The fate of traitors
Mr Modin also recalled that after the war, when Mr Cairncross was working in the British Treasury, at the heart of government, he gave the Russians information about NATO. Philby also continued to work for Russia during the cold war, but he too had his defenders, among them Graham Greene, who wrote an introduction to his memoirs.

Britain has not always been compassionate to those regarded as traitors. William Joyce broadcast propaganda from Germany to Britain in the second world war. A British court found him guilty of treason. Because his nationality was in question, he may have been tried illegally. But Joyce was regarded as a yob who sneered at Britain in its finest hour, and he was hanged. Oswald Mosley, an aristocrat who would have been Britain's Führer had Germany won the war, was merely detained in some comfort. Cynics looking at the leniency extended to the Cambridge five say that a superior education and some polish remain useful protections in Britain. America has been notably tougher with treachery. Julius and Ethel Rosenberg were executed in 1953 after being found guilty of passing

information about nuclear weapons to the Soviet Union.

Anyone seeking some quirk in Mr Cairncross's upbringing, some early disenchantment with society, would be disappointed. His Scottish childhood home was austere but secure. His mother was a teacher and his father ran a shop. After excelling at Cambridge he topped the Foreign Office entrance examinations and was quickly promoted. He told people close to him, including members of his family, that he was never a communist, unlike the other spies at Cambridge.

But Peter Wright, a British security-service officer, said in his book *Spycatcher* that Mr Cairncross told him he had not only become a communist at Cambridge but, "with characteristic Scottish tenacity", remained one. Getting the truth about spies is inevitably difficult, as lying is an important part of their skill. But, ideology apart, Mr

Cairncross's actions in helping Russia during the second world war were at least partly motivated by intellectual arrogance; an assumption that he, rather than the idiots who were running the war, was better able to judge what needed to be done to hasten victory. Possibly he was right. It was also possible that, despite his academic brilliance, his judgment was flawed. The two qualities do not always go together.

After Mr Cairncross was rumbled he was allowed to resign discreetly from government service. From 1952 he lived mostly abroad: in America, where he got an academic job, in Rome, where he worked for the United Nations, but chiefly in France. He had skill as a linguist. Before going to Cambridge he had gained a degree at the Sorbonne. In France he built up a reputation as an authority on its greatest comic dramatist, Molière. *Tartuffe*, a play about pretence, was one of his favourites. ∎

Jeanne Calment

Jeanne Louise Calment, the world's oldest person, died on August 4th 1997, aged 122

FOR 100 years nothing much happened to Jeanne Calment. Centenarians are commonplace these days. But as she lived on, and on, she became famous, first in her home town, Arles, in southern France, then nationally, and eventually as the person with the longest proven life of anyone in history. France, always happy for new evidence that it is, in every way, the most desirable of countries to be born in, was gratified when (in October 1995) Mrs Calment passed the lifespan of a Japanese who had previously held this most competitive of records. Mrs Calment, it was noted, attributed her staying power to olive oil and good French wine.

Each birthday, reporters would be dispatched to write about Mrs Calment's career in longevity. But extracting the gems of her experience was not easy. In her final years Mrs Calment's sight and hearing had almost gone. There is a certain amount of repetition in these birthday accounts. One much-told story is that in 1965, when Mrs Calment was 90, a local lawyer made a deal with her to take over her flat when she died, meanwhile paying her the equivalent of $500 a month. But the lawyer died first, 30 years after the deal, having paid Mrs Calment several times the value of her flat and ensuring that she lived out the rest of her time without money worries. "It happens in life that we make bad deals," Mrs Calment was reported to have said.

The lawyer story is probably true. But as Mrs Calment grew ever older and frailer, the tales about her became suspiciously improbable. Did she really remember Van Gogh when he had both his ears, or was this a piece of embroidery by a journalist who worked out that the painter lived in Arles when Jeanne Calment was a girl? Did she really say, off pat, "I've been forgotten by God"?

The claims and the proof

Perhaps it does not matter. For most people, the interest in Mrs Calment was her durability. We all live under sentence of death. How did she put it off so long? And was it worth it? Research into ageing is one of the newer disciplines. The University of California's department for "the economics and demography of ageing" has located more than 20,000 centenarians in the United States and quite a few "super centenarians" aged at least 110. It studied the life of Jeanne Calment for clues to her endurance. "Here was someone of the greatest age and one we could authenticate," said a worker in the department. Since Methuselah, said to be 969, and his less-famous son Lamech, a mere 777, many claims have been made for long life. But Mrs Calment had the papers to prove that she was born on February 21st 1875, the year that Tolstoy published *Anna Karenina*. Her father was a shopkeeper and Jeanne was married within her class to another shopkeeper. The couple had one child, a girl. Mrs Calment seems to have had no endangering illnesses. Putting aside her faith in the life-sustaining qualities of olive oil, the Californian researchers assumed that Mrs Calment's otherwise

unexceptional life had been prolonged because of her genes. It seems the best chance of attaining a great age comes from having long-lived parents. Mrs Calment's father lived to the age of 94 and her mother to 86. But it doesn't always work. Her daughter died at 36.

People generally are living longer in the rich countries. In some, average life expectancy has doubled over the past century. There will be 1.3m American centenarians by 2040, according to present projections. The Californian researchers are unwilling to point to a maximum age beyond which no one could live, although they take the view that no one could live for ever. Would anyone want to? As it happens, in the week that Jeanne Calment died, 44% of Germans who took part in a survey said they did not want to live beyond 80, and only 18% hoped to be centenarians. They may change their mind nearer the time.

The nasty ailments, cancer, Alzheimer's and heart disease, tend to strike those aged between 50 and 80. Survive beyond that period and you could still live a life without being a nuisance to your nearest and dearest. Another American group, the National Institute on Ageing, reckons that many octogenarians can climb stairs, go for a walk and do their shopping. At the age of 85, Bernard Baruch, an adviser to American presidents, wrote, "I will never be an old man. To me, old age is always 15 years older than I am." He was to live another ten years.

Mrs Calment may have simply grown weary. "Journalists visit her," said her doctor, "but she no longer enjoys them." The journalists are now keeping a watch on Christian Mortensen, a Danish-born American, who will be 115 on August 16th. Others are contesting his claim to be the oldest living person, among them a Brazilian woman who says she is 126 and a Lebanese who smokes 60 cigarettes a day and is sure he is 135. But Mr Mortensen has the all-important birth certificate, and has already held his first press conference, reminiscing about his early days as a cowboy. A promising start. ■

Alec Campbell

Alec William Campbell, a veteran of Gallipoli, died on May 16th 2002, aged 103

IN THE first world war 324,000 Australians volunteered to fight overseas, an extraordinary number in a nation of fewer than 5m people. Of the 60,000 Australians who died in the war, 8,700 were lost in a few months during a hopeless attempt to capture Gallipoli, a small piece of territory in Turkey. In the words of a piece of doggerel at the time, "In five minutes flat, we were blown to hell / Nearly blew us right back to Australia."

The story of Gallipoli and the Anzacs, the name given to members of the Australia New Zealand Army Corps, became a legend in Australia (and indeed in New Zealand, which lost 2,700 men). Nine Australians were awarded the Victoria Cross, Britain's highest military honour. Australians talk of the Anzac spirit, rather as the British of a certain age talk of the Dunkirk spirit (both refer to managed retreats that softened the sting of defeat). A lot of Australian homes are simply called Anzac. Each year the battle is commemorated on April 25th, the anniversary of the Anzacs' landing in Gallipoli in 1915, in what is now known as Anzac Cove.

This year, as on many previous occasions, the main commemorative procession was led by Alec Campbell, who because of his age was allowed the comfort of riding in a car. When Mr Campbell died a few weeks later flags were flown at half mast throughout Australia. He was given a state funeral on May 24th and the prime minister, John Howard, cut short an official visit to China to be there.

Mr Campbell was uneasy at his growing fame as one by one newspapers reported the deaths of the few remaining Gallipoli survivors. One of the last was Roy Longmore, who died last year aged 107. The last survivor on the Turkish side, Adil Sahin, died in 1998. When it seemed likely that Mr Campbell was the only remaining witness of Gallipoli he was increasingly referred to in Australia as a "national treasure".

An ordinary chap

Alec Campbell was not so sure about that. He said, correctly, that he was an ordinary chap, but he politely answered reporters' questions about his life. He was born into a farming family in Tasmania. Queen Victoria was still reigning. Australia had not yet seen a motor car. He worked on a cattle station, then as a carpenter, then as a civil servant. He gained an economics degree in his 50s, studying part-time. He taught himself to sail and took part in several big races in Australian waters. He was married twice and fathered nine children. It was a respectable life, although perhaps not an extraordinary one. Now, Mr Campbell, what about Gallipoli ...?

The decision to land in Turkey was a consequence of the lack of success by Britain and its allies on the western front in France. Turkey, which had sided with Germany only reluctantly, was reckoned to be a soft target. Land forces, aided by the navy, would advance to Constantinople, and Turkey would surrender. The way would be open to supply Russia with much needed arms through the Dardanelles, the strip of water that separates Europe and Asia, and the Russians would march triumphantly to Berlin. What would now be called a multinational force of some 500,000 men was assembled from the far reaches of the British empire; and a disparate bunch they were, among them the Assyrian Jewish Refugee Mule Corps, believed to be the first Jewish unit to fight since 70AD, when the Romans attacked Jerusalem.

The Turks defended their territory well, killing 33,000 of the invasion force. The Anzacs were given a particularly tricky stretch of Gallipoli to attack. The beach where they landed was dominated by well-fortified high ground. The Anzacs lost 2,000 men on the first day. Alec Campbell arrived at Gallipoli some time after the initial attack, when the Anzacs were barely holding on. He was only 16, was still not shaving, but insisted he was 18.

Older Aussies called him the Kid, and did their best to protect him He was given the job of running water to the men in the front line. That was dangerous enough. Every day runners would be picked off by Turkish snipers. "They kept you on your toes," he said. "To stick up your noddle was nearly always fatal." Mr Campbell's tour of duty ended after two months when he fell ill with a fever and was invalided home. He was asked how many Turks he had killed. "None," he replied, probably truthfully. But in later life, fed up with the question, he said "Dozens."

A British government report conceded that the attack on Turkey had been "ill conceived". In Australia the criticism was earthier, and if anything the bitterness that followed the massacre of its young men has grown over the years. If Australia ever decides to become a republic, the memory of Gallipoli may play a part. Mr Campbell voted for a republic in the referendum in 1999. But he was not by nature a propagandist. If he spoke of the folly of war, of the need for peace, of the idiocy of politicians, they were the casual views of an ordinary man. He was admired partly because he was so ordinary, an accidental hero.

Alec Campbell made a return visit to Gallipoli in later life and found a trench used by the Anzacs, now overgrown by wild flowers. He said, "It was a lovely place, you know, if conditions had been better ..." ∎

Marcel Carné

Marcel Carné, whose "Paradis" turned to pain, died on October 31st 1996, aged 90

WHILE IN his thirties Marcel Carné made "Les Enfants du Paradis", considered by some critics to be the world's best film. Although the film was a triumph, it came to be a personal burden. For ever after, at festivals and other gatherings, people would come up to Mr Carné and praise "Paradis". He would smile courteously and seek to move the conversation to his latest project. But nothing Mr Carné made in the 50 years of his life after "Paradis" was judged to be in the same class.

Critics said he had lost his touch, or belonged to a bygone era, or whatever. Orson Welles (1915–85) suffered similarly. Anything he did was liable to be measured, adversely, against "Citizen Kane", regarded as his masterpiece, and made when he was 25. Like Orson Welles, Marcel Carné never lost his enthusiasm for film. He turned up at the Cannes film festival as recently as 1992. But, like Welles, he was edged to the periphery of the business, when once he had occupied the centre.

Was "Paradis" the best film ever made? The critics who voted it number one were French. But less nationalistic critics elsewhere have consistently put it in their "ten best" list. The film is shown every Saturday in one Paris cinema, and presumably this will continue for as long as the building stands. (Paris likes this agreeable type of memorial: for the past 40 years the Théâtre de la Huchette has been putting on for six nights a week two plays by Eugène Ionesco.) More generally, the film is revived from time to time, but usually in cinemas known in the trade as "art houses". *Variety*, an American showbusiness newspaper, once called the film "beautiful" but, perhaps reflecting a Hollywood view, said it was "downright dull". There are no car chases, no shoot-outs, no violent language. Take your seat for three hours and a quarter and immerse yourself in improbable love stories set in theatrical Paris of the 19th century.

Gestapo in the studio

However it looks now, when "Paradis" was released at the end of the second world war, it came as a total surprise. Mr Carné's pre-war films had tended to be pessimistic. "Paradis", made in Paris during the German occupation, was a sumptuous fantasy. What had been going on in wartime France?

After France surrendered, Joseph Goebbels, Germany's propaganda chief, saw the French as "sick and worm-eaten" and a market for cheap "corny pictures" made by German-run companies. French directors had to endure the presence of Gestapo officers in their studios. Some collaborated, some escaped abroad, usually to America. Those that resisted did so by trying to make films of the highest quality. "Les Visiteurs du Soir", made by Mr Carné in 1942 (and which some saw as a symbol of occupied France), is a meticulously crafted film. "Paradis" has sets and costumes created regardless of cost: at the time it was the most expensive film made in France. Throughout, Mr Carné was anxious for the safety of the Jews he employed on the film; while Arletty, one of his stars, was having an affair with a German

but most were either dismissed by critics or, perhaps worse, received token praise from those reluctant to knock him. As a film-maker he came to be thought of as a poor financial risk. The backers of "Mouche", promised as a new "Paradis", withdrew after shooting started, and the film was never made.

He was further wounded when critics turned to his early career in the 1930s. This period is regarded as a golden age of French cinema. Mr Carné worked as an assistant to two of the most gilded directors, René Clair and Jacques Feyder, and then made a number of much-praised pictures of his own, among them "Le Jour se Lève" (also on some "best" lists). Mr Carné's detractors now suggested that his films of this period owed more to the scriptwriter, Jacques Prévert, than to the director. Prévert, a poet as well as a scriptwriter, did make his own mark on Mr Carné's films. His dialogue captured the drifting hopelessness of France in the 1930s. "Cinema and poetry are almost the same thing," he said. But he thought of himself as simply one of the large team assembled by Mr Carné. "He is a great director," Prévert said, "and an extraordinarily modest man." The modest Marcel Carné never claimed for "Paradis" that it was the world's best. It was enough to have made a good film, he said. "Too much praise only creates enemies for you." ■

officer. An extra was arrested in the studio and never seen again. Mr Carné said he would relive that scene for ever.

While Mr Carné survived the war, a more dangerous threat to his career lay ahead in peacetime. This was the emergence of a "new wave" of French film-makers such as François Truffaut and Jean-Luc Godard. They made films on small budgets, shot on location to cut costs, and used non-professional actors who made up their own lines, all features that were anathema to Mr Carné. "The new wave assassinated me," he recalled. "But then it assassinated the cinema too."

Mr Carné was not killed off. He made more than a dozen films after "Paradis",

Barbara Cartland

Barbara Hamilton Cartland, a romantic, died on May 21st 2000, aged 98

OVER THE past year or two the name Barbara Cartland has been mentioned by writers in *The Economist* at least six times, usually as a synonym for romanticism of one sort or another. No doubt other publications have found it equally useful. Perhaps the adjective Cartlandish may even creep into the dictionaries. Barbara Cartland would have approved of that. She was worried about her prospects for immortality, as indeed she had reason to be. Some time ago she sent to the editors of London newspapers a thick folder containing "The History of Barbara Cartland", and subtitled "How I want to be remembered."

Such an offering was bound to be treated with suspicion by the media's guardians of truth, even though, as

in Barbara Cartland's case, it was bound with pink ribbon and smelt of scent. Those who actually read it were intrigued with its detail. Being made a dame (a knighthood for a woman) was recorded, of course. But so was being honoured by the National Home Furnishing Association of Colorado Springs. Her entries in reference books show the same anxious attention to detail. For the benefit of scholars delving into her oeuvre she notes helpfully that "Cupid Rides Pillion", one of her 723 novels, is also known as "Dangerous Love". Her entry in "Who's Who" is the longest in the book.

There might indeed be a doctorate awaiting someone brave enough to read through her millions of words and offer plausible conclusions about why she became a household name. An early surprise might be that as a young woman Barbara Cartland showed signs of being a gifted writer. In those days she took a year over a book, not the couple of weeks she gave to her later work. She worked too for the *Daily Express*, which under Beaverbrook never allowed a sentence of sloppy writing. But she was perpetually hard up, a grave inhibition for a pretty woman who wanted to enjoy the high life of London. She decided that the quickest way to get rich was to write trash. Lots of writers do that, but she was among the best, becoming a power in the vast trash industry that envelops popular culture, in pop music, films, television and in the arts.

When the moon beams

Respectability was important to Barbara Cartland. No one "rolls around naked in my books", she said. "I do allow them to go to bed together if they're married, but it's all very wonderful and the moon beams." She said she was born into a more innocent age than today's. She claimed that Muslims appreciated the moral tone of her books. Colonel Qaddafi of Libya was said to be a fan.

But the Cartland novels have their own artful form of foreplay, extended over the first 100 pages or so, with relief finally provided by the sanction of marriage. Just as the routine of courtship is constantly renewed in humans, so the Cartland stories are served by a simple plot in which only the scenery and the characters are changed. She liked historical settings. She wrote a biography of Metternich, though academics were discouraged by its title, "The Passionate Diplomat". Her quickie method of dictating a book to a team of secretaries resembled that of Edgar Wallace, a thriller writer famous in the 1920s, although he managed a mere 175 novels.

Wallace's name never made it into a dictionary, but some of his quotable remarks have survived. A highbrow, he said, is a man who has found something more interesting than women. If being quotable is the way to be remembered, Barbara Cartland did her very best. She was asked in a radio interview whether she thought that British class barriers had broken down. "Of course they have," she said, "or I wouldn't be sitting here talking to someone like you."

She came from a middle-class family, but had aristocratic yearnings. Her daughter, Raine, married the father of Princess Diana. Barbara Cartland thus became Diana's step-grandmother, and was fiercely defensive of her against other members of the royal family. "This royal family are Germans," she said. "The princess is English." Like many of her generation in Britain, she found it difficult to regard Germany as other than an enemy. Her father was killed in the first world war and her two brothers in the second.

She lived in a statelyish house in Hertfordshire, where journalists were always welcome, and they usually came away with the material for a readable article. Sometimes she would abandon her prudish public mask and talk about sex with remarkable candour. Yes, she believed that a woman should remain a virgin until she was married, but that a man should be experienced, so that one of the partners would know what to do. How would the man get experience if all women were virgins? He would go to a brothel, of course, she said.

She told a photographer, "I have the body of a young girl, without a line in it." By then she was an old old lady, and looked it, despite the layers of make-up. He declined her offer to be photographed in the nude. Perhaps, despite her strong will and intelligence, Barbara Cartland's human weakness was to see herself as eternally young. ∎

Bonnie Cashin

Bonnie Cashin, designer of America's new look, died on February 3rd 2000, aged 84

O N A visit to Japan in the 1950s Bonnie Cashin was told that if the weather was chilly, Japanese talked of a "nine-layer day". That is, they wore numerous light garments against the cold, instead of a single heavy one. Miss Cashin was shown how to wear a kimono, an artfully structured garment of many layers. Back in New York she introduced the idea of layering into western fashion. Quite likely, people throughout the world, and not just in Japan, had for centuries wrapped themselves in whatever was available to face the rigours of a bitter day. But fashion writers are ever grateful for something that looks new, and for a while layering was praised as the big new idea.

American fashion was in dire need of new ideas. Its designers were little known outside the United States, and not much there. Americans had all the money, but Paris, irritatingly, seemed to have all the business. American painters were doing their best for their country. Was not New York the art capital of the world? Now it was time to show those uppity Europeans the American way of dress.

"Fashion evolves from need," Miss Cashin told a reporter. What did Europeans need? Not an American version of the kimono, a garment which took half an hour to put on (with assistance), was rather stuffy, and was falling into disuse even in Japan. Miss Cashin turned to another source for inspiration. During the second world war she had designed uniforms for women in the armed forces. The mass-produced uniforms were comfortable, protective and allowed freedom of movement. The clothes she now designed had these practical qualities. They were made of hard-wearing materials, including canvas and leather, had useful pockets, toggle fastenings and industrial-size zips. If Miss Cashin's clothes had the look of a tunic, they were done with a civilian casualness. In the fashion lexicon her clothes are said to have the sportswear look, but this is the look of most women's clothes today. When some of her clothes were exhibited in New York's Metropolitan Museum of Art in 1997, the catalogue said they reflected "democracy's magnitude and the consequence of independent and intrepid women". Despite that, European women loved them.

You like it? It's yours

Intrepid, though, is perhaps not a bad adjective for the long career of Bonnie Cashin. She had no formal training as a designer, just what she had picked up from her mother, a dressmaker. She reckoned that her father, a photographer, had given her an eye for a good design. While still at school, she persuaded a Los Angeles ballet company to give her a job as a dress designer. A year or two later she was designing the costumes for the troupe of dancing girls that gave performances between movies at the Roxy Theatre in New York. She took her needle and sketchbook to Hollywood. "Anna and the King of Siam" is probably the best known of the 60 or so films she designed costumes for.

She had a reputation for generosity.

Anyone who admired something of hers was quite likely to be given it. Whether she intended to or not, Miss Cashin seemed to mirror the disposable nature of fashion: that a product is almost out of date the moment it goes on sale. She was mildly surprised that some of her designs that had survived the dustbin had become collectors' items. A Cashin leather shoulder bag of the 1960s fetches several hundred dollars, and the market is rising. Jackets in

good condition with the Cashin label intact fetch much more. But she was not herself sentimental about the past. Museums and collectors' pieces were not for the living. You must move on, she said. A cartoon in her New York flat shows a trapeze performer saying, "You've got to know when to let go."

This idea of constant change is nothing new, of course. "Woman is always fickle and changing," Virgil complained. An exasperated Prince Albert, Queen Victoria's husband, lamented "the unreasoning laws of markets and fashion". But fashion has become a pacemaker of the throwaway society. In the cities of the rich world no woman is expected to wear a garment until it is worn out. (Men, unaccountably, tend to hold on to their clothes for years, but the industry is working on the problem.) The clothes industry would be in a pickle without a constant supply of clients dissatisfied with the contents of their wardrobes. The fashion round, what's in, who's out, is associated with the poise of Paris, the newness of New York. Without it, the fashion weeks in New York and London, this month's boost to the clothes industry, would not last a day.

There are no reliable figures for the phenomenal growth of the fashion industry, chiefly because its reach is so wide – not just clothes, but everything that goes with them, from buttons to scent. What can be said is that a single idea can give birth to a product worth infinite millions. What used to be called plimsolls have been transformed into vastly expensive trainers. Denim, a humble material whose virtue was its cheapness, became as valuable as satin when turned into jeans. Jeans and trainers are the foremost innovative fashions of recent decades. Bonnie Cashin's "democratic look" is a reasonable runner-up. ∎

Charles Causley

Charles Causley, a defiantly unmodern poet, died on November 4th 2003, aged 86

THE PUREST poetry, it can be argued, springs not from urban angst or cloistered academies, nor even from the passionate contemplation of nature. It grows from the soil, and is best expressed in the simple songs of ordinary people. Just as a line of hills, or the edge of a wood, can move an English heart in inexplicable ways, so too can the plain, quiet words of "The Sally Gardens" or "Linden Lea", even before a Benjamin Britten or a Ralph Vaughan Williams has added woodwinds to them.

Yet for centuries, from the decorous Augustans through the blazing Romantics to the solid Victorians, no one paid much attention to the ballads of England's drinking houses or the rhymes of its playgrounds. The odd little snatches chanted in Shakespeare's plays by Puck or Ariel had a certain haunting power, but no poetic virtue. These were primitive things. Only poor half-mad William Blake, buffeting the wind on Hampstead Heath, gained some sort of audience for "songs" that deliberately confused the worlds of the adult and the child. And only Rudyard Kipling gave soldiers' slangy ballads an honoured place in his work.

Charles Causley not only embraced this sort of poetry, but became its best modern practitioner. He called his poems ballads, carols, serenades, rondels and nursery rhymes, and wrote them as if they should be danced to. He delighted too, like Blake, in making poems that could be read by children and adults alike. He did not believe in the distinction, and in his work the observer always kept both perspectives. The world was disturbing as well as magical, and the eye that saw it both

innocent and knowing. In "Timothy Winters", he wrote of a wild schoolboy with the boy's defiance and the teacher's frustration:

> When teacher talks he won't hear a word
> And he shoots down dead the arithmetic-bird
> He licks the patterns off his plate
> And he's not even heard of the Welfare State.

while in "Recruiting Drive", one of many poems born out of his naval experiences in the second world war, the "lily-white boy" is both a pitiable piece of cannon-fodder and a character from a fairy tale:

> Under the willow the willow
> I heard the butcher bird sing,
> Come out you fine young fellow
> From under your mother's wing ...
>
> You must take off your clothes for the doctor
> And stand as straight as a pin,
> His hand of stone on your white breastbone
> Where the bullets all go in.

Even his rare non-ballads could not leave childhood songs aside, as in "Convoy", about a drowned sailor in the Arctic:

> He is now a child in the land of Christmas:
> Watching, amazed, the white tumbling bears
> And the diving seal.
> The iron wind clangs round the ice-caps,
> The five-pointed Dog-star
> Burns over the silent sea,
>
> And the three ships
> Come sailing in.

Because such writing looks easy, and because the common man understands and likes it, Mr Causley was often scorned as simplistic and old-fashioned. His insistent rhymes and metres got on the nerves of those who thought only free verse or broken rhythms could express the modern muse. Yet the best poets – Philip Larkin, Ted Hughes – knew how deep simplicity could go, and admired him.

His natural shyness did not help him. He was brought up poor, and remained keenly aware of his working-class roots. His mother took in washing, but also saw that her son learned piano, where he encountered the bitter songs of the first world war. His own experiences in the next war, he always said, made him decide to be a poet. Before that he had worked as a clerk for a builder's firm and an electrical company. Though he travelled widely, he kept returning to the slate-and-stone town of Launceston in Cornwall, where he was born. Like most good poets, he thought the voyages of his imagination more important than travels round the world.

In that sense, too, he was true to his balladeer's calling. The old songs are rooted in local earth and feeling, and so, too, were his: not in England, properly speaking, but in Cornwall, that misty Celtic promontory running out into the Atlantic. Though he wrote of many other places, the core of his work was set in Marazion, Porth Veor, Lezant or Bodmin, on granite moors or under hawthorn hedges, and constantly within sight or hearing of the "long salt fingers" of the sea. Many Cornishmen wanted him for their official Poet Laureate, cocking a deliberate snub at their long-felt colonisation by Anglo-Saxons.

This is also a land peopled with giants, devils and saints, as Mr Causley saw them. Giant Winter lies over Wilsey Down, "the snow flossing his blue coat and his buckles/Drifting his lip and his eye." A demon is shot down by St Michael, the "silver bowman", over Helston, and Judas Iscariot returns as Jack O'Lent, running across the moors in search of redemption. All this, too, is in the style of ancient carols, which translated the Christian mysteries to local places and contemporary dress. But it is hard to think of any modern caroller who could pick up Mr Causley's pen. ■

Régine Cavagnoud

Régine Cavagnoud, France's brightest sporting star, died on October 31st 2001, aged 31

ONE WAY to look at the short life of Régine Cavagnoud is that it was thrown away recklessly and needlessly. She died after colliding with a ski coach who was on the slopes. The collision seems not to have been her fault. Indeed, no one has been blamed. In Europe it is difficult to find high-quality skiing sites to practise on this early in the season, and the one used by Miss Cavagnoud may have been crowded. That said, there seemed to be an inevitability about the tragedy. Many times previously Miss Cavagnoud had been badly injured on the slopes while pushing herself to her natural limits, and probably beyond, in her drive to become a world champion.

Since her death, there have been cautionary words generally about the need for more regulation, and some observers have expressed surprise that she was on the slopes at all so soon after being injured in a skiing accident in Chile in August. But no such adverse comment has been heard in her native France. There she is, quite simply, a national heroine.

The French prime minister, Lionel Jospin, said Régine Cavagnoud had come "to embody" France's passion for skiing. Mr Jospin, not by nature an emotional man, used the verb *incarner*, with its religious overtone. At her funeral last week, much covered on television, there were similar sentiments. The French do take their sport seriously; and Miss Cavagnoud, with her red hair and blue eyes and her blazing courage, was seen as a goddess by sports writers and their readers. She was only 31 and looked younger. She could become a candidate for the popular immortality that is sometimes, and mysteriously, bestowed on those who die young. James Dean, who made only three films before crashing his sports car at the age of 24, is one of the youthful pantheon. Buddy Holly, who died in an air crash at 22, is another. Some would be happy to beatify Princess Diana. Like her, Régine Cavagnoud died with her promise unfulfilled.

A catalogue of injuries

Her earliest recollection of skiing was when she was three. Her father was a carpenter at La Clusaz, a town in the French Alps where she was brought up. But when winter came he helped out at the local ski lifts, and Régine went with him. In the snowy places of the world children soon learn to ski, but Régine showed enough talent to be spotted when she was a teenager by scouts for the French national team. She joined the junior section at 16. A year later she had the first of the injuries that were to mark her career for the next 15 years. She tore the ligaments in her left knee. A little later she hurt her right knee. She broke a shoulder bone and several times hurt her back. Once she skied while wearing a surgical collar. Still, between injuries she became a regular with the French team. "After every injury", she said, "I told myself that it was not over. My passion for skiing just carried me through."

Her talent was slow to show results. In Japan in 1993, seven years into her skiing career, she could only manage 11th place in a downhill event. Medals

slither at turns, class skiers seek to check the slide to keep up their speed. On her last fatal run Miss Cavagnoud was travelling at such a speed that she just could not avoid a crash. There was something in her make-up that demanded speed. When she wasn't on the slopes she was roaring along mountain roads on her powerful motor-bike. "Twice I have given myself a fright," she recalled, but she would not give up biking. Hunter Thompson, an American writer, put the urge like this:

Faster, faster, until the thrill of speed overcomes the fear of death.

were rare in the next few years. Still, the French had faith in her. She took part in three Olympics and would have been a probable choice for the Olympics at Salt Lake City next year. She became a world champion in February at St Anton in Austria, winning the coveted title known as the super-G. The G stands for giant slalom, the winding course that takes its name from the Norwegian word for a sloping track. Miss Cavagnoud was the first Frenchwoman to win a world skiing title for 17 years.

Hurtling down a mountain on skis is the fastest a human being can travel on land without a mechanical aid. The record is 248km per hour (154mph). When slaloming in the super-G you go at less than half that speed, but it is still a heart-stopping way to travel as you manoeuvre the twists and turns. Unlike recreational skiers, who tend to

Miss Cavagnoud did feel fear. Considering the risks involved, there have been relatively few deaths on the slopes: 11 in first-class skiing over the past 30 years. Ulrike Maier of Austria was the previous woman skier to die on the slopes: she broke her neck in 1994 when she hit a post. But many skiers are badly injured. Miss Cavagnoud dreaded ending up in a wheelchair. But even more, she said, she dreaded doing badly. As some actors do, she had psychiatric help to relax her for her next performance. If there was something of an actor in Régine Cavagnoud, she saw the admiring people of La Clusaz as her audience. They elected her to the local council. When she won her world title they wanted her to give up competing. She said she thought she would soon. "I really want to have children," she said. ■

Eddie Chapman

Arnold Edward Chapman, a patriotic crook, died on December 15th 1997, aged 83

THE FILM, called "Triple Cross", was made in 1966 but it was a lively yarn and turns up occasionally on late-night television. A crook, Eddie Chapman, becomes a spy in the second world war, pretending to work for the Germans but really employed by the British. The Germans award him the Iron Cross and the British acclaim him as a hero, happily pardoning him for his crimes.

The film was almost true. But the real-life tale of Mr Chapman was even better, for those who like real life. Christopher Plummer, who played Mr Chapman, made him a Bond-like character, shrewd, attractive to women, handy with his fists. But Eddie Chapman was, at least in his early life, far from being an elegant figure. He grew up in Sunderland, in the industrial north of England, and for a time worked in the shipyards. But when work became scarce in the 1930s, he joined the army. He was not considered a good soldier and, after several spells in army prisons, he was thrown out. He took up crime; at first smashing shop windows and grabbing what he could, and then learning the more profitable trade of safe-breaking.

In 1940, when the Germans occupied the British-owned Channel Islands, Eddie Chapman was in a local jail. The Germans took an interest in him. Here was a man who appeared to have a grudge against Britain. Would he like to work for the fatherland? Mr Chapman said he would, very much. He was sent to France to be trained as a spy, and one night in December 1942 he parachuted out of a German aircraft over eastern England. He was equipped with a radio transmitter, a pistol, a bottle of invisible ink, a wallet full of British money and, just in case things got desperate, a cyanide pill.

Little Fritz

The British were waiting for him. For all the Germans' much-vaunted efficiency in other enterprises, their wartime spy organisation, the Abwehr, was a dud. The Germans' codes had been broken. British intelligence already knew a great deal about the man the Germans called, not very originally, Fritzchen (Little Fritz). As German agents arrived in Britain they were arrested and given a choice: work for the British or be hanged. Did Mr Chapman want to work for the British? He did, very much. In any case, he told Sir John Masterman, an intelligence chief, his whole purpose in pretending to collaborate with the Germans was to get to Britain to fight for king and country.

The task Fritzchen had been given by the Germans was to blow up a factory which was making an aircraft called the Mosquito. This was one of the war's most revolutionary aircraft, made of wood for lightness and the fastest thing in the air. Using the services of Jasper Maskelyne, who in civilian life had been a conjuror, the British faked extensive damage at the Mosquito factory. Newspapers were allowed to report the "explosion", and aerial photographs taken by a German aircraft convinced the Abwehr that Fritz had done extraordinarily well. They had no reason to doubt the truth of subsequent messages that flowed from Mr Chapman's radio, compiled by the creative minds of the intelligence service.

The Abwehr told him to return to Germany to be briefed for further missions, and offered to fetch him in a U-boat. The British preferred to allow him to return via Portugal, formally a neutral country but under the thumb of Germany. In Lisbon Mr Chapman picked up his German salary and a bonus for good work, went on a long holiday in Norway and then to Berlin to get his Iron Cross.

In 1944 he was again dropped on to England. The Germans wanted to know whether their missiles – the forerunners of the space rockets – were reaching the cities they were aimed at. The misleading information Mr Chapman sent them probably saved many civilian lives. The British were grateful and, within the confines of wartime, Mr Chapman lived a comfortable life. He received a pardon for any crimes committed before the war. But as an agent he had one great drawback. He could not keep a secret. To his old cronies he would hint of his daring exploits. Whether they believed him or not, a talkative agent was a menace to the intelligence service. Mr Chapman was retired. In any case, Germany was almost beaten.

After the war he wrote about his experiences. An account was published in a French newspaper, but Mr Chapman found himself in a court of law when he sold his story to a British newspaper. He was accused of disclosing official secrets and fined. He was again in trouble for a currency offence, but a government official softened the heart of the judge by stating that Mr Chapman was "one of the bravest men who served in the war". He was in the news again when he was deported from Tangier for smuggling. And in 1966 he had his moment of glory in the Christopher Plummer film. In a war that has produced many extraordinary stories, Mr Chapman's was among the oddest. Just how much glory there was is a matter of conjecture. But this is the season of goodwill. ∎

Eugenia Charles

Dame Mary Eugenia Charles, prime minister of Dominica, died on September 6th 2005, aged 86

THE PRESS photographs did no justice to how Eugenia Charles felt as she stood beside Ronald Reagan, at the White House, in October 1983. They showed a rather grim and melancholy woman, in a white cravat and executive striped suit. Only a vestigial twinkle in Reagan's eye suggested the truth: that Miss Charles was having the time of her life. "Mr President," she told him afterwards in her lilting *basso profundo*, "you have big balls!"

She had just invited him to invade Grenada, and he had done so secretly, at once. That island, in the same chain as her own state of Dominica in the eastern Caribbean, had been taken over by Cuban-backed thugs and the moderate prime minister murdered. Miss Charles had raised the spectre of Cuban infiltration all over the region; Reagan, ever ready to wage clandestine

war against Commies, had gallantly responded. A navy flotilla with marines had been diverted from its voyage to Lebanon to carry out her wishes and liberate the island. This was power.

Grenada was a member of the British Commonwealth; but even Margaret Thatcher was not told, a matter of some satisfaction. Miss Charles became impatient with the endless comparisons that were made between them. True, they were both hard-working daughters of the bourgeoisie, Red-haters and pioneers in male-dominated worlds. Both liked to let their hair down, at the end of a hard day of governing, by kicking off their shoes and indulging in something rather vulgar (Lady Thatcher swigging a large whisky, Dame Eugenia gnawing on a stick of sugar cane). Both made their opinions absolutely plain and were fearless in argument. The Iron

Lady and the Iron Lady of the Caribbean met, and admired each other. But Miss Charles thought Mrs Thatcher had got too fancy in her years in power.

She herself, though she ruled Dominica for 15 years, from 1980 to 1995, had little chance of hubris. Dominica was a tiny, troubled place, covered in volcanic jungle and short of everything but drug-runners and bananas. It was famous mostly for the slowness of its post, much of it being redirected from the Dominican Republic.

The year before Miss Charles became prime minister, Hurricane David wrecked the island. Whatever grand schemes she had for health care or education took a back seat to simple restoration of roads and power: "concrete and current", in her phrase. Eventually, by dint of IMF loans, eco-tourism, economic reforms and favourable terms for Caribbean bananas, for which she haggled tirelessly, the island stabilised somewhat. It remained, like all its neighbours, vulnerable to everything.

The aunt type

Her enemies said she governed like a headmistress, and there was something in that. In her second term, all the big portfolios – finance, the economy, foreign affairs, defence – were in her capable hands. She banned casinos, night clubs and duty-free shops from Dominica, convinced that they brought bad elements in, and championed banana-growers because, if "yellow gold" failed, they would just grow ganja instead. The island's minute defence force was summarily disbanded in 1981 for disloyalty, reluctance to wield a shovel after the hurricane, and selling marijuana to Rastafarians. Miss Charles weathered two coups with withering disdain, once quietly leaving by the back door while soldiers piled in at the front.

At first she was a reluctant politician.

Her training was in law, which she studied in Toronto and London. Back in Dominica in 1949, the first woman ever to set up a legal practice there, her energies were engaged in that for almost two decades. But government corruption increasingly outraged her. When, in 1968, a left-wing government brought in the Seditious and Undesirable Publications Act (the "Shut-Your-Mouth Bill", as she called it) to suppress dissent, she led the opposition to it, got it withdrawn and was made the leader of the Dominica Freedom Party.

Miss Charles was never, however, the party type. She was the aunt type: a true Caribbean matriarch (though unmarried and childless), ruling the roost and dispensing wisdom with no feckless male around to steal the limelight. The men could bum in the sun; she would "look after the things that need looking after". This was the extent of her ideology. Though she did various free-market things, to America's delight, she was no free-trader, and approved of co-operative ventures at every level. Her favourite reading was not Hayek, but Mills & Boon.

Her greatest political influence was probably her father, "J-B", with whom she lived until he died at the age of 107. It was he who encouraged her to argue at the dinner table (conduct frowned on at the Convent of the Faithful Virgin, where she went to school). He also suggested she should take a secretarial course and practise her shorthand in the magistrate's court, which led to her career in law. J-B Charles was many things: a planter, a fruit-exporter, a land-speculator, a politician and, in the fishing village of Pointe Michel where the family lived, the founder of a "penny bank" to encourage poor farmers to save. Thrift, debate, self-reliance, self-improvement: it all sounds very like the moral and political training of a certain grocer's daughter from Grantham. ∎

Ray Charles

Ray Charles Robinson, music-maker, died on June 10th 2004, aged 73

IN THE small town of Greenville in northern Florida, round the corner from Western Avenue, Wylie Pittman used to run a joint called the Red Wing Café. With its upright piano and its juke box, this was Greenville's answer to a night club in the 1930s. There was nothing much else round about but the railway, poor blacks and pine forests.

A black boy called "RC" haunted the café. His deserted mother took in washing for a living. His sight was failing, and by the age of six he was blind from glaucoma. But Pittman let him play the juke box: Nat King Cole, Count Basie, blues from Tampa Red, and the whole of the Classical Selection. After that, plumping him down on a stack of soda crates, he would take his small hands and let him loose on the piano, encouraging him when the boy hit on something good.

Of the many influences on Ray Charles's career, those sessions at the Red Wing Café were perhaps the most fundamental. The singer who wooed, teased and thrilled audiences the world over for 50 years, swaying on the piano stool in his sparkling lamé jackets, was still the delighted little boy teetering on the soda crates. He never saw the bright lights that surrounded him for much of his life, but he told his biographer that lights were his best memories of the years when he could see: flaring matches, lightning he tried to catch, and the sun blazing through the tall trees in the woods he used to explore.

Mr Charles felt the music was there even earlier, like an extra limb or a sixth sense, as soon as he was born.

It was "one of my parts", he said, "like my blood", or a force inside him, "nothing separate from me". However he struggled to describe it, one thing was clear: if you wanted to stop him playing and singing, "You'd have to remove the music surgically."

Which music was it? A mixture of almost everything he had ever heard, from Minnie Pearl to Sibelius, from Art Tatum to Chopin, from the Baptist choir in Greenville (in which he sang) to hillbilly players strumming on their guitars. At the start of his career, as an orphaned teenager travelling round Florida, he imitated the rural musicians with whom he played, though already he had a formidable ability to orchestrate music in Braille. A little later, living on scant savings in the red-light district of Seattle, he modelled himself on the crooner Cole. But after realising he was known only as an imitator, a "boy" with no name of his own, he determined to make a music that was distinctively his.

That music turned out to be an amalgam mostly of gospel and blues, with the gospel hotter than anyone imagined. Mr Charles's first act of daring, in 1954, was to transform the hymn "My Jesus is All the World to Me" into "I Got a Woman". His second, in 1959, was to use moaning and wailing gospel-choir techniques in a song called "What'd I Say?" to suggest the sexual play between a woman and a man. Banned on radio stations all across America, it sold a million copies.

To those who complained of blasphemy and abomination, and who

saw unleashed black sexuality as a threat to America second only to Soviet missiles, Mr Charles gave an innocent rejoinder: he was only singing what he felt. He was talking about a woman as he would talk about God. The fact that women in his act lingered round him like sirens, in skin-tight turquoise dresses, and that he was hooked for years on heroin and promiscuous sex, was somewhat smoothed by the knowledge that his music had sprung both out of a desperately hard life and, however wildly, out of church.

Songs for the general Joe

Mr Charles did not invent "soul", as he came to call it. But he put his stamp on it so thoroughly, as unmistakably as the gravelly baritone and the dark glasses, that he may as well have done. It was the same with "his" songs. After hearing him sing "Georgia on My Mind", few remembered that it had been written by Hoagy Carmichael; and after his renditions of "America the Beautiful", most famously at the tearful Republican convention that re-crowned Ronald Reagan in 1984, the anthem was more or less declared to be his property.

He was seldom, however, an overtly political figure. At first he seemed no more angry about segregation – in which, even at the blind school he attended in Florida, the white and black children were kept apart – than he did about his own blindness, whose effect on his life he dismissed as "nothing". But he began to protest when he found that blacks and whites could not sit together at his concerts. He soon became friends with Martin Luther King, though he believed his role in the struggle was different. As a music-maker, he wanted to sing about "the general Joe" and the hardships suffered by both blacks and whites as they tried to settle, love and earn a living. As a star, he had no trouble raising money for King's legal costs.

At bottom, Mr Charles felt that music could do the job of integration. He believed it could do anything. At his concerts, he was well aware of holding audiences in the palm of his hand: wildly roiling them one moment, making them cry the next, and then sliding to a silence in which you could hear a pin drop. This was power; to revert to his seeing days, this was lightning you could catch. ■

Julia Child

Julia Child, cookery teacher, died on August 13th 2004, aged 91

ST PAUL saw the light on the road to Damascus, Archimedes while soaking in the bath. Julia Child's moment of illumination came in a restaurant in Rouen in 1948. The meal was simple: oysters on the half-shell, sole *meunière*, green salad, a bottle of Pouilly-Fuissé, *café filtre*. But the whole experience, she later wrote, was "an opening up of the soul and spirit for me."

Until that moment, Mrs Child knew nothing of French food. She had never tasted *crème fraîche* or encountered a shallot. Nor had most Americans. Their menus revolved around Jell-O, Cream of Wheat and a single, rubbery, species of cheese. Almost single-handedly, Mrs Child was to change all that. Under her trilling and exuberant guidance, Americans came to embrace at least the cooking of France.

The main problem, she understood, was fear. The language was foreign, the recipes long, the ingredients difficult

to get, and the whole enterprise shot through with French superiority. Mrs Child determined to show that French cooking could be fun; that even a frazzled New Yorker, after a day at the office, could cobble up a mean *boeuf bourguignon*.

Her eruption on television, in 1962, made the point superbly. She had just produced 734 pages, in two volumes, called "Mastering the Art of French Cooking". This, the work of ten years, was still a mite intimidating. But Mrs Child appeared on set with a frying pan, a portable hot-plate, an apron, a whisk and a dozen eggs, and merrily whipped up an omelette as she was being interviewed. In the book, the process took ten pages; on screen, it took two minutes. She was launched as a star.

Americans had seen TV chefs before, but not like this one. The towering Mrs Child was a maniac with blades, never meeting a knife she didn't like; she once jointed a chicken with a sword, and was spoofed bleeding to death on "Saturday Night Live". Dishes were tasted liberally, and fingers licked. She drank as she went, recommending a glass for any tired cook, and her sing-song aristocratic tones ("*Bon appétit!*") grew steadily more extravagant.

Mistakes were summarily dealt with. An offending loaf was tossed over her shoulder among the potted plants; a misflipped potato pancake was scraped off the range and back into the pan; her false teeth were firmly readjusted in front of the camera. She began her demonstration of *coq au vin* by dropping a whole chicken on the floor, dusting it off and remarking: "It's OK. No one's looking."

Behind the fun lurked a stickler for exactitude. French cooking, she believed, was about rules; it was as much science as art. As a scientist, she was obsessed with discovering how to make perfect French bread with American all-purpose flour in an American oven. It took two years, 284 pounds of flour and all the ingenuity of her husband, Paul, who lined her stove with quarry tiles and, to produce the necessary burst of steam, dropped a brick into a pan of hot water at the bottom of the oven. Within two or three decades, Americans had no need to go to the trouble; they could buy good French bread in shops across the country. But that too, you could argue, was Julia's doing.

Butter and cream

Nothing in her background made her a gourmet. She ate prodigiously as a child, but so did her equally tall sisters. Though they were a rich family, the food was poor; her mother, who kept a cook, could make only biscuits and Welsh rarebit. Julia misbehaved, and smoked her father's cigars; she remained a smoker half her life, despite the risks to a discerning palate.

She thought she might be a novelist, or preferably a spy. During the second world war she joined the Office of Strategic Services, the forerunner of the CIA, and was sent to Ceylon (now Sri Lanka); there she met Paul Child, a serious foodie as well as her first and last love. His posting to Paris sealed her fate. After the Rouen epiphany *en route*, Julia enrolled at the Cordon Bleu school in 1949; on graduation, she started her own cookery class. By this time, she had discovered that her greatest joy was shopping and eating as the French did, and teaching how to do it. She went on almost until the day she died.

As a national institution, with her turquoise kitchen and copper pans eventually enshrined in the Smithsonian, she was excused from changes in fashion. She loved red meat with a passion, while America switched squeamishly to chicken; her cookery included lashings of eggs, butter and cream, when the national waistline was alarmingly expanding. "Just slowly incorporate another stick of butter," was Mrs Child's soothing response to emergencies with sauce. She could hardly think of another larder essential, except potatoes; and these too, when cooked, demanded to be buried in butter and cheese.

In 2000, when she was awarded the Légion d'Honneur for bringing the delights of France to Americans, she was served all her favourite things: oysters, caviar, Dover sole, duck, profiteroles and a good deal of champagne. Her life could appear one long indulgence of comfortable houses and perfect meals. Yet Julia was no snob. She encouraged all the clumsy, aspiring cooks who wrote to her and sought her autograph; and when stuck in an airport she would eat a hamburger quite happily, *comme tout le monde.* ∎

Ion Cioaba

Ion Cioaba, self-proclaimed gypsy king, died on February 23rd 1997, aged 62

WHEN ION Cioaba proclaimed himself King of all the Gypsies Everywhere he found himself short of loyal subjects. About 5,000 followers turned up for his coronation in Romania in 1992 at a monastery he had borrowed for the occasion. They cheered as a solid gold crown, made in Switzerland, was lowered on to his head. But many other gypsies "everywhere" – some 10m in 40 countries – felt that the notion of kingship contradicted their scattered existence.

Unlike the other great diaspora, the Jews, the gypsies have never desired their own nation state. If they had, it would not have been Mr Cioaba's Romania. It would have been somewhere in central India, from which a low caste tribe, the Dom, famous for its singing and dancing, fled to escape from Muslim invaders. Dom became corrupted into Rom, hence Romany, the gypsy language, a mixture of Sanskrit and acquired words. (Gypsy was the name given to the tribe by the English, in the erroneous belief that it had originated in Egypt.)

Whatever Ion Cioaba's ungypsylike ambitions, no one doubted that he did his best for his much maligned people. Perhaps because of their chosen exclusivity, gypsies are often seen as a threat by communities close to their encampments. Not even the politically correct have fought to suppress the nursery rhyme, "My mother said that I never should / Play with the gypsies in the wood". The Soviet Union sought to suppress the gypsy culture, tried to get gypsies to assimilate, and had the ultimate sanction of the gulag. In the United States, which has more than 1m gypsies, some states have passed laws banning fortune telling, a move apparently directed against gypsy women. However, American gypsies appear to be well organised, with the country divided into "economic territories", each controlled by a gypsy group.

Hiding the gold

Romanian gypsies had the misfortune to live under, first, a fascist dictatorship and then a communist one. During the second world war several members of Mr Cioaba's family were among the 40,000 Romanian gypsies deported to German concentration camps (where more than 500,000 gypsies from European counties died: Auschwitz had its own gypsy section).

The post-war ruler, Nicolae Ceausescu, did not persecute the gypsies – at least no more than he exercised a rule of fear over all Romanians. Gypsies gave up wearing in public the gold earrings and other ornaments they were fond of, knowing that the police would seize them. But their closed society gave them some protection from the excesses of the state. Gypsies traditionally do not marry non-gypsies and they avoid inessential dealings with them, preferring to work for themselves. They have their own god, called Del, but no clergy, although some are Roman Catholic or Orthodox Christian. They have purity codes and are pacifists. That said, anyone who attends the World Romany Congress is likely to bump into

academics, scientists and others with jobs usually held by *gaujes*, Romany for outsiders. They are happy to be thought of as gypsies, just as American Indians who become industrialists like to tell of ancestors who fought against Custer.

Mr Cioaba kept a foot in both worlds. Some of his critics said he had collaborated with the Ceausescu regime. He was president of a state-registered trade union, the unlikely sounding Union of Nomadic Metalworking Gypsies, but this may have arisen simply because his clanspeople were metalworkers. In 1986, accused of cheating the government over a copper deal, he was jailed and, he said, tortured. He claimed that the real reason for his imprisonment was that he made himself a nuisance by demanding rights for gypsies.

He drove a Mercedes car, which upset some Romanians. But not all gypsies are poor. Mr Cioaba belonged to the Kalerash, a rich gypsy clan. At any rate, when the Ceausescu regime was toppled in December 1989 Mr Cioaba was judged to be on the right side and served on the Provisional National Council, the country's frail start towards the democracy it achieved only in 1996. In a triumph for bureaucratic language, Romania formally recognised gypsies as a "transnational non-territorial minority". Mr Cioaba formed the Gypsy Party and stood for parliament. But neither he nor the party got anywhere. He turned to the world stage and claimed to be the United Nations spokesman for gypsies everywhere. He demanded that gypsy children be accepted in their local schools, and set up a centre for teaching adult gypsies to read and write (Mr Cioaba was illiterate).

In an interview with a German television company, Ion Cioaba argued for compensation for the families of gypsies who died in the camps, and some money has since been paid. But the gypsy life disturbs the German sense of order. Because of this, and worries about its unemployed, Germany has been deporting gypsies to the countries from which they migrated. Mr Cioaba did not much care for national borders. Gypsies, he said, were the only true pan-Europeans. There's a thought. ■

Eddie Clontz

Eddie Clontz, master of tabloid journalism, died on January 26th 2004, aged 56

THE RELATIONSHIP between truth and reporting has ever been a tricky one. No scene remains undistorted as it passes the eye of the beholder, and none reaches the page exactly as it was. But while living with this discrepancy, many journalists struggle with a much baser temptation. What they really want to put into their copy is that extraordinary "fact", that jaw-dropping story retailed by a single source down a crackling telephone line, which would earn them a banner headline if they could only stand it up.

Eddie Clontz felt this more than most, and he never resisted the temptation. As the deviser and, for 20 years, the editor-in-chief of *Weekly World News*, his delight was to run the wildest stories he could find. He described himself not as an editor but as a circus-master, drawing readers into his tent with an endless parade of fantasies and freaks.

The *News* had, and has, an unassuming look, a black-and-white tabloid with blurry graphics that sits at supermarket checkouts across America, among the chewing gum. But its headlines, in inch-high sans serif, are another matter. "ARCHEOLOGISTS FIND MIDDLE EARTH IN NEW JERSEY SWAMP!" "SEVEN CONGRESSMEN ARE ZOMBIES!" "TINY TERRORISTS DISGUISED AS GARDEN GNOMES!" ("These guys are typical al-Qaeda operatives,' says a top CIA source, 'with beards down to their belt buckles'.") Such stories, all from one recent issue, would have made Mr Clontz proud.

The *News* for which he was hired, in 1981, was a sorry affair, a dumping ground for stories that failed to make the *National Enquirer*. It had been started mostly to make use of the *Enquirer*'s old black-and-white presses after the sister-tabloid had gone to colour. Mr

Clontz soon shook it up. Out went the tired celebrity gossip; in came space aliens, dinosaurs, giant vegetables, and a "Psychic" column in which his brother Derek would find readers' car keys. Circulation soared. In a good week, it can reach well over a million.

Two stories in particular got Mr Clontz noticed. In 1988, his organ revealed that "ELVIS IS ALIVE! (King of Rock 'n' Roll Faked his Death and is Living in Kalamazoo, Mich!)". A few years later, the News reported that a bat boy, with huge ears and amber eyes and "eating his own weight in insects each single day", had been found by scientists in a cave in West Virginia.

Both items were followed up for years. Elvis went on appearing; Bat Boy escaped, was recaptured by the FBI, fell in love and endorsed Al Gore for president. Readers wrote in with their own sightings, bolstering whatever truth the nation believed was there. In 1993, Mr Clontz dared to kill the resurrected Elvis ("ELVIS DEAD AT 58!") – only to reveal some time later that this death, too, had been a hoax.

Scallops to scoops

Sheer chance seemed to bring Mr Clontz to this strange outpost of journalism. After dropping out of school at 16 and trying his luck as a scallop fisherman, he became a copy boy on his local paper in North Carolina. He moved next to a Florida paper, and from there to the disreputable corner office in the Enquirer building, in a run-down resort near Palm Beach, from which he was to entertain and terrify America.

His own politics were mysterious. Under the pseudonym "Ed Anger", he wrote a News column so vitriolically right-wing that it possibly came from the left. Anger hated foreigners, yoga, whales, speed limits and pineapple on pizza; he liked flogging, electrocutions

and beer. No, Mr Clontz would say, he had no idea who Anger really was. But he was "about as close to him as any human being."

Mr Clontz also always denied that his staff made the stories up. It was subtler than that. Many tips came from "freelance correspondents" who called in; their stories were "checked", but never past the point where they might disintegrate. ("We don't know whether stories are true," said Mr Clontz, "and we really don't care.") The staff also read dozens of respectable newspapers and magazines, antennae alert for the daft and the bizarre. When a nugget was found, Mr Clontz would order them to run away with it, urging them to greater imaginative heights by squirting them with a giant water-pistol.

Yet he also showed care for authenticity. If a story resisted tracking down, he would give it the dateline "Bolivia". If it relied on "scientific research", he would make sure the scientists were Bulgarian. Writers who made up the names of Georgia natives terrorised by giant chickens would be asked to check in the telephone book to make sure they did not exist. Loving editorial attention was given to the face of Satan when he appeared in a cloud formation over New York.

The result of this was that many readers appeared to believe Mr Clontz's stories. Letters poured in, especially from the conservative and rural parts of the country where Ed Anger's columns struck a chord. If a sensible man like Anger kept company with aliens and 20-pound cucumbers, perhaps those stories too were true. When the News reported the discovery of a hive of baby ghosts, more than a thousand readers wrote in to adopt one. But the saddest tale was of the soldier who wrote, in all seriousness, offering marriage to the two-headed woman. ∎

Christopher Cockerell

Sir Christopher Sydney Cockerell, hovercraft inventor, died on June 1st 1999, aged 88

THE STORY most often told about Christopher Cockerell is that he invented the hovercraft by experimenting with a device made from two empty cans and a vacuum cleaner. Some accounts say one of the cans had contained cat food and the other coffee. Some maintain that both were coffee cans. In other versions a pair of kitchen scales is mentioned. Sir Christopher (as he later became) seems not to have clarified these technical points. He was content for this homely story to become part of inventors' folklore, unencumbered by too much detail.

Everything was stacked against becoming an inventor, he once said. People did not really want new ideas, even when they offered a better way of doing something. He had first learnt this as a child, when his mother declined to have her sewing machine powered by Christopher's steam engine. But "some silly chaps seem to be driven" to inventing. Britain, he believed, needed more silly chaps like George Stephenson, James Watt and Richard Arkwright, who had given the world its first industrial revolution. What could be more encouraging to their successors than the knowledge that a great invention could be given birth with a couple of cans salvaged from the dustbin?

This was an antidote to the gloomy notion that would-be inventors these days needed to work in the sort of scientific palaces where Nobel prize-winners seek drugs that will enable people to live for ever. Simple-tech was still with us. As a piece of engineering, the Cockerell hovercraft, travelling on a cushion of air and released from the friction of water, was in the elegant tradition of Stephenson's steam locomotive. There would always be a market, too, for what might be called primitive-tech. In someone's mind there was surely an idea waiting to be born as brilliant as the paper clip and the safety pin. Sir Christopher never found that golden fleece, but he never gave up the search and in the course of a long life patented more than 70 inventions.

The rewards
With all these inventions to his credit, Sir Christopher felt that he should have been rich. The hovercraft, versatile, fast, able to operate independently of harbours, was in demand throughout the world after the prototype first crossed the English Channel successfully in 1959. This conveyance, described in its patent as "neither an aeroplane, nor a boat, nor a wheeled land-vehicle", was, it was claimed, the all-purpose craft of the future. To a large extent this claim has been realised. It is reckoned that in the past 40 years some 600m people have travelled by hovercraft. But not all of them have travelled in a hovercraft more than once. The vehicle's movement, especially over choppy seas, can encourage nausea. Hovercraft still ply the English Channel, where the craft first flew, but many people prefer the steamers or the tunnel. Its future may be more as a transport for uncomplaining soldiers. American marines are enthusiastic about the hovercraft and it is widely used in the Russian army. In Finland coastguards have found that it

GH·900

the government took the hovercraft off the secret list and put up some money to develop it commercially; and later still helped to set up a corporation to market the vehicle. Sir Christopher surrendered his patents to the corporation. In 1969 he received £150,000 ($1.6m in today's money) in settlement of his claims, a knighthood from a grateful government and the admiration of his colleagues. "Numerous medals", he notes in a biographical entry in a reference book.

"I've enjoyed life," Sir Christopher remarked, "but it would have been nice to treat my wife to dinner once in a while." He may have felt bitter, but he was never poor. He had a comfortable childhood in Cambridge, where his father was director of the Fitzwilliam Museum. He gained an engineering degree and worked for Marconi. During the second world war at Marconi he was part of the team that invented a radio direction-finder which was fitted to British bombers.

He liked messing around in boats, and after the war bought a boatyard in Norfolk. As a business it was a failure, but it was here that he first experimented with his tins; and mulled over the possibilities of generating electricity from the movement of sea waves, an idea that once seemed silly but now seems less so. But for the silly chaps, said Christopher Cockerell, we would still be living in the stone age. ■

goes well over ice. Car-size hovercrafts have become a toy for the rich. In America there are hovercraft races.

One way or another the hovercraft has been quite a success. The name has gone into the language. "Hovercraft will always be around," Sir Christopher predicted. Had he been an entrepreneur as well as an inventor he might indeed have made a fortune. But creativity and salesmanship do not always go together. In 1955 he had shown an early model of the craft, about two feet long, to the British government. A bad move to involve the bureaucrats, perhaps, but he was a patriot and thought the hovercraft might have a military use. The government agreed, and classified it as a state secret. Later

The Columbia seven

Columbia's crew of seven died on February 1st 2003

THE SPACE shuttle *Columbia* took off on its last flight without particular ceremony. Shuttles have been America's space workhorses for more than 20 years. They are regularly rocketed into space loaded with satellites, or supplies for a space station, or boxes of plants to see how they grow without gravity; that sort of thing. Yet, humdrum or not, getting a ride in a shuttle, joining the still tiny group of people who have viewed the world from the heavens like gods, is greatly coveted. All seven in *Columbia*'s crew had served long apprenticeships in more earthbound activities before being considered for a space trip. All seven were in their 40s; the five men with receding hairlines; the two women doing their best to look alluring in their working clothes. No movie director would have cast them for a space epic. Yet each had a personality more interesting than that suggested by the routine grins offered to cameramen.

Kalpana Chawla, an Indian-born naturalised American, had for years radiated star quality, particularly in Karnal, the small farming town in northern India where she grew up. She said that J. R. D. Tata, who flew the first mail flights in India, had been her childhood hero. The *Times of India* and *India Today*, a news magazine, ran pictures of Miss Chawla as she prepared for her mission. Readers were told when to watch the skies of southern India as *Columbia* passed over in orbit during the 16-day journey.

Miss Chawla had had an earlier trip into space in 1997 after studying aerospace engineering in India and America, and learning to pilot practically anything that could fly, from gliders to airliners. For Indian politicians her career has for years been an argument that technology promised a hopeful future for all Indians, a powerful message in a country where millions live in poverty. When technology failed Kalpana Chawla last weekend, Karnal turned to its old, trusted ways. Incense was burnt and marigolds were placed on her photographs.

The symbols
The United States turned to its own trusted symbol, the flag. All over the country flags were lowered to half-mast. Israel did the same. Ilan Ramon, an Israeli air force colonel, was the only non-American in the crew. In the aftermath of the shuttle disaster, Israel, perhaps understandably, sought to emphasise its links with the United States. Ariel Sharon, the Israeli prime minister, said that "at times like these" the two countries felt their "common fate, identity and values, and shared vision". Just as Indian newspapers had dwelt on Miss Chawla's qualities as a symbol of the new India, the Israeli press recounted Mr Ramon's exploits in defence of his country. In 1981 he had taken part in an air attack on a nuclear reactor being built in Iraq. He was a modest soldier. "There was no knife between his teeth," said a colleague. Mr Ramon recalled that an Arab, Sultan bin Salman of Saudi Arabia, had flown in a space shuttle in 1985, so he was not the first astronaut from the Middle East. As

Front: Chawla, McCool, Husband   Back: Ramon, Anderson, Clark, Brown

well as Israel, he represented "all our neighbours".

Mr Ramon was one of a number of foreigners who have been invited from time to time to take part in shuttle flights. He had been training with the rest of the crew since July 1998. As *Columbia*'s "payload specialist" he had the most peaceful of the 59 scientific tasks being carried out: studying the effects of sandstorms on climate.

Three of the Americans in *Columbia* were on their first space flights. Laurel Clark was a physician and much of her previous experience had been in submarines, where she worked on escape techniques. The day before the shuttle burnt up, she sent to her family an e-mail, now a footnote in space history, describing the trip. David Brown was another doctor. As a young man he worked in a circus as an acrobat. He said it taught him the value of team work. William McCool, the pilot of the shuttle, was a former test pilot. Rick Husband, the shuttle's commander, was on his second space flight. He was working with a team designing spacecraft for possible trips to the moon and beyond.

This was the first shuttle mission for three years to be given over entirely to scientific experiments, rather than as a space truck carrying cargoes to a space station being assembled 200 miles above the earth. Michael Anderson, an African-American, had the job of checking that all the experiments were going well. He, like Miss Chawla and Mr Ramon, was aware that he carried an extra burden in his job: as a role model for young blacks. Impressively, he had logged more than 200 hours in space. One of his trips was to *Mir*, a Russian station that has since been abandoned after years in space.

It is obvious to say that the seven made a unified group. If you work together towards a common objective over a period of several years there is likely to be a unity. But for the *Columbia* seven there was more than that. Some people call themselves Europeans, some Asians, some indeed Americans. Kalpana Chawla said, "When you are in space and look at the stars and the galaxy, you feel that you are not just from any particular piece of land, but from the solar system." ■

Charles Conrad

Charles Peter Conrad, the third man on the moon, died on July 9th 1999, aged 69

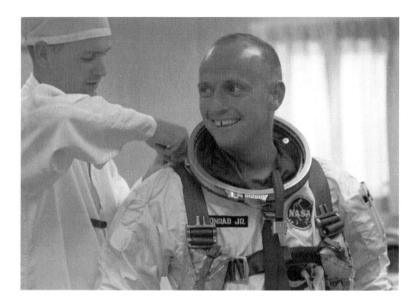

ANYONE INTERESTED in space travel can probably name Neil Armstrong as the first man to step on the moon 30 years ago, uttering the carefully scripted words, "That's one small step for man, one giant leap for mankind." Perhaps the name of his companion, Buzz Aldrin, may also come to mind. Charles Conrad, though, was in the second moon landing four months later, and for him memories have faded. Nice guys come last, as the cruel American aphorism puts it, or, in the case of Mr Conrad, third. He was a nice guy; everyone said that. A nicer man never put on a space suit. He could also be amusing, and this may have been one reason why he was not selected for the first moon trip.

Going to the moon was a very serious undertaking: only a successful landing would justify the colossal amount of money spent on space research and, most important, would put one over on the Russians, who had sent up the first satellite and whose Yuri Gagarin had been the first person to circle the earth in a spacecraft. Neil Armstrong was serious to the point of shyness, and was preferred as leader of the first moon trip even though Buzz Aldrin had had more experience in space.

But Mr Conrad was a wild card. During his training as an astronaut he had made light of the physical and psychological tests that spacemen had to endure. He scoffed at attempts to probe his mind, and was convinced that the medical staff had an unhealthy obsession about enemas. When the diminutive (5ft 6in) Charles Conrad made his first step on to the moon, his slightly mocking words were, "Whoopee!

Man, that may have been a small one for Neil, but that's a long one for me." There were more shudders among the space people when Mr Conrad appeared in a television advertisement for the American Express bank. "Do you know me?" he said. "I walked on the moon."

Up in the air

Those who did know Charles Conrad had a high regard for his competence. Getting off the ground, he said, was a family tradition: his father had been a balloonist observing enemy lines in the first world war. Father had come down to earth and had made a fortune as a stockbroker, providing Charles, or Pete, as his parents called him, with a privileged childhood. The 1930s were the heroic days of flying. Mr Conrad remembered assembling crates and chairs to resemble the aircraft in which Charles Lindbergh had made the first solo non-stop flight across the Atlantic, "then sit inside it for hours pretending to fly".

He studied aeronautical engineering at Princeton and made a career as a navy airman. In the early 1960s he was taken on for training by America's space agency. In the fragile contraptions that first took Americans into space, Mr Conrad's small stature and light weight were great assets. Waiting for lift-off, he recalled, you had fears "just like bullfighters have fears of being killed by the bull", but once you started "it's all business" because that is what keeps you alive.

The Apollo craft, called *Intrepid*, that took Mr Conrad to the moon provided him with business that no one had expected. A minute after lift-off the craft was struck by lightning, and all the warning lights in *Intrepid* began to flash. Mr Conrad declined to abort the mission and carried on to make a perfect landing on the moon. He and his companion, Alan Bean (who now became the fourth man to walk on the moon), spent nearly eight hours there. Mr Conrad returned with what he called "the world's greatest cold". They also collected bits of moon rock and took lots of pictures (but mislaid a spool of film, presumably still on the moon). Neither these souvenirs nor those collected on the first moon flight seemed much to show as a return on the costly investment. But getting to the moon cheered up America, and but for the clever engineering involved we might not have gadgets such as the mobile phone. So be grateful.

Mr Conrad never went to the moon again, although there were four more successful missions. Twelve people in all have walked on the moon, all of them American. Mr Conrad did take part in extended space flights, one of them lasting for 28 days. To him, space was just another workplace. He did not see his moon trip as a religious experience. Those that did, such as James Irwin, who later led six expeditions to Turkey in search of Noah's Ark, were, said Mr Conrad, religious before they went, and remained religious when they got back.

He predicted that, not too long in the future, there would be tourist flights into space, providing the costs could be kept down with reusable craft. There would be plenty to see. The earth, he said, resembled "a beautiful blue marble suspended against a black velvet blanket". Space was healthy, he said, colds aside. He never suffered any ill effects from his space travels: he died in a motor-cycle accident.

Mr Conrad was asked whether there was life in other worlds. He said there probably was. "After all, there's plenty of unearthly looking things moving around in my refrigerator, so there's always a chance of life springing up almost anywhere." He liked a joke, did Charles Conrad. ■

Alistair Cooke

Alistair Cooke, smoother of transatlantic tensions, died on March 30th 2004, aged 95

FOR AS long as anyone can remember, Alistair Cooke was the perfect embodiment of the special relationship. British ambassadors sometimes take Washington by storm, but more usually blend in with the scenery. British prime ministers sometimes forge real personal bonds with American presidents, but more often have to do with the make-believe kind. Mr Cooke, a BBC broadcaster, was different. For more than half a century he formed a solid, though urbane, one-man bridge between the two cultures.

Every Thursday, for 58 years, he wrote his "Letter from America". He would compose in his Manhattan flat, picking away at his typewriter, with the trees of Central Park laid out before him. The letters were generally pegged to some current event, but anything less like the urgent hectorings of foreign correspondents would be hard to imagine. Mr Cooke was a master of the perambulatory style. Each letter wandered for 15 minutes down all sorts of highways and byways only to end up, just when it seemed he must have lost his way, at his intended destination.

His voice alone lured listeners on. It was a treasure, light and high, with a jaunty breathiness honed by decades of smoking, and with a curious accent that floated somewhere in the mid-Atlantic. And this was where he belonged, patiently explaining one side to the other.

He had first seen America in the early 1930s, travelling on a Harkness Fellowship. Even in the Depression, its energy and vitality astonished him. "The landscape and the people", he once said, "were far more gripping and dramatic than anything I had ever seen." Until then, his interest had lain vaguely in the theatre. From then on, it shifted to what he saw as the real drama unfolding in the world – the United States. In 1941, he became an American citizen.

Mr Cooke made his analysis of his new country sound easy, but it was not. As he well knew, the superficial similarities between Britain and America hid differences that lay deep and needed careful unravelling. "The stress will tend always to be on the springs of American life, whose bubbles are the headlines, rather than on the headlines themselves," he told the BBC as the letters began, in 1946.

In his first, he told weary Britons that even New York was a war casualty, driven to burning filthy soft coal and hoarding butter. In his last, delivered a month before his death, he reminded his audience that Bill Clinton might well have invaded Iraq but for the Monica Lewinsky affair. "By the time Clinton was ready to mobilise an American or allied force, he didn't possess the moral authority to invade Long Island." In the almost 3,000 letters in between – he missed only three broadcasts – he covered all the most important events in modern American history, from Watergate to September 11th, from the black market in beef to the Black Panthers, from Vietnam to the California recall.

Mr Cooke was almost as influential in shaping America's image of Britain. As the host of "Masterpiece Theatre" for two decades, he carefully nurtured the idea that Britain continued to play Greece to America's Rome. He sat in his easy chair surrounded by books and enveloped by civilisation, but with no trace of that superiority that sometimes seems natural to Limeys. "As empires go," he once told his American audience, "the British empire was a wink in the eye of history."

A necessary man
In 1976 his adopted country paid him the highest compliment imaginable, when Congress chose him to give the keynote address at its bicentennial celebration. It was all a very long way from Salford, near Manchester, where he had been born as plain Alfred Cooke, the son of a metalworker. His elder brother left school at 15 to become a butcher. But Alfred shinned up the scholarship ladder, to grammar school and Cambridge, before winning that fateful Harkness Fellowship.

Though known mostly as a broadcaster after 1938, when the BBC made him its chief commentator on American affairs, Mr Cooke was also for 27 years the chief American correspondent for the *Manchester Guardian*. He short-changed neither employer, at one stage sending the newspaper 4,000 words a day. Yet, as he admitted, he was seldom present at "a single accidental convulsion of history". The few exceptions became fodder for his most compelling letters, as when he found himself in the hotel pantry where Robert Kennedy was shot in 1968. That place, he told his audience, "I suppose will never be wiped out of my memory: a sinister alley, a Roman circus run amok, and a charnel house. It would be quite false to say, as I should truly like to say, that I'm sorry I was there." For once, his journalistic instincts were trumping his good manners.

The world that produced Mr Cooke has gone. Americans increasingly see British journalists not as civilised gentlemen but as drunken spongers, like Peter Fallow in Tom Wolfe's "Bonfire of the Vanities". The *Guardian*, the descendant of Mr Cooke's old paper, routinely presents Americans as bloodthirsty lard-arses. The two countries, ostensibly allies, too often view each other suspiciously and lovelessly. At Mr Cooke's death, the special relationship had never needed him more. ∎

Maurice Couve de Murville

Maurice Couve de Murville, a French patriot, died on December 24th 1999, aged 92

DURING THE 1960s France practised what are remembered as the "politics of grandeur". They were the creation of Charles de Gaulle, the French president from 1959 to 1969, and his foreign minister, Maurice Couve de Murville. They sought to imbue in the minds of their countrymen a new and glorious France, untarnished by defeat. Historians are divided on whether they succeeded, and if they did whether their success has been lasting. What is clear is that in its pursuit of *la gloire* France managed to upset, and sometimes anger, its closest friends, notably Britain and the United States, creating distrust for French policies that persists to this day.

One view of Mr Couve was that he was simply a servant, reporting to his master on Friday mornings and receiving his instructions for the following week. It was an excusable mistake. How could anyone be other than servile to the towering De Gaulle? But it is probably more accurate to think of Mr Couve as a Jeeves, the highly intelligent interpreter of his master's wishes and the quiet dissuader of his eccentricities.

But an unsmiling Jeeves. Mr Couve was known for his chilly silences. Ask him a question and he might simply look at you without speaking, undermining your confidence by the second. Was the question so idiotic? Eventually Mr Couve would pronounce. "Our thinking is different," he replied to a journalist who asked about France's differences with the United States. Different in what way? Another silence. The questioner found out in 1966 when, to show its independence from

the "Anglo-Saxons", France withdrew from the NATO command structure and expelled its American-led staff from Paris. For years Britain was made to look foolish trying to get into the Common Market, the forerunner of the European Union, when the De Gaulle-Couve partnership had decided its entry to the club would weaken French influence. Even the Germans and others in the club deferred to the French, who for months in 1965 boycotted all market affairs until their farmers could be assured of favoured treatment. For Mr Couve, De Gaulle wrote in his memoirs, "nothing in life" was more important than that France should "survive in the first rank of nations".

Vichy days

When France was defeated by Germany in 1940 Maurice Couve de Murville at first worked for the puppet government in Vichy. He had been a senior civil servant in the pre-war government, specialising in financial matters. In Vichy he was said to have done his best to stop the Germans seizing France's gold reserves. He was then in his early 30s, married with a young family, and Hitler was the master of continental Europe. Like many Vichy officials who later had successful post-war careers, his time as a collaborator was not held against him.

In 1943 he left France and eventually joined De Gaulle's government in exile. The two men seemed immediately to hit it off. Apart from having a common purpose in liberating France, they saw themselves as near nobility with a duty to defend traditional values. Mr Couve's

father, a lawyer and later a judge, had added the aristocratic "de Murville" to the family name. De Gaulle claimed as an ancestor a knight who fought at Agincourt, although perhaps not hard enough as England won.

De Gaulle was briefly the leader of post-war France before resigning in disgust over the country's political system, which he considered unworkable. In 1958, at a time of deep crisis for the country, he returned, first as prime minister and later, having changed the constitution, as president. By then Mr Couve had become ambassador to West Germany. De Gaulle made him foreign minister, a job he was to hold for ten years, longer than any other occupant of that post; longer even, he observed, than Talleyrand, the foreign minister under Napoleon, who was also ambitious for France.

Although the 1960s might seem to have been an exhilarating time for France, there is little evidence that most ordinary French people shared the Gaullist view of history, destiny and all that. The tenth anniversary of De Gaulle's rule in 1968 was marred by student riots and a general strike, ostensibly against the Vietnam war but which developed into a protest against authoritarian, centralist government in general.

The French franc came under attack and a chastened government had to apply for an emergency loan to the International Monetary Fund, an organisation that De Gaulle had attacked as the villain of "dollar hegemony". Mr Couve was made prime minister with a brief to sort out the mess and bring France to order. But the clever diplomat was no politician. His chilly silences might be a formidable weapon in the conference room, his cerebral qualities were undisputed, but to the voter he was seen as a cold fish. He was too old to learn populist tricks; and anyway would have regarded them as unprincipled. De Gaulle stood down in 1969 after losing a referendum on proposed reforms that had been drafted by Mr Couve. Georges Pompidou was elected president, and after a few months dropped Mr Couve as prime minister. It was time for France to repair its friendships. ∎

George Dawson

George Dawson, who discovered literacy late in life, died on July 5th 2001, aged 103

FOR THE first 98 years of his life George Dawson could not read or write. He was persuaded that it was never too late to learn and turned out to be a remarkably able student. In his remaining five years he became a celebrity in the United States. Television programmes were made about his life. He was awarded honorary degrees by two universities. A school was named after him.

Literacy, or rather the lack of it, can be a touchy subject in countries whose people are materially rich but may have difficulty in constructing a decent sentence. According to the World Bank, 99% of Americans can read and write. But a report by the OECD in April shattered any complacency about this figure for the world's richest country by claiming that 60% of Americans aged 16 to 25 were "functionally illiterate", meaning that when it came to, say,

filling in a form they were stumped. A test of simple numeracy was included by the OECD, which involved the reading of a timetable, unfairly say some, realistically say others. The United States came top of the OECD's list of shame. Finland and Denmark did best of the industrialised countries, each having only 10% of illiterate young dunces.

So here was the improbably-aged Mr Dawson. If he could at least learn to stop signing his name with an X, surely those young slackers could make more of an effort to cope with the hard stuff. Such was the theme of Mr Dawson's philosophising in his appearances at schools, universities and, most importantly, on television.

"I am still learning," he would say, in his rolling southern accent. He was born in Texas, whose rapid development as an agricultural state in the early 19th century had been based on slavery. George Dawson was the grandson of a slave. So, as well as becoming a teacher's pet, Mr Dawson was taken under the wing of black reformists. He obliged them with tales of a harsh life. When he was ten, he said, a friend of his was lynched. You could not trust the white man, he said.

How long a life?

Along with educationalists and reformists, George Dawson was adopted by what might be called the long-lifeists, an important group in the United States. To get to a great age is an accomplishment; to do so and remain clear minded is a bit of a marvel. The long-lifers' heroes are the likes of John Glenn, who circled the earth at the age of 77, and Goya, who was still painting rather well at 80. One group names a "centenarian of the month", who is closely questioned about how he or she made it.

Mr Dawson, its choice for October 2000, catalogued a life of continuous manual labour, starting at the age of four as a farm hand. It had some variety. He had worked in the gangs that had laid railways in Texas; he once travelled to Canada to see what snow was like. He had tamed wild horses. He once played baseball professionally. He had outlived his four wives, his four siblings and two of his seven children. But his experiences did not offer a clue to a reliable elixir anxiously sought by long-lifeists. Even his diet was ordinary: a beef sandwich for lunch, fish for supper. He seemed to have reached a great age more by luck than scheming.

The sight of Mr Dawson on television, looking fit and wise, aroused mixed feelings among Americans. For the rich, long life has come to be regarded as the new human right. The United Nations itself lists longevity as one of the criteria

for determining quality of life. But what of those people who have outlasted their quota of threescore years and ten only to be kept in a state of half-life by the skills of medicine? Such questions have dimmed much of the sentimentality attached to America's extraordinary number of centenarians – some 70,000 and rising. A writer in the March issue of *Psychological Science* observed, "Our society is living longer, and the issue is, if you live longer, what are those last years like, and is length itself a good thing?"

At the age of 102 Mr Dawson the scholar gained fresh attention by relaunching himself as an author. He published a book of memoirs, albeit written in collaboration with a schoolteacher. Some people were surprised by the book's Panglossian title, *Life Is So Good*, when previously Mr Dawson had given the impression that much of his life had been pretty awful. Like many biographies some bits ring truer than others. This is one of the truer-sounding bits:

> I kept it a secret that I couldn't read ... When I travelled somewhere I could never read a sign. I had to ask people things and had to remember. I could never let my mind forget anything. I listened to the news and had to trust what I heard. I never read it for myself. My wife read the mail and paid our bills ... People wonder why I didn't go to school earlier. But when I was young I had missed my turn to go. One day, out of the blue, a man came to the door. He handed me a piece of paper which I couldn't read. He said there were some classes for adults. My turn had come. I always thought I could drive a spike as good as any man and cook as good as any woman. I just figured if everybody else can learn to read, I could too.

A quite complex man had discovered happiness in an unconsidered pleasure. For nearly 100 years, George Dawson said, his name was X. "Writing my real name was one of the greatest things in my life." ■

Magda Denes

Magda Denes, a hidden child in the second world war, died on December 28th 1996, aged 62

FOR MOST of her life Magda Denes preferred not to talk of her experiences as a child in the second world war, which she spent in hiding. In later life Dr Denes rose to eminence in her profession of psychoanalysis, both in private practice in New York and in academic posts, but interviewers who sought to delve deeply into her own psyche for early recollections drew a blank. "Hidden children try to forget what happened to them," she said.

The number of children who were confined to secret places for long periods to escape the concentration camp appalled her: perhaps as many as 100,000 in Germany and the territories it occupied. And these were only a fraction of the million or more children who were caught and died in captivity, the best known of whom was Anne Frank, a Dutch girl who has come to exemplify the fate of Jewish children in the war.

Many victims of that time have tried, but with only limited success, to overcome the privations of their early years. Two of the more famous were Primo Levi, a scientist and writer who was interned in concentration camps, and Bruno Bettelheim, a psychologist who later used his experience in the camps to treat disturbed children in America. Both committed suicide.

From her work in psychology, Dr Denes may have decided that the hidden portion of her life should best be faced. Whatever the reason, she did eventually feel compelled to write of her childhood and did so at length. It was almost the last thing she did. Her book, *Castles Burning: A Child's Life in War*, is published this month in America (W. W. Norton).

Dr Denes had planned to tour the United States and Europe in connection with the book. Her death at this moment might have seemed to her typical of the kicks from a brutal world. For age did not mellow her. Anne Frank's memorialists in films and books have tended to avoid arousing hate against her oppressors. But Dr Denes never stopped loathing the Germans and their wartime surrogates in her native Hungary.

The last fairy tales

Magda Denes was born into a privileged household. Hungary was poor. It had been on the losing side in the first world war and the victors had awarded two-thirds of its territory to Yugoslavia and other neighbours (creating problems that still exist). But the Denes family was well off. Magda's father was a successful publisher in Budapest. There were servants and other luxuries. Magda does not seem to have been an appealing child. In her mother's eyes, Magda said, she was "impossibly sarcastic, big-mouthed, insolent and far too smart". Still, at five, she must have had some charm. Magda recalled stories being read to her "in the dark of night, when I couldn't sleep", about Hungary's magical castles, stories that always had a happy ending. The castles in the title of her book started burning in her imagination in 1939, at the outbreak of the second world war, when Magda's father abandoned his family and left for America.

The bitterness Magda felt towards her father persisted throughout her life. Indignantly, she listed the luggage he took with him, including 12 suits and 45 shirts. No doubt her father had his reasons for leaving. He had been critical of the Hungarian dictator, Admiral Horthy. Jews in Hungary were already coming under threat from Arrow-Cross, the local Nazis. Parts of Budapest were barred to Jews. Denes *père* may have thought that, by leaving, he would make his family safe.

What happened was that for years Magda, her brother Ivan and their mother were constantly on the move. Once Magda had to hide in an oven. Ivan was caught and shot.

After the war Hungary became a Soviet satellite. Magda experienced "a deep rot" that "ate away" her life. She got to America by way of Austria and Cuba. Meeting her father again was not a happy reunion. He thought her a rather unpleasant girl. She said that starving, while being eaten by lice, "tends to corrode one's pleasant side".

Her life in New York was almost conventional. She had an education, rose in her career, got married and had two children. She became a psychologist, she said, because of her early experiences. "Survivors identify with the damaged. To help is a self-healing process." She was drawn into feminist issues. One was abortion, or, as euphemists like to term it, being "pro-life" or "pro-choice". How did Dr Denes feel about the unborn child in its "hiding place"? She spent two years interviewing staff in abortion clinics, and her report, published as a book that has become a classic of its type, reflected the mental agonies she had undergone. Abortion, she said, was murder, whatever it was called. "No physician involved with the procedure ever kids himself about that." That sounds like an anti-abortion message, and some of the detail in her report has been used by "pro-life" campaigners. This upset her, for her conclusion, after considering the many reasons for abortion, was that it was killing "of a very special and necessary sort". Any distracting sentiment in Magda Denes was crushed from the age of five. ■

Jacques Derrida

Jacques Derrida, French intellectual, died on October 8th 2004, aged 74

"IN HIM France gave the world one of the major figures of the intellectual life of our times," announced Jacques Chirac, the French president, on the day after Jacques Derrida's death. Mr Derrida himself disagreed with pretty much everything anyone said about him; but he may have let that encomium pass. The inventor of "deconstruction" – an ill-defined habit of dismantling texts by revealing their assumptions and contradictions – was indeed, and unfortunately, one of the most cited modern scholars in the humanities.

He was also the most controversial. In 1992 a proposal to award him an honorary doctorate at Cambridge University caused such howls that the university was forced to put the matter to a ballot – the first time this had happened in 30 years. Amid charges that Mr Derrida's work was absurd, vapid and pernicious, the degree was awarded in the end, by 336 votes to 204.

The academy is often fractious, but this was different. It is not that Mr Derrida's views, or his arguments for them, were unusually contentious. There were no arguments, nor really any views either. He would have been the first to admit this. He not only contradicted himself, over and over again, but vehemently resisted any attempt to clarify his ideas. "A critique of what I do", he said, "is indeed impossible."

There has always been a market for obscurantism. Socrates railed against the followers of Heraclitus of Ephesus for much the same reasons that Mr Derrida's critics berate his unfortunate disciples:

If you ask one of them a question, they draw out enigmatic little expressions from their quiver, so to speak, and shoot one off; and if you try to get hold of an account of what that one meant, you're transfixed by another novel set of metaphors. You'll never get anywhere with any of them.

Subjected to his weak puns ("logical phallusies" was a famous example), bombastic rhetoric and illogical ramblings, an open-minded reader might suspect Mr Derrida of charlatanism. That would be going too far, however. He was a sincere and learned man, if a confused one, who offered some academics and students just what they were looking for.

Mr Derrida's father was a salesman of Sephardic Jewish extraction. Born in a suburb of Algiers, Jacques was expelled from his school at the age of 12 because of the Vichy government's racial laws. With some difficulty, in 1952 he succeeded in entering the elite Ecole Normale Supérieure in Paris and attended the lectures of Michel Foucault. He began to lecture at the Ecole Normale in 1964. Two years later, at a conference at Johns Hopkins University in Baltimore, he laid the foundations of his reputation in America with a bold new way to approach literary texts and lay bare their ideological presuppositions. Three books followed in 1967, including "Of Grammatology" and "Writing and Difference". A radical star was born.

Mr Derrida's style of deconstruction flowered especially in American departments of comparative literature, where it became interwoven with Marxism, feminism and anti-colonialism.

Although by the early 1980s French academics had largely tired of trying to make sense of him, America's teachers of literature increasingly embraced Mr Derrida. Armed with an impenetrable new vocabulary, and without having to master any rigorous thought, they could masquerade as social, political and philosophical critics. Mr Derrida always denied any responsibility for the undisciplined nihilism of his imitators, who gave the strong impression that deconstructionism had somehow succeeded in undermining, or even in refuting, the notion of objective truth. But his work could not easily be interpreted in any other way.

The fog of words

A crisis came in 1987. The *New York Times* revealed that Paul de Man, a friend of Mr Derrida's and one of America's leading deconstructionists, had written anti-Semitic articles for a pro-Nazi Belgian newspaper in 1940–42. Coincidentally, also in 1987, evidence began to emerge of the hidden Nazi past of the German philosopher Martin Heidegger, who had been a major influence on Mr Derrida. Mr Derrida's response was disastrous. He used deconstructionist techniques to defend the two men, laying down a fog of convoluted rhetoric in a doomed attempt to exonerate them. This fed straight into the hands of his critics, who had always argued that the playful evasiveness of deconstruction masked its moral and intellectual bankruptcy. The *New York Review of Books* quipped that deconstruction means never having to say you're sorry.

Mr Derrida also pursued far worthier causes. He fought for the rights of Algerian immigrants in France, opposed apartheid and campaigned for Czech dissidents. As his influence waned, his fame grew. Abandoning his earlier reticence, he submitted to interviews and photographs. He confessed to disliking Woody Allen's comedy, "Deconstructing Harry". The books continued to flow (80 volumes in all) as his concerns moved away from literary and philosophical texts to ethical and political subjects, but they were no easier to follow. In his final years he became increasingly concerned with religion, and some theologians started to show interest in his work. God help them. ∎

Correction: Jacques Derrida
In our obituary of Jacques Derrida, we gave "logical phallusies" as an example of his weak puns. We were wrong; it was not his coinage. But "phallogocentrique" was (see, if you will, "Éperons: Les Styles de Nietzsche", 1978). Our apologies.

The Duke of Devonshire

Andrew Cavendish, 11th Duke of Devonshire, died on May 3rd 2004, aged 84

THE VILLAGE of Edensor in Derbyshire is a pretty place. Its houses are eccentric, with Tudor chimneys and Italian doorways, and they sit around a spacious green planted with laburnum trees. The church boasts both a tower and spire, and it is here that Andrew Cavendish now lies along with many of his forebears. Edensor was moved and rebuilt by the sixth duke in the 19th century because, sitting as it used to on a ridge east of Chatsworth, it spoiled the view. It now blends seamlessly into the wide sweep of parkland that leads down to the great house, and knows its place: a tiny settlement amid 35,000 acres of moorland, woodland, meadows and gardens, all owned by one family.

The 11th duke could never quite believe he possessed all this. Delightedly, he would count his Chatsworth assets: 297 rooms, 112 fireplaces, 56 loos, 2,084 lightbulbs. The beauty of the house, stacked with books, paintings and sculpture collected by the Cavendishes for 450 years, constantly enthralled him. Chatsworth, he once remarked, was his idea of heaven; that, and drinking tea in the hall at Brooks's Club in St James's.

Nor was this all. He owned another 40,000 acres, including Bolton Abbey, the most romantic ruin in Yorkshire; Lismore Castle in Ireland; a chunk of the West End and a goodly extent of Eastbourne, a shabbily genteel resort on the Sussex coast. Each year the duke would spend a week there in his own hotel, the Cavendish, relishing the end-of-the-pier shows and the distant blare of military bands.

If he never took any of this for granted, strolling through life with an air of the utmost diffidence and happiness, it was because he had never expected it. As the second son of the 10th duke, he was told he would inherit nothing. He was vaguely preparing himself for a career in publishing when his elder brother was killed in action, in 1944, and everything was his.

Having stumbled by sheer luck into the Cavendish inheritance, he then almost lost it again. His father's sudden death in 1950 saddled him with almost £7m in death duties, or 80% of the estate. Drastic measures were necessary. Hardwick Hall, another ravishing Elizabethan house in Derbyshire, was sold to the National Trust. Several Rembrandts, Van Dycks and Raphaels went to galleries, and the Caxton and Shakespeare first folios to America. The duke himself was driven to working as a minister of state in the government of his uncle, Harold Macmillan: a reward, he supposed, for having given him some good shooting. Around 150 staff had to be dismissed, including 15 gardeners. It was touch and go whether the magnificent cascades could be kept flowing and the topiary trimmed.

At this desperate point the duke took a leaf from the book of his hero and exemplar, the sixth duke. William Spencer Cavendish had been a member of the Whig party in the early 19th century: a liberal reformer and anti-slavery campaigner who, though a grandee to his fingertips, empathised with the common man. He eventually opened Chatsworth to the public every day, especially making sure that the great fountain was working for them to see. Whatever new wings he built, or new sculptures he acquired in Italy, he believed should be shared with the gawping crowd.

Noblesse oblige

The 11th duke, pushed on by his "bossy" Mitford duchess, decided to do the same. Chatsworth was made over to an independent charitable trust, with the family renting their quarters, and the doors were flung open to visitors. Every possible means of making money was employed, as long as it was consonant with dignity; the duke had no wish to make his house a "circus", like Woburn or Beaulieu. A shop was opened, the first of its kind, selling branded cushions, teapots and hand cream; a farm shop offered Stilton and game. A hotel was built, then a conference centre. The duke happily attached his name to a hamper, retailing at £499, containing sloe gin, sausages and chutney. By 2002, Chatsworth was making a profit and bringing in 500,000 visitors a year.

The taxman, you could argue, had forced him to this pass. But the duke was also devoted to a far more ancient concept, *noblesse oblige*. Having been so fortunate, and having done nothing, as he said, to deserve it, it was incumbent on him to be generous to others. He opened his vast "back garden" to ramblers, where his grandfather had used his gamekeepers to send them packing. In 1991 he founded the Polite Society after an aged taxi-driver, pressing his hand, told him how good it felt to be thanked. He was active in all kinds of charities, and helped to save the Chesterfield football team from extinction.

Those with no stomach for feudalism remained unimpressed. They muttered about his fortune (£1.6 billion, by some estimates), his gaming and horse-racing, his pretty young mistresses, his self-declared "dimness", and all the usual failings of the English upper classes. They were scandalised by his pledge to break the law if fox-hunting was banned, and by his patronage of the Europhobic UK Independence Party. But his Chatsworth staff, more than 600 of them, all of whom felt he had known and respected them, put on their uniforms and lined the road that led through the deer park to Edensor. ∎

Diana, Princess of Wales

Diana Frances Spencer, Princess of Wales, died on August 31st 1997, aged 36

IT WAS easy to get caught up in the cult of Diana, which became as strong for the Princess of Wales as it was for her mythological Roman namesake. When she was married in 1981 *The Economist* itself gushed, "God save the next queen." Now the cult is immeasurably greater than it was 16 years ago. Books await to be written, perhaps are already being written, about how a 19-year-old kindergarten helper became the most famous woman in the world, and was seen at her death to be an icon of her age. But whatever puzzles the writer may encounter, there will be no shortage of material to ponder over.

One of the oddities of many of the articles written about Diana during the past week is that they dwell on her search for privacy. True, she had no privacy, but she appeared content to be constantly on public view. After Lenin died the Soviet government employed researchers to make a record of every day of his life. The reporters and photographers who made Diana their career did the same, and more efficiently. She mostly smiled on their dog-like attention and occasionally threw them a bone which would turn up in a tabloid next day as a "world exclusive".

Her friends were privy to her more intimate thoughts and these too would become public property. The princess went on television to give answers to the most searching questions about her life in a BBC programme that was sold around the world. As a product, Diana never palled. There was always some event to keep her public keen, a new lover, a new cause, some painful disclosure about her physical and mental health. Privacy is a luxury still available to the rich, albeit with difficulty. Princess Diana preferred to display her infinite variety.

Enter the bride
Despite her humble job looking after tinies, Diana Frances Spencer was born a lady. Her father was an earl, her mother the daughter of a baron. For centuries the Spencer family had been close to the monarchy, holding whimsically named posts: a grandmother was a woman of the bedchamber. When Prince Charles was looking for a bride fit to be a queen, Diana was high on his list. Like the Roman goddess, she was apparently a virgin, a rare qualification among the prince's girlfriends. She was pretty and, as shown in many of the pictures subsequently taken of her, she could look beautiful in a sympathetic setting. She had received little formal education, but that did not seem to matter. Her youth suggested that she could be eased without difficulty into the royal mould. The Queen Mother, who had never given the monarchy a moment's anxiety since she married into the royal family in 1923 (and is now a hale 97), was the model, and for a while she chaperoned Diana. The princess did her duty, providing two splendid sons, one of whom is in line to be king if he and the monarchy survive. She went along with the formalities expected of a prince's wife, becoming, for example, colonel-in-chief of the Royal Hampshire Regiment and a patron of numerous charities long cherished by the royals.

But her fancy was for more offbeat causes, AIDS sufferers, lepers and, most recently, land-mine victims.

She gave them valuable, if brief, publicity, and her support made all the more impact by being unusual coming from a royal. She was up to date. The National Marriage Guidance Council changed its name to the snazzier Relate, with the princess as its patron. The prince also had his favoured causes, concern for the environment, the preservation of architectural standards, but a picture of Diana cuddling a handicapped child was what caught the eye. According to Diana's accounts, she found the prince's family boring and offhand. Although the prince was a mere 13 years older than she, Diana saw him as an old fogey, approaching middle age. Worse, Charles kept up his friendship with Camilla Parker Bowles, an old flame. "There were three of us in the marriage," she said famously on the BBC.

The British public was slowly eased into the knowledge that what had been seen as a fairytale marriage had been deeply miserable. A separation was announced in 1992. On that television programme in 1995 Diana hinted that the prince might never become king. As for herself, she would like to be "a queen of people's hearts". The put-upon real queen had had enough. She told the couple to get divorced as soon as possible. Diana fought her corner and, after long and sometimes bitter negotiations partly over money, the couple were divorced in 1996. Diana remained a princess but was no longer the future queen, no longer even "her royal highness". One of her first actions was to drop the patronage of some 100 charities.

Still, in the public eye, Diana could do nothing mean. Indeed, her seeming lapses, her adulteries, her conspicuous extravagance, seemed only to support the view that she was a real person. The manner of her death, in a speeding car crashed by a drunken driver, with her latest lover by her side, could merely have been shocking. For millions it confirmed that Diana the goddess was a victim of "fate", whatever that may mean. ■

Manuel Elizalde

Manuel Elizalde, protector of minorities, died on May 3rd 1997, aged 60

W HEN MANUEL Elizalde announced the discovery of a tribe in the Philippines uncorrupted by civilisation, he touched a sympathetic chord among the ordinary corrupted millions who sometimes allow themselves to muse on the appeal of the simple life. Here, it seemed, was the modern version of Rousseau's noble savage, a people who lived in harmony, had no word for war, and whose modest needs were provided by the rain forest which had sheltered them from contact with the outside world. Their basic food was the wild yam, a root vegetable, flavoured with grubs and small fish, with wild bananas for pudding. Their homes were caves. They made fire by rubbing sticks together. They ran naked in this Eden or dressed in clothes made of leaves.

Immediately, there was scepticism from experts doubtful about any surviving human dodos. How could the Tasaday, as the tribe called itself, have remained undiscovered until 1971 in a country of more than 40m people which was a battleground in the second world war? Mr Elizalde came under deep suspicion. He was from one of the rich families that in the Marcos era ran the Philippines, and, largely, still do. After leaving Harvard he had gained notoriety in Manila newspapers as a playboy. Were the Tasaday people an elaborate hoax?

It would be tidy to close the story there, as one more example of a mischievous anthropological joke, comparable to the Piltdown man, the "missing link" in human development found in 1912 and not exposed as a forgery until 1953. However, the Tasaday discovery is not a Piltdown. Whatever controversy may surround the Tasaday, Mr Elizalde did not invent the tribe.

In the jungle

When Manuel Elizalde first spoke publicly of the Tasaday he had put aside his wild days. He served for a time as president of his family's vast industrial conglomerate – steel, fibres, sugar, mining, broadcasting – and later became head of the government department responsible for minorities in the Philippines. Some years before Mr Elizalde disclosed the whereabouts of the Tasaday he had been told of the tribe by a trader from another tribe in the region.

Mr Elizalde was personally interested in minorities: he and his wife had adopted 50 orphaned children from minority families. He knew from experience of surveying his family's estates that parts of the Philippines were almost impenetrable. Since 1952 three Japanese soldiers had been holed up in the jungle in the Lubang islands, unaware that the war had ended five years earlier, and shooting at anyone who approached (the last one gave up in 1972). But the Tasaday homeland in Cotabato, in the impoverished deep south of the Philippines, was coming under the eye of the loggers. Mr Elizalde decided to make contact with the tribe and give it protection. "It was us or the lumbermen," he recalled.

When Mr Elizalde arrived with his party in a helicopter he was treated

like a god. An ancestor of the Tasaday had predicted that one day someone "who loves us" would come from the outside world. Mr Elizalde did his godlike best, getting President Marcos to make the jungle inhabited by the tribe a reserve barred to loggers and farmers. The subsequent Aquino and Ramos governments have retained the ban.

Yet doubts remain among some anthropologists about how complete has been the tribe's isolation. A writer in the *National Geographic Magazine* in 1972 claimed that "as stone age cave dwellers [they] are unique: their like has not been found before in our time". But later research suggests that the Tasaday may have once lived elsewhere in the Philippines, perhaps as fishermen, but fled into the jungle some hundreds of years ago after clashing with another tribe, or possibly to escape an outbreak of plague. Over a number of generations they then "reverted" to a primitive culture. Neither were they unbelievably peaceable. It turned out that they had knowledge of violence and had bows and arrows. Their "simple life" was a

struggle for existence which had reduced their numbers to fewer than a hundred. Anyone seeking a break from civilisation would be better advised to take up something less arduous, like sailing alone around the world or doing up a cottage in Provence.

The publicity given to the Tasaday has overshadowed Mr Elizalde's work protecting other minorities, equally deserving, though less newsy. All over the world there are threatened "unreached peoples", sought by anthropologists (and enthusiastic Christian missionaries). Mr Elizalde became interested in minorities in Latin America, and moved to Costa Rica in 1983 after falling out with the Marcos regime. He returned to the Philippines in 1988 and was in line to become ambassador to Mexico but withdrew after being attacked for his Marcos links. Most recently, he was educating some members of the Tasaday into the ways of the outside world. At least one Tasaday is learning fast: he is contemplating legal proceedings against an anthropologist who said the tribe was a fake. ∎

Juan Fangio

Juan Manuel Fangio, racing driver, five times grand prix world champion, died on July 16th 1995, at the age of 84

ONE DAY Juan Fangio's record of being five times the world champion racing driver may be beaten. But even if that happens many people will continue to regard him as the greatest grand prix driver of any generation. Better than the gifted Ayrton Senna, three times the world champion, who was killed in 1994? Better than Stirling Moss, who twice outraced Mr Fangio? Or was there something special about motor racing in the 1950s, when Mr Fangio gained his fame, that stays in the memory and adds to his lustre?

Nostalgia plays a strong part in distorting assessments of sporting heroes. That is also true of another sportsman, Harold Larwood, an English cricketer, who died on July 22nd at the age of 90. He was the most feared – and controversial – fast bowler of his time. He aimed at the batsman's body in order to induce a catch. In 1926 the England team, with Mr Larwood its hero, beat the Australians, who were left whimpering that this was not cricket. This is a happy memory, especially these days when England mostly loses. People may argue about whether Mr Larwood was as great a bowler as, say, some of the recent West Indians, but the nostalgia for old cricket, before sponsorship, before body armour, will only grow with the story-telling.

The same sentiment may be felt for Mr Fangio. The drivers in his day were plainly visible to the crowd, riding their mounts like cavalry, their arms bare to the wind, their goggles streaked with oil if something had gone wrong, as often it did. The cars of Mr Fangio's time were not really made to go as fast

as they were driven. Once, Mr Fangio's seat came adrift when the securing bolts broke. Somehow he clung to the cockpit with his knees.

The elegant touch
If a car crashed it would probably explode. At least 30 top drivers were killed between 1951, when Mr Fangio first became world champion, and 1958, when he retired having driven the cars of four great marques, Alfa Romeo, Maserati, Mercedes-Benz and Ferrari. Motor racing sometimes seemed like a Roman blood sport, with Juan Fangio as a surviving gladiator, saluted by the chequered flag, a cigarette dangling from his mouth, acknowledging the cheers with a casual wave. In those days no one squirted champagne. It would have been considered vulgar.

Mr Fangio took care to cultivate a non-vulgar style. When taking a corner, most drivers would not be too bothered if they shaved the straw bales put there to protect the crowd. Mr Fangio would elegantly just miss them. Neither did he care for speed for its own sake. If he was going to win anyway he was content to cruise home. "A car is like a creature that lives, with its own emotions and its own heart," he said. "You have to understand it and to live with it accordingly." Such "understanding" seemed to enable Mr Fangio to cajole an extraordinary performance from his car when the need arose. One of his tricks was the "four-wheel drift", a controlled skid for taking corners at high speed. It was used with effect in 1957, at the German grand prix at the Nurburgring, 500km (313 miles)

immigrants. At 13 he was a car mechanic. In his 20s he was winning long distance races, including one from Buenos Aires to Lima and back, about 6,000 miles. Stamina was one of his many admired qualities, although he got tired like anyone else. Chewing coca leaves kept him awake. Later, in Europe, he used pep pills.

The Argentines acknowledged his growing fame by naming a new dance the "Fangio Tango". He received the blessing of Juan Peron, then the dictator of Argentina. Publicists in the racing world sought to link him with pretty women. Gina Lollobrigida was one. But Mr Fangio was not one of the sports world's lechers. For years he was greeted at the end of a race by

round and round the Eifel mountains, with numerous bends. He started with a light load of fuel, reckoning that he would build up enough lead to refuel comfortably during the race. But the refuelling was bungled. His lead of 28 seconds became a deficit of 51 seconds. In what was probably Mr Fangio's finest race, he pushed on ferociously, passing the leaders with one lap to go.

Stirling Moss said Mr Fangio was a gentleman "not of birth, but of being". He was an Argentine, born the fourth of six children in a family of Italian

a matronly woman who was assumed to be his wife. But she wasn't. Their friendship apparently ended and Mr Fangio never married.

Rather than being a heart-throb Juan Fangio might be considered an inspiration to the elderly. He would have been happy with that encomium. At the time of his greatest successes he was in his 40s, a pensioner in motor-sport terms. Later, he attributed his great age to living simply – plenty of sleep, healthy food, and a special Fangio tip: don't go faster than you have to. ■

Joey Faye

Joey Faye, among the greatest of second bananas, died on April 26th 1997, aged 87

IN THE art of making people laugh it was probably better to be the second banana than the top banana. The second banana was the clown taking the rise out of the straight man. Joey Faye was one of the greatest of all second bananas. Some people say he was one of the last. It is true that bananas of Mr Faye's background are close to extinction, surviving mainly only in the memories of those in America old enough to have seen vaudeville or burlesque or, in England, music hall. But he showed during a career of nearly 70 years that comedy is immensely accommodating to whatever audience is out there waiting to be diverted.

Mr Faye himself became a banana when technology, in the form of radio, was starting to give people the excuse to take their entertainment at home rather than going out to a theatre. This was in the early 1930s, when Mr Faye was taken on as a comic at Minsky's, a New York theatre that specialised in burlesque. "Those were depression days," Mr Faye recalled. "But there was always room for burlesque comedians, because burlesque did business."

Burlesque had a sexy reputation: that was part of its appeal. But in retrospect it seems an innocent sort of sexiness compared with the accepted prurience of today. Gypsy Rose Lee, a fellow star with Joey Faye, became famous for her striptease act. But she did not remove all of her clothes. The mayor of New York, Fiorello LaGuardia, would not allow such an exhibition. He feared that the sight of nude bodies would corrupt young people. Neither, observed Mr Faye, was "rough" language allowed on stage, such as "hell" or "damn".

The new humour
Whatever its reputation, burlesque was no more than the latest version of a popular entertainment that had its origin in the 19th century in touring minstrel shows and which had expanded into permanent variety theatres to cater for the massive growth in America's population. By the 1920s the urban population of America had grown to 55m, with thousands more pouring in on every tide eager to do well, and the country was already the world's largest economy, with an expanding entertainment industry to match.

The cultural and racial mix of the new Americans was reflected in showbiz. Just as jazz was born in the seaport of New Orleans from a blend of African and European sounds, so New York humour was shaped by talented immigrants. Mr Faye's parents were Italian immigrants called Pallandino. Signore Pallandino worked as a barber, and his clients, in the captivity of their chair, would be told stories of his ancestors in the *commedia dell'arte*, an improvised song and dance entertainment that is the basis of English pantomime.

One thing Mr Faye's family folklore taught him was that there was no such thing as a new joke in showbiz, just new ways of pushing a joke for laughs. He admired Lupino Lane, probably Britain's best-known comic of the time, whose book *How to Be a Comedian* is still a reliable guide to a perilous trade.

Mr Faye's pay at Minsky's rose from $25 a week to $300, about $3,700 in today's money. Even bigger bucks beckoned. Mr Faye had parts in 36 Broadway shows, one of them called *Top Banana*. He was in *Man of La Mancha*, a musical version of *Don Quixote*, playing Sancho Panza, Cervantes's second banana. But for all bananas the lure was Hollywood. Such performers as Laurel & Hardy and Abbott & Costello had shown how the skills learnt on the boards before a live audience could be made to look as funny on the movies.

In showbiz reference books Mr Faye lists a dozen films in which he supplied comic diversion to the likes of Gary Cooper, John Wayne and Cary Grant, and a dozen shows in which he starred on television. But curiously, or perhaps not so curiously, he notes that his favourite part was as Gogo in *Waiting for Godot*, played in a theatre in Los Angeles. In Beckett's play Gogo and Didi speak about the futility of life while waiting for the elusive Mr Godot.

Gogo: Why don't we hang ourselves?
Didi: With what?
Gogo: You haven't got a bit of rope?
Didi: No.
Gogo: Then we can't.

"In the comedy world there is nothing new," he wrote, "but it's not impossible to put your own new coat on an old coathanger."

The old coathangers for comics in vaudeville and burlesque were, Joey Faye recalled, "big shoes and a red nose". He started wearing "straight clothes" on stage. And, he found, you did not have to throw yourself about to hold an audience. A critic wrote of Mr Faye's "quiet misbehaviours". It was the start of something new. Other second bananas took to wearing jackets and ties, with perhaps a funny hat as a reminder of their old costume.

The passage usually gets a laugh, but it takes a great banana to put it over well. ■

Thomas Ferebee

Thomas Wilson Ferebee, the bomber of Hiroshima, died on March 16th 2000, aged 81

MANY TIMES Thomas Ferebee was asked if he felt guilty about dropping the atomic bomb on Hiroshima. Invariably, he said he did not. There was a certain logic in his reply. Assuming that someone was guilty – still a matter of unresolved argument – others would seem more culpable than Mr Ferebee and the 11 other airmen in the *Enola Gay*, the bomber that destroyed the Japanese city on the morning of August 6th 1945. What about Robert Oppenheimer, the leader of the team of scientists who designed the bomb? But he did not give the order for the bomb to be dropped. That responsibility fell to Harry Truman, the American president. Truman's defenders, though, might shift the blame to Franklin Roosevelt, who set in motion the Manhattan Project, the name given to

the making of the bomb. But Roosevelt took his momentous decision apparently as the result of a letter he received from Albert Einstein, pointing out that such a weapon was possible.

Einstein was troubled by moral questions posed by the bomb, and how much his work on theoretical physics had contributed to its creation. He was a pacifist. But as a Jew, forced to leave Germany, he was desperately worried that the Germans might build the bomb first. Thomas Ferebee's thoughts on the bomb he dropped were not all that far from those that divided Einstein the pacifist from Einstein the fighter against the forces of tyranny. Like most people in democracies, he became a soldier only because he lived in a time of war. He was a farmer's son from North Carolina. He fancied a career in baseball, and was good enough to be given a trial by the Boston Red Sox. After America entered the second world war in 1941, he chose to be an airman and became, in Shakespeare's phrase, a warrior for the working day.

He was posted to England and took part in the first American bombing raid on German-occupied Europe. Despite its name, the Flying Fortress, the standard American long-range bomber, was vulnerable. Losses were high. In England Mr Ferebee survived an astonishing 63 missions. Not only was he lucky but on many occasions his pilot was Paul Tibbets, an outstandingly skilful airman who was to command the *Enola Gay*.

Mission 13

In 1944 Paul Tibbets was told about the Manhattan Project and ordered to pick a crew for what was called special bombing mission number 13. He chose Mr Ferebee as his bombardier. Striking an enemy target was then a hit and miss affair, as indeed it still is, despite claims to the contrary. Much depended on the experience and steadiness under fire of the bomb aimer. At Tinian Island, in the Pacific, where mission 13 was based, Mr Ferebee and the rest of the crew trained and re-trained. A team of psychologists checked that they were staying sane.

Mr Ferebee recalled that he, and presumably others in the crew, were given cyanide tablets in case they were captured. The Japanese often beheaded captured airmen. But the 13-hour flight went smoothly, if that is the word. Mr Ferebee slept for most of the journey. The bomb he released, sighted on a bridge, turned out to be accurately placed. At least 70,000 people are believed to have been killed in the explosion, and many others died later from radiation. This was not the largest number killed in a single raid: about 83,000 people died in a "conventional" raid on Tokyo in March that year. But

no previous weapon had been so destructive. Three days later a second atomic bomb was dropped on Nagasaki, and Japan surrendered unconditionally six days after that.

Mr Ferebee took the view that dropping the bomb that was foretold by Einstein shortened the war. Had it lasted, many more people would have been killed. "Everybody wanted the war to end, and that's what I wanted," he said. Morally, yes, Hiroshima was horrible. But had the enemy invented the bomb first, that too would have been horrible. In Europe, he had seen the new type of total warfare invented by the Germans and inflicted on London. What would they and the Japanese have done with the bomb?

Most people seem to agree with this argument, but many do not. They say the bomb should never have been used under any circumstances, and Japan was ready to surrender anyway. Millions of words have been written and spoken on the subject, without, perhaps, changing many minds. In 1995 the National Air and Space Museum in Washington planned to put on show the *Enola Gay* in connection with an exhibition about the second world war, but the plan was scrapped after it stirred up controversy over Hiroshima.

Thomas Ferebee did not leave the air force until 1970. He said he had become used to the comradeship. As he saw his former comrades in the Hiroshima expedition die one by one, he felt a duty to keep alive a defence of their actions. He was always willing to give interviews or speak from a public platform or answer letters from those interested in the weapon that changed the world. He and Einstein were accidents of history. Einstein said he would rather have been a watchmaker than a physicist. Thomas Ferebee regretted not making it in baseball. ∎

Ibrahim Ferrer

Ibrahim Ferrer Planas, a Cuban musician, died on August 6th 2005, aged 78

NEGLECT IS the essence of Cuba. Washing flaps from the balconies of what used to be thriving banks, and their once-grand elevators are caked with rust and grime. Colonial columns and cornices crumble along the back streets of Havana, and rubbish and waste water fill pits that span the roads. In elegant abandoned villas damp stains the outside walls, and mildew rots the draperies still hanging in upstairs rooms.

For years, Ibrahim Ferrer's music was treated with similar indifference. He was a band singer, fronting the orchestras that used to tour Cuba's beach resorts and casinos in the years before the 1959 revolution. When Fidel Castro came to power, those orchestras – with their evocation of Palm Court ballrooms, American tourists and capitalist *joie de vivre* – suddenly seemed unsuitable fare for hard Communist times.

The music itself, however, had always been joyously eclectic. Cuba's musicians borrowed everything, from Spanish flamenco to African drumming, from European dances to tribal litanies, to the work-songs of coffee-pickers and sugar-cane pounders. They made instruments of anything that came to hand: conch-shells, wooden boxes, metal cups. Mr Ferrer, when a child in the village of San Luis in Oriente province, played rumba with bottles and spoons at the corner of his street. He grew up to the rhythm of that, and to tango, mamba and *son*, as heard at the Social Club dances held at his grandfather's house. At one such dance, his mother had gone into labour with him. The rhythm, he liked to say, had reached him in the womb and got into his blood.

Of all these different rhythms, none pleased him so much as the *bolero*. Orphaned at 12, struggling to make his way in the world by selling peanuts in the street and singing at parties, he would hear a tango or a *son* dance number and instinctively slow it down into the lilting, romantic *bolero* style. Yet, as he complained later, he was seldom allowed to sing *boleros*. When he worked with the Chepín-Chovén orchestra and with Benny Moré in the 1950s, he was told that his voice – soft, light and pure, and as caressing as a Caribbean breeze – was too small for them. He gained his reputation improvising faster dance numbers. And then "the revolution triumphed", in his words, and the world moved past him anyway.

For 35 years, he found other ways of earning a living. His recordings, unplayed, lay in the vaults of the Egrem state recording studios. His family was large, money short; he became a docker, a builder, a lottery-ticket seller. He shone shoes and imagined that, approaching his 70s, he would never make music again. Then, in 1996, buffing a pair of white shoes one morning outside his apartment, he was hailed by Juan de Marcos González, bandleader of the Afro-Cuban Allstars. Mr de Marcos wanted him at the Egrem studios straight away. There was no time even to wash the polish from his hands.

Mr de Marcos was taping Cuba's old music masters for a compilation. A Texan guitarist, Ry Cooder, engaged on a similar project, was listening in. Mr Ferrer – improvising, as he remembered,

with his equally elderly *compadre* Rubén González on piano – launched into a racy *son* called "Candela" and then a classic *bolero*, "Dos Gardenias". Mr Cooder, astonished, recorded both, and Mr Ferrer was shortly to become as famous a singer of *boleros* as he had ever wished to be.

The band of ancient *muchachos* Mr Cooder had assembled produced the "Buena Vista Social Club" album, which sold 4m copies and won a Grammy. There were sold-out concerts and tours. Suddenly, Cuban music swept the world. Mr Ferrer was not only the voice of it, but also the face, pictured on the sleeve of the album strolling down a Havana street in one of the golfing caps he always wore. At the tender age of 72, he went solo; he made two albums, each of which won Latin Grammys. He did not know too well what a Grammy was, only that the Americans thought him too dangerous to go to the United States in 2004 to collect it. But he was enormously, radiantly pleased.

Some of Miami's sadder Cuban exiles claimed that he was a poster-boy for Mr Castro's regime. Certainly Mr Ferrer criticised the embargo and made fun of America's stupidity at keeping him out, as well he might. He also thought Cuba a "lucky" and "strong" country. But if he was a poster-boy for anything, it was for Castroite neglect. The film that was made of the Buena Vista Social Club, itself nominated for an Oscar, showed him sitting in his tiny, decaying apartment, with a rusting refrigerator and ceiling tiles buckled by humidity, still poor. "If we Cubans cared about possessions," he said stoically, "we should have died out long ago. But we've learned to resist."

Inside the apartment, most of his care was lavished on a Santería shrine to Saint Lazarus. He did powerful work, Mr Ferrer believed, especially for the poor. He had two Lazarus figures of ebony, one to carry about with him and the other to be honoured with candles, honey, fresh flowers, tots of rum and meringues, if his wife had made any. Mr Ferrer would spray his Lazarus copiously with perfume, then spray himself before he went out. And it had proved lucky; like Lazarus, he too had been restored to life. ∎

Virginia Fiennes

Lady Virginia Twisleton-Wykeham-Fiennes, organiser of explorers, died on February 20th 2004, aged 56

THOUGH WOMEN have seldom had much say in the matter, history owes a great deal to spouses who champion their husbands' interests while staying discreetly in the background. Ulysses would not have come to much without Penelope, rebutting suitors with a flick of her shuttle while her husband floundered between Circe and Sirens. And Wordsworth would surely have starved or frozen to death, deep in the Cumbrian fells, if both his wife and his sister had not devoted their lives to cooking his meals and washing his shirts. In pensive solitude, he wrote the poems; in the steamy chaos of the kitchen, his womenfolk made the poems possible.

Virginia ("Ginnie") Fiennes was soundly in this tradition. As a 20th-century woman, she too could drive Land Rovers across British Columbia, hike across the desert and endure the temperatures of the Arctic and Antarctica. Indeed, it was often her idea to do so. But as the wife of perhaps the greatest and most eccentric modern explorer, Sir Ranulph Fiennes, she preferred to leave the adventures, and the triumphs, mostly to him.

As his chief promoter, she made it her job to find the agents, the sponsorship and the boats, plan the routes, help pick the teams, and set up the radio communications necessary to keep track of her husband as he struggled through sandstorms or polar ice. He was sometimes away for years at a time; she grew used to sitting over a crackling, whining radio in some godforsaken spot, listening for the dull tap of Morse code that would tell her where he was. Orders from the explorers tended to be terse and peremptory. Told to have a Boston Whaler ready in 20 days at Inuvik, or light canoes waiting at Spitzbergen, Lady Fiennes snapped to it at once.

The most rigorous test of her

organising powers was the Transglobe expedition of 1979–82, the first circumnavigation of the world along the polar axis. Typically, this was her idea. Her husband thought it "absurd" and "romantic rambling"; she called him pathetic for rejecting it just because it had never been done. Besides, in 1972, early in their marriage, they needed the money. He, though titled, had no income except what he could earn by lecturing about his travels. Why not undertake the most daring trip of all?

The planning and sponsor-finding took seven years. Lady Fiennes, the only woman in the team, had to learn not merely to be a wireless operator (when, according to her husband, her technical expertise was "nil"), but to set up radio masts in solid ice, and replace coaxial cables snapped by sheer cold or eaten by Arctic foxes. At the Ryvingen base in the Antarctic, her radio hut was made of cardboard and wooden floorboards she had dragged into place herself. She took comfort in cigarettes; one day, venturing out to check something, her Zippo lighter burned its cold metal shape into her thigh. The soup she cooked for the adventurers had to be hammered out of the bowls, and raw eggs, broken from the shell, bounced on the floor like golf balls.

Missing the Poles
As her husband often gently hinted in his accounts of their expeditions, Lady Fiennes was not cut out for this. She much preferred deserts to snows. *Woman's Own* magazine once commissioned her to live for two months as the nominal third wife of an Omani sheikh; this suited her much better, and she grew so fond of Arabia that she organised four expeditions to find the lost frankincense city of Ubar in Oman. Out in the desert, she could pick out half-vanished camel trails from cooking pots and saddles abandoned in the sand.

The Transglobe expedition, all 35,000 miles of it, was a huge physical challenge. Slightly built, Lady Fiennes could manage only two laps of a running track before she had to lie on the grass. She was scared of heights, and too claustrophobic to make snow tunnels to her radio huts. In the Antarctic, she thought she saw ghosts; in the Arctic, where her husband always slept with the window open, she took a hot-water bottle and endured the draught.

She had known him a long time, since he was 12 and she was nine. Their first expeditions had been down the Lod river in Sussex or through the nearby woods. Her father tried to separate her from the wild adventurer, but failed. Since her husband was impelled on these extraordinary journeys, she showed little emotion whenever he left. Her Jack Russell, Bothie, became her chief companion in the long absences. Even so, Lady Fiennes let Bothie go to both the South and the North Poles, the first dog ever to do so, while she stayed back at base. Bothie made his mark in the usual way, not far from the Union Jack.

In 1979, in South Africa, a baffled woman reporter asked her why she went on these expeditions in such a self-effacing way. She replied that she simply wished to be where her husband was. "I'm not here proving that a woman can do anything a man can," she said. "Women are not as suited or better at doing anything that is normally done by men." She added, "I'm not brave." When her husband went on his latest half-crazy endurance test, running seven marathons in seven continents in seven days while recovering from a massive heart attack, she refused to tell him of her own cancer diagnosis in case it made him abandon his goal. ∎

Bobby Fischer

Bobby Fischer, an unsettling chess-player, died on January 17th 2008, aged 64

PEOPLE WERE always coming to get Bobby Fischer. And he was ready for them. In a locked suitcase he kept bottles and bottles of vitamin pills and herbal potions and a large orange-juicer, in case they tried to put toxins in his food. His most precious memorabilia – match notebooks, photo albums, letters from President Nixon – were kept in a filing cabinet in a safe behind two combination locks in a ten-by-ten storage room in Pasadena, California. In the end, as he railed to radio talk-show hosts in Hungary and the Philippines, even all this couldn't keep him safe from Russians, or Jews, or "CIA rats who work for the Jews". But he had tried.

They tried to disrupt his chess games, too. As he wrestled for the world championship against Boris Spassky at Reykjavik in 1972 they poked whirring TV cameras over his shoulder. They made the board too shiny, reflecting the lights, and fidgeted and coughed until he cleared out the first seven rows of the audience. By the third game he insisted on retreating to a tiny back room, where he could think. He was always better in dingy, womb-like spaces: the cabinet room of the Marshall Chess Club in New York City, where as a boy he skipped school to spend his mornings reading through old file-cards of 19th-century games; a particular table in the New York Public Library, where he sat for hours immersed in chess history, openings and strategy; or the walk-up family flat in Brooklyn where, once his mother and sister had moved out, he set up continuous chess games beside each bed, ignoring the outside

sunshine to compete against himself. If you could see inside his brain, as his enemies no doubt hoped to, you would find it primed to attack and defend in every way possible, with a straight-moving rook or a sidling bishop, or with both in his favourite Ruy Lopez opening, or with the queen swallowing an early pawn in the "poisoned" version of the Sicilian, or a thousand others. At Reykjavik, when Mr Spassky was advised between games by 35 Russian grand masters, Mr Fischer had a notebook and his own long, lugubrious, clever head. And he won.

That made him a cold-war hero. The quirky individual had outplayed the state machine, and America had thrashed the Soviet Union at its own favourite game. But Mr Fischer, for all his elegant suits and childhood genius, his grandmastership at 15 and his 20-game winning streak at championship level in 1968-71, was always an unsettling poster-boy. His objective, he told everyone, was not just to win. It was to crush the other man's mind until he squirmed. And, in proper capitalist style, to get rich. At his insistence, the championship money was raised from $1,400 to $250,000; from the rematch with Mr Spassky in 1992, which he also won, he took away $3.5m. Since few venues, even Qatar or Caesar's Palace, offered him enough to make public playing worth his while, he spent the years after 1975 (when he forfeited his world title by refusing to defend it) largely wandering the world like a tramp, castigating his enemies. Only cold, eccentric Iceland welcomed him.

A house like a rook

What exactly was
wrong with Bobby
Fischer was a subject
of much debate. The
combination of high
intelligence and social
dysfunction suggested
autism; but he had
been a normal boy in
many respects, enjoying
Superman comics
and going to hockey
games. He had got
mixed up in the 1960s
with the Worldwide
Church of God, a crazed
millenarian outfit, and
perhaps had learned
from them to hate
and revile the Jews;
though he was Jewish
himself, with a Jewish
mother who had tried
psychologists and the
columns of the local
paper to cure him of too much chess,
but who still couldn't stop the pocket set
coming out at the dinner table.

Possibly – some said – he had been
unhinged by the American government's
stern pursuit of him after the 1992
rematch, which was played illegally
in the former Yugoslavia. He cursed
"stinking" America to his death, and
welcomed the 2001 terrorist attacks as
"wonderful news" – at which much
of the good he had done for chess in
his country, from inspiring clubs to
instructing players to simply making the
game, for the first time, cool, drained
away like water into sand.

Perhaps, in the end, the trouble was
this: that chess, as he once said, was life,
and there was nothing more. Mr Fischer
was not good at anything else, had not
persevered in school, had never done
another job, had never married, but
had pinned every urgent minute of his
existence to 32 pieces and 64 black and
white squares. He dreamed of a house in
Beverly Hills that would be built in the
shape of a rook.

Within this landscape, to be sure, he
was one of the world's most creative
players; no one was more scathing about
the dullness of chess games that were
simply feats of memorising tactics. Most
world-championship games, he claimed,
were pre-arranged, proof that the "old
chess" was dead, and rotten to the core.
He invented a new version, Fischer
Random, in which the back pieces
were lined up any old how, throwing
all that careful book-learning to the
winds. Yet the grid remained and the
rules remained: attack, defend, capture,
sacrifice. Win at all costs. From this grid,
and from this war, Mr Fischer could
never escape. ∎

Paul Foot

Paul Foot, a British investigative journalist, died on July 18th 2004, aged 66

"THERE ARE more people walking the streets of Britain who have been freed from prison by Paul Foot than by any other person." Mr Foot was far from being vain or self-seeking, but he must have been pleased by this compliment from one of his editors at the *Daily Mirror*. It was a vindication of his work as a campaigning journalist whose efforts on behalf of victims of injustice were not only tireless and brave, but also capable of bringing about results that would change people's lives. Though he wrote articles of every kind, and books too, his innovation was the investigative column, a device that worked because it was based on hard research rather than mere prejudice and polemic.

Not that he was short of prejudice and polemic. Far from it: they were the starting-point of all his inquiries, for Mr Foot was a committed socialist of a largely unreconstructed kind, with a particular admiration for Leon Trotsky. Indeed, many of his energies were devoted to the cause of the Socialist Workers Party, a Trotskyite outfit. How could anyone with views such as his produce balanced journalism? Mr Foot could not. He did not even try. But that was not the point. He still could, and did, produce excellent work. Doggedly – the word aptly describes the terrier in him – he dug out information that powerful people did not want to see published.

The tradition of radical journalism goes back a long way in Britain, to William Hazlitt, William Cobbett, Tom Paine, John Wilkes and beyond. These 18th- and 19th-century essayists and pamphleteers were not self-described neutral observers who meticulously separated facts from opinions, discarded the opinions and then left readers to form their own judgments. They were committed campaigners who had a point of view and made no apologies for expressing it. Mr Foot was in that tradition.

He was also in the tradition of British satire, whose most notable exponents have usually been writers, such as Jonathan Swift, or caricaturists, such as James Gillray and Thomas Rowlandson. In the 1960s, the genre enjoyed a wonderful renaissance, bursting out on every front – the stage ("Beyond the Fringe"), night clubs (The Establishment, in London), television ("That Was The Week That Was") and, most enduringly, the magazine *Private Eye*.

Born to rebel

By circumstance and breeding, Mr Foot slipped easily into this world of satire and dissent. His grandfather, Isaac Foot, a devout Methodist, had been a Liberal MP, as was his uncle Dingle, though he later defected to Labour. Another uncle, John, became a Liberal peer, and a third, Michael, was to lead the Labour Party. His father, Hugh (later Lord Caradon), was a diplomat and colonial servant whose career included terms as governor of Cyprus and Britain's ambassador to the United Nations.

The taste for satire started at Shrewsbury School, where he wrote for the school newspaper, as did his near contemporaries, Christopher Booker,

affairs. To most people his politics seemed potty. His revelatory journalism was different. Though equal scepticism greeted his first inquiries into potential scandals, his diligence and persistence nearly always won him admiration in the end. Those who fell foul of him included politicians (Jonathan Aitken, Jeffrey Archer, Reginald Maudling), union leaders (Clive Jenkins), architects (John Poulson), journalists (notably his boss at the *Mirror*, David Montgomery), businessmen (the list is long), as well as disc jockeys, civil servants and countless others. His exertions to right injustice were equally impressive: the Birmingham Six, the Bridgewater Four and the Cardiff Three were all freed from prison after campaigns led by Mr Foot.

Richard Ingrams and Willie Rushton. This trio went on to found *Private Eye* in 1961, which Mr Foot was to join six years later. Though he wrote for many other publications over the years – the *Daily Record* in Glasgow, the *Daily Mirror*, the *Guardian* among them – and edited the magazine *Isis* while up at Oxford in 1961 and later *Socialist Worker*, he never cut his links with the *Eye*.

Yet Mr Foot was unlike the others on *Private Eye*. For most of them, such as John Wells, an Oxford friend, the main aim was to puncture pomposity and make people laugh. Mr Foot had a sense of humour and could be a devastating exponent of mockery, but he was above all a polemicist and muck-raker. His contributions to the *Eye* were not cartoons like Rushton's or spoof diaries like Wells's; they were the scandalous revelations in his "Footnotes" column.

These, too, were different from the classical writings of British radical journalists, and they – and Mr Foot's other investigative books and articles – were his real contribution to public

On two occasions, Mr Foot stood for public office. The first time, in 1977, when he tried for Parliament, he gathered only 377 votes. He did better in 2002, as candidate for mayor of Hackney, in east London, but still came third. Clearly, his heart was not in it on either occasion. He wrote, after all, that "responsible office in capitalist society ... leads inevitably to arbitrary and demeaning behaviour towards others." Perhaps he really agreed with one of his heroes, Percy Bysshe Shelley, that "Poets are the unacknowledged legislators of the world." So far as is known, Mr Foot did not unearth a scandal involving poetry. ■

Gerald Ford

Gerald Rudolph Ford, an accidental president of the United States, died on December 26th 2007, aged 93

THERE WERE many times in his long life when Gerald Ford felt he had reached the top of the tree. The moment when, puffing out his teenage chest, he was made an Eagle Scout after earning 21 badges (Cooking, Camping, Civics, Lifesaving, Bird Study, First Aid). The afternoon when, his big bland face still running with sweat under his leather cap, he was named most valuable player for Michigan against Minnesota in the 1934 football season. The day in 1948 when he beat Bartel Jonkman, darling of the powerful Dutch Calvinist community, to win the Republican primary for the Grand Rapids congressional seat by nearly 10,000 votes; and the morning when, wearing one black shoe and one brown one, he walked down the aisle with Betty Warren, the prettiest single woman in the city.

The moment he became vice-president of the United States felt somewhat less portentous. Spiro Agnew had resigned in October 1973 after charges of tax evasion; the leaders of Congress had picked Mr Ford to succeed him. There was a telephone call. Mr Ford, after 13 terms as a congressman, had risen to become a popular minority leader in the House, with no ambitions but to be speaker one day if control swung back to the Republicans. Still, as he told Betty, the vice-presidency would make a "nice conclusion" to his career.

It was not the conclusion. The moment he reached the top came on August 9th 1974, when Richard Nixon, worn down by the Watergate scandal, resigned the presidency. Mr Ford, like the rest of America, watched the broadcast on television. Then he went to bed. "My feeling is you might as well get to sleep," he said later. After becoming the first unelected vice-president, he was now the first unelected president of the United States. He snored happily on.

Mr Ford disliked fuss. His philosophy was to put his head down, work "like hell" and not fret about what might have been. His straightness and squareness made him the antithesis of the wriggling, tormented man he replaced. As he made his inaugural speech in the East Room of the White House – "just a little straight talk among friends" – the very flatness of his Michigan vowels, his stumbles over words, his mistiness whenever he talked about prayers, seemed like a gale of fresh air.

But straightness could also be disconcerting. Americans found that out when, after a month in office, Mr Ford gave Nixon a "full, free and absolute" pardon for anything he might have done while president. All inquiries, charges, rootings through the evidence, rehashings of the past were short-circuited; America would move on. The president's hordes of critics suspected a deal had been done, and certainly one had been floated by Nixon's chief of staff, Alexander Haig. But Mr Ford had not agreed to it. He had pardoned Nixon – as his speech at the time made clear, and as remarks made public after his death confirmed – both to calm things down, and because he was his friend. Buddies should stick by each other.

For an average congressman thrust accidentally into power, Mr Ford made a

fairly good fist of things. Forces beyond his control helped somewhat. The galloping inflation he inherited was cooled by a mild recession; sky-high energy prices fell gradually of their own accord; Vietnam was definitely lost to the Vietcong, and the last American troops had no option but to leave. The post-Watergate Congress swarmed with cocky, virtuous Democrats, but Mr Ford, an instinctive fiscal conservative, managed to veto most of the spending bills he disliked. He also refused – with a certain pleasure, it seemed at the time – to bail out the bankrupt Democratic city of New York.

He felt proud, looking back, of what he had done to bind up his damaged country. Under him, Nixon's besieged White House became a relaxed and open place, in which a large loping golden retriever shadowed the large loping president, and the powers assumed by the executive branch began to be scaled back again. America, still outraged by the pardon, did not thank him, ejecting him in 1976 in favour of a Georgia peanut farmer. That hurt; for all his diffidence in coming to the job, Mr Ford had grown to like the life of

a president, and so had Betty. But he "wasn't going to sit and cry about it". He would smoke his pipe, write his memoirs, and play golf with Bob Hope.

On time for dinner

The curious wondered what made him so very assured in the top job; for, despite all his tumblings on the ski-slopes or down the steps of Air Force One, assured he was. Mr Ford gave pious credit to his mother, who had made him recite Kipling's "If" whenever he got in a temper, and whose rule-of-the-house had been "Tell the truth, work hard, and come to dinner on time." Cod psychologists noted that Mr Ford revered his paint-seller stepfather and had a soft spot for another Midwestern retailer, Harry Truman; both, perhaps, had inspired him to be decent, conciliatory and industrious.

He himself, in retirement, was still surprised at what he had done. Oddly, he remarked, he had never felt "more secure, more certain of myself", than when he was in the White House, at the top of the tree. Some might say that he had never had enough imagination to be scared. ■

Antonio Fortich

Antonio Fortich, fighting bishop of the Philippines, died on July 2nd 2003, aged 89

THE CEREMONIAL opening of the Martial Law Museum in Manila in 1999 was carried out by Antonio Fortich, a bishop in the Roman Catholic church. He was handed wire-cutters and snipped through the barbed wire that was thought more appropriate to the occasion than a ribbon. Those who had suffered under the martial law regime of Ferdinand Marcos felt that the bishop had done as much as any public figure in the Philippines to oppose the dictatorship. More than that the bishop, known to his supporters as Commander Tony, was still in fighting mood long after Marcos had been deposed. The

museum conveyed a "sense of horror", he said, but for millions of people in the Philippines their horrors had not ended when Marcos quit in 1986. The subsequent restoration of democracy had meant little to his own people in Negros.

Negros is a large island in the southern Philippines. Antonio Fortich was bishop of Bacolod, its main town. Negros has long been the sugar bowl of the country. From an aircraft you can see a vast stretch of green cane that covers much of the land. The United States expanded Negros's sugar industry when it took possession of the Philippines after defeating Spain in 1898, and it continued to be its main export market after the Philippines gained independence in 1946. The landowning families of Negros, mostly of Spanish stock, became rich, providing welfare for their sugar workers in return for subservience. But America eventually developed its own sugar industry. In the 1980s the price of Philippine sugar crashed.

The sugar barons were no longer making money, and the welfare system for the workers was collapsing. Hundreds of children were dying of malnutrition. Bishop Fortich said that what was known as *tiempo muerto* (the dead season, after the sugar has been harvested) had expanded and become *tiempo del muerto* (a time of death). The island, he believed, could become a "social volcano".

A sparrow's tale

The poor in Negros turn to the church or the communists. In its hunt for communists, the army made Negros an area of "low-intensity conflict". Many communists were killed, but many innocent people died too, either because they were accused of helping the communists or because they were caught in crossfire. Bishop Fortich rushed to a church hall in Negros where 500 villagers were being threatened by army "death squads" and persuaded the soldiers to leave. He once showed reporters a dead sparrow he had found. The bird, he said, was just like any poor citizen caught in the crossfire of contending ideological forces. The bishop had the sparrow stuffed and mounted and kept it on his desk.

Bishop Fortich said he did not support any ideology. But in the Philippines, as in Latin America, not even a priest can escape politics. For many in authority priests are still considered to be as dangerous as in Graham Greene's *The Power and the Glory*. Bishop Fortich's superior, Cardinal Jaime Sin, archbishop of Manila, provides guidelines to his clergy: like the bishop, he thundered in the pulpit against the iniquities of Marcos, but granted him the blessings of the church.

Bishop Fortich probably stretched the guidelines. He spoke against the hanging judges of Manila who called themselves the Guillotine Club. He was one of the first people to alert the government to the activities of timber bandits who had stripped hundreds of acres of forest in Negros. He supported the election of Joseph Estrada as president of the Philippines; it was clear that he was the overwhelming choice of the ordinary people, sick of successive governments being run for the benefit of the rich. He persuaded the president to release 200 political prisoners. It was only when it became clear that Mr Estrada had betrayed his supporters by lining his pockets that the bishop withdrew his support.

In keeping his flock together, he sought to show that the church was a better fighter for their interests than the communists. He said the sugar barons should be more generous to their workers. Cutting sugar cane, swinging a machete all day and loading lorries is a tough job, made worse in the suffocating heat by having to wear thick clothing to provide protection from the sharp leaves. After paying his employer for food a worker might be left with only a few pesos at the end of a month. To tide him over he would get in debt, which would grow year by year.

Bishop Fortich set up a co-operative composed of small landowners and sugar workers, to show what could be done. He wanted the great sugar estates broken up and land distributed to small farmers, who would grow other crops. The Philippines no longer exports sugar. To satisfy its sweet tooth, most years it imports some, at a price lower than the home-grown cane. The sugar barons accused the bishop of being a traitor to his class: after all, his parents had themselves been landowners in Negros. As a warning, a hand grenade was lobbed into his house in Bacolod.

He was nominated for a Nobel peace prize, praised by Pope John Paul II, and many of his followers thought of him as a saint. Cardinal Sin said that he was sure that, in heaven, the bishop would "intercede for us". ■

Janet Frame

Janet Frame, a chronicler of mental turmoil, died on January 29th 2004, aged 79

"THIS BOOK ... is a work of fiction. None of the characters, including Istina Movet, portrays a living person." The disclaimer to Janet Frame's second novel, "Faces in the Water", published in 1961, fooled no one. Istina Movet was herself in the thinnest disguise, enduring the full barbarities of the treatment of mental illness in New Zealand in the mid-20th century.

Miss Frame was first institutionalised in 1945, when she was 21. The doctors diagnosed incipient schizophrenia. As she explained it, a great gap had opened up between herself and the world, "drifting away through a violet-coloured sea where hammer-nosed sharks in tropical ease swam side by side with the seals and the polar bears." No comforting god appeared to remove "the foreign ideas, the glass beads of

fantasy, the bent hair-pins of unreason" embedded in her mind. She needed "treatment" – electro-convulsive therapy at the Seacliff hospital in Dunedin.

Every part of this therapy was horrific to her. The sleek, cream-painted machine with its knobs and lights; the smell of methylated spirits, rubbed on her temples so that the shock would take; the grey woollen socks she would compulsively wear on treatment days, "to ward off death"; the stifled, choking cries of other patients; and the shock itself, a trap-door dropping open on darkness. As she came round afterwards, her tears kept falling "in a grief that you cannot name".

For almost a decade, Miss Frame moved in and out of institutions. Since electric-shock treatment did little for her, it was decided in 1952 that she needed a lobotomy. She had often seen such patients returning from the hospital, "with plaster over their shaven heads ... and the pupils of their eyes large and dark as if filled with ink." Now she, too, was to be "changed" into someone biddable and quiet.

But she had also been writing while in hospital. In the nick of time, "The Lagoon", a collection of short stories, was published and won New Zealand's highest literary prize. "I've decided that you should stay as you are. I don't want you changed," said Seacliff's chief surgeon. As Miss Frame later agreed, "My writing saved me."

It was to go on doing so. "Faces in the Water" was written as a therapeutic exercise on the advice of her psychiatrist at London's Maudsley hospital, where she admitted herself as an outpatient in 1957. To the end of her life she used writing as therapy, not caring whether she was published. Her autobiography (which was made into the film "An Angel at My Table" in 1990) was meant to set the record straight and show that she was not disturbed. She loathed being labelled a "mad genius".

Yet as her fame spread abroad, leading last October to her nomination for the Nobel prize for literature, she admitted that madness was a mantle for her. When her Maudsley doctors had told her that she was not schizophrenic, she remembered wistfully

> how ... I had accepted [my schizophrenia], how in the midst of the agony and terror of the acceptance I found the unexpected warmth, comfort, protection: how I had longed to be rid of the opinion but was unwilling to part with it. And even when I did not wear it openly I always had it by for emergency, to put on quickly, for shelter from the cruel world. And now it was gone ...

A railway child
If she was not mad, perhaps her strangeness, shyness and social ineptitude sprang from her background. She was born in Dunedin, in New Zealand's far south. Her father worked on the railways, and the family moved constantly from small town to small town: Outram, Glenham, Wyndham, Oamaru. They were poor but artistic; her mother, a poet and Christadelphian, encouraged her children to "wondrous contemplation" of stones, stars and words.

At four, Janet made up her first story. At around that age, too, she had what she described as "my first conscious feeling of an outside sadness", as she stood on the long white road that ran past the Outram swamp and heard the wind sighing in the telephone wires. Already, "Outside" and "Inside" were in strong conflict in her life. At school, red-haired and gawky, she found her inner world of books taking over the "real" world, "the literature streaming through it like an array of beautiful ribbons through the branches of a green, growing tree."

As she grew older, having lost two sisters by drowning, she sought the Inside more and more: in imaginary diaries, in the huts where she hid to write, or in the linen cupboard at Seacliff, with its little dusty window looking over lawns to the sea:

> ... the prospect of the world terrified me: a morass of despair, violence, death with a thin layer of glass spread upon the surface where Love, a tiny crab with pincers and rainbow shell, walked delicately ever sideways but getting nowhere.

Miss Frame came to terms with the world eventually, but never needed its approval. Nor did she lose her restlessness. When she was nominated for the Nobel prize, an honour that did not excite her, she was asked how she would spend the prize money. She said she would use it to buy back New Zealand's now-privatised railways, the fabric of her tortured past. ■

Betty Friedan

Betty Friedan, campaigner for women's rights, died on February 4th 2006, aged 85

ONCE UPON a time, behind the door of almost every ranch house on almost every suburban street in America, a beautiful creature could be found. She wore a housecoat, sheer stockings and a turban that kept her hairstyle neat when she was dusting. Rubber gloves preserved her flawless hands as she washed the dishes after breakfast. Her husband's homecoming was welcomed every day with new recipes from the *Ladies' Home Journal* and, after lights out, complaisant sex.

She had never been to college or, if she had, put her intelligence aside. Her life was to ferry children in the station wagon, make peanut-butter sandwiches, choose new drapes, do the laundry, arrange flowers. At eleven in the morning she would open her enormous refrigerator, cut a slice of pastel-frosted cake and wash down, with coffee, the pills that kept her smiling.

For almost a decade, in the 1950s, Betty Friedan's life was much like this. In her rambling house in Grandview-on-the-Hudson, New York, she brought up three children, cooked meals for her theatre-producer husband and "messed about" with home decoration. Obviously, she did not work in the proper sense of the word. She was a wife and mother and, as a woman, was happy to be nothing else.

One glance at Mrs Friedan, though, suggested that matters were more complicated. Short, stocky, with an enormous nose and hooded eyes, she was far from the sweet Bambi creature promoted in womens' magazines. Argument-wise, she could give as good as she got, complete with smashing crockery and the whole gamut of screams. She had majored in psychology and won a research fellowship at Berkeley, though she gave it up when her boyfriend felt overshadowed. At college she had gone, dressed in twinset and pearls, to a squalid New York office to try to join the Communist Party. For years she had been a left-wing journalist, writing about race and sex discrimination for union news-sheets, and she had fearlessly gone on working after marriage until, on her second pregnancy, she had been fired in favour of a man.

In Grandview-on-the-Hudson, her radicalism buried, Mrs Friedan asked: "Is this all?" Despite her education she was doing no better than her mother, whose misery had filled their nice house in Peoria with temper and recrimination. Her father, once a button-hawker, had risen to own a jeweller's shop; her mother's creativity began and ended at the front yard. Most women, Mrs Friedan believed, felt the same. In 1957 she surveyed 200 classmates from Smith College, now housewives, most desperate; but when she catalogued their despair in an article, no women's magazine would publish it. Mrs Friedan determined to write a book, and in 1963 threw a firebomb into American society whose effects are still reverberating.

"The Feminine Mystique" was rambling and badly written, but it identified precisely why women were miserable. Oddly enough, since Mrs Friedan had been a keen Freudian at college, much of the problem lay with

and, in 1970, celebrating 50 years of women's suffrage by leading the Women's Strike for Equality, some 50,000 souls, through New York City.

Much was achieved, especially on abortion law, but it was not plain sailing. Mrs Friedan's sharp tongue made enemies everywhere. She rapidly fell out with the daft fringe of the women's movement, the bra-burners and ball-breakers and militant lesbians (the Lavender Menace, as she called them), who wanted all-out war. The impatient disliked her incrementalist approach; the class-conscious condemned her for rooting the "woman problem" in the pampered white suburbs, rather than in ghettos and factories.

Freud, whose theories were now so popular. He had thought of women as inferiors, racked with penis envy, whose only route to fulfilment lay through men. Garbage, cried Mrs Friedan. Women needed simply to be treated as equals and freed to become themselves.

Black eyes under make-up

Grateful letters poured in from women readers. Critics, mostly but not merely male, spluttered that she was a danger to the state and a proof of the folly of sending girls to college. But women now had the political wind behind them. Mrs Friedan got busy, co-founding in 1966 the National Organisation for Women (NOW) campaigning for equal pay, maternity leave, abortion choice and decent child care, fighting for the still unpassed Equal Rights Amendment

Part of the difficulty was that she loathed political correctness, gender politics and the gender studies that came to clutter the curriculums of American universities. She also approved of marriage and refused to hate men. Though she claimed her own husband abused her, giving her black eyes which she hid under make-up (in 1969, she divorced him), she insisted that men were victims of women's frustrations as much as women were. This was less a sexual problem than an economic one. It would be solved with equal work, worth and incomes.

When Mrs Friedan died, that Utopia was still distant. But at least she had made sure that post-war America's Ideal Woman was buried at some suburban crossroads, her hair still unmussed, and with a stake through her perfectly calibrated heart. ∎

Imre Friedmann

Imre Friedmann, an extreme microbiologist, died on June 11th 2007, aged 85

LIFE STANDS no chance at all on the surface of the planet Mars. Fields of reddish oxydised rocks stretch out to the horizon. Carbon dioxide fills the atmosphere, and ultra-violet radiation burns through it. Deep cold and dryness reign everywhere. There has probably been water, for the poles have ice caps and the ground shows channels, gullies and the shifting shoreline of what may once have been an ocean. But water, in itself, is not a proof of life.

So science says. Human curiosity says otherwise. The lines on Mars are surely canals; the dark patches may well be forests; random flashes of light suggest volcanic activity. Move on a notch, and there are little green men, glowing slightly and with their eyes out on stalks, peopling the scene. Or there are far more terrifying creatures, "intellects vast and cool and unsympathetic" as H.G. Wells described them, with grey tentacles and slobbering mouths, hammering together their metal war machines and howling with each death-flash of their Heat-Rays, "Aloo! Aloo!"

Imre Friedmann's version of life on Mars was less noisy but, to him, no less exciting. It lay inside a squarish grey lump of rock known as ALH 84001, a meteorite picked up in 1984 in the Allen Hills of Antarctica. Traces of gas inside it seemed to prove that it came from Mars. And there too, like a microscopic "string of pearls" as Mr Friedmann described it, were flexible chains of crystals that could only have formed by some organic process. They seemed to be the fossilised internal "compasses" of magnetotactic bacteria, similar to kinds that still exist on Earth. And since such bacteria need oxygen, their presence suggested that photosynthesising organisms must once have lived on Mars too.

This discovery, announced in 1996, was the apogee of Mr Friedmann's long search for life in the most daunting places possible. The organisms he found were nothing much to see. They lay under the stony floor of deserts like the Negev, the Gobi and the Atacama, or in the dry valleys of the Antarctic. He called them "cryptoendoliths", hiders-in-rocks. Most of them were cyanobacteria, familiarly known as blue-green algae, clinging precariously to life in the most extreme conditions of heat, cold, dryness or salinity.

For years the scientific world was indifferent to Mr Friedmann's studies of these organisms. Fame suddenly engulfed him in 1978, not long after the first *Viking* landing on Mars, when NASA had disappointingly concluded that the planet's soil was sterile. Some NASA scientists recalled then that, two years before, Mr Friedmann (with his wife Roseli Ocampo, also a microbiologist) had published a paper on bacteria surviving in terrain almost as hostile as Mars; and the dead rocks began to suggest a different story.

Mr Friedmann himself always felt a peculiar tenderness for his cryptoendoliths: "always hungry, always too cold, in this grey zone". "In human terms", he said, "you could compare them to the most miserably living generations of pariahs in India. They are born, they live, and they die in the gutter." Like pariahs; or like him when,

as a Jew growing up in Budapest, he was debarred from university, forced into a labour camp, driven into a life of hiding from both Germans and Russians bent on killing him, as though he was the most contemptible form of life.

Seaweed in the desert

His enthusiasm for science had started in boyhood and in his mother's kitchen; but his taste for extreme microbiology began in the 1950s, at Hebrew University in Jerusalem. He had gone there, a refugee, to restart his academic career. As a student of seaweed, he had the "outlandish" idea that he might find single-celled versions of seaweed in the desert; and he did indeed find, under the limestone surface of the Negev, a greenish layer like a copper compound that turned out to be algae, alive.

When he moved to Florida State University and when, with NASA's interest, money began to come in, he travelled frequently in search of more. Well into old age he could be spotted, in bright red parka and with frozen beard, lying full-length on the Antarctic sandstone to snap some tiny life-containing fissure in the rocks. Or he could be seen in the Atacama, gently attaching sensors to rocks as if they were living bodies, so that his data boxes could record for seven years the least intimation of something happening inside them.

Of course, any such movement on Mars had long since ceased. About 3 billion years ago, by the best estimates, life had died out there. But Mr Friedmann was fascinated by the thought that Mars might well have been warm, wet and biologically pulsing before Earth was. This provided another data point from which to explore the origins of life. It was possible, too, that life had originally come to Earth from Mars, since it was much easier to make the journey that way than in reverse, and that it had come in the form of bacteria locked up in meteorites like ALH 84001.

Almost as a dare, Mr Friedmann suggested that future voyagers might "terraform" Mars by reintroducing as "pioneer organisms" the cyanobacteria he had discovered. Like the Martian dreams of most Earthlings, it seemed beyond all bounds of probability. But Mr Friedmann's plucky little organisms, life at its most resistant, could never be counted out of anything. ∎

Takeo Fukuda

Takeo Fukuda, prime minister of Japan in 1976–78 and twice its finance minister, died on July 5th 1995, at the age of 90

ACCEPTING THAT politics is a cynical game, Takeo Fukuda resolved to make it more so. He spent two decades at the top of government in Japan, a span long enough for him to hold most senior cabinet jobs, to stab most of his colleagues in the back and to go through vast sums of ill-gotten money. And yet, improbable though it might sound, many think fondly of him. He was one part scoundrel, and two parts mystery.

Mr Fukuda went to considerable lengths to avoid consistency. He was elected to the Diet (parliament) in 1952, after a bribery scandal forced him to quit his first career as a finance ministry bureaucrat. He managed nonetheless to spend most of the ensuing years posing as the respectable face of the ruling Liberal Democratic Party. For a time he led a campaign to rid the LDP of factions, the channels for dirty campaign funds. Yet this did not prevent him from heading a faction of his own. In 1976 he engineered the downfall of a genuinely clean prime minister, Takeo Miki, in order to clear the way for his own succession.

As finance minister in 1965, Mr Fukuda broke with tradition by running a budget deficit, and took the credit for the high growth that followed. Yet he denounced the inflation that followed too, and by the early 1970s he had emerged as chief guardian of Japan's public finances. For many years a supporter of Taiwan, Mr Fukuda nonetheless devoted much of his energy when prime minister to concluding a peace treaty with communist China. Japan's aid to Asia doubled during his

term. A large slice of it probably landed up in the coffers of his faction.

Among the hawks

Mr Fukuda's two years as prime minister will be remembered by some for the immodestly named "Fukuda doctrine", which promised that Japan would never again become a military power. Most domestic tributes to Mr Fukuda have dwelt on the supposed idealism of this pronouncement. Yet the doctrine was a con. It gave little away, since the constitution imposed on Japan after the second world war excluded war in any case; and there is little evidence that Mr Fukuda meant it seriously.

In 1978, a year after crafting his doctrine, Mr Fukuda said: "Japan can possess any type of weapon if it falls within the necessary minimum for self-defence purposes, even if this means nuclear or bacteriological weapons." The comment placed him squarely among the hawks set on a minimalist reading of the constitution's war-renouncing clause. Mr Fukuda had, moreover, entered politics as a protégé of Nobusuke Kishi, a war criminal turned prime minister who supported rearmament.

Mr Fukuda's personal loyalties were no more constant than his principles. In 1973–74 he was happy to serve as finance minister in Kakuei Tanaka's government; yet the "Kaku–Fuku war" divided the LDP between their camps for the ensuing decade.

In 1976 Mr Fukuda became prime minister on the understanding that he would relinquish the job to Masayoshi Ohira after two years. Mr Fukuda tried

prime minister. The machine served Mr Fukuda's friends and family too: his son and son-in-law still sit in the Diet.

Mr Fukuda's reputation survived all this: the nepotism, the corruption, the ambitious hypocrisy. For this he must thank his arch-rival, Mr Tanaka. The two men operated in similar ways: through factions based on dirty cash. Mr Tanaka was the more successful at this game. By the 1980s he commanded far more cash, and his faction had grown to nearly twice the size of Mr Fukuda's. As a result, Mr Tanaka, rather than Mr Fukuda, is remembered as the architect of Japan's contemporary corruption.

Another factor in the buoyancy of Mr Fukuda's reputation is the power of snobbery in Japan. Whereas Mr Tanaka was a self-made upstart, an entrepreneur, a folksy, rough-voiced charmer, Mr Fukuda was a patrician, a graduate of Tokyo University's law school with a patina of respectability burnished by his years in the finance ministry. Mr Tanaka seldom laid claim to high principles or sophisticated vision; Mr Fukuda spent his later years convening worthy symposiums. Mr Tanaka was surely the less hypocritical of the two. But Japan is in awe of its mandarin elite, so Mr Fukuda is remembered as the more honourable. ■

to wriggle out of the deal; in 1980 he helped destroy Mr Ohira's government.

Mr Fukuda sometimes compared himself to the feudal barons of old Japan. Like them, his only real loyalty was to relatives and neighbours. His family farmed silk in Gunma prefecture; and the men at Gunma's cocoon-futures exchange still tell stories about how deeply their patron interested himself in sericulture. Mr Fukuda's electoral machine in Gunma is said to have mustered 50,000 members at its peak – enough to ensure that its master won more votes than his local rival, Yasuhiro Nakasone, when Mr Nakasone was

John Kenneth Galbraith

John Kenneth Galbraith, economist and public intellectual, died on April 29th 2006, aged 97

ABOVE A large oak bookcase in John Kenneth Galbraith's elegant sitting room in Cambridge, Massachusetts, a framed sampler was displayed. "Galbraith's First Law", read the meticulous red and blue cross-stitch: "Modesty is a vastly overrated virtue." He thoroughly believed it. Save for his humble origins on a farm in Ontario, little about Mr Galbraith or his life was modest.

At six foot eight, he was a giant. Intellectually he was equally towering, a man who spent more than seven decades either on the stage of American public policy – as a bureaucrat in Franklin Roosevelt's New Deal, a confidante of John Kennedy and adviser to countless other Democrats – or loudly lambasting Washington from offstage left, as a Harvard professor.

For several of those decades, Mr Galbraith – much to the chagrin of his academic colleagues – could claim to be the best-known economist in the world. His books, more than 40 of them, were spectacularly successful. All this made him an extraordinary public intellectual. But for many, particularly on America's left, he was much more. Mr Galbraith embodied a creed (a broad scepticism of markets and unshakeable belief in a strong state to balance them) and an era, the 1960s, when that sort of liberalism reached its peak. In many eyes, and perhaps his own, Mr Galbraith was America's Great Liberal Economist, the intellectual heir to John Maynard Keynes, whose contributions to economics are underappreciated by a profession obsessed with mathematical formulae.

He was certainly Keynes's heir in his passion for the trenches of public policy, his recognition that economics could and should be accessible, and his way with words. A devotee of Trollope and Evelyn Waugh – "Scoop" was a favourite – Mr Galbraith strove to perfect his prose, reworking each passage at least five times. "It was usually on about the fourth day that I put in that note of spontaneity for which I am known," he once admitted.

Bons mots, however, seemed to come naturally to him. "Economists are economical, among other things, of ideas; most make those of their graduate days last a lifetime." "Wealth is not without its advantages, and the case to the contrary, although it has often been made, has never proved widely persuasive." As Kennedy's ambassador to India, Mr Galbraith preferred to write to the president direct: sending letters through the State Department, he told Kennedy, was "like fornicating through a mattress".

Where Mr Galbraith differed from Keynes, and from other Great Economists such as Milton Friedman, was that he produced no robust economic theories. Robert Skidelsky, Keynes's biographer, thought that he lacked "the theoretical brilliance, or perhaps merely interest". In fact, Mr Galbraith disdained a theoretical approach to economics. This was more than a simple aversion to mathematical formulae. The greatest problem with economics, he argued, was its "wilful denial of the presence of power and political interests". By positing an idealised world of perfect competition, economic theory assumed away the factors that drove societies.

Mr Galbraith was thus less an economist than a mixture of sociologist, political scientist and journalist. His three most influential books were snapshots of the America of their time. In "American Capitalism" (1952), giant firms were balanced by the "countervailing power" of, for instance, unions; in "The Affluent Society" (1958), massive private consumption coexisted with public decay; in "The New Industrial State" (1967), producers held all the economic power and competition was irrelevant. Time proved especially unkind to that idea.

His faith in government, born of the searing experience of the Depression, verged sometimes on the bizarre. In 1973, for instance, he argued that America's few-hundred biggest companies should be brought into public ownership. Yet if Mr Galbraith was often wrong, he nonetheless gave much to American public life. "The Affluent Society" not only changed the way the country viewed itself, but gave new phrases to the language: "Conventional wisdom", "the bland leading the bland", "private opulence and public squalor". Amartya Sen, the Indian economist, said that reading it was like reading "Hamlet": "You realise where [all the quotations] came from".

Competition in Gstaad
Long after Mr Galbraith's brand of big-government liberalism fell out of favour, he remained its standard-bearer. His acerbic comments on public policy were always worth reading. In private matters he was not partisan, and could count Bill Buckley, the conservative intellectual, among his closest friends. In the local bookstore in Gstaad, where they both went skiing, they would battle to get their books the best spot in the window.

A decade ago, Mr Galbraith lamented that old age brought an annoying affliction he called the "Still Syndrome". People would constantly note that he was "still" doing things: still "interested in politics" when he showed up at a meeting, "still imbibing" when he had a drink and "still that way" when his eyes lit up on seeing a beautiful woman. The Still Syndrome lasted an immodestly long time. Its passing has left America poorer. ■

Allen Ginsberg

Allen Ginsberg, who howled about life in America, died on April 5th 1997, aged 70

WHEN ALLEN Ginsberg was being shown around an Oxford college he asked to see the rooms Shelley had used. His companion was uncertain of their whereabouts, but pointed hopefully to a door. Mr Ginsberg entered, dropped to his knees and kissed the carpet, much to the surprise of the occupant, who was making tea. Shelley would have been amused. He would have recognised a fellow romantic and quite likely invited him along to meet Keats and Byron. And as a connoisseur of dope, the American must have a chat with De Quincey about the virtues of opium.

The curious era in American culture that produced the beat generation (from beatitude or deadbeat: take your pick) was in some ways a reliving of England's 19th-century romantic movement. The beats rejected the rationality of normal living. In their pursuit of "flower power" some sought a return to nature. Mr Ginsberg was their outrageous Byron, although far from handsome and in love with men rather than women.

"Coming out", green politics, feminism, trash fashion and much else that today hardly raises an eyebrow, made its bow in the late 1950s and early 1960s. Mr Ginsberg and his friends, among them Jack Kerouac and William Burroughs, would not claim to have begotten all these innovations, but they were a catalyst. Although the Eisenhower presidency (1953-61) is thought of as a stodgy period, the civil rights movement was growing and in 1961 America sent its first soldiers to Vietnam. Civil rights and draft dodging were oxygen to the beats.

The start of fame

Allen Ginsberg, though, grew up in a nine-to-five world. His parents were Jewish immigrants from Russia determined to make good. His father was a teacher, and wrote poetry of a traditionalist style. Young Allen went to university and was expected to become a lawyer. This ordered life came apart. His mother, who for years had had bouts of schizophrenia, was confined to a mental home. Mr Ginsberg dropped out and had a series of jobs, including a spell writing copy for advertisements. He settled in San Francisco because of its "tradition of Bohemia" and wrote "Howl", the poem that made him famous.

Just as an earlier generation first heard of *Ulysses* when it was banned, "Howl" became famous by being prosecuted for obscenity. In the course of a long and widely-publicised trial its opening lines were read by millions who would not normally pick up a book of poetry. Unlike *Ulysses*, with James Joyce's peculiar syntax, "Howl", whatever its merits as poetry, is a pretty straightforward read: "I saw the best minds of my generation destroyed by madness, starving hysterical naked, / dragging themselves through the negro streets at dawn looking for an angry fix."

Even better for a public avid for novelty, Allen Ginsberg turned out to be a character, a bald-headed bearded lump in sandals, never short of a lively opinion and, if there was a photographer around, happy to play the buffoon. He travelled across America reading his poems to large, mainly young audiences

who seemed not to mind that he was often incomprehensible, perhaps because his admirers were themselves blotto on drugs.

Even during his travels abroad he was often in the headlines. He was expelled from Cuba and Czechoslovakia for advocating homosexuality, and from India, where he sought "eastern mysticism" and was accused of being an American spy, and from various countries in Latin America where he said he was looking for new drugs. At a party in London he took off his clothes and hung a hotel notice, "Do not disturb", on his penis. "Poetry is best read naked," he said. John Lennon, not a man usually offended, shielded his wife and walked out in disgust. Back home, Mr Ginsberg practised yoga and other forms of meditation, declaring them to be superior to drugs, and became a devotee of a guru who dressed his staff as English butlers. He once bemused police at a civil rights demo in Chicago by chanting the mantra "om" for seven hours.

The *New Yorker* published a sly version of "Howl": "I saw the best minds of my generation / Reading their poems to Vassar girls / Being interviewed by *Mademoiselle* / Having their publicity handled by professionals."

Nevertheless, Allen Ginsberg was said to be a generous man, giving support to less famous poets and other writers. He pioneered poetry designed to be read aloud. He turned down offers from big publishing houses and stuck with the small firm that first put him in print. He produced a mountain of work published in some 40 books. On one day just before he died he was said to have written a dozen poems.

Will his poetry endure? Some of his poems are now in anthologies. "Kaddish", about his mother's death, is well regarded. But while every poet may hope to outlive fashion and be read for ever, there are not many Shelleys. The judge who heard the "Howl" case decided that the poem had "social importance". That, anyway, was true enough. ∎

Françoise Giroud

Françoise Giroud, a French writer and politician, died on January 19th 2003, aged 86

THE BRAVE ambition of Françoise Giroud was, as she put it, "to move France out of its rut". Americans, she thought, had the right idea. They never seemed to get into a rut. On her first visit to New York soon after the end of the second world war she had been struck by "the degree of optimism, the exhilaration" she had found there. That view stayed with her: "There is a strength in the United States that we in Europe constantly tend to underestimate." Miss Giroud's views were not always well received by the French, who do not consider themselves in any way inferior to the Americans, or indeed to anyone else. They denied they were in a rut, but even if they were it was one of elegant and enviable proportions.

Miss Giroud's weapon to give more pace to French life was language. During her long life she worked in films, was a journalist and a government minister. The thread that linked these jobs was a way with words. For many French people she became an addiction, whether they agreed with her or not. She edited two magazines entirely new to France, *Elle* and *L'Express. Elle* aimed to be provocative. An article Miss Giroud wrote in 1951 was entitled "Is the Frenchwoman clean?" A woman would buy a new dress because she wanted to look good, she wrote. "But under the dress, what are you wearing? A garter-belt that has not been washed in two years. That is the national average." The indignation Miss Giroud aroused by discussing personal hygiene quickly became of lesser importance

amid a national debate that ensued over whether La France herself was clean. In the years after the second world war many French people were feeling that the stain of the German occupation, and its accompanying collaboration by the Vichy government, had not been cleansed. Others argued passionately that France had to give up Vietnam and Algeria and abandon the dirty ways of colonialism. *Elle* offered Frenchwomen a view of the world beyond the home.

L'Express, France's first weekly news magazine, was a challenge to xenophobic French. The French, Miss Giroud said, were among those westerners "most ill-informed about themselves". News magazines keep Americans informed. Try ours. The French did and they liked it. Perhaps they were moving out of their rut.

Through the fog

In 1974 Jacques Chirac, the then prime minister, created for Françoise Giroud the new job of minister of women's affairs. She was later made culture minister. But although she came to be described as a feminist, she was never a campaigning American-style sister. Nor was she in the philosophical mould of Simone de Beauvoir. More practically, she sought to help French women find their way through what she called "the fog" of a male-run world. Women bought most of the products consumed in the home, but were ignorant of how they were made or the economics of their marketing. In politics, especially, the fog was thick, and remains so. In the lower house of the present French parliament fewer than

"A complete German absurdity," she writes. Miss Giroud shared the shame of those French who believed the government should have fought on in 1940, but she had been sure that the Germans would be defeated. "I never for a minute doubted the moral superiority of England, and for me that explained how it was able to hold out."

She had little education to speak of. She left school at 14 and worked first in a shop, then as a typist, after her father, a journalist, died and her mother had no money. Or, it could be said, she gradually acquired a broad education

11% of its members are women, one of the lowest proportions in Europe. Three women are in the cabinet but, said Miss Giroud, "we have had women ministers for decades". Nor did she approve of the jobs they were often given. A ministry for women was "a shallow answer to a non-existent problem".

As Miss Giroud became well known she was pressed for details of her own life, and obligingly offered some colourful stories, such as when she was an aide to Jean Renoir in 1937 while he was making *La Grande Illusion*, regarded as one of the greatest of anti-war films. "You have gifts," he told her.

In her book *I Give You My Word* she tells of being arrested towards the end of the war by the Gestapo on suspicion of helping the resistance. She was released and her confiscated watch was returned to her by a helpful German.

through reading. Two of her heroines were Marie Curie, a pioneer in the study of radioactivity, and Alma Mahler, who gained rather more notorious fame as a result of her love affairs. Miss Giroud was to write biographies of both women. She preferred to say little about her own love life. She was married briefly and had two children, a son who died in a skiing accident, and a daughter who survives her. She said, "The men who helped me, and they are legion, were my friends, not my lovers."

She was writing a regular column, for a news magazine, up to a few days before her death. A recent article was about the conflict in Israel. She chides both sides, but characteristically avoids a rush to judgment. She once said, "Off the rack solutions, like bargain basement dresses, never fit anyone." ■

Elizabeth Gordon

Elizabeth Gordon, defender of American "style", died on September 3rd 2000, aged 94

IN AN essay entitled "The threat to the next America" Elizabeth Gordon sought to show that some modern architects, mainly from Europe, were undermining traditional American values. Their buildings, she told a reporter, were an expression of communism. Communism? Wasn't that a bit hard on buildings that did not happen to be to your taste? Miss Gordon stood her ground. The buildings we lived in reflected our view of society. There was the rich, earthy American style, which had evolved alongside a desire for liberty and space. And there was the rigid "international" style, of steel and concrete, which was being urged on Americans by a sinister cultural elite.

Miss Gordon was involved in what might be called the politics of architecture. A debate between supporters of the old and the new had been going on for much of the 20th century and continues today. But until her essay in 1953 the debate had been largely confined to specialist publications. Miss Gordon opened it up to a wide audience. She was editor of a popular magazine called *House Beautiful*, and told her readers there was more to design than matching the carpets with the curtains. Beware the austere "less is more" look, she said.

Equating modernism with communism helped Miss Gordon's cause at a time when America was being told by Joe McCarthy that the government was full of reds. The pioneers of the international style were indeed mostly socialist: it went with being members of the avant garde.

The Bauhaus, a group of architects and artists founded in Germany after the first world war, was a big influence. It was closed down after Hitler came to power in 1933. The Bauhaus was led for a time by Ludwig Mies van der Rohe, who coined the phrase "less is more", hated by Miss Gordon. He later moved to the United States, where his ideas were enthusiastically received by his disciples. But for Miss Gordon an even worse influence than Mies van der Rohe was Le Corbusier, a Swiss-born architect famous for the Unité d'Habitation, a vast block of flats in Marseilles. He confirmed her fears about the inhumanity of the new architecture by observing on a visit to New York that its skyscrapers were far too small.

Her godfather

So who did get Miss Gordon's approval? That's easy. Frank Lloyd Wright. She called him her god. For her, he was America's greatest artist. He, modestly, was content to call himself her godfather. It is unclear whether he wrote any of her 1953 essay, but it was certainly written under his influence. After it was published he sent a note to her, "Am at your service from here on. Godfather." Wright was then 87, the most famous architect in America and still working, but in the eyes of younger architects, especially those dazzled by the international style, a bit old-fashioned.

Miss Gordon was flattered by her attention from Wright. She had had no training in architecture. After university she had first got a job writing advertising copy and had then taken up journalism.

What Elizabeth Gordon had to offer Wright was a sharp pen and her magazine to use as a "propaganda tool". She set out to make him the symbol of all that was worthwhile in design. On three occasions, she devoted an entire issue of her magazine to his work.

Like Frank Lloyd Wright, Miss Gordon was born in the wide open spaces of the northern midwest. She instinctively liked his rambling "prairie style" houses, as he called them. Wright was, in his time, as much a revolutionary as Mies van der Rohe. Among other things he invented open-plan, and many millions of interior walls have been demolished in traditional homes as a result. Just as Britain pioneered suburbia with its cosy mock Tudor, Wright created a new vernacular for American architecture, which can be seen in homes throughout the country in some degree. He designed hundreds of buildings but was fastidious about which should be built. He once said, "The physician can bury his mistakes, but the architect can only advise his client to plant vines."

The Wright/Gordon relationship was much admired in architectural exhibitions where Wright designed the house and Miss Gordon furnished it. She put together a collection of about a thousand photographs of Wright buildings, which is now in a museum. Wright was grateful to his most loyal fan, and designed a bed for her and her husband, Carl Norcross, an authority on town planning. "Frank was fun to be with," she said. He loved to talk "and he always liked my hats."

In the heated arguments about the progress, or non-progress, of architecture, Elizabeth Gordon was sometimes accused of being xenophobic. It was probably unfair. She did take the view that, as a world power, America should be confident about its native artistry. But during her 25 years as editor of her magazine she, as much as anyone, introduced Japanese furnishing design to Americans. She visited Japan half a dozen times and wrote about *shibui*, which translates roughly as serene good taste. For publicising Scandinavian design, Finland made her a knight and awarded her a medal. There cannot be many editors of furnishing mags who have the Finnish Order of the Lion, first class. ■

Robert Graham

Robert Graham, who probed the secrets of the Vatican, died on February 10th 1997, aged 84

THE ROMAN Catholic church is not easily rattled. It seeks to rise above what it regards as petty attacks. "Confident in its destiny," Robert Graham wrote in his book *Vatican Diplomacy*, the church "does not reckon in terms of years but of centuries". All the same, in the 1960s Catholic leaders became worried by persistent stories that Pope Pius XII, the church's head during the second world war, had chosen to ignore German atrocities against the Jews and others.

The crisis facing the Vatican had something in common with the claims now being made by a new generation that Switzerland was Germany's willing banker during the Nazi period. Both Switzerland and the Vatican, tiny in area but a sovereign state nevertheless, claimed neutrality in a Europe mainly under fascist rule. Did their accommodation with Europe's masters extend to the unspeakable: to condoning the Holocaust, the name Jews give to the mass killing of their people?

Mr Graham was a clever choice by the Vatican to probe the career of Pope Pius. He was an American, so was distanced, at least geographically, from the Vatican cabal. He had a mildly colourful background. His father, Charlie Graham, had played professional baseball for the Boston Red Sox. But Robert Graham was, as he put it, "batting for God". He belonged to the Jesuits, a Catholic order noted for its rigorous discipline and scholarship.

His *Vatican Diplomacy* was not only a first-rate piece of scholarship, it was elegantly written. Mr Graham's skill as a communicator had been honed while working for *America*, a Jesuit magazine with a reputation for tackling controversial subjects and reporting them with a pithiness unusual in religious publications. Clearly the place to start the most important investigation of his career was in the archives of the Vatican. Mr Graham packed his bag and his typewriter and headed for Rome. He stayed there for most of the rest of his life.

Under pressure

Whatever pithiness Mr Graham had acquired in America was abandoned when he immersed himself in the archives of the Vatican. His report on Pope Pius runs to a dozen volumes. Those interested in exploring the thinking of a pope under extreme worldly pressures can find details of many of the documents unearthed by Mr Graham in the library of Georgetown University, which has thoughtfully put them on the internet. Although any summary stands the risk of seeming a distortion, it is fair to say that Mr Graham emerged at the end of his inquiries as a strong defender of Pope Pius.

The main complaint of the pope's critics was that he did not make a public statement condemning the murder of Jews when the extermination camps first came to the knowledge of the Vatican. Such a statement, it was argued, might have halted the massacre. At least, a pastoral letter stating that killing Jews was a sin might have deterred collaborators from delivering them to the Germans.

appointment, he said nothing about the invasion. This time the papal silence was more conspicuous.

However, despite Mr Graham's efforts, it is unlikely that many critics of Pope Pius changed their minds, just as Switzerland's name will remain besmirched for many people even if every Swiss banker turns out to have been a secret resistance leader. *The Deputy*, a play by Rolf Hochhuth, a German, which first caused a stir in the 1960s by depicting Pope Pius as a German collaborator, is still being performed in various places. *The Statement*, a novel by Brian Moore and currently selling well, is about an elderly French war criminal sheltered by the Catholic church. Mr Graham, though, believed that the future would provide a less prejudiced audience for his work; that history had a more open mind.

Mr Graham said that Pope Pius, working quietly behind the scenes, helped the underground to rescue more than 800,000 Jews from the gas chambers, hiding them in churches and in the Vatican itself. Speaking in public against the oppressors would, the pope believed, have made matters worse for Jews and Catholics. In Dachau, a concentration camp, 2,000 Catholic priests were held. A speech against the Germans would have invited reprisals.

Pope Pius has also been accused of favouring Germany's attack on the godless Soviet Union. Mr Graham noted that Germany tried to get the pope to give his approval to the Russian campaign, and even to declare it a crusade. But, to Germany's dis-

In his researches in the Vatican's and other archives Mr Graham came across many an embarrassing skeleton, not directly connected with the war. In a file he labelled "hoaxes, howlers and humbug" there is an account of an American spy planted in the Vatican who filed colourful, and entirely imaginary, reports of chats with the pope. Robert Graham "unloaded all my stuff before I pop off", and told his colleagues in the Vatican that it was time for him to return home to his native California. In a few months he was dead. ■

Paolo Gucci

Paolo Gucci, designer of fashionable goods, and black sheep of his family, died on October 10th 1995, aged 64

THE FAMOUS families of Italy have had mixed fortunes. "I can find no one who can definitely suggest a basis for agreement among them," observed Machiavelli, normally a cool customer, trying to keep his temper in his dealings with Cesare Borgia, the head of the nastiest family in Italian history. Machiavelli might have been equally at a loss had he had to deal with the Guccis. This is one of the industrious families that have been the driving force of Italy's economy. But the family ended up by destroying itself. Simple quarrels led to assault, litigation and betrayals. Paolo Gucci has been mostly blamed for the destruction of the family. He was

said to be the black sheep. His defenders say that at least he was a designer of brilliance and had vision.

Italy's talent for creating agreeable things has been a redeeming feature in a century that otherwise has not treated the country well. Its most famous politician, Mussolini, was the mentor of Hitler. Italy chose the losing side in the second world war, and its post-war politics have been steeped in corruption on a massive scale. But it has produced great film-makers, such as De Sica, great novelists, such as Moravia, and at least one key group of artists, the Futurists. For Paolo Gucci this was the real Italy, creative and civilised. And, because he was born into a rich family, he could indulge himself in its pleasures.

Grandpa Guccio Gucci had founded the family fortunes in the early years of the 20th century with a leather goods shop in Florence. By the 1950s there were shops in posh districts of other cities, including New York. Paolo Gucci, the designer of nearly all the delectable Gucci products, then proposed to sell them to a wider market than that provided by the family shops.

Blood in the boardroom

These days this seems an obvious idea, with such firms as Armani and Cartier cultivating a mass-market while still suggesting exclusivity. As far back as 1899, Thorstein Veblen, an American economist (whose pioneering book on consumerism Mr Gucci probably read), had predicted that, as wealth spread, people would buy things that enhanced "their esteem and envy" among their fellows. But Mr Gucci's father, Aldo, and an uncle, Rodolfo, wanted to continue to produce items only for the select few. Eventually they were persuaded, though reluctantly, by Paolo's promise of untold riches.

He was spectacularly successful, particularly in America. His designs, bearing the Gucci logo and a band of green, red and black, became a mark of personal affluence. So many political lobbyists wore his shoes in Washington that their favourite stamping ground became known as Gucci Gulch. At one time around 14,000 items carried the Gucci logo, not just handbags, headscarves and scent, but coffee mugs and key-rings. It may be a sort of compliment that in Asia they were the most pirated of western products.

Despite the profits involved, Mr Gucci's father and other members of the family turned on him for popularising, and, worse, Americanising, the family name. In their view he had turned his back on Italy. Even his private life was seen as more American than Italian. He had been divorced, had abandoned a second wife and lived openly with a third woman. Traditionalist Italians are supposed to stay married, with mistresses a tolerated secret. Once Mr Gucci emerged from a board meeting with blood pouring from a gash in his face. "You see what happens when the Gucci board of directors meets," he shouted to delighted reporters. He claimed his attackers had included his father and others in the family. He sued them, and the case drifted on expensively for years. Whatever the provocation, Italy was shocked when, as a result of information provided by Mr Gucci, his 81-year-old father, Aldo, was jailed in America for tax dodging. Mr Gucci was sacked by the family firm, but ran his own business for a time, trading, not very successfully, as "Paolo Gucci". Then there was Maurizio, a cousin who ran part of the Gucci empire. He was accused by Aldo Gucci of falsifying his father's will. An unknown gunman killed him in Milan in April.

The Gucci business no longer belongs to the family. In the 1980s sales slipped, possibly because of a general dip in the fashion business, possibly because the family lost heart. The family sold out to an investment group. The Gucci company has now been granted a listing on the New York stock exchange. On October 24th, the first day of trading, the company was in demand.

Aldo, Rodolfo, Maurizio and now Paolo are dead. But the Gucci quarrels may not yet have subsided. Mr Gucci is believed to have left property worth about £3m ($4.7m), including a country house in England and a number of racehorses. His will, if he left one, could be of interest to two brothers, one wife, one ex-wife, a mistress and five children. ∎

Thom Gunn

Thomson William Gunn, poet and rebel, died on April 25th 2004, aged 74

SOMETIME IN the late 1950s, in northern California, Thom Gunn came across a roaring company of bikers in their leather gear. The sight was not unusual in those days, but it was strange for that particular place, in open fields that had been haunted until then only by blue jays and swallows. Mr Gunn began to muse on the natural instinct of the birds and the crowd-compulsion of the bikers, both flocking noisily, and wrote what was to become his best-known poem, "On the Move":

> Much that is natural, to the will must yield.
> Men manufacture both machine and soul
> And use what they imperfectly control
> To dare a future from the taken routes.

For some readers, however, these verses were less about instinct and will than about the thrill of leather, steel and muscle. By moving from England to America in 1954 to live with his male lover and to explore the California bath-house culture, Mr Gunn had acknowledged himself a homosexual, and he was to become perhaps the best gay poet writing in English. But it was many years before he dared to come out in his poetry. Had he done so, in the 1950s, he would never have got his teaching job at Berkeley.

Not merely the need for a job restrained him, but the forms and traditions of poetry itself. Mr Gunn, a fine and deliberate wordsmith, revered the rhythms of Spenser, Milton and Dante all through his writing career. Accordingly he also clung to the themes beloved by older poets, including heterosexual love. His first book of verse, "Fighting Terms", published just after his graduation from Cambridge in 1953, opened with a battle poem based on Homer's "Iliad". It then moved on, via homage to Donne ("To his Cynical Mistress") to coy games between men and women:

> Even in bed I pose: desire may grow
> More circumstantial and less circumspect
> Each night, but an acute girl would suspect
> That my self is not like my body, bare.

The book also contained a poem to his lover, Mike Kitay. It was carefully disguised not only in Elizabethan stanzas but in an Elizabethan metaphor, of tamer and hawk:

> Even in flight above
> I am no longer free:
> You seeled me with your love,
> I am blind to other birds –
> The habit of your words
> Has hooded me.

Mr Gunn's self was not laid bare for a long time. He left England hoping, in his words, to be someone new. The English always wanted to categorise him, lumping him with Kingsley Amis and Philip Larkin as a "Movement" poet (though he had never met Larkin), and anthologising him with Ted Hughes because he was young and angry, though he had nothing of Mr Hughes's primal violence. In fact, he was more often lyrical and tender: instead of scraggy crows, soft-footed cats.

America, however, quickly became a succession of masks and intense experimentation. In 1966 he gave up teaching, telling colleagues that he wished to devote himself to poetry. On

the contrary he wanted to take drugs, pick up lovers and listen to rock concerts in the park. In his verse, he took on the voices of drop-outs and speed-sellers. Formal metre ("filtering the infinite through the grid of the finite", as he once put it) remained a cover for him; even on LSD, he could still scan.

> Landscape of acid:
> Where on fern and mound
> The lights fragmented by the roofing bough
> Throbbed outward, joining over broken
>   ground
> To one long dazzling burst; as even now
> Horn closes over horn into one sound.

As he grew older he relaxed, as poets tend to. He wrote a little more about his past: a childhood on the North Kent coast, lingering in the marshy graveyard of Dickens's "Great Expectations", and a bookish Hampstead boyhood, lying on Parliament Hill with Lamartine's poems. In 2000 he managed at last to commemorate his mother's suicide, which he had stumbled on at 15, by using the third person and "withdrawing" the first.

He also relaxed into his homosexuality, now serenely domesticated, and into free verse,

shocking his readers far more with that. "Jack Straw's Castle" (1976), a collection named after a gay cruising spot on Hampstead Heath, seemed to be a celebration of exuberantly broken rules. But times changed. As the AIDS epidemic began to kill his San Francisco friends in the 1980s, Mr Gunn turned back instinctively to formal metre to mourn them, as in "The Man with Night Sweats":

> I wake up cold, I who
> Prospered through dreams of heat
> Wake to their residue,
> Sweat, and a clinging sheet.

As his friends died around him, Mr Gunn often questioned why he had been spared. Their deaths, he wrote, "have left me less defined/It was their pulsing presence made me clear." Nor could he feel anything but emptiness beyond them. "On the Move" had ended with lines reminiscent of T.S. Eliot:

> At worst, one is in motion; and at best,
> Reaching no absolute, in which to rest,
> One is always nearer by not keeping still.

"I'm not sure that the last line means anything," he told an interviewer in 1999. "Nearer to what?" ■

Kenneth Hale

Kenneth Locke Hale, a master of languages, died on October 8th 2001, aged 67

SOMETIMES KENNETH Hale was asked how long it would take him to learn a new language. He thought ten or 15 minutes would be enough to pick up the essentials if he were listening to a native speaker. After that he could probably converse; obviously not fluently, but enough to make himself understood. To those whose education, however admirable in other respects, had provided only rudimentary language skills, Mr Hale seemed a marvel.

And so he was. He had a gift. But he was also an academic, a teacher of linguistics at the Massachusetts Institute of Technology (MIT). He was aware that many otherwise clever people are dunces at learning a second language. He sought to find laws and structures that could be applied to all languages. As well as studying the common languages, French, Spanish and so on, the search took him into many linguistic byways, to the languages of native Americans and Australian aborigines and the Celtic fringes of Europe. As many of these languages had no written grammar or vocabulary, and indeed were spoken by few people, Mr Hale picked them up orally. His tip for anyone who pressed him for advice on learning a language was to talk to a native speaker. Start with parts of the body, he said, then common objects.

After learning the nouns, you can start to make sentences and get attuned to the sounds. Still, there was much more to language than that. Noam Chomsky, like Mr Hale a teacher of linguistics at MIT, wrote:

Language is really weird. Although speaking a language is for normal humans an effortless task, there is nothing else in the natural world that even approaches its complexity .... Although children receive no instruction in learning their native language, they are able to fully master it in less than five years. This is all the more confusing as language is much more computationally complex than, say, simple arithmetic, which often takes years to master ... It is often hypothesised that language is an innate human faculty, with its own specialised system in our brain.

Some students of linguistics believe that such a system, if it exists, is normally shut down in the brain at the age of 12. But for Mr Hale it was around this age that his interest in language was just starting.

In cowboy boots
Kenneth Hale's childhood was on a ranch in Arizona and he started his education in a one-roomed school in the desert. Many years later, lecturing at MIT, he still felt most comfortable in cowboy boots. On his belt was a buckle he had won at a rodeo by riding bulls, and he had the slightly bowed legs of a horseman. His students were impressed that he could light a match with his thumbnail.

Mr Hale had discovered his talent for language when playing with Indian friends who taught him Hopi and Navajo. Learning languages became an obsession. Wherever he travelled he picked up a new tongue. In Spain he learnt Basque; in Ireland he spoke Gaelic so convincingly that an immigration officer asked if he knew English. He apologised to the Dutch for taking a whole week to master their somewhat complex language. He picked up the rudiments of Japanese after watching a Japanese film with subtitles. He sought to rescue languages that were dying out. One Indian language at its last gasp was spoken by the Wopanaak, the tribe that greeted the Pilgrim Fathers in 1620. It is now spoken again by several thousand people around Cape Cod. A Wopanaak who studied under Mr Hale is preparing a dictionary of her language. "Ken was a voice for the voiceless," said Noam Chomsky.

Mr Hale could converse in about 50 languages, perhaps a world record, although he was too modest to claim one. But some tongues, such as Australia's Lardil, died with its last seven speakers. Mr Hale was the last person on earth to speak some languages. Hundreds are disappearing, he said. "They became extinct, and I had no one to speak them with."

How much did Kenneth Hale contribute to an understanding of the apparently innate human capacity for speech? He made a number of what he called "neat" discoveries about the structure of language, and had an

instinctive sense of what all languages had in common. After his retirement from MIT in 1999, he said he would "really get down to work", an ambition he was unable to achieve. And linguistics itself is a fairly recent discipline. He is likely to be remembered by *The Green Book of Language Revitalisation*, which he helped to edit and which was published shortly before he died. It was warmly welcomed, especially by those who may be a touch aggrieved by the spread of English, which is blamed for brutally sweeping other languages aside.

A scholarly argument surfaces from time to time about the desirability of keeping alive languages that, in medical parlance, are brain dead. Occasionally the argument turns nationalistic. For example, is what Mr Hale called the "revitalisation" of Welsh merely a nuisance in Britain where, obviously, English is the working language? Kenneth Hale had an indignant answer to that question. "When you lose a language," he told a reporter, "you lose a culture, intellectual wealth, a work of art. It's like dropping a bomb on a museum, the Louvre." ∎

Lionel Hampton

Lionel Hampton, jazz musician, died on August 31st 2002, aged 94

HAD THIS newspaper been running an obituary page at the time, Louis Armstrong, who died in 1971, would have been a natural choice. Duke Ellington (died 1974) and Bessie Smith (died 1937) are among others who would have made it. Lionel Hampton was of that flowering, and had the good grace to live to 94.

Until a few years ago he would still take to the stage with a band. Once at the piano or vibraphone, an electronic instrument he introduced to jazz, the marks of age would fall away and the sweaty passion that he had first brought to jazz back in the 1930s would be relived; and "Flying Home", his most famous composition, would soar for the hundredth, or perhaps the thousandth, time. Among the legends attached to "Flying Home" is that it depicts an American Flying Fortress bomber, damaged in a raid over Germany, with

its crew urging on the aircraft as it strives to reach its base in eastern England. Listening to a recording of the number made during the second world war, with Mr Hampton's driving solos and his grunts of excitement as the pace quickens, it does seem to convey a will to win.

Never mind that "Flying Home" was written before the Americans went to war in 1941; Lionel Hampton, like Glenn Miller, provided much of the background music to the war. The young men and women who danced to his music until the floor creaked danced just as energetically when they went into uniform. Their children and grandchildren are still dancing to the derivative music of bands such as the Rolling Stones. Who invented rock and roll is an unsettled argument, but Mr Hampton had a hand in it. Perhaps because of his association with one of the more limited offshoots of jazz, the range of his gifts may have been overlooked.

The "beat in me"

At the age of six Lionel Hampton discovered what he called the "beat in me" while attending church in Alabama, where the congregation clapped along with a guitarist and other performers. What distinguishes the beat in jazz is that it is slightly delayed. It makes jazz sound relaxed. However many decibels Mr Hampton produced, however much excitement he generated, however much pandemonium he created on the dance floor, there was always in his music the delayed beat that underpins much of great jazz.

It is especially distinctive in a number of records he made with Benny Goodman. Although Goodman ran a successful swing band, he is remembered by connoisseurs for his quartet in which Mr Hampton played the vibraphone with melodic simplicity. Remarkably for the time, the group was racially mixed: Lionel Hampton and Teddy Wilson, the pianist in the quartet, were black. As his fame grew Mr Hampton was courted by politicians after the black vote. Harry Truman, a Democrat, was a fan and got Mr Hampton to play at his presidential inauguration. But Mr Hampton favoured the Republicans: unlike the Democrats, he said, Republicans helped blacks "without ballyhoo".

The Republicans were pleasantly surprised. Mr Hampton was undoubtedly an asset to the party that sees itself as the promoter of self-reliance. He had learnt the rudiments of music from a nun at a boarding school where he was placed after his father was killed in the first world war. He worked as a newspaper seller to pay for tuition at a music school. By his late teens he was a professional musician in Chicago,

playing piano, vibraphone and drums. Chicago was then the country's main jazz city, where Armstrong recorded "West End Blues", considered by some to be America's finest piece of music, jazz or classical. Mr Hampton worked for a while with Armstrong, as he did with most jazz musicians over the next 50 years, many of whom, such as Dizzie Gillespie, became famous as innovators. Mr Hampton remained a conservative in his musical style. "All those altered scales and harmonic extensions people were calling modern in the 1940s, I knew all about years earlier," he said.

He was conservative too in his life offstage. Unlike musicians who blew their money and their minds on drink and drugs, Mr Hampton was a careful saver. He owned a record company and several blocks of flats in New York's Harlem district. He set up scholarships in music schools. Academe rewarded him with a dozen honorary doctorates. One of his vibraphones is in a Washington museum, along with Goodman's clarinet.

Mr Hampton became head of a group called Black Republicans. He campaigned for, among others, Richard Nixon, Ronald Reagan and George Bush, senior. After they were elected they sent Mr Hampton on world tours to promote American culture. The Germans especially appreciated his concerts. There is a road in Berlin called Hamptonstrasse.

Big-time politics was a temptation. He served on New York's Human Relations Commission and could perhaps have made it to Congress. The politician in him said, "I always liked to be taking bows." But he was getting old. It was music, rather than the slog of politics, that made him feel young again; with the mallets falling on the vibes and the driving rhythm that got the crowd going. "Flying Home". One more time. ■

Pamela Harriman

Pamela Digby Churchill Harriman, ambassador and courtesan, died on February 5th 1997, aged 76

IF YOU collected a dozen or so of Pamela Harriman's fancier lovers and put them round a dinner table, you had the makings of a world government. Not in the sense of cabinet ministers and presidents – that would have been far too crude and plodding for the stylish Mrs Harriman – but in the sense that her galaxy of fellows and husbands could, together, have bought much of the world and made it spin.

Imagine the dinner party. Her first husband, the drunken Randolph Churchill, might have brought along his father, Winston. There could have been a general or two, from either side of the Atlantic, whom Mrs Harriman helped win the second world war. The airwaves would have been vibrant enough: Bill Paley of CBS owned a lot of them; Ed Murrow, America's greatest wartime correspondent, was their master. Fine wine at dinner? Elie de Rothschild, owner – among other things – of Château Lafite, would see to that. Nice pictures on the wall? Even without her Murillos and Renoirs, Carter Brown, director of Washington's National Gallery, could help out.

Want to go racing tomorrow? Aly Khan, the Aga's heir, would give you a tip. Something soapy after dinner? Step forward Frank Sinatra. Or something still more soothing? Then why not a late-night viewing of *The Sound of Music*, courtesy of husband number two, Leland Hayward, who produced it (and left the royalties, trickling in every year, to darling Pamela). If you wanted to leave in a hurry, Gianni Agnelli, who owned Fiat, could provide fast wheels. A more sedate exit? How about one of Stavros Niarchos's yachts? Mrs Harriman's life was an astonishing tale of sex, money and – far sweeter smelling than both those coarse commodities – power.

From pigs to riches
But it was not how she started. Her father, the 11th Baron Digby, was charming and gentle, knowledgeable about pigs and other rural matters. She was red-headed, bouncy more than pretty, always a bit pushy, and slightly unpopular with her crowd. But when she was 19 she met and very quickly – and disastrously – married the only son of the man shortly to be prime minister. When he was away at war, she took up with the rich and famous and glamorous – and never looked back. She rapidly divorced, then played the field for 14 years. Her second marriage, to Hayward, lasted from 1960 until he died, in 1971. Soon after, she married a mega-rich former lover, Averell Harriman, and became an American. Harriman was once governor of New York, ex-ambassador to the Soviet Union and Britain, and one of the Democratic Party's biggest benefactors. When he died in 1986, leaving her assets worth over $100m, her storm-tossed ship had finally come home.

She became, in her own right, the doyenne of Washington hostesses, giving power-meals largely in the cause bequeathed to her by Harriman: the resurrection of the Democratic Party. She helped promising lads from Hicksville – like a certain Bill Clinton. They were grateful. He gave her a lovely embassy in Paris. At last she was both rich and powerful in her own right. She had won.

Why did she do it? How did she manage it? And did it, in the end, make her happy? From an early age, despite – perhaps because of – her rather dozy background, she was driven to succeed. Perhaps her unpopularity in early life egged her on – to "show those bitches" who was best. She liked glamour. She adored money – not so much for hedonistic reasons as for the sense of security she hoped it would bring. Power, perhaps, became an additional aphrodisiac. Having the ears of presidents and prime ministers as well as tycoons and film stars was marvellously satisfying.

How did she do it? She was tough and manipulative, though not especially subtle. She was not very clever, certainly not bookish. She had little interest in ideology – if Harriman or Clinton had been Republicans, she wouldn't have minded a jot. Although not a great beauty, she kept a trim figure. Doubtless she was expert between the sheets. The key to her success, though, was her ability to fix her concentration on one man – one at a time; and convince him that she was utterly enthralled. It is a recipe that few could resist. After Harriman died, the prospect of her financial backing was an additional allure. She was loyal to most of her friends. A deal with Pamela, it was said, was a deal. She was good to her two later husbands when they were dying.

Was she happy, though? She sparkled. But, at the end of the day, despite all those luxuries, it was a harsh life. Old British friends, especially, mocked her transparent ambition (which Americans took more at face value). Lovers she hoped to marry dumped her. Her husbands were difficult. Her stepchildren liked her. Even the goal of financial security eluded her in the end as relations clawed back much of Harriman's estate.

Was there not always, at the very back of her mind, just a nagging feeling that she was being laughed at, even scorned? Her façade was shiny. It is not certain that, as the French say, she really felt *bien dans sa peau*. ■

George Harrison

George Harrison, a Beatle, died on November 29th 2001, aged 58

SO MUCH has been written and broadcast about the death of George Harrison that it might be thought that there was nothing left to say. But to hazard such a rash prediction would be to underestimate the resourcefulness of what might be called the Beatles generation, now steeped in melancholy. This may prove to be a long goodbye. The large sections of newspapers that have been devoted to Mr Harrison's career could be merely the opening bars of a requiem. Already there is talk of biographies and memorial record albums, along with television and radio retrospectives and perhaps a film.

Those who were not even born in the 1960s, when the Beatles were at their most active, may have been surprised that, to take a random example, the *Daily Telegraph*, a London newspaper that prides itself on the quality of its readership, should have cleared its front page of other news to report Mr Harrison's death, continuing the saga inside for five more pages. Other British newspapers were equally proliferative. American and European newspapers were more restrained, but generous in their treatment of the famous Brit. Not since the death of Princess Diana, and before that of Churchill, had there been so many tears in print.

Still, the young are mostly tolerant of the eccentricities of the middle-aged. Those who had once courted and cuddled to the music of the Beatles and now ran the media were entitled to their harmless indulgence. The death of Mr Harrison seemed also the death of their era. When it was proposed that a minute's silence should be observed no one objected, even though such an obsequy is normally reserved for the war dead. After all, it wasn't often that an era died.

It may seem odd that the same vast coverage was not given to the death in 1980 of John Lennon, the founder Beatle. But Lennon was shot dead. The reporting was extensive, but hurriedly put together. George Harrison had been ill for a long time. By the time he died the essays on his life by his admirers had been written and polished. Mostly they were moving, although perhaps avoiding Voltaire's dictum that "to the dead we owe only truth".

Never again

The story of George Harrison's life can be simply told. He was a busman's son who left school at 14 and worked briefly as an electrician's mate. He won a place in John Lennon's little group in Liverpool because he played the guitar a bit better than either Lennon or Paul McCartney. He has been called the "quiet Beatle"; perhaps shy is a more accurate adjective. He found it difficult to cope with the publicity that underpinned the Beatles' success, and for a dark period in his life was addicted to drugs. Like the other Beatles he made huge amounts of money. He bought a house with 120 rooms, and shut himself away from the screaming fans saying, "I would never want that again." The British film industry was grateful to him for backing several productions during one of its customary hard-up periods, among them "Monty Python's Life of

Brian". He was married twice. Of Mr Harrison's songs perhaps "Something" is the best known. Frank Sinatra thought it great.

A mixed life, but a better one perhaps than mending fuses. He had luck, just as the Beatles had luck. Their luck started when they were taken over by Brian Epstein, who ran a record shop in Liverpool near the Cavern Club, where the Beatles were regularly performing. The role of Epstein has tended to be minimised in the golden memory of the Beatles, perhaps because he was thought to be too fond of young men. But Epstein was the one who groomed the Beatles to look cuddly rather than rough, to brush their hair and to wear neat suits rather than leather.

In 1962, after two years spent hawking their demo tapes around reluctant record companies who said that guitar groups were finished, he got the Beatles their first big deal. Epstein said he would make them "bigger than Elvis", and so he did. By the mid-1960s they were the most important pop group in Europe and the United States. Any Beatles memorabilia from that time tends to become a museum piece. A few days before Mr Harrison died his first guitar, bought for pennies, drew a bid at an auction in London of £25,000 ($35,500). After Epstein died in 1967 the group began to break up with its members going their own way, sometimes as soloists, sometimes forming new groups, sometimes doing not much. George Harrison for one said he was tired of going "round and round the world singing the same ten dopey tunes".

A talent for publicity cannot in itself explain why they did so well. And musically they have probably been overpraised. Epstein managed other groups, among them Gerry and the Pacemakers, but although successful they never matched the appeal of the Beatles. Nor did the Rolling Stones with their pastiche of American blues, although some preferred their fiercer music. To use an expression that flourished in the 1960s, it seems that the Beatles more than other groups caught the *Zeitgeist*, the spirit of the age. "All You Need Is Love", declaimed against a pounding background of cellos, could be hypnotically compelling, although hardly a message of Voltairian truth. ∎

John Harsanyi

John Charles Harsanyi, a pioneer in game theory, died on August 9th 2000, aged 80

IT SOUNDS pretty obvious: life is all a game. Charles Lamb (1775-1834) put it rather elegantly: "Man is a gaming animal. He must always be trying to get the better in something or other." What John Harsanyi and other economists did was to apply mathematical logic to this human urge and make game theory, as it is called, part of their tool kit. At its humblest level, game theory is useful in saving the players from going mad. In devising a strategy you know that your rival may know what you are planning, and he knows that you know he knows, and so on... Even skilled chess-players can feel mentally wounded.

In chess and comparable real-life games, each side has basic information about the other. The problem of Charles Lamb's gaming animals is that they usually have imperfect knowledge about their opponents. They guessed, or relied on "intuition" or, as Napoleon said of his favourite generals, they were lucky. Until quite recent times, this was the way countries and great companies dealt with their rivals.

Mr Harsanyi's contribution to game theory was to show that such games need not be played in a fog, or at least not much. It was possible to analyse such games and provide guidance about the probable moves and their out-comes. This advanced game theory was employed, at least by the Americans, in their negotiations with the Soviet Union on arms control. Kennedy and Khrushchev used game theory in their tussle over Cuban missiles in 1962.

Game theory is widely used in commerce, as happened this year when, with great success, the British government sold licences for mobile phone services in an auction designed by an Oxford economist, Paul Klemperer. Some economists are watching with fascination the contest between the European Central Bank and the currency market over the future of the euro, which has at least the look of an exercise in game theory. A Dutch team of economists applied the theory to international football and concluded that a bad team playing at home is more likely to score than a good one playing away. One effect of game theory is to make economists seem quite human.

By other names

As often happens when an idea becomes fashionable, there has been some argument about who first thought of game theory. Mr Harsanyi, who shared a Nobel prize in 1994 with two other economists in the same field, John Nash and Reinhard Selten, was happy to acknowledge that game theory had been around in some form for a long time. Players of poker, and of course chess, had been using game theory without calling it that. Philosophy has a claim: it seeks to rationalise the behaviour of people with conflicting interests. As a young man in Budapest Mr Harsanyi had studied philosophy and mathematics and, to please his parents, who ran a pharmacy, he added chemistry.

Hungary entered the second world war on the side of Germany and Mr Harsanyi, a Jew, was imprisoned. He was with a group about to be sent to a

What triggered his interest in game theory appears to have been the work of John von Neumann and Oskar Morgenstern, who in 1944 published a book entitled "The Theory of Games and Economic Behaviour". Von Neumann was an American mathematician who, by coincidence, had also been born in Hungary and had attended the same school as Mr Harsanyi. He and Morgenstern may have been the first to show how the philosophical idea of rational behaviour could be applied to economics. They did not develop the idea. In his short life, von Neumann especially had many other interests, including work on quantum theory and the design of the first electronic computers. In paper after paper, Mr Harsanyi and his colleagues took the theory further. It is still being polished.

concentration camp when he removed the yellow star that Jews had to wear and walked away. A guard stopped him, but not all his fellow countrymen were Nazis, and he let him go. After the war Hungary became a communist state. Mr Harsanyi put up with it for a time, and continued with his studies, but in 1950 he left for Australia, about as far away from Europe as he could get.

The Australians did not recognise his Hungarian degrees, so he worked in a factory for several years and studied part-time until he gained some Aussie ones. Mr Harsanyi made his way quite swiftly up the academic ladder, first in Australia and then in the United States, where he was a professor in the business school of the University of California at Berkeley for 26 years.

The philosopher in John Harsanyi saw in game theory a means of improving the human condition. He promoted the idea that the rightness or wrongness of an action depended on its consequences, an ethical theory known as utilitarianism. The connection between game theory and ethics is a complex one. His book on this theme, "Essays on Ethics, Social Behaviour and Scientific Explanation", is a hard read, just as game theory itself demands lots of tricky mathematics. No one would blame you for sticking to Charles Lamb. ■

Sir Joshua Hassan

Sir Joshua Abraham Hassan, defender of Gibraltar, died on July 1st 1997, aged 81

IN JUNE 1969, Spain, then a dictatorship under General Franco, closed its border with Gibraltar. Sir Joshua Hassan, the chief minister of the Rock, reckoned that this was the 15th siege the place had faced since it was taken by the British in 1704. He had no doubt, he assured Gibraltarians, that it would survive the latest threat. Sieges, survival: Sir Joshua often stiffened his language with a military turn of phrase, a practice that he had probably picked up in the second world war when, as simply Gunner Hassan, he had served in the army on the Rock.

In the war Franco had resisted Hitler's calls to attack the Rock, fearing that Britain would take the Canaries in retaliation. Now Spain was appealing to the United Nations. Surely it was time, Spain argued, for this colony in Europe to be restored to its rightful owners. The UN was worryingly sympathetic to Spain, but it agreed with a British proposal that the matter should be put to a referendum. Urged on by Sir Joshua, the people of the Rock decided by 12,138 votes to 44 to remain British. It was Sir Joshua's finest hour.

Spanish pride was hurt. The border remained closed long after Franco died in 1975. It was re-opened in 1985, and then only after a threat by Britain, under Margaret Thatcher, to veto Spain's entry to the European Community.

Spain remains surly about Gibraltar. Its border controls with the Rock are the most tiresome in Europe, with travellers in cars subjected to petty hassles. There are no direct air and sea links between Spain and the Rock. On July 1st, the day Hong Kong became China's (and Sir Joshua died), some Spanish politicians commented on Gibraltar's future. Gibraltar was passed to Britain "in perpetuity", they acknowledged, but, as the surrender of Hong Kong island showed, this did not necessarily mean "for ever". Britain, though, seems likely to hold on to this remnant of empire whose 32,000 people were granted British citizenship (unlike most Hong Kongers). One way or another, prompted by Sir Joshua, this two and a bit square miles of southern Europe has turned into a mini Britain.

England's strong arm

Oppression was familiar to Sir Joshua's family. His ancestors were Spanish Jews who fled from Spain to Morocco and eventually settled in more tolerant places, including Gibraltar, where Hassan père was a cloth merchant. One ancestor was Don Pacifico, a Gibraltarian who was living in Greece. Pacifico's house was burnt down in an anti-Jewish demonstration. In 1850, Palmerston, the British foreign secretary, sent a gunboat to demand compensation, and Greece paid up. "The watchful eye and strong arm of England," said Palmerston in a stirring speech to Parliament, would always protect its subjects "against injustice and wrong". If that sounds old-fashioned, it did not bother Sir Joshua. His Gibraltar was happily old-fashioned, perhaps the last refuge in the world of the tea-dance.

Sir Joshua was a lawyer and ran a successful practice, but his heart was in politics. One of his first campaigns was to persuade Britain to allow civilians who had been evacuated from the Rock to return after the war. It was no use being a politician without constituents. Gibraltar gradually gained autonomy, first through a city council, then through a legislative council and in 1969 through its own parliament, the House of Assembly.

Sir Joshua headed each one. He was chief minister in 1964-69 and 1972-87. In the intervening three years he lost power to the Integration with Britain Party, which claimed to be even more pro-British than Sir Joshua's more modestly named party, the Association for the Advancement of Civil Rights.

As a young man Sir Joshua expressed republican views, and may have retained them privately all his life. But publicly he was a monarchist, proudly welcoming the queen to Gibraltar in 1954, and gratefully accepting a knighthood in 1963. He was a populist, if that description can be applied to the leader of such a small constituency. He was said to know every Gibraltarian by name. Long into old age he made himself available once a week in a pub called Sir Winston's Tavern to anyone seeking advice.

Spain's argument with Britain over Gibraltar rumbles on, complicated these days by the well-meant intentions of Brussels, which favours limitless discussions on sovereignty, and by the worries of NATO, expressed at its Madrid meeting this week, that Gibraltar's value as a military base is limited without Spain's co-operation. Britain appeared to be weakening in 1982 in favour of a deal with Spain, but the Falklands war put a stop to that. Gibraltarians seem to remain staunchly opposed to a change in their status. "Sir Joshua", wrote the *Gibraltar Chronicle* in a tribute, protected "the people from Spain's claim". It may be that even if Britain were willing to give Spain a say in Gibraltar, the move would be stymied by the Rock-like constitution granted in 1969, which Sir Joshua helped to make wriggle-proof. Under it, Gibraltarians have the last word on their future. Failing a Palmerstonian gunboat on call, this was the next best thing. ■

Edward Heath

Sir Edward Heath, a former British prime minister, died on July 17th 2005, aged 89

THE TRIBUTES spoke of his integrity, his long service and the strength of his convictions. Many of his fellow Conservatives were especially keen to emphasise his love of music and sailing. Unspoken, at least for a few hours after his death, were the thoughts uppermost in many minds: his general grumpiness, his undisguised bitterness and in particular his loathing for "that woman" – in this context the person who replaced him as party leader, Margaret Thatcher. And, just as difficult for many of today's Tories to stomach, there was also his unqualified loyalty to Europe. This was the man who had taken Britain into what is now the European Union, and had never had the grace to apologise.

Although he resigned his seat in Parliament only in 2001, Sir Edward Heath already seems like a politician from another age. Awkward in public and ill at ease before the cameras, he had an off-putting voice and an off-putting appearance – all jowls and teeth and heaving shoulders. A bachelor, he was a million miles away from metrosexuality. At lunch or dinner he could make Calvin Coolidge seem like a chatterbox. And he disdained the tricks of the modern politician's trade. He had principles, stuck to them and made no effort to

present himself as something he was not: he trimmed not, neither did he spin. How on earth did he become leader of the Conservative Party, let alone prime minister?

The answer is that in the 1960s he seemed a thoroughly modern sort of Tory. For a start, he was of lowly origins, humbler than those of any previous prime minister and certainly humbler than those of the grandees – most recently the Earl of Home – who had led the party before him. The son of a Kent carpenter and a former lady's maid, Teddy, as he was first called, went to grammar school and thence to Oxford, where he soon won an organ scholarship. He read politics, philosophy

and economics and was elected president of the Union, the university debating society.

From Grocer Heath to grocer's daughter

Then followed a "good" war – he became a lieutenant-colonel – a spell in the civil service and a couple of other jobs before entering Parliament in 1950. His abilities were soon clear, and within ten years he was in the cabinet. When, in 1965, the party needed a leader to take on Labour's Harold Wilson, presented as a thrusting technocrat, capable Ted Heath won in a three-cornered election. It was the Tories' first: all previous leaders had simply "emerged" through a haze of cigar smoke.

The Tories knew they were getting an ardent pro-European. Sir Edward's belief in European integration had been apparent since his maiden speech in the House of Commons. It had remained undiminished even by the French veto of Britain's application to join the European Economic Community (EEC) in 1963, for which he had been chief negotiator. Two other Heath qualities soon also became manifest. First, in 1968, Sir Edward showed his loyalty to the concept of "one-nation" Toryism by sacking Enoch Powell from the shadow cabinet after his infamous "rivers of blood" speech on immigration. Second, he showed the strength of his self-belief when he, almost alone, insisted the party would win the 1970 election, which it did.

In many ways his 3½-year prime ministership was a failure. Beset by IRA bombers, quadrupling oil prices and, most damagingly, striking miners, dockers and power workers, he made mistake after mistake: U-turns in economic policy, a bad industrial-relations bill, support for internment in Ulster, and so on. They culminated in a badly timed election, which the Tories just lost. But even this failure was not without honour: his reluctance to go to the country earlier had largely reflected his desire to avoid an election fought, as he saw it, along class-warfare lines. And in one respect his prime ministership was a triumph: thanks in large part to his personal diplomacy with France's President Georges Pompidou, he gained French acceptance for Britain's bid to join the EEC – and then won the vote in Parliament. It was a rare example in politics of clarity of purpose combining with mastery of detail, and resulted in a change that could aptly, and unusually, be called historic.

But after a second general election in 1974, the Tories had lost three out of the four elections he had taken them into. They wanted a change, and chose "that woman", who went on to do much of what Sir Edward would have liked to have done, albeit in very different style. Certainly, his work was to some extent a precursor for hers. He, however, did nothing to conceal his contempt and she, when she won the 1979 election, made no effort to heal the rift, passing him over for the foreign secretaryship that he wanted and that precedent suggested. The Great Sulk was thus doomed to last the rest of his life.

Eurosceptical Tories have, perhaps rightly, put Mr Heath's belief in Europe down to his wartime experiences. His memories of 1930s unemployment may have done as much to form his views on industrial relations. This obstinate and often rude man was always honourable and usually sensitive. He was also a highly successful sailor – winner of the Sydney-to-Hobart yacht race in 1969 – and an accomplished musician. In short, he was a man of parts – another way in which he differed so strikingly from politicians of today. ■

Freddy Heineken

Alfred "Freddy" Heineken, a brewer and salesman, died on January 3rd 2002, aged 78

SERIOUS BEER drinkers will tell you that beers differ from place to place, as wines and cheeses do. That is true, but most people are content to accept whatever beer is available as long as it is pleasant and clean. The world's most widely drunk beer, made by various brewers, is a mild version of a lager that was created by Czechs in Pilsen in 1842. The one popularised by Freddy Heineken is sniffed at by connoisseurs for, they say, not having a lot of character, but it is difficult to dislike and goes down smoothly. The Dutch firm grew rapidly to become one of the global giants in brewing, its beer selling in some 170 countries, rivalled only in size by Anheuser-Busch and Miller in the United States and Belgium's Interbrew.

If it had a secret ingredient it was Mr Heineken's talent as a salesman. During two years in New York as a young man he fell under the spell, as he put it, of American advertising and marketing. It was liberating, especially after the staid world of the Netherlands. Advertising lived on ideas, some of them quite mad ones. That was their appeal. Mr Heineken never rejected an idea simply because it seemed mad. Some of his colleagues thought it a little mad when he proposed to sell Heineken beer overseas in green-glass bottles. Why not brown bottles, the usual containers for beer? Green would be more distinctive, Mr Heineken said. The firm had to sell distinction.

In its green bottle, with "export" on the label, and priced to match its suggestion of exclusivity, it caught on in the United States and elsewhere as a beer for special occasions. People were amused by, and perhaps even believed, its claim to be the beer that "refreshes the parts that other beers cannot reach". Mr Heineken said he wasn't really selling beer. "I was selling warmth, gaiety."

The friendly traveller

Freddy Heineken's father was also a clever salesman. He taught Freddy that beer travels well. It is remarkably neutral, with no threatening nationalistic message, no enemies. When in the second world war the Japanese occupied the Dutch East Indies, now Indonesia, they were happy to drink Heineken beer. Heineken senior was the first foreign brewer to ship beer to the United States after prohibition ended in 1933. He was also a boozer, and in 1942, possibly under the strain of living in a country under German occupation, he sold most of the family's shares in the brewery that could trace its roots back to 1592.

In the 1950s, when Freddy succeeded his father on the Heineken board, he borrowed enough money to buy a controlling share. He was chief executive from 1971 to 1989, guiding the company to great prosperity, buying out competitors or taking stakes in them, and becoming the richest man in the Netherlands. He retained the chairmanship of Heineken's holding group until last November.

It amused him to claim that he was a financial dunce, uninterested in such matters as debt-to-equity ratios. Had his father not floated the company, he said, he would have kept it private. He said he relied on intuition, a sense of the market:

with Two Pussies. The Dutch loved Freddy stories, and he did his best to oblige them. In 1983, after being released from three terrifying weeks in the hands of kidnappers, he joked that he had never been so relieved to see so many policemen all at once.

It may be that eventually Freddy Heineken became a little bored with the beer he made famous. He was careful not to say so. For a Dutchman to say he was bored with beer would be akin to knocking Rembrandt. But he did say that had he not been a brewer he would have liked to have made a career in advertising. The "refreshes the parts" campaign was said to be his idea. One of his wilder proposals, never tried, was to sell beer in square bottles. Instead of being thrown away, the "world bottle", as he called it, could be used as a brick to build homes in poor countries, or even rich ones.

He supported research into saving the ozone layer and was interested in communication with other possible worlds. He set up a foundation to promote the arts. He was sympathetic to the European Union's aim of ending war by hobbling the old troublemakers. But a better plan, he said, would be to divide up the continent into numerous states – 75, he suggested – each with the same number of inhabitants. Quite mad, said his critics, as though that were a reason for rejecting it. ■

more female drinkers, the move to beer among wine drinkers, the demand for low-calorie drinks. In the end a healthy balance sheet and steady profits were what matter, he said soothingly. Unsoothed financial experts believed the share price should have been higher, and they will be watching for any changes in the company following the death of its guiding light.

He was born Alfred, but the name Freddy stuck from childhood and even Heineken shares are called Freddies. The name seemed to suit his engaging personality, his love of life and his rough sense of humour. A woman journalist he was showing around his Amsterdam headquarters, called the Pentagon, was mildly surprised by a picture in a bedroom next to his office of a naked woman with a cat, entitled *The Woman*

Ernest Hendon

Ernest Hendon, an unexpected survivor, died on January 16th 2004, aged 96

THEY SAID Ernest Hendon did not look his age when he stood, two years ago, in front of the Alabama House of Representatives in Montgomery. His back was straight, his eyes bright. He felt good, he told reporters; and better still now that the Alabama House had expressed regret for what had been done to him. "I feel this means that it won't happen again," he said happily.

Limelight was the last thing he had ever expected. He was born a poor black sharecropper's son in Macon County, Alabama, and was a sharecropper himself. Nothing came easily to him or his neighbours. They hoed small plots of red earth in the pine woods, lived in wooden shacks, and picked cotton in the season. There was little money around and small chance of seeing a doctor, though syphilis was more rampant there than anywhere else in the South. From time to time, the Ku Klux Klan lit their fiery crosses in the hills.

Mr Hendon remembered the day the bus arrived, in 1932. It carried doctors and nurses who had come to do a study among the syphilitic sharecroppers. In exchange for their help they would get free medical examinations, burial insurance, free transport to and from the hospital in Tuskegee and – a rare treat – the chance to stop and shop in town. On the days they were examined, the men got a free hot meal. Along with 398 others, Mr Hendon, then 24, signed up to take part.

He was already unwell, though he himself, like most of the men, was not sure what was wrong with him. The doctors called it "bad blood", a term that also covered anaemia and general weariness. Some of the volunteers were given, for a while, the fierce and ineffective syphilis treatment of the time: injection with arsenic compounds and

mercury ointment for the crusted ulcers on their skin. Mr Hendon, like many of the others, was not. He was given "pink medicine", or aspirin, and "some kinda brown-looking medicine", which was iron tonic. When a "last chance" for free treatment was offered, Mr Hendon turned up and was given a spinal tap: "They give me a test in the back and they draw something out of me." "They said it would do you good," he said later.

None of it did him good. The doctors and nurses were not there to cure, but to observe the progress of untreated syphilis. Patients who are untreated sometimes develop no symptoms, and sometimes spontaneously recover; but they can also suffer liver deformity, heart damage, paralysis and insanity. Burial insurance was offered because the data for the study was to come from the men's autopsies. But none of this was communicated to them.

For 40 years, the Tuskegee Syphilis Study continued. Mr Hendon went for his examinations and, after 25 years, got a certificate of appreciation from the surgeon-general. The men especially liked Eunice Rivers, a motherly black nurse who made them feel at home in the hospital. Several of the doctors and nurses were black, and the Tuskegee Institute, which ran the hospital, was a black university. There was dignity in the proceedings, and a sense that the doctors cared about the health of poor blacks. At that time, few others did.

Ignoring penicillin
Yet the study also showed clearly the parternalistic racism of the age. The federal Public Health Service (PHS) wanted not only to compare the effects of syphilis in blacks and whites, but also to stop black "degeneracies" spreading to the white population. It made no secret of this. The Tuskegee study was mentioned in reports and cited at conferences. The fact that it was doing nothing to cure Mr Hendon or the others was, however, kept quiet.

Certain moments were tricky. In 1942, the army drew up a list of likely recruits from Macon County. Many subjects of the study were on it, presumably including Mr Hendon, who was the right age. Having seen them, the local recruiting board ordered them to be treated for syphilis; but the assistant surgeon-general intervened to have their names removed from the list.

The next year, penicillin became an effective treatment for syphilis. It was not given to the Tuskegee subjects unless they asked for it. By 1948 the Nuremberg Code, inspired by revelations of experiments in the Nazi death camps, set standards for medical studies on human subjects. In Tuskegee, things went on as before.

No serious questions were asked until 1972, when a whistle-blower from the PHS talked to the Associated Press. Once exposed, the study was ended immediately. That very year, the surviving subjects filed a lawsuit against all the individuals and institutions involved. The government agreed to pay out almost $10m, of which Mr Hendon's share was $37,500, with free health care for life.

He had confounded expectations by living so long. More than 100 of the subjects died of the disease or related complications, together with at least 40 unwitting wives, and 19 children contracted syphilis at birth. A longer-lasting legacy was black distrust, which continues, of government doctors and clinical trials.

Mr Hendon was too ill to go to Washington when President Bill Clinton apologised, in 1997. Instead, he watched by satellite. But five years later he was in smiling form when Alabama said sorry. "I survived," he said. "That's good." ∎

María Julia Hernández

María Julia Hernández, fighter for human rights, died on March 30th 2007, aged 68

WHEN FORENSIC teams from Argentina dug in 1992 into the earth at El Mozote, in the mountains of eastern El Salvador, they first came upon a reddish rubble, mixed up with the roots of thorn-plants and weeds. A little deeper they uncovered small, thin skulls, some of them blackened by fire. Underneath these were bundles of what seemed to be brown rags: the blood-soaked cotton dresses, trousers and socks of what had once been children, killed more than a decade before. The pockets of some still held their lucky plastic toys.

The forensic work at this, the most dreadful killing-field of modern Latin America, was memorably reported by Mark Danner in the *New Yorker*. But it might never have been carried out, and the massacre of 794 people, overwhelmingly civilians, in December 1981 might never have been forced to the world's attention, if María Julia Hernández had not been on the case. She was in charge of the Socorro Jurídico, later the Tutela Legal, which during El Salvador's murderous civil war of 1980–92 kept track of human-rights abuses for the archdiocese of San Salvador. She was therefore the person to whom Rufina Amaya Márquez first told her story.

Rufina had been the sole survivor of the massacre. When the troops of the elite Atlacatl battalion of the Salvadoran army had come to the village to flush out leftist rebels, she had been locked up with the other women. She had seen her husband beheaded with a machete; her baby daughter had been torn from her breast. But as the women were led away Rufina managed to hide beside a crab-apple tree, and the screaming of the others distracted the soldiers from seeing that she had gone. When night fell she crawled away into the maguey plants, her skirts knotted up so as not to hamper her, and dug a little hole into which she could press her face to weep without being heard.

Miss Hernández took all this down. She was a homely, sympathetic sort, who in her old-fashioned print dresses looked much like a priest's housekeeper; but she had been a professor of law at the University of Central America in San Salvador, and would fix those who tried to deceive her with a stony, intellectual stare. Since 1978, as El Salvador slid into disorder, she had been compiling for the archdiocese a book of the dead. These were the corpses left by right-wing death squads in the city streets most nights, their faces dissolved by battery acid and their backs or chests scored with the tags of their killers. Her colleagues would take photographs, and relatives of the missing would come to her office to leaf through the portfolio in the hope, or fear, of finding them. But El Mozote was an atrocity beyond any of this.

For years, with a lawyer's thoroughness and steely determination, Miss Hernández amassed the evidence. The government would not help; it denied that anything had happened, and dismissed Tutela Legal as a guerrilla front. The Reagan administration, intent on stamping out communist infection, agreed that Miss Hernández was a trouble-maker. She was undeterred. In 1989 six Jesuits were shot dead at

her old university; Tutela Legal did the first investigation, and found that the army had ordered it. In 1991 her office published the first investigation into El Mozote, including the names of all the dead.

The signing of peace accords the next year ended the civil war, set up a Truth Commission and led to the dig at the site of the massacre. Miss Hernández had the names of those responsible; but in 1993 the new government declared an amnesty for all of them. She kept going, campaigning to overturn the amnesty and to bring the killings before the Inter-American Court of Justice. On her death the case had been reopened and, with her help, evidence was slowly being gathered again. She was also publicising corruption and brutality in El Salvador's police force.

The heart entire

Her life was full of risks, cheerfully faced. Each day, settling to her work in a room as bare as a nun's cell, she began with a prayer: "Well, God, will I see you today, or will you leave me a bit longer, fighting?" Papers carrying death-threats were often pushed through the door. She drew strength from her dearest

friend, Oscar Romero, who in 1977 had become archbishop of San Salvador and had set up the human-rights office. Like Christ calling the disciples, as she liked to remember it, he had summoned her from the university, "and I didn't really know how to [follow him], but I said yes." Once she went searching for the archbishop, out into the countryside, and found him saying mass for the *campesinos* under a tree. From him she learned to love and defend the poor; and when he too was murdered by a death squad, at the altar, in 1980, she felt bound to continue the work he had begun.

She died relatively young, from a heart attack, in the same month that Romero had been killed and on the very day of his burial. Salvadorans found a fascinating symmetry in that. Miss Hernández had liked to show visitors where he was buried and to tell the story that, though he had been shot in the chest, his heart had been undamaged. She was sure it was still whole under the earth, evidence of his continuing power to encourage her, just as the reddish soil at El Mozote had preserved, in blood and bones, the truth. ■

Charlton Heston

Charlton Heston, America's prophet, died on April 5th 2008, aged 84

SOME SAID it was the nose: high, majestic, aquiline, magnificently broken in a high-school football game. Some said it was the jaw, rugged as Mount Rushmore and packed almost too full of white, clenched teeth. Or the eyes, blue and far-seeing, as if they measured out panoramas of Western mountain and desert. The body matched: tall, muscled, buffed, bronzed. In Charlton Heston, a whole American landscape seemed to have heaved itself into human shape, stretched out its arm, and received from God the tablets of the Law:

> A well regulated Militia, being necessary to the security of a free State, the right of the people to keep and bear Arms, shall not be infringed.

The National Rifle Association was never so lucky as when it elected as its president, in 1998, a man who, barefoot on the real Mount Sinai, had led his people out of bondage; or who, up to his waist in the freezing Colorado river, had baptised Jesus Christ; or who, at the end of "The Planet of the Apes", had rolled in the surf bewailing the sight of the Statue of Liberty shipwrecked in the sand. Moses, John the Baptist and the Last Man Alive were all rolled up in one, together with El Cid propped dead on his horse, Gordon falling at Khartoum and Michelangelo, flat on his back, painting the Sistine Chapel. All these towering figures had, in the scope and restlessness of their ambition, something American about them. In a cable network series of 1992, Mr Heston even played the voice of God; and God,

he believed, had plans for His country, once the right side had triumphed in the culture wars.

Long before the NRA, however, it was Cecil B. DeMille who had the luck to chance on Mr Heston, and vice versa. There was never so good a face, especially in a black fedora, to play the circus-manager in "The Greatest Show on Earth" in 1952. And there was no other director, Mr Heston thought, who could so definitively have rescued him from his round of TV dramas and failed Broadway shows, of cold-water tenements and tinned-macaroni suppers, in post-war New York. DeMille offered glorious wide-frame spectacle, and Mr Heston was exactly the type for it. In drawing-room comedies he was clumsy as a giant; but put him in the desert in "The Ten Commandments", staff in hand, and 8,000 extras would part for him like the waves of the Red Sea itself.

This would have gone to most actors' heads. Occasionally it went to Mr Heston's. The first chapter of his autobiography, "In the Arena", opens with "In the beginning ... the earth was without form, and void." But for all his apparent command before that "mysterious black beast", the camera, he was shy. Health, energy and good parts were the key to his success, he thought; not talent. He had always pretended to be people who were better than himself, starting in childhood with Tom Sawyer and Davy Crockett. Hollywood fed that compulsion. Painstakingly he taught himself chariot-racing, sketching (for Michelangelo) and long tracts of the Old Testament. He never learned to dance, as

Ava Gardner found out the hard way in "55 Days at Peking".

To the Promised Land

A generation knew him as Judah Ben-Hur, whipping four white horses into a frenzy round a Roman arena. But his tunic-and-loincloth roles, though they made his name (and won him an Oscar for "Ben-Hur" in 1960), sometimes annoyed him. He preferred to be explicitly American: wearing buckskins, making Westerns, handling a six-gun, or playing President Andrew Jackson, that "giant figure in American memory". He delighted in his childhood in the north woods of Michigan, when, "seriously overgunned", he had hunted rabbits, fished through ice and, like Lincoln and Reagan, chopped logs. There in a one-room schoolhouse he had learned his lessons, in the days before the destruction of the public-school system.

His politics were not always so right-wing. He was active in the civil-rights movement, and a paid-up Democrat until the Robert Bork debacle of 1987. But there was something inevitable about his rightward slide. It was not just the rise of Reagan, his friend from the Screen Actors Guild, or the growing blight of political correctness, which he called "tyranny with manners". It went deeper than that.

Mr Heston's favourite of his film characters was no genius or prophet, but the taciturn, determined cowboy in "Will Penny" (1968). His favourite scene was where Penny, carrying a dead cowboy, rode through the rain to apply for the dead man's job, only to be mocked. Mr Heston saw this as the plight of every white, rural, Protestant, god-fearing, gun-owning male in America. Their voices, too, went unheard. But they would knock the water from their hats and carry on.

He knew where that "blood-call" would take them. He had been there himself for "The Big Country" in 1958. On some mountain-top, as the sun rose, they would look west into a shining place where freedom and greatness still invited them: "where you could pray without feeling naive, love without being kinky, sing without profanity, be white without feeling guilty". To that mythical America, the Promised Land, he would stretch out his bronzed arm and lead his kind. ∎

Thor Heyerdahl

Thor Heyerdahl, the *Kon-Tiki* man, died on April 18th 2002, aged 87

THE FIRST publishers that were offered Thor Heyerdahl's *Kon-Tiki* thought there would be little public interest in a scientific voyage on a raft across the Pacific. "Did anyone drown?" one publisher asked hopefully. Mr Heyerdahl said that he and his five companions had felt a bit tired when they landed on a Polynesian reef after 101 days at sea, but were otherwise fit. Well, in that case...

Eventually Mr Heyerdahl did find a publisher brave enough to take on his saga. The book sold more than 30m copies and was translated into 67 languages. A triumph, and a satisfying smack in the eye for those who had turned him down. But the most important result for Mr Heyerdahl was that money from his writing allowed him to spend a vastly interesting life pursuing a number of unorthodox notions, some of them plausible, some of them cranky, all of them infuriating to those whose theories he was challenging.

Kon-Tiki, while a success with the general public, was knocked by some anthropologists who disputed Mr Heyerdahl's claim that many Pacific islands had received their first people from South America. The orthodox view was that they had been first settled from Asia as part of the slow drift eastwards of humans from Africa; everyone knew that. Everyone except, it seemed, Thor Heyerdahl. He saw cultural and genetic links between South Americans and Polynesians, and set out to show that such a voyage between the two territories would have been possible in

ancient times. Using balsa wood and other materials that would have been available in antiquity, Mr Heyerdahl built the *Kon-Tiki*, named after a mythical South American king said to have been fleeing for his life, and launched her from Peru. As he had predicted, she was carried by currents and wind to Polynesia 4,300 miles away. The raft stood up to Pacific storms and Mr Heyerdahl and his friends supplemented their diet with algae strained through cloth.

The voyage showed only that contacts had been possible among the ancients across vast stretches of ocean, not that they had happened. But Mr Heyerdahl was well satisfied. He had in mind a Big Idea. The *Kon-Tiki* expedition was just the start of his efforts to shape it.

As Adam and Eve

Thor Heyerdahl's mother ran a museum in his hometown Larvik, a port city in southern Norway. Helping her, he said, he first became interested in what he called "natural things". At Oslo University he studied zoology and geography. In 1936 his indulgent parents provided him and his new bride with enough money to spend a year in the Pacific, partly as a honeymoon, partly so that Mr Heyerdahl could gather material for a doctorate on Pacific life. In fact the couple chose to live as a modern Adam and Eve on the island of Fatuhiva in the Marquesas. But modern stomachs turned out to be unsuited to roots and berries. His bride became seriously ill and discovered that modern medicine had its charms.

Still, the Pacific had Mr Heyerdahl in its grip. After the second world war (when Norway was occupied by Germany and Mr Heyerdahl served with the Allies) he mulled over how the islands had been settled. After his *Kon-Tiki* experience he posed the question: if such voyages took place in the Pacific might there have been similar voyages elsewhere in the ancient world? Were the oceans less a barrier isolating people, more an avenue connecting them? Mr Heyerdahl became convinced that this is what had happened. "The ocean is a conveyor and not an isolator," he said. He rejected the assumption that Europeans were the first to discover distant lands. Columbus was not the first to sail to America; nor even Mr Heyerdahl's fellow countryman Leif Ericsson.

> We Europeans are so one-track minded when it comes to our own history that we say to the world that Europe discovered the whole world. I say that no European has discovered anything but Europe.

Mr Heyerdahl was intrigued by the number of step pyramids found in different parts of the world. These tend to be smaller and of more ancient origin than true pyramids with their smooth sides. Did the knowledge of their construction spread from Egypt to Mexico, Peru and the Canary Islands? To show that an Atlantic crossing was possible with the technology that existed in ancient times, in 1969 he built a ship of reeds called *Ra* based on an Egyptian design and launched her from the former Phoenician port of Safi, in Morocco. The ship survived in the Atlantic for 56 days before she became dangerously leaky. A second reed ship reached Barbados safely.

Mr Heyerdahl's surmise that the old civilisations were linked by sea, exchanging ideas and materials, remains a matter of debate, if not scepticism, for many anthropologists. Similarities between ancient cultures are assumed to be coincidences. Nevertheless, Thor Heyerdahl extended the role of anthropology. He was a marvellous stimulant: everyone who met him came away with their head buzzing with ideas. In Norway he was simply a hero. In 1999 he was voted Norwegian of the century. So there. ■

Albert Hofmann

Albert Hofmann, chemist, died on April 29th 2008, aged 102

HIS FIRST experience was "rather agreeable". As he worked in the Sandoz research laboratory in Basel in Switzerland on April 16th 1943, isolating and synthesising the unstable alkaloids of the ergot fungus, Albert Hofmann began to feel a slight lightheadedness. He could not think why. His lab was shared with two other chemists; frugality and company had taught him careful habits. And this was a man whose doctoral thesis had revolved around the gastrointestinal juices of the vineyard snail.

Perhaps, he supposed, he had inhaled the fumes of the solvent he was using. In any event, he took himself home and lay down on the sofa. There the world exploded, dissolving into a kaleidoscope of colours, shapes, spirals and light. It seemed to have something to do with lysergic acid diethylamide, LSD-25, the substance he had been working on. He had synthesised it five years before, but had found it "uninteresting" and stopped. Now, like some prince in faery, he had got the stuff on his fingertips, rubbed it into his eyes and seen the secrets of the universe.

The next Monday, ever the good scientist, he deliberately took 0.25 milligrams of LSD diluted with 10cc of water. It tasted of nothing. But by 5 o'clock the lab was distorting, and his limbs were stiffening. The last words he managed to scrawl in his lab journal were "desire to laugh". That desire soon left him. As he cycled home with a companion, perhaps the most famous bike ride in history, he had no idea he was moving. But in his house the furniture was ghoulishly mutating

and spinning, and the neighbour who brought him milk as an antidote was "a witch with a coloured mask". He realised now that LSD was the devil he couldn't shake off, though in his senseless body he screamed and writhed on the sofa, certain that he was dying.

After six hours it left him. The last hour was wonderful again, with images "opening and then closing themselves in circles and spirals, exploding in coloured fountains." Each sound made colours. His doctor found nothing physically wrong with him, except for extremely dilated pupils. The substance evidently left the body quickly, and caused no hangover. But the mind it flung apart, reassembled and profoundly changed, leaving him the next morning as fresh as a newborn child.

Over the next decades, Mr Hofmann took an awful lot of LSD. He ingested it listening to Mozart and looking at red roses. He learned not to take it when tired, or with amphetamines (a very bad trip). As head of the natural products division at Sandoz, he revelled in its potential for psychiatry. Though he also developed derivatives of ergot that helped circulation and respiration, and had a drawerful of useful pharmaceuticals to his name, it was LSD that filled him with "the joy of fatherhood". And the sense it had given him, of union with nature and of the spiritual basis of all creation, convinced him that he had found a sacrament for the modern age: the antidote to the ennui caused by consumerism, industrialisation and the vanishing of the divine from human life.

Yellow and purple and green

It proved disastrous for him that Timothy Leary at Harvard had the same idea. When the professor told his students in the 1960s that LSD was the route to the divine, the true self and (not least) great sex, use of the drug became an epidemic. People ingested it, in impure forms, from sugar cubes and blotting paper. They blamed it for accidents, murders and wild attempts to fly. The media flowered in psychedelic shades of orange, purple, yellow and green, and in the melting shapes and dizzying circles of a world gone almost mad. Mr Hofmann in 1971 met Leary in the snack bar at Lausanne station; he found him a charmer, but because of his carelessness LSD had by then been banned in most countries, and production and research had been stopped. They never resumed.

Mr Hofmann turned his chemist's attention to other things: the Mexican magic mushroom, whose active compounds he synthesised into little white pills, and the LSD-like properties of the seeds of the blue morning-glory flower. He continued his self-experiments with both of them – noting that on his mushroom trip his very

German doctor became an Aztec priest who seemed about to slice his chest open with an obsidian knife. He loved his work, but still mourned the disappearance of his "problem child". LSD, treated with respect, could have powerfully instructed men and women in the glories of the spiritual dimension of life. But they had abused it, so it had given them terrors instead.

Without it, however, Mr Hofmann knew it was still possible to get to the same place. As a child, wandering in May on a forest path above Baden in a year he had forgotten, he had suddenly been filled with such a sense of the radiance and oneness of creation that he thought the vision would last for ever. "Miraculous, powerful, unfathomable reality" had ambushed him elsewhere, too: the wind in a field of yellow chrysanthemums, leaves in the sunlit garden after a shower of rain. When he had drunk LSD in solution on that fateful April afternoon he had recovered those insights, but had not surpassed them. His advice to would-be trippers, therefore, was simple. "Go to the meadow, go to the garden, go to the woods. Open your eyes!" ■

Bob Hope

Leslie Townes (Bob) Hope, comedian, died on July 27th 2003, aged 100

THE SONG most associated with Bob Hope was "Thanks for the Memory", which he first sang in a film called "The Big Broadcast" in 1938. He made it his theme tune, adapting its originally bittersweet words to the needs of the time. So in the second world war he was introducing his act with, "Thanks to our brave allies / You gallant Russian bear / You British everywhere..." As Russians became less gallant and British influence shrank, the words were changed. Topicality was always one of his strengths. But Bob Hope himself seemed to remain the same.

He belonged to a period that retains a persistent nostalgia sustained in the memory mainly by old films on television: a period, say, from the 1930s when he was building his career, followed by the war years when he made *The Road to Morocco* with Bing Crosby, the best of the "Road" series, and touring the world to raise the spirits of millions of American soldiers as they prepared for combat; and after the war making numerous films, mostly duds, saved only by his brilliance.

So, he had a notably creative period of perhaps 20 years, from age 30 to 50, although he worked on into old age. Ask a teenager about Bob Hope and it is quite likely, and understandably, that the response will be a shake of the head. The *Daily Telegraph*, a London newspaper that tries to please the young as well as its loyal readership of old fogies, devoted six pages to George Harrison, a Beatle (Obituary, December 8th 2001), but allocated a mere two pages to Bob Hope. But mention Woody Allen to a teenager; no problem. It would be unfair to say that he is a copy of Bob Hope, but he is one of a generation of comedians who learnt from him. He once said, "When my mother took me to see "The Road to Morocco" I knew exactly what I wanted to do with my life." His idea of a "weekend of pure pleasure", he said, would be to watch half a dozen Bob Hope films. He "combined a thin story with great jokes". The jokes were indeed often good. Bob Hope said he was the first comedian to admit that he employed a team of scriptwriters to keep him supplied with new material. "Other comedians fostered the illusion that all those funny sayings came right out of their own skulls." But it was the way the jokes were told that mattered.

A test of nerve

Bob Hope was much praised for his timing. You could write a thesis about timing. Henri Cartier-Bresson's photographs are beautifully timed, capturing the telling moment. Michael Vaughan, England's present cricketing hope, has match-winning timing, judging to the instant when to send a hurtling ball soaring to the boundary. Bob Hope had this kind of gift. Perhaps there is a gene for it. It takes nerve to hold your audience in suspense for microseconds until you judge it is ready for the punchline. For Bob Hope the talent always seemed to flow easily, even on occasions when he was not on stage. "I feel very humble," he said to President Kennedy when he was being presented with a gold medal for "services to his country". Then the follow-through that sent laughter through the White House: "But I think I have the strength of character to fight it." Bob Hope's material was not hurtful or obscene. That style had to wait for a later generation of comedians.

Even a good gene has to be encouraged. He was born in England, the fifth of seven sons of a hard-up stonemason who brought his family to America when Bob was five and settled in Cleveland, Ohio. There seems to have been little formal schooling. While in his teens he made a start in showbusiness in what the Americans call vaudeville and the British call variety, an overcrowded profession with some 20,000 performers in competition, many of them ambitious "foreigners" like Bob Hope. At one time he was doing four shows a day, followed by a stint at a nightclub. In "The Cat and the Canary", a film he made later, a character asks him if big, empty houses scared him. In a line that Bob Hope may have written himself he replies, "Not me. I was in vaudeville."

Whatever the size of the audience, being a stand-up comedian, alone on the stage in front of an audience that may or may not be friendly, with only a microphone to hold on to, is agony if you flop, and ecstasy if it likes you. That was his schooling. Broadway and the movies were to follow. It should be said that there were others who had the same polished timing, notably Jack Benny. It was a fortunate time for American audiences, with great entertainers, gifted songwriters and novelists such as Ernest Hemingway who were breaking new ground.

Bob Hope never won an Oscar, although he was awarded several honorary ones. He received 54 honorary degrees, while some 500 towns presented him with their keys. Britain made him an honorary knight. He stayed married to one woman for 69 years, and they lived in the same house for 60 years. They adopted four children. He made loads of money, invested it wisely and gave much away to charity. Almost no one had a bad word to say about him. Marlon Brando once grumbled that Bob Hope would go to the opening of a phone booth in a petrol station as long as he could play to a camera and three people. He was, Brando said, a junkie for applause. But isn't everyone? ■

Ulrich Inderbinen

Ulrich Inderbinen, the world's oldest mountain guide, died on June 14th 2004, aged 103

T HE MATTERHORN in Switzerland, with its bent, jagged peak and steep glacial ridges, is frequently climbed these days. As on many popular yet difficult mountains, ropes and ladders are fixed permanently into the rock and ice, and huts line the route to the summit. But the Matterhorn has long had a reputation for deadliness – half the members of the first group to climb it, in 1865, perished on the descent – and it remains one of the world's most dangerous peaks. Crowds make it more so, as novice climbers are tempted by its fame.

This awesome mountain was a hugely important place in Ulrich Inderbinen's life. He was born in 1900 in Zermatt, at the mountain's foot: a remote village of only 750 people, with tourism a small but burgeoning industry. Mr Inderbinen rarely left the region of his birth, and was 20 before he took the train to the nearest town. To make up for it, he climbed out of the valley

quite often – almost daily for nearly 70 years. He scaled all 14,700 feet of the Matterhorn more than 370 times, though he is said to have lost track of the exact number.

Mr Inderbinen thought the Matterhorn "the most beautiful mountain in the world". Although it was only one of many mountains he climbed over the course of the 20th century, guiding innumerable clients up and down with inexhaustible good cheer, no other so engrossed him. On his first ascent, at the age of 20, he went with his sister Martha and a friend of hers. The girls wore long skirts and their ordinary shoes, and the lanterns they were carrying kept blowing out. Since none of them knew the route, they followed scratch-marks made by previous climbers on the rocks. On his last ascent, bent double under his ropes at the age of almost 90, he conquered the mountain in four hours.

Mr Inderbinen met life with the same equanimity as the mountains, his dry wit punctuating his monumental energy. When asked if he ever got bored, climbing the same peaks again and again, he replied, "Only when the clients walk too slowly." When one journalist pointed out an enthusiastic review from an American client in the 1930s, Mr Inderbinen replied: "Perhaps he did not know any other guides."

But rivalry was by no means absent from Mr Inderbinen's life. As a young guide, he would walk for four hours each morning to catch visitors disembarking from the train above Zermatt. He took up ski-racing at 82 when he realised that, with no other competitors in his age-group, he could win every race – which he did. Until almost the end of the century he continued to take climbers up easier local peaks, proving to other guides how sure he still was. For his 95th birthday he was given an ice-axe as a present, which he put to good use. One of Mr Inderbinen's few regrets was his family's veto of an attempt to climb Mount Kilimanjaro, the tallest mountain in Africa, when he was 92.

On larch-wood skis

Mr Inderbinen might have been a farmer like his parents. Much of his early life was spent herding cows and picking edelweiss for tourists. He did not get his first skis, made from local larch, until he was 20. But he eventually chose mountain-guiding in emulation of his uncle Moritz, a famous guide when Mr Inderbinen was a child.

At first, business was slow. Between customers, Mr Inderbinen had to cut trees and shovel snow. Then came the second world war, with no visitors at all. For a while Mr Inderbinen served in the ski patrol of the Swiss army. He would glide in the mountains above Zermatt,

often alone and often at night, forbidden even to switch on a torch. Whether or not he truly helped the war effort, it was a billet that suited him exactly.

His chosen profession allowed for a bit more camaraderie in peacetime. Indeed, the profession of a guide entailed a paradoxical combination of solitude amongst the high glaciers and sociability among his fellow mountaineers. And once visitors poured back to Zermatt, he began to be in demand. Unusually in the climbing business, he sought fame through service – guiding others safely up mountains, rather than conquering them for himself.

Mr Inderbinen's life was notably harmonious. He had no car, telephone or even bicycle, and chopped his own firewood deep into old age. He made his living on his feet or his skis, proceeding steadily; he did not believe, he said, in doing anything hastily, on the slopes or elsewhere. (This, however, was not always true; he gave up mountain-guiding, at 97, when he realised he had taken ten minutes longer than he should have done to decend the Breithorn.) He built his house with his own hands, finishing it in 1935, and lived in it for the rest of his life. He knew what he wanted, and had it close by. Especially, he wanted those particular mountains.

George Mallory, a British mountaineer who tried to conquer Everest and died on it, famously said he wanted to climb the peak "because it is there". Mallory crystallised a romantic vision of the mountaineer, chasing after dreams on ice-wrapped summits far from home and hearth. Ulrich Inderbinen could not have been more different. He went up mountains not because they were there, but because he was. He died gently, in his bed. And though he may not have been the first to climb the Matterhorn, he seems to have climbed it best. ∎

Steve Irwin

Steve Irwin, crocodile hunter, died on September 4th 2006, aged 44

SOME OF his fans thought he was dead long since. Bitten by a venomous snake that had left the real Steve Irwin out in the bush-grass, dead as a maggot. Chomped in half by a croc as he gave it a loving hug. Paralysed by some spider that had crept into those teeny-tiny shorts and sunk its fangs into him. Pricked by a beetle that had burrowed into his ear, into his brain. But "Nah!" he would cry, jumping up and waving his arms: "I'm still here, mate."

Thousands of bits had been taken out of him by the animals he loved and provoked. One croc had "caved" his face, another had grabbed his hand and dragged him under. No worries: nothing poisonous had ever got him. Sure, he felt nervy when he "went in on" apex predators, but fear was good. It let him survive. Besides, if a poisonous snake didn't bite him in the first 30 seconds, he knew it was a softie that would settle in his hands and slither round his neck like a tie. Only parrots he was scared of. They had this uncanny desire to peck him completely to death.

For 169 episodes of "The Crocodile Hunter", "Croc Files", and "Croc Diaries", watched by 500m people in 136 countries, Mr Irwin diced with death-by-animals. He got close, really close. His smooth blond face filled the screen, eyes goggling, tongue flicking out to kiss a flickering snake's. Creep up to a sleeping mamba, tweak it by the tail. Crikey! Run a lawnmower at a croc, see it launch itself right into the air to seize him. Help! "There's a cheetah. Wanna see that cheetah?" Steve would whip his camera from his little green back-pack and poke

it practically into the creature's mouth, scanning the molars. Aaarrrghhh! Better run! Danger, danger, danger.

His excitement had been going at full tilt for years. As a toddler he put his foot deliberately on a large brown killer snake; it seemed to like it. At six he got 12 feet of scrub python for his birthday, and spent his days at the creek catching frogs for it. At nine his father, a naturalist who had started a reptile park on the Queensland coast, taught him to stalk crocs at night and lug them out of the water. He made a living from that for a time. While other young men were chundering and barracking in the bars of Brisbane he was up to his arse in a mangrove swamp, tormented by mozzies, roping rogue crocs single-handed for the Queensland government.

Though he played the boofhead both onscreen and off, he was serious about wildlife. His clowning was to get interest going. He eventually owned not just his parents' reptile park (turned into the Australia Zoo, "Where Crocs Rule!") but 30,000 hectares in Australia, Vanuatu, Fiji and the United States, which he kept as natural reserves. He railed against the farming of animals for leather, fur or ivory and the culling of kangaroos by the Australian government: "You never save any wild animal by killing it." He abominated his country's determined land-clearing. In Timor-Leste, to local astonishment, he caught and penned up two crocodiles to stress that they should be respected.

Could Mr Irwin himself be respected? Australia was divided. He did stupid things, such as feeding a chicken carcass

to a crocodile while cradling, as tenderly as a six-pack of Castlemaine XXXX, his month-old baby son. (He never gave a rip, either; he had been "completely in control".) To promoters of Australia as an urban, sophisticated, cosmopolitan place, he was a prancing horror, a big-booted oaf from the outback who reminded everyone of the rough edges of Australian life. Even in the good cause of conservation he was loud, bloody loud, in his unmodulated Strine. And he was naive in a wide-eyed, right-wing way, almost genuflecting to John Howard as he called him "the greatest leader in the entire world".

The face of Australia

A few wowsers yearned for a different face of Australia, such as Olivia Newton-John. But Mr Irwin won out. He loved his country with a passion, and people the world over took him as its exemplar. Americans raised on "Crocodile Dundee" now assumed that all Australian men could wrestle with tigers and anacondas while getting over cruciate-ligament surgery, as Stevie once showed them live on campus ("G'day

LA!") at the University of California. He brought tourists to Australia by the plane-load, though they half-dreaded what they would find there.

He was filming again, diving off the Great Barrier reef for a children's TV series, when a stingray got him. It would probably have ignored him, floating quietly by, but Mr Irwin went over the top of it, almost on its back, observing. Its tail, venom-coated and serrated, pierced his chest and stopped his heart. He managed to pull the barb out, but not fast enough.

He had always got away before, but it had often been a close-run thing. After the poking, joking and prodding would come a shot of Steve retreating, tumbling, shouting, hands up to his face, as the creature came after him. He was not that quick. He was human.

Australia, plunged into grief despite its carping, talked of holding a state funeral for him. But the last word on Steve Irwin seemed to belong to Africa's greatest crocodile-hunter, Khalid Hassen, bagger of 17,000 crocs the easy way, with a rifle, who said it simply didn't seem right that a fish should have killed him. ∎

Junius Jayewardene

Junius Richard Jayewardene, Sri Lanka's "old fox", died on November 1st 1996, aged 90

AT A conference in San Francisco in 1951, called to discuss a peace settlement with Japan, Junius Jayewardene spoke for magnanimity towards the old enemy. It was an unexpected sentiment at the time. Japan's cruelties in the 1930s and in the second world war, which even now, many years later, continue to be a disturbing subject, were then fresh in people's minds. Mr Jayewardene, appealing especially to Asians at the conference, asked them to extend "the hand of friendship" and close "this chapter in the history of man". His speech, the shortest at the conference, was received with acclamation. The Japanese prime minister, Shigeru Yoshida, usually an impassive figure, burst into tears.

Some would call Mr Jayewardene an opportunist who appreciated that Japan, backed and protected by America, was rapidly rising from its ashes. Not for nothing was he known as "the old fox", a nickname he rather relished. Certainly, Japan never forgot his gesture in San Francisco, and has treated Sri Lanka with generosity ever since. But, equally, it can be claimed that Mr Jayewardene had vision, looking beyond the world of the moment.

Asia, he said, had to put aside the past and find solutions to the daunting problems of the future. The most important of these was how best to make a living. Today, the free market and privatisation are everyone's ideology. But in 1977, when Mr Jayewardene at last became prime minister of Sri Lanka and was able to put his ideas into practice,

liberalisation was new, especially in Asia. He ended the protectionism of the previous socialist government under Mrs Sirimavo Bandaranaike, dismantling controls on imports and foreign exchange. "Let the robber barons come in," he said happily. Since then, much has changed in Sri Lanka. It has had to endure a civil war. Mr Jayewardene's party has lost power to a coalition led by Mrs Bandaranaike's daughter, Chandrika Kumaratunga. But the economy continues to be run mostly as Mr Jayewardene would wish.

His Scottish governess

For the first 40 or so years of Junius Jayewardene's life, Ceylon, as Sri Lanka used to be called, was still ruled by the British. The Jayewardenes had prospered. Mr Jayewardene's father, a judge in Ceylon's Supreme Court, believed the British empire would last for a thousand years, a view shared by other eminent Asian families who took on themselves a bit of the empire's grandeur. Young Junius had a Scottish governess, a Miss Munroe, and later kept a picture of her on his desk. He became a lawyer, as his forebears had done for four generations. But politics lured him. One of his heroes was Benjamin Disraeli, a Victorian politician who did much to turn Britain into a world power. Mr Jayewardene helped to found the pro-western United National Party, and after independence in 1948, with his party in power, he held a number of ministries. But he had to wait until he was almost 71 to become prime minister and to reform the economy. The gains were immediately apparent, but from 1983 Sri Lanka saw its resources, including its young men, increasingly wasted in a conflict, still going on, between the Hindu Tamils, a minority who live mainly in the north, and the Buddhist Sinhalese.

Mr Jayewardene, a Buddhist, is blamed by some Sri Lankans for misjudging the conflict. His economic reforms did not benefit the Tamil areas. While the rest of the country prospered, the Tamils continued to live in a poor ghetto. But it is uncertain whether, as some believe, the Tamils could have been wooed away from their demand for independence. The Tamil guerrillas, known as Tigers, have never wavered from their demands for a separate homeland. Generous offers by the present government, of autonomy within a form of federalism, have been rejected by the Tigers. India may be more to blame for the viciousness of the conflict. During Indira Gandhi's rule the Tigers were trained and armed by India. That policy was ended by Rajiv Gandhi, Indira's son and successor (who was later to be murdered by the Tigers). In 1987 India sent 50,000 troops into Sri Lanka as "peacekeepers", but they withdrew after suffering heavy casualties from the guerrillas they had trained too well.

A desperate Sri Lanka could have become a military dictatorship, the fate, for long periods, of its South Asian neighbours Pakistan and Bangladesh.

Mr Jayewardene was often accused by opponents of being a dictator, particularly after he put through constitutional changes that made him executive president on the French model. But he believed that strength at the top was needed to keep Sri Lanka from falling into anarchy. Mrs Kumaratunga has clung to the presidency, although in opposition she promised to restore the British-style system. Junius Jayewardene retired without fuss in 1989 after ruling for 11 years. Afterwards, politicians and others often came to his home (called Braemar, his governess's birthplace) to get his thoughts. He would welcome them, even his critics. "There is nothing," said the old fox, "that gentlemen cannot discuss over a drink." ■

Roy Jenkins

Roy Jenkins, political reformist, died on January 5th 2003, aged 82

FOR THE first 67 years of his life he was Roy Jenkins. For the remaining 15 years, in a curious British exercise in metamorphosis, he was a lord. The elevation suited him. He had a natural and agreeable grandeur, If you had to have lords, you could not do better than making Lord Jenkins the prototype. He usually had something interesting to say and said it well. He pursued some of the most progressive ideas in British politics over the past 50 years, but managed to be good humoured to his opponents as well as his supporters. To British voters, not terribly interested in politics between elections, he was nevertheless a character they warmed to, made all the more likeable by an engaging lisp and a taste for good living.

For all that, his political career could be judged a failure, although Enoch Powell,

a gloomy seer, said that was the fate of all politicians unless they died early. He held two of the highest offices of state, home secretary and chancellor of the exchequer (finance minister). He was reckoned to be a careful manager of the national purse, and he matched the tolerant mood of the 1960s by promoting laws that scrapped the censorship of the theatre, allowed abortion, stopped the punishment of flogging and ended the hounding of gays. But the big prize, that of prime minister, eluded him. As if in compensation, other rewards came his way. For three years, from 1977, he was president of the European Commission. In 1987 he was elected chancellor of Oxford University. His 19 books, mainly on political history, were well received. In 1993 he was appointed to the Order of Merit, a royal honour limited to 24 people.

In later years Lord Jenkins ruminated that although, in his view, he would have made a good prime minister, he lacked the ruthlessness that takes you to the very top. It was an odd contention by a political historian. To get anywhere in politics requires a degree of ruthlessness. More likely, he failed to make the final leap because, to quote Powell again, the position of prime minister "is filled by fluke".

Goodbye to lunacy

In the obsequies that have followed Lord Jenkins's death this week it has been claimed that the policies of Britain's present Labour government are, in essence, his creation. The argument goes like this. In 1981, after he had left the European Commission, and the chance of leading the Labour Party and becoming prime minister was long past, he helped to form the Social Democratic Party. It rejected the "lunatic" leftist policies of the Labour Party and sought the "civilised" centre-left ground. The party had some by-election successes but never "broke the mould of British politics", as it had hoped, and eventually merged with the Liberal Party to form the present Liberal Democrats, an opposition group in Parliament. However, the Jenkinsite ideas lived on and, so it is argued, were taken up by Tony Blair and his team, leading to a landslide victory in 1997 by New Labour, as it was now called.

Mr Blair was generous in his praise of "one of the most remarkable people ever to grace British politics" but he stopped short of saying that he had pinched his ideas. Blairites went through agonies ditching Labour's traditional policies, and do not want to share their success with anyone. If Lord Jenkins was indeed Mr Blair's mentor, his protégé has been a touch wayward, refusing to ally New Labour with the Liberal Democrats in Parliament, declining to reform the voting system to benefit the Liberals and refusing, so far, to swap the pound for the euro. An unusually irritated Lord Jenkins said that Mr Blair had a "second-rate mind".

No one doubted that the Jenkins mind was first rate. It was moulded in the valleys of Wales, a proving ground for many spinners of words, notably David Lloyd George and Dylan Thomas. His father, Arthur Jenkins, worked in the coal mines from the age of 12 for 24 years with a two-year break at Ruskin, an Oxford college for working people, and in 1935 became a Labour member of Parliament. Young Roy went to Oxford too, to Balliol, where he gained a first. In the second world war he worked at Bletchley, a country house where clever people broke enemy codes.

During Labour's first post-war government he entered Parliament as its youngest member. In Harold Wilson's government, which first took office in 1964, he rose rapidly. In 1965, aged 45, he was the youngest home secretary for 55 years. In 1970 he was deputy leader of the party and, as misleadingly happens in politics, was regarded as unstoppable. What may endure are his elegant words. Arguing for change in a much quoted lecture in 1979 he said:

> Some societies, France in the second half of the Third Republic, pre-revolutionary Russia, the Austro-Hungarian empire, have been still less adaptable than our own. But they hardly provide grounds for comfort. Compared with post-war Germany, post-war Japan, Fifth Republican France (industrially at least), the United States for virtually the whole of its history ... modern Britain has been sluggish, uninventive and resistant to voluntary change, not merely economically but socially and politically as well. We cannot successfully survive unless we can make our society more adaptable.

He usually had something interesting to say, and said it well. ■

Elrey Jeppesen

Elrey Borge Jeppesen, a pioneer of safe flying, died on November 26th 1996, aged 89

THE JEPP, short for the Jeppesen airway manual, is a kind of road atlas of the skies. Anything a pilot may need about the route from departure to destination, and the unpleasant obstacles in between, is there. Having such a seemingly old-fashioned aid may come as a surprise to air passengers who assume that aircraft are guided effortlessly on their way by computers, with a bit of help from satellites. Many are, and airlines reasonably encourage a sense of technological well-being among their passengers. But aircraft come in all sizes and degrees of sophistication. However, even jumbos carry Jepps, or other navigation manuals, as well as navigational equipment. Pilots can still get that uncertain feeling in parts of Africa and China and other places where air-traffic control may be rudimentary. Until recently, the jumbos of some major airlines carried sextants, and some airliners still do. "You can't be too careful," a pilot remarked to the writer of this article.

Being careful may not have been uppermost in the mind of Elrey Jeppesen when he started flying in 1927, in an ex-army Jenny biplane he had bought for $500. He seems to have been a natural as a flyer. As a boy, he recalled, he would watch for hours eagles soaring above his home in Oregon. He went solo after about two hours' tuition and made a living in what was called barnstorming: performing low-flying stunts over towns to get people to pay a few dollars for a ride. Sometimes, to stop a few hearts, he walked along the wings. "God, it was fun," he recalled later.

Flying still seemed new. Orville Wright was still telling people how he and his brother had got their early contraptions into the air. As head of America's aviation authority, Orville had signed Mr Jeppesen's pilot's licence. The licence, with his Danish name spelt incorrectly, is part of the memorabilia at a terminal in Denver airport named after him. They think a lot of him in his old home territory in America's west. Denver has a statue of him. A museum in Seattle traces the history of flight from Leonardo da Vinci to Elrey Borge Jeppesen.

When the engine failed

Elrey Jeppesen turned from barnstorming to flying mail, and life became more serious. If flying seemed new, air navigation was very new. Mostly it consisted of looking over the side of the cockpit and hoping you recognised the landscape. Some of Mr Jeppesen's mail runs took him over the Rockies. It was reckoned to be the most dangerous mail run in America, and paid well accordingly ($50 a week, plus 14 cents a mile, double for night flights). Sometimes the head wind was so strong that the little aeroplane with a sack of mail in the open cockpit was flying backwards. Sometimes the engine would cut out and Mr Jeppesen would glide down, hoping for a soft landing. In one winter four mail-pilots on the Rockies run were killed. Mr Jeppesen started to keep a careful record of the terrain. "Never pass this beacon on the north," he noted, "or you'll smack a hill." "At this intersection, turn right and

direction if your compass misbehaved was to search the ground for an outhouse lavatory. The door of the outhouse usually faced south.

A business that began in the basement of his home, run part-time with his wife between flights, grew and grew. In the second world war his manuals were used by allied air forces. Aircraft flying spies to occupied Europe found Mr Jeppesen's hints about following railway lines and rivers were particularly helpful.

He sold his business in 1961. Jeppesen Sanderson is now a world-wide company with more than 1,000 employees. It sells flight information in diverse ways that would have amazed the pioneers. "JetPlan IV," it announces, is a "state-of-the-art client-server" designed "to produce the most fuel, time or cost-efficient flight plans between any two points in the world". But the navigation manuals remain the company's most famous product. Elrey Jeppesen approved of anything that made flying safer, but he never lost his affection for the days when he first started charting the landscape of America. "Those old open airplanes, you felt like a bird," he once reminisced to a reporter. "It was so damn much fun. You could feel the wind in your face, the wind on the stick and the rudder." Today, he said, you might just as well get on a train. ■

follow the railroad track." And so on.

What began as entries in a pocket notebook turned into a sizeable manual. Mr Jeppesen amplified his observations made from the air with information gained from travelling along the mail routes by car, and picking the brains of local people. He would climb a mountain or a factory chimney with an altimeter to check how low an aircraft could go in safety. He noted the phone numbers of farmers who could be called for a weather report.

In 1933 he put the first Jeppesen air manual on sale for $10. In it a pilot could learn not only the best landing approaches to some 50 airfields, but also that one way to check your

John Paul II

Pope John Paul II, a colossus of the Catholic church, died on April 2nd 2005, aged 84

LONG BEFORE he died, the world was counting down the last days of Pope John Paul II. Each month he grew frailer, shrivelling inside the carapace of his white robes, his limbs trembling more violently, his ceremonial cross apparently all that kept him standing. Yet that, he believed, was the point. God kept him working, insisted on it, whatever the state of his body. And not just working at a desk like Pius XII, sustained by hot milk, but flying to India, Brazil and Africa, preaching to anyone who would hear him. Even his last trip, to Lourdes in August, was not for healing but to proclaim Our Lady's love. In each new country his first act, after stepping from the aircraft, was to kiss the earth. When his body no longer let him, as in Cuba, the earth was raised on a tray to him.

His body took punishment all through his life. In 1981 he was shot by a would-be assassin; in 1992 a tumour the size of an orange was cut out of his gut. He skied until he was made an archbishop, and swam well into old age. Such vigour was one of his most welcome qualities when, as Karol Jozef Wojtyla, he was made pope in 1978. His Polishness made him a curiosity of papal history. But it was his moral, physical and intellectual strength that commended him. His predecessor John Paul I, an amiable but delicate man, had died soon after his election, and the Catholic church itself was close to disarray. The reforming zeal of the Second Vatican Council had run into the sand; churches were emptying, vocations falling, and Paul VI's encyclical condemning birth control,

"Humanae Vitae", had driven millions of devout western Catholics to furtive disobedience. The second Pope John Paul offered a vigorous return to certainty.

It was not always the sort Catholics wanted. Above everything, Pope John Paul was an authoritarian and a centraliser. On bishops and laymen tentatively starting, after Vatican II, to organise things their own way, he strenuously imposed obedience to the diktat of the Holy See. Compromises worked out on the ground to respect the cultures of Africa or Latin America tended to die in dim offices in Rome, stifled by the men in black or red. Having helped to defeat communism in eastern Europe, Pope John Paul spent his next years attacking consumerism and capitalism for the similar illusions they offered.

Within the church itself, dissenters were harshly silenced. Prickly or distasteful issues – the ordination of women, the celibacy rule for priests, paedophile scandals among American clergy – were either ignored or put aside. Pope John Paul considered that church teaching on these topics was simple and right, and that rules set by popes before him were not to be overturned simply because the fecklessly modernising world had shifted once again.

Over the 26 years of his papacy, Catholics were increasingly torn between wishing that, by his going, he would let the church breathe, and loving the uncompromising faith he represented. The young, in particular, seemed drawn to that, and he to them, almost feeding off their energy in his

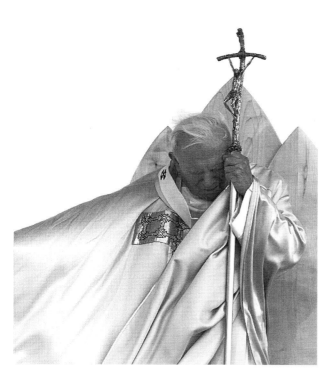

a frequency already dying out in western countries. Some of Pope John Paul's most admirable acts were speeches made to oppressed peoples, within earshot of their leaders, appealing to them to treasure their human rights and agitate to be free. He did this in Chile, Cuba and the Philippines, as well as in communist Poland.

This was also a pope who could spring surprises. He was good at ecumenism, visiting both synagogues and mosques. As a Pole from a town once full of Jews, he felt a special obligation to respect them, and was the

last years. But many Catholics found the world too complex for this pope, and his formidably intelligent encyclicals both inspiring and impossibly demanding.

A voice for the oppressed
The church Pope John Paul treasured and promoted was essentially the one he had known in Poland. He was born in 1920 in the town of Wadowice to a mother who died young and a father who first sowed the idea of priesthood in him, making him study in a cold room to improve his concentration. He began his priestly training, in 1942, in an underground seminary kept secret from the Nazis; after his ordination, in 1946, he worked in a church that was a brave alternative to atheistic secular power. Priests were heroes, and the ordinary people, making acts of political defiance as much as faith, went to Mass, communion and confession with

first pope to push a folded prayer-note between the stones of the Wailing Wall in Jerusalem. In 2000, startlingly, he read out a long apology for the church's bad behaviour over the centuries. Some noted that it was church members, not the church itself, for whom he apologised. Nonetheless, it was a rare marvel that a man so certain of the church's possession of the truth should criticise those who had believed it with equal fervour, but had taken things a bit too far.

The most frequent surprise, however, was the strength of spirit – of soul, he would say – that kept him going. He carried on largely in order to display, to a cynical world, the power of God at work in him and the needlessness of the fear of death. Now that he has been called back to source, his bruised and worried church feels, more than anything, the lack of his confidence. ■

Lady Bird Johnson

Claudia Alta (Lady Bird) Johnson, first lady and environmentalist, died on July 11th 2007, aged 94

NOVEMBER 22nd 1963 started in drizzle, but soon turned bright. The sun shone on Dallas, the breeze was light, and Lady Bird Johnson enjoyed the drive in the open limousine, even when the Secret Service man thrust her husband down to the floor, even when the car screeched so violently round the corner by the hospital that she feared they would be flung out of it. Looking towards the first limousine, she saw what looked like "a drift of pink blossom" on the back seat. It was Jackie Kennedy lying across her dying husband.

Mrs Johnson saw beauty even at that moment, when her life turned upside down. It was instinctive; she could not help it. Her lonely, motherless childhood had been made bearable by roaming the pinewoods, fields and bayous round Karnack in east Texas, delighting in magnolia blooms and the first spring daffodils and the touch of Spanish moss against her face. She found beauty, too, in a marriage to Lyndon Baines Johnson that seemed to friends, at least for its first 20 years, to be a sojourn in hell.

She knew he was a handful at first sight: lanky and good-looking, impossibly full of himself and his political ambitions, bossing her about from the first date onwards, rushing her so precipitately into marriage in November 1934 that they had neither a proper ring nor flowers. But he gave her "a queer sort of moth-and-flame feeling", so she followed. The orders continued: to bring him breakfast in bed, to have a hot meal ready whenever he and his congressional cronies came home, to serve him seconds instantly ("Bird, bring me another piece of pie!"). A snap of his fingers, and she would run across the room. A public dressing down for her dowdiness and shyness ("Bird, why can't you look nice, like Connie here?"), and she would take it on the chin. Her unwavering smile would make the house beautiful. Her steadiness would calm Lyndon down. And it was love and orderliness, rather than subservience, that made her lay out his clothes each morning with his pen, filled up, in one suit pocket and his cigarette lighter, filled up, in another, and the cufflinks in the shirt-cuffs, and the shoes shined.

She applied the same sense of grace and neatness to America. Long before it was fashionable, she encouraged Americans to care for the place they lived in. From 1938 onwards, as Lyndon rose from congressman to senator to vice-president to president, she fretted about the junkyards and billboards that lined the highways between Texas and Washington, DC, vowing to replace them with bluebonnets and pink morning primroses. Driving through Washington itself, she imagined the weed-filled parks and triangles filled with dogwoods, azaleas, tulips and chrysanthemums, red oaks rising on Connecticut Avenue, crape myrtles throwing shade over F Street. As first lady, starting in 1964, she filled the city with flowers.

It seemed to some a lightweight occupation, especially at a time when her husband was being sucked into the slough of Vietnam. But Mrs Johnson had the solid core of a determined southern liberal. She had brought her own money to the marriage (money enough to give her, at 16, a Buick to drive to school and an unlimited charge account at Neiman Marcus), and used it both to bankroll Lyndon's first run for Congress and to buy a low-power radio station, KTBC, which made the family a telecoms fortune. The mouse, ignored at her own parties, would note the books people mentioned and go away and read them herself. For months at a time, when

Lyndon was on navy service or felled in 1955 with a heart attack, she ran his office. During the 1964 campaign she found the strength to make speeches and train tours through the South in the cause of civil rights. In the White House, as her husband battled with demons of drink, heart disease, depression and the war, she became indispensable to him.

Just as beauty was indispensable to the country. When she first conceived "beautification" (a "prissy" word, one that never pleased her), she found it was like "picking up a tangled skein of wool; all the threads are interwoven – recreation and pollution and mental health, and the crime rate, and rapid transit and the war on poverty, and parks ... everything leads to something else." Her efforts in Washington included clearing rubbish and trapping rats in run-down projects, in order to plant white azaleas there. Her own version of Lyndon's great social programmes began, as her Aunt Effie had begun with her, by "opening [the] spirit to beauty".

Lyndon, too, was now on board, pushing her bills through Congress for her. A presidency remembered for horror abroad and disintegration at home also made green politics legitimate. She made sure her husband withdrew from the Democratic race in March 1968, inserting into his speech the words that made it irreversible, but did not keep him long thereafter. More than 30 years of widowhood were spent campaigning nationally for preservation and conservation of the landscape and wild flowers.

At the end of her life, almost blind, she saw what she could: the "mighty big" clouds above Texas, or single blooms through a magnifying glass. Failing this, she would listen to the birds. Before that beauty, the years of chaos at the heart of American politics would recede like some extraordinary dream. ■

Yousuf Karsh

Yousuf Karsh, photographer of the famous, died on July 13th 2002, aged 93

SO MUCH praise has been heaped upon Yousuf Karsh that it is tempting to believe that he was the world's greatest photographer. But then you think of Henri Cartier-Bresson, Robert Capa, Ansel Adams and a dozen others, all of whom produced pictures that have an enduring quality. Mr Karsh was, though, for half a century perhaps the greatest portrait photographer in the monumental manner. Unlike Mr Cartier-Bresson, the master of the Leica, Mr Karsh preferred to use a camera that looked hardly different from the weighty apparatus of the Victorian pioneers. It stood on a hefty tripod and the image was captured on a glass negative almost the size of this page.

Intimidated by this awesome instrument the sitter was expected to be patient as Mr Karsh composed the lighting, a hot light here, a softer one there. The camera is focused, and Mr Karsh emerges from under a dark cloth. The negative holder slides in. The sitter is expectant, and probably restless. It can't be long now. But Mr Karsh is not quite ready. He once said, "Look and think before opening the shutter. The heart and mind are the true lens of the camera. If it is a likeness alone, it's not a success."

Mr Cartier-Bresson would no doubt concur. Whether the image is falling on 35mm film or on a glass plate, the aim is to capture what Mr Karsh called the "brief moment" of truth. How is it done? No one is sure, not even the photographer. Whatever it is, great photographers have it. The many millions of happy snappers do not.

Mr Karsh's portraits have been faulted, by those reckless enough to criticise him, for all looking the same: impressive, solemn, usually in black and white to heighten the feeling of drama. It is said he could make the woman next door look like Queen

Elizabeth. His admirers retort that this was his style. It was like complaining that Rembrandt's paintings did not make you laugh. No one expressed surprise that Karsh and Rembrandt could be mentioned in the same breath.

When fame came

Yousuf Karsh was a Canadian by adoption: Karsh of Ottawa is how he signed his photographs. But he thought of himself as an Armenian. After hundreds of years as an independent state Armenia had been eventually divided between Turkey and Russia. Mr Karsh had the misfortune to be born in the part ruled by Turkey, whose policy towards Armenians was to exterminate them. In his teens he joined the flow of Armenians who found refuge in North America. An uncle in Canada who was doing well as a portrait photographer gave young Yousuf a job and a cheap camera of the time called a Box Brownie (with which he won a prize). A few years later he was taken on by John Garo, a well-known Boston portrait photographer of that era, who also happened to be an Armenian.

In the 1930s Mr Karsh had his own business in Ottawa. His leisure time he spent with a local drama group, experimenting with lighting. What transformed him from a journeyman photographer into a star was a chance opportunity to photograph Winston Churchill, who in December 1941 was on a brief visit to Ottawa. Mr Karsh set up his equipment in a room in the Canadian parliament. Churchill was led in, grumbling. "Why was I not told of this?" He said Mr Karsh could have two minutes and no more to take his picture and lit a cigar. "Forgive me, sir," Yousuf Karsh said, removing the cigar from Churchill's lips, and releasing the shutter on his camera.

Looking at the picture now, and knowing the story behind it, you can imagine Churchill, slightly petulant, deprived of his dummy. But at the time the expression matched the widespread feeling about the British leader, pugnaciously leading a brave nation against an all-conquering foe. *Life* magazine bought the picture for $100. Mr Karsh did not haggle. He just wanted to see his work in print. Eventually it became the most reproduced portrait in the history of photography.

Mr Karsh was never again looking for work. The work came looking for him. Over the years practically anyone who was anyone had their picture taken by Yousuf Karsh. "People of consequence", he called them, politicians, royalty, popes, writers, scientists, actors. To be "Karshed" proved that you had arrived. It was almost like buying immortality. There are Karsh portraits of a succession of 12 United States presidents. Mr Karsh loved the famous. "It's the minority that make the world go around," he said.

He seemed to be aware that his gift could be misused. It was clever to make a politician look like a statesman, but was this artistically truthful? Mr Karsh confronted this tricky question in an essay in which he considered the difference between photographing the merely famous and "the challenge of portraying true greatness adequately".

He reckoned that he had met the challenge with Albert Einstein, Ernest Hemingway and Pablo Casals, among others. As a preliminary to a "challenge" he would get to know as much about a subject as possible; read biographies, speak to the subject's friends. But any photographer could do that. Why did Mr Karsh quite often capture, as he said, "the essential element that has made them great"? He did not know how the magic worked. "And I am not going to make inquiries." ■

Genichi Kawakami

Genichi Kawakami, the "emperor" of Yamaha, died on May 25th 2002, aged 90

IN THE 1970s, Steinway, perhaps the grandest of America's piano makers, became alarmed at the success of Asian competitors, notably Yamaha of Japan. Yamaha offered well-made pianos at much lower prices than American ones. Several American manufacturers were unable to stand the competition and closed down. Yamaha's president, Genichi Kawakami, having captured an enviable slice of the American market, was now after a more elusive prize: the sort of status that went with a Steinway piano. And not just equal status. Mr Kawakami predicted that a Yamaha would eventually come to be regarded in the United States and Europe as the piano of choice.

Steinway's strategy was not to let its worries show. "A Steinway is a Steinway," said John Steinway, whose family had been making pianos since 1853. The simple, if pompous, pronouncement seemed to strike a faultless chord with its traditional public for whom a grand piano was a necessary icon, whether or not anyone in the family could play it; and, even more distressing to Mr Kawakami, it made sense to ambitious Americans who hoped one day to have a home graced with their own grand piano as a symbol of high achievement and cultural taste.

Mr Kawakami could also play the history game. He pointed out that his firm had been started in 1887 by Torakusu Yamaha. A Yamaha piano and organ won a prize at the St Louis World Fair in 1904. Mr Kawakami's father became president of the firm in 1927. Ten years

later Mr Kawakami joined the firm and subsequently took command, adding many other products, notably motorbikes (now made by a separate company), to the Yamaha brand, and passing the baton to his son Hiroshi in 1983. Three generations in the same family. It was, declared Mr Kawakami, like a symphony in three movements. Americans enjoyed the tussle of the giants, but Steinway's reputation remained defiantly intact.

The mystery

Genichi Kawakami was sure that Yamaha pianos sounded every bit as good as the American product. Indeed, he was assured by his experts that they were superior. But this mysterious quality, status, has bewildered, and irritated, many Japanese manufacturers who set out to take on the world. Japanese cameras are among the finest you can get, used by professionals the world over. Yet, for your ordinary rich Japanese Germany's Leica carries the real prestige. If you can lay your hands on an early one (the miniature camera was invented by Leica in 1925), so much the better. Japanese cars are known for their reliability and style, but a Mercedes or a Rolls, polished until it glows like an old painting, still has the edge. Who would prefer a cumbersome Harley-Davidson motorbike to a slim, racy Japanese model, a Yamaha perhaps? Quite a lot of people.

Mr Kawakami's worries over status may have cast a cloud over a career that in every other way was extraordinarily successful. He was one of the tycoons who helped to make Japan's economy the second largest in the world. The beginnings were modest. The firm that he took charge of in 1950 made pianos, mouth-organs and wind-up gramophones. It had a respected name in Japan, but not much else in the way of assets. The Japanese were too busy rebuilding their ruined country after the second world war to indulge much in such luxuries.

In 1953 Mr Kawakami toured the United States and western Europe. He observed that the victorious countries were prospering and spending happily, although perhaps not happily enough to buy a wind-up gramophone, however carefully made. In the culture of the jukebox, even the piano seemed old-fashioned. Playing the piano was something that parents might do, but not their children.

Mr Kawakami decided that to sell his pianos in any number he first had to create a new market. "Put yourself in the shoes of the user and build world-class products," he said. It was a statement of the obvious; what was special was that, in marketing Yamaha pianos, Mr Kawakami pursued the obvious with great tenacity. In 1954 in Hamamatsu, where his factory was located, he started a class to teach the rudiments of music to young children. This evolved into a worldwide chain of franchised schools of music, many with a showroom for Yamaha musical instruments. More than 5m students are reckoned to have passed through the schools. By the late 1980s, Yamaha had become the world's leading maker of musical instruments of all kinds, not just pianos. In Japan alone, Yamaha had 55% of the piano market. In a country of mostly minute homes, Mr Kawakami was able to persuade many Japanese that a piano was a necessity.

He never seemed to stop. "Diversification was his hobby," Mr Kawakami's son remarked. "He got bored with old businesses." During the 33 years Mr Kawakami ran the firm either as president or "supreme adviser" he kept boredom at bay by expanding Yamaha into all kinds of products. These days, along with Yamaha pianos and motor-bikes, there are water scooters, tennis rackets, golf clubs, machine tools. Japanese newspapers called him the "emperor" of Yamaha. Genichi Kawakami quite liked that. ∎

Noel Keane

Noel Keane, America's father of surrogate parenting, died on January 25th 1997, aged 58

IT WAS the strangest of requests, even to a lawyer. The couple in Noel Keane's office wanted a child. The woman was not able to bear one herself, but a woman had been found who was prepared to be impregnated with the man's sperm and to hand over the baby as soon as it was born. Mr Keane was asked to prepare a document to safeguard the interests of all parties. This, as far as is known, was the first formal contract for surrogate motherhood.

Mr Keane devoted the rest of his life to this speciality: not simply looking after the legal side, but starting what he called "infertility centres" throughout the United States where couples could meet women willing to bear their child. These days there are numerous agencies offering to arrange surrogate parenting, but in 1976 Mr Keane, for better or worse, seems to have been the innovator.

Surrogacy is a novelty of the rich world. While a desire to have children may be common to all, this has conflicted in poor countries with a concern about rising populations. If there are surrogate births in China or India, no one is reporting them.

In America and Europe, producing a child is seen as a right. Being deprived of a child, it can be argued, takes away that right. The traditional remedy has been adoption, but, with the growth of welfare services, fewer single mothers now surrender their babies, while others will have chosen abortion. Medicine has sought to fill the gap. Sometimes an egg collected from an "infertile" woman will grow in the surrogate mother. However, even if the surrogate's egg is used, the baby should at least be a bit like Dad.

One of the charms claimed for surrogacy is that a baby can be partially designed to order. So a white, fair-haired infant may eventually grace the nursery, if that is what the couple wants. The surrogate baby is formally turned over to its biological father whose wife can then adopt it. But what if the surrogate mother is so attached to the child that she refuses to hand it over? This is what happened in 1986 in the celebrated "Baby M" case arising out of a surrogacy arranged by Mr Keane.

A modern Solomon
The surrogate mother, Mary Whitehead, asked a court to allow her to keep Baby M. The case went to a higher court, where the judge did his best to play Solomon. The father who had ordered Baby M was given custody but Miss Whitehead was awarded visiting rights. In a separate case Miss Whitehead sued Mr Keane for not screening her adequately and there was an out of court settlement. In another case involving Mr Keane's firm, a baby died because, it was said in court, the father did not have "parenting skills".

The Baby M and other cases brought surrogacy great publicity, much of it unfavourable. Some American states made surrogacy illegal. Latterly, Mr Keane has had a practice in Indiana, where it is legal as long as all the parties involved in a surrogacy live elsewhere (most surrogate law is confusing). In Britain, surrogacy is legal but soliciting for surrogate business and advertising were banned under a law passed in 1985.

Some American firms see Britain and other European countries as a promising market, but prospective clients usually have to go to the United States to choose a surrogate mother and arrange the contract.

There can be snags bringing home a baby born abroad. What is its nationality? What happens if twins are born and the contracting couple will take only one child? Lawyers try to rise to such challenges. Surrogacy is a new, interesting and profitable business. A baby, nominally free to a normal couple, becomes an expensive product in the marketplace. Only luxury items take nine months to make. Miss Whitehead was paid $10,000. Today a surrogate mother may charge a lot more. Some agencies in America reckon on a bill to the happy couple of up to $65,000, to include the costs of doctors and psychologists as well as the fee to the surrogate mother. A Russian agency offers a similar service for a competitive $25,000. Comes the market, comes the product. Advertising on the internet, a prospective surrogate mother (blonde hair, green eyes, Caucasian) is reassuring: "My husband is very supportive."

Apart from distaste about the commerce of surrogacy, some critics claim that the baby suffers psychologically. A woman is not a hen producing eggs, goes the argument: the baby bonds with the surrogate mother in her womb and is upset when handed over to a stranger. No one knows if this is true, so anyone can join in. Mr Keane kept his counsel in the moral, religious and medical arguments that kept the chat shows busy but, according to friends, was hurt by much of the criticism. He was an outgoing personality, one of five children of parents who had come to the United States from Ireland. He took a simple view of his work: some women could have children, some could not. What was wrong with the have-nots being given a helping hand? He reckoned that he had arranged the births of about 600 children (and had two sons of his own). Some parents were so grateful that their child was named Noel, or, if appropriate, Noelle. ■

Karl Kehrle

Karl Kehrle (Brother Adam), saviour of the bees, died on September 1st 1996, aged 98

THE ACHIEVEMENT of Karl Kehrle, a Benedictine monk, was to breed a very decent British bee. Wherever in the world apiarists meet they speak in awe of Mr Kehrle's sturdy bee, which produces lots of honey and is reluctant to sting. Like the British themselves, it is a mongrel, combining the virtues of the native bee with those of worthy bees from elsewhere. Mr Kehrle once heard of a promising bee said to be found only in central Africa. Although in his 80s, in poor health and carried on the back of a friend, he tracked the bee down on the slopes of Mount Kilimanjaro.

Selective breeding has been going on in a random way for thousands of years since animals and plants were first domesticated. Gregor Mendel (1822-84), like Mr Kehrle a monk, laid the foundations of what has come to be called genetics. Mendel did clever things with garden peas, but had no success with bees, whose sexual practices remained a mystery to him. Queen bees, it is now known, mate with a drone, or several drones, while on the wing. Then, loaded with sperm, they return to the hive for several years, producing huge numbers of bees. Mr Kehrle pioneered artificial insemination for bees, impregnating his queens with the sperm of immigrant bees. "A very delicate operation," remarked a colleague of Mr Kehrle.

His Buckfast bee, named after the abbey in Devon where Mr Kehrle was a monk, became an unusual export, earning many thousands of pounds for the order. Numerous Buckfast bees have been imported by commercial honey producers in the United States, where disease has caused widespread damage. (The Benedictines, a fairly liberal order, have a talent for making money: their abbey in northern France makes a liqueur, much in demand despite being too sweet for some tastes.) Mr Kehrle became a celebrity within the bee world, lecturing here, picking up an honorary doctorate there, written up in bee journals, made a vice-president of Britain's International Bee Research Association. A species of bee was named after him. It wasn't a bad career for someone who, as he occasionally remarked, had no formal education at all.

The Italian clue
Karl Kehrle was born in Germany. His mother, a keen Roman Catholic, heard that the monks rebuilding their abbey at Buckfast, shut down in the reign of Henry VIII, needed workers. So Karl, not quite 12, was sent to England. He wasn't strong enough to lift stones, so he helped with the bees. By 1919, aged 21 and now a monk named Brother Adam, he was the abbey's master beekeeper. He set out to save the native British bee, which was being wiped out by a disease called acarine. He cross-bred Italian bees, which were free of acarine, with some of the abbey's bees that had eluded the disease. The cross-breeding was a process that was continued under Mr Kehrle over subsequent years with the help of other foreign bees.

Some bee people, while admiring Mr Kehrle's skill as a beekeeper, note that his innovations owed much to the work of Ludwig Armbruster, a fellow German (later a victim of the Nazis), who, following up the work of Mendel, published research on bees and genetics. Mr Kehrle was, by contrast, a hands-on, practical man. But this was no bad

thing. Someone has to turn theory into practice. He was unsurpassed as a breeder of bees. He talked to them, he stroked them. He brought to the hives a calmness that, according to those who saw him at work, the sensitive bees responded to. He was very upset when two of the abbey's queen bees were stolen, and remarked on the frailty of humans. Bees, he said, would never behave like people. "He loved the bees almost as much as he loved God," said a colleague.

A mischievous comment, perhaps. Yet even in the brotherly community of an abbey little jealousies can arise over a colleague who seems to have got more than his fair share of attention. In 1991 Mr Kehrle asked the abbey to provide him with a qualified assistant to help with research into the varroa parasite, which, like the acarine disease of the 1920s, is threatening British bees, and is at present controlled, although only partially, by chemicals. The abbot turned down the request, and apparently felt that, after 80 years at the abbey, it was time for Brother Adam to part from his bees and spend the remainder of his life on monkish duties. "I am sure that he would consider himself a monk first and a beekeeper second," said the abbot, not entirely convincingly. Mr Kehrle handed over his hives to young monks, but was never unwilling to give advice.

He said he wanted to live to 100. The astonishing thing is that he lived as long as he did. Physically, he was not strong. His journeys abroad in search of bees, often partly on foot or by donkey, were exhausting. He suffered several heart attacks. Doctors routinely told him he would never work again. Several times he received the last rites of his religion, but clambered from his bed to see how his bees were managing without him. If an interest in life can keep you going, it certainly worked with Karl Kehrle. ■

Stanley Kubrick

Stanley Kubrick, cinema's master of pessimism, died on March 7th 1999, aged 70

IT IS the dialogue that seems especially puzzling in "2001: A Space Odyssey", Stanley Kubrick's best-known film. Why is it so awful? The film is marvellous to watch. The use of a Strauss waltz, "The Blue Danube", as accompanying music is both innovative and successful. But the wooden words? Still, Mr Kubrick was forgiven when the film came out in 1968. Even great directors should be allowed to make mistakes.

That view, though kind, was itself mistaken. As the film has been watched and watched again, and increasingly admired, the dialogue has come to be accepted as appallingly accurate. This is the new minimalist language, call it min-lan, invented by Houston's space people and now used wherever simple messages need to be put over quickly. Motorway signs, advertisements, even television soaps, all use min-lan. Mr Kubrick anticipated a world where a tiny spoken vocabulary, and even fewer written words, were all you needed to get by. The eloquence of, say, "Casablanca", made in 1942, had been superseded by the frugality of Hal, the talking robot in 2001. Of all the horrors, existing and potential, confronted in Mr Kubrick's films, the abandoning of literacy is perhaps the most dismaying. Books, newspapers, if they survived at all, would be for an elite, and regarded in an urgent world as irrelevant as medieval manuscripts.

Stanley Kubrick himself did his best to insulate himself from what he regarded as the pains of modern living, which included cars, flying and the attentions of reporters, while carrying on with his career as a maker of films with a world-wide audience. In the 1960s he moved from Hollywood to England and bought a statelyish house near, but not too near, London. Here he lived with the fourth of his wives and three daughters. When making a film he would be driven each day, at not more than 30 miles an hour, to Pinewood studios, a well-equipped survivor from the days when Britain had a large and flourishing film industry. During his time in England he gave few interviews and avoided having his picture taken, which is why published photographs of him are as a younger man.

Absolute control

The young Kubrick had a quick success. He took a snap of a man selling newspapers reporting the death of President Roosevelt. *Look* magazine bought the picture and offered him a job. He was poised to go to university, but at 17 who could turn down such a chance? Later, Mr Kubrick was to disparage formal learning, as self-educated people sometimes do. "I never learned anything at all at school," he said. He was, anyway, hardly a teacher's favourite: films were his only real interest. In New York he could see practically every film that was ever made, either at the commercial cinema or at the Museum of Modern Art. He said that seeing so many bad films made him feel he could do better. He left *Look* and, with money borrowed from his father, a doctor, he made a number of short documentaries which he sold to a Hollywood company. Hollywood was sufficiently

impressed by his talent to allow him to make some low-cost feature films, among them "Paths of Glory", set in the first world war, his first critical success, in 1957. Two years later he was given real money to spend on "Spartacus", a Roman epic. At 29 Mr Kubrick was regarded as a major director who could name his own terms. But he disliked working as part of a team. He sought control of the script, the editing, the lighting, the music, as well as the direction, as he had in his early shoestring movies. Only then could he accurately convey his dark view of the world, which in some ways accords with that of Thomas Hobbes, a 17th-century English philosopher remembered for his observation that life in the state of nature is "nasty, brutish and short". Stanley Kubrick's great films, "Dr Strangelove", "A Clockwork Orange", "Lolita" and "2001", are, as far as Mr Kubrick could order things, untouched by any hand other than his.

England gave him freedom. Far from the moguls of Hollywood, he could indulge his costly obsession for perfection. He shot the closing of a car door more than 70 times before he was satisfied it looked right. Actors would be taken mercilessly through a scene again and again. Some would quit, fleeing into the arms of their psychiatrist. Actors were flattered to be asked to work in a Kubrick film, but for some once was enough. "You don't have to be nice to be talented," Kirk Douglas said of Mr Kubrick. 2001 took so long to make that its backers asked if they would have to wait until then to see it.

His final film, "Eyes Wide Shut", was 12 months overdue when it was completed just before he died. Mr Kubrick has been customarily secretive about it. Little has been revealed, although there are rumours that in it Tom Cruise wears a dress. The film is due to be shown in July or thereabouts, and the moguls seem confident that it will be successful, commercially and critically as most Kubrick films have been. Stanley Kubrick might have been odd, but in the end he delivered the goods, and such goods. ∎

Konrad Kujau

Konrad Kujau, forger of the Hitler diaries, died on September 12th 2000, aged 62

AS A forger, Konrad Kujau began modestly, getting free meals with fake luncheon vouchers. He had stumbled on a truth, pithily expressed by Shakespeare, that the world is a "great stage of fools". He was not at all surprised when the fools lined up to acclaim his most ambitious work, the Hitler diaries. The diaries were bought by *Stern*, a German magazine, Britain's *Sunday Times* and America's *Newsweek*. This, they claimed, was the scoop of the century. Hugh Trevor-Roper, an authority on the Hitler period, was among the luckless academics who dispelled doubts about their authenticity. Yet the diaries were later shown to be forgeries by the simplest of scientific tests. The paper and the ink had been made long after Hitler had died. Mr Kujau had made the paper look old by soaking it in tea.

The gullibility of those taken in by the diaries may be excused, or at least explained, by the fact that Hitler was, and remains, the most intriguing monster of modern times. By the 1980s, when *Stern* first got wind of the diaries, it seemed that everything about Adolf Hitler had been found, sifted, published, and published again. Now here was a rich new seam of Hitleriana. There was this entry in 1936 when Germany staged the Olympic Games: "Must not forget tickets for Eva."

No editor of a popular paper could resist the evident charm of Hitler as a human being, and so banal. Better get me the file on Eva Braun. Was she sexy? Konrad Kujau was sent to jail for four and a half years for his deception. Some Germans felt he had got off too lightly, and in fact he was released after three years. But most felt he had done no real harm. In 1996 he ran for mayor of Stuttgart and received 901 votes. A television film was made of his career, treating it with much heavy German humour. It was considered a riot by everyone except Mr Kujau, who felt that not enough credit had been given to his talent as an artist.

The shop in Stuttgart
He did have a gift. He could paint. And he had what painters call a "good eye" for detail. As a young man Konrad Kujau had studied art in Dresden, in what was then East Germany. He moved to the West in 1957, worked in menial jobs and saved up enough money to open a shop in Stuttgart. His wares were Nazi memorabilia and autographs of personalities from the Hitler era, which he forged along with his luncheon vouchers. Aware that there was a market for anything connected with Hitler himself, he forged some poems, an opera and watercolours by the Führer and his diary covering a few months in 1935.

Gerd Heidemann, a *Stern* employee who patronised Mr Kujau's shop, was intensely interested in the diary. Where did it come from? Were there any more like that? The story that Mr Heidemann subsequently told *Stern* was that diaries kept by Hitler over a period of 12 years had been salvaged from a German aircraft that had crashed after leaving Berlin just before the city fell to the Russians and were now for sale. The story seemed to add up. A plane had crashed in the locality and at the time

It was the sheer volume of the diaries that fooled the experts. Hugh Trevor-Roper noted that the collection "coheres as a whole". There was plenty of source material – biographies of Hitler, contemporary newspapers and so on. Sometimes Mr Kujau wore a general's uniform of the Nazi period to get him in the mood. After a time Mr Kujau felt that he was Hitler. "As I wrote about Stalingrad, my hand began to shake." Many forgers have had a similar experience. The most famous was Thomas Chatterton, an 18th-century writer who forged poems that he said were written by one Thomas Rowley, a medieval monk, and which continue to be much admired.

specified. Who knew what dirty dealing went on in East Germany? *Stern* agreed to buy the diaries under conditions of strict secrecy, and several million dollars were passed to Mr Kujau via Gerd Heidemann, who took a generous commission (and, like his accomplice, was later jailed).

For two years Mr Kujau laboured in a back room in his Stuttgart shop, penning the thoughts and deeds of Hitler in a fair copy of the Führer's spidery handwriting, using a steel nib. One by one the volumes were handed over, 62 in all, to a grateful and marvelling *Stern*.

Mr Kujau was proud of his skill and, in later life, was always happy to give a quick lesson on forgery to reporters. He was upset when a German archivist, late in the day, called his work "superficial".

Some of Mr Kujau's work may continue to be admired only, as it were, by proxy. After his release from jail he opened a gallery in Stuttgart specialising in fakes, many of them painted by him. His fakes were also on sale in Majorca, and much in demand by tourists. The work of many modern painters is easy to forge and while they may be sold originally as "honest" fakes, they can pass into the market and be taken as originals. Hitler's paintings have growing value as curiosities, but it is difficult to tell which are his and which are Konrad Kujau's. But perhaps Mr Kujau's life will be remembered chiefly as a cautionary tale. No one offered such fool's gold would be likely to be taken in again. Would they? ■

Stanley Kunitz

Stanley Kunitz, American poet, died on May 14th 2006, aged 100

IN A very long life, Stanley Kunitz did not seem to move around much. Apart from a spell in Pennsylvania in the 1930s and a lecture tour of the Soviet Union in 1967, he spent almost all his days in New York or New England, and most of those in Massachusetts. A line drawn through Worcester, Cambridge and Provincetown, in Cape Cod, where he grew roses in the Atlantic blasts, could neatly contain his world.

Yet Mr Kunitz was a poet, one of America's best of the past century, and therefore travelled incessantly. Much of the time he was on the sea, voyaging to the ends of the earth. In imagination he "strode years; stretched into bird;/ Raced though the sleeping country where I was young." He could sink deep into his own mind, through gorges and ravines, "from the known to the unknown to the unknowable". Or he could coil through life like a fish in a river.

> If the water were clear enough,
> if the water were still,
> but the water is not clear,
> the water is not still,
> you would see yourself,
> slipped out of your skin,
> nosing upstream,
> slapping, thrashing,
> tumbling
> over the rocks

This transformation happened as he read about the Pacific salmon in *Time*. The words began to flow, and he followed them. His sense of poetry-making – and few could explain so well the mysteries of it – was an almost animal instinct. As soon as he could feel his own "interior rhythm" in what he observed, whether slithering fish or falling leaf, he knew the poem would work.

His own rhythm took time to discover. Robert Herrick's songs, recited unexpectedly by a teacher at high school, first drew him into poetry; but it was Gerard Manley Hopkins's "God's Grandeur", pulled down by chance from a shelf in a Harvard library, that showed Mr Kunitz the scope of what he could write. Over the years he moved from Elizabethan high style to simple, almost conversational free verse, "wringing out the water", as he put it, and aiming for a poetry that was natural, luminous, deep and spare.

That was difficult, because Mr Kunitz felt his human heaviness so intensely. When a whale beached itself at Wellfleet, Massachusetts, he made it a metaphor of himself, "crushed by your own weight,/ collapsing into yourself ... disgraced and mortal." In his first collection, "Intellectual Things" (1930), he dreamed of stripping "The tender blanket from my bone" and rising "like a skeleton in the sun", but did not have much faith he would.

Nor, despite Hopkins, did he write about God. The "Father" he invoked in his poems was his own, who had killed himself before he was born. He had drunk carbolic acid in a park in Worcester, leaving Stanley's mother to support her children by dressmaking. Mr Kunitz followed this ghost obsessively: across the bloody grass, through plum orchards, to the edge of a river, where

> Among the turtles and the lilies he turned to me
> The white ignorant hollow of his face.

He wrote frequently of family, but almost never of his Jewishness. When rebuked for that, Mr Kunitz, who had been barred as a Jew from teaching at Harvard in 1927, made a sharp reply: "I am an American free-thinker, a damn stubborn one, and my poetry is not hyphenated." His rebelliousness showed again when he insisted on being a conscientious objector during the second world war; it showed, too, in his refusal to write fashionable stuff. To be a metaphysical poet entranced with nature, rather than a cynical observer of men and cities,

was the wrong flavour for the mid-20th century. Mr Kunitz paid for his contrarian streak by being dismissed as too abstract and ignored by the critics. Had Theodore Roethke and Robert Lowell not befriended him, he might have stayed as sunk in pastoral obscurity as John Clare, and perhaps as mad.

Two hits on the tree

Loneliness seemed engrained in him. Out of school, his childhood was spent by himself in the woods throwing stones at a tree (two hits, he would be a poet), or testing how far he could climb up a perpendicular cliff. Later in life he kept the usual poet's habits, shut up by himself, writing in scrupulously neat longhand with no deletions. Every decade or so, a book of poems would appear. Very gradually, out of this slim

oeuvre, a reputation grew and prizes came. In 2000, at the age of 95, he was made poet laureate of the United States.

Yet the lonely, searching poet could also be almost gregarious. He loved teaching, at Bennington, Yale and elsewhere, persuading his students, he said once, that every one of them could be a poet. He set up two centres, in Provincetown and New York, where writers could live and work in company with other artists, discussing their explorations.

As for his own endless travelling, each poem hinted at an end to it. "I have the sense", he said, "of swimming underwater towards some kind of light and open air that will be saving." Or,

Becoming, never being, till
Becoming is a being still. ∎

Akira Kurosawa

Akira Kurosawa, emperor of Japanese films, died on September 6th 1998, aged 88

WATCHING A film made by Akira Kurosawa is not always fun. "Rashomon" is set in medieval Japan. A murder has taken place, and probably a rape. Four witnesses to the events describe what they have seen. Their accounts are contradictory. The message of the film appears to be that truth is elusive.

The film had an indifferent reception when first shown in Japan. Reviewers judged, no doubt correctly, that Japanese moviegoers were not keen on messages. Soft porn and simple stories are what pack the cinemas of Tokyo. The critics at the Venice film festival in 1951 were made of sterner stuff. *Rashomon* gained their top award. They

had taken their seats expecting to see a cliché Japan of geishas and cherry blossom. They emerged in the grip of a subtle mind. The film has gained a kind of immortality in the phrase "Rashomon-like", meaning uncertainty. For the first time a Japanese director won international recognition. The Japanese became proud of their world-beater. Mr Kurosawa was awarded the Order of the Sacred Treasure, the first film director to receive it. But, for choice, most Japanese have continued to feel there is nothing to beat a spicy boy-meets-girl story.

For all the critical praise heaped upon him, Mr Kurosawa never found it easy to raise money for his films. In 1971, when he was 61, his spirits were so low that he attempted suicide; presumably a cry for help as Japanese suicide attempts tend to be final. At other times he tried to make films with an obvious popular appeal, which are best forgotten. Orson Welles had a similar experience. "Citizen Kane", made when he was young, is considered by some to be the best film ever, but for the rest of his career he only scraped a living as a director.

The samurai

Akira Kurosawa and Orson Welles were innovators in an industry that mostly prefers tried and tested formulae. There are of course other directors whose talents are argued over by the minority who see film as an art as well as mass entertainment. But the list is fairly small, and belongs to no one country. In the 1920s, the most critically admired films were German and Russian, in the 1930s they were French, in the 1940s British and Italian. As in a great painting, there is always something new to see in, say, "The Bicycle Thieves" (Vittorio De Sica, 1948) or "La Grande Illusion" (Jean Renoir, 1937). Mr Kurosawa saw these and many other films made in the West. As a child he had had a free pass to a cinema where his brother was a narrator of silent movies. At a time when Japan was authoritarian and fiercely nationalistic, Mr Kurosawa became an admirer of western ideas. Shakespeare was an obvious master, but so was John Ford, the maker of American westerns of pace and atmosphere. "The Seven Samurai", perhaps Mr Kurosawa's best-known film, is a sort of Japanese western, in which poor villagers hire a group of unemployed warriors to protect them from bandits. Hollywood remade it as "The Magnificent Seven", which has some of the shine of the original. "Yojimbo" was remade as "A Fistful of Dollars", starring Clint Eastwood. Hollywood was grateful. It awarded Mr Kurosawa three Oscars.

When in 1970 Hollywood decided to make "Tora! Tora! Tora!", an epic about the attack on Pearl Harbor which brought America into the second world war, Mr Kurosawa seemed just the man to direct the Japanese scenes. He was enthusiastic, but pulled out long before the film was completed. One story told at the time was that he wanted the Japanese in the cast to have military training to ensure authenticity. Whether that is true or not is unclear; it doesn't seem a bad idea. What is clear is that Mr Kurosawa insisted on absolute control of the Japanese scenes.

This was his way. He was *tenno*, the emperor, of his world. One of his actors recalled that he would scream, "The rain isn't falling like I want it to." He was a perfectionist, but necessarily a frugal one. His most expensive film was "Ran", made in 1985, and based on the story of "King Lear". It cost $10m, a lot of money for a Japanese film but trifling by Hollywood standards. He kept costs down by working fast. In many of his films he used the same team of reliable actors, headed by Toshiro Mifune, who died last year. Each scene was filmed by three cameras in different positions. Each night Mr Kurosawa would edit the day's filming, so that when the filming was finally finished he had a rough draft of the movie.

He left an oeuvre of 30 films produced over a period of about 50 years, the final one, "Madadayo", about an elderly academic, as recently as 1993. Although no one questioned that he was world class as an artist, some Japanese, still among the most nationalistic of people, wondered whether he was too fond of western ideas. Mr Kurosawa would point to his collection of antiques. Alongside Japanese lacquerware was French glass. Both were beautiful. Japan and the West, he said, lived side-by-side in his mind. ■

Freddie Laker

Sir Freddie Laker, airline pioneer, died on February 9th 2006, aged 83

IN A lifetime dedicated to piloting and managing aircraft of all sorts, Freddie Laker rarely felt scared. But there were exceptions. In the winter of 1948–49 he found himself flying old Halifax bombers over Germany, going to the relief of Berlin after it had been blockaded by the Russians. Ice coated his windscreen. More ice would have clogged his wings, had he not smeared thick grease over them. Russian planes buzzed him and, unable to get much height, he could watch Russian guns firing at him from the ground.

In these planes – "deathtraps" and "junk" as he thought of them – he and his team flew 4,700 sorties in 54 weeks. Under each plane, roughly in place of the bomb chamber, hung a pannier containing oil, coal and potatoes. Though the oil added to the hazard, the coal was worse, covering him with black dust as though he had been down a mine. But Mr Laker could not have cared less. "It was all about freedom," he said later.

Flying and freedom were inseparable in his mind. They had been so ever since, as a yobbish teenager eating fish and chips in the street with his mates, he had looked up to see the German airship *Hindenburg* and a Handley Page biplane flying at the same moment over Canterbury Cathedral. Home life was a struggle in a cold-water flat, school a dead end, but up there was limitless. For the rest of his life, whenever high spirits seized him, the big, ebullient, grinning Mr Laker would spread out his arms and mimic a plane.

Yet the sky, he was soon to find, was not as open as all that. Commercial air routes had been neatly divided up between big carriers and, after the war, the Labour government nationalised the industry. On both sides of the Atlantic, politicians and national airlines colluded with each other to keep ticket prices high. The ordinary man could only dream of flying. The wide blue yonder was out of his reach.

That it is not so these days is largely due to Mr Laker. Any passenger who now jets to Italy or Greece for the price of a train fare to the suburbs is following the trail he blazed. Mr Laker in 1977 introduced the first outrageous discounts, £118 ($206) to fly the Laker Skytrain from London to New York, and the first taste of no frills: if staff were scarce, he sometimes loaded bags himself. And he offered these benefits on long-haul flights, something his brash young acolytes – from Southwest Airlines to Ryanair to easyJet – have yet to attempt.

The public loved it. By the end of its first year, Skytrain had made profits of £3m and the number of passengers from Britain to America had shot up by 30%. Within five years, it had 20 aircraft. Then, inexorably, the big carriers closed in. Since restrictive trade agreements, underpinned by legislation, could not keep Mr Laker out, they slashed their own prices to undercut him. This, and the world recession of 1980–81, drove Laker Airways into bankruptcy. Only when the creditors sued did the airlines plead guilty to predatory pricing. Mr Laker's best advice to his disciple and friend Richard Branson, when Mr Branson was setting up cut-price Virgin

Atlantic, was to sue the bastards before, not after, going belly-up.

Car-boot sales

Up until 1982, Mr Laker had thrived on luck and opportunism. By meeting a useful man in 1941, he learned from scratch to fly four-engine aircraft. His first enterprise was to sell aeronautical spare parts out of the boot of a car, his second to strip the platinum points off the spark-plugs of Bristol Hercules engines. The Berlin airlift ("the best piece of luck I ever had", since he just happened to have bought 12 of those second-hand bombers) got him easily and profitably into the cargo-delivery business. This led him to think of ways to wriggle into the commercial passenger trade.

He made his play deviously and slowly. In the 1950s he converted a fleet of DC4s to take passengers and cars from Southend, which the big carriers did not use, to Calais. Then in 1966 he observed that a loophole in the law allowed independents to take "affinity groups", such as clubs, abroad. Immediately, his passengers were made members of the Right Wheel Group or the Left Wing Club, and Mr Laker would

appear at Gatwick with a Bible on which they would swear club allegiance if the airline snoops were watching. Once the Department of Trade had rumbled him, in 1971, he began to think of a different ruse to break the cartel: running an air operation that passengers would treat like a train. The rest was history.

His adventure with Laker Airways earned him a knighthood from a red-faced Labour government and the devotion of Margaret Thatcher. He bought boats, Rolls Royces and race horses, and regularly changed wives. After the crash he left England, feeling unappreciated, to toy with low-cost airlines in Florida.

His last venture, in 1996, flew out of the Bahamas. This one was rather different to the others he had managed. There were leather seats and gilt-edged dinner plates; wines were served in crystal glasses. Mr Laker had made flying, once again, an occupation for the elite. Nonetheless, the man on the 9.30 from Stansted to Palma, crushed in a middle seat between crying children and with a home-made sandwich as his sustenance, should raise a plastic cup to freedom and to Freddie. ■

Alice Lakwena

Alice Auma Lakwena, warrior and spirit-channeller, died on January 17th 2007, aged 50

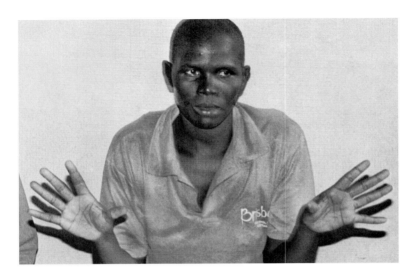

AT A place called Wang Jok, in Paraa National Park in northern Uganda, the Nile flows strongly among trees and over rapids. This is a magic spot: coins, pots and human figures sometimes mysteriously appear from the river. And if you had visited Wang Jok in May 1986 you might have seen, sitting beside the water, a young woman of 30 apparently talking to herself.

People from Opit, the railway town where she lived, knew her as Alice Auma. She sold fish and flour with another woman and had had two husbands, both of whom had deserted her because she was barren. But it was not Alice Auma who was sitting by the Nile. She was possessed by a spirit called Lakwena, and he was holding a consultation with all the animals of the park.

They swarmed round him in a huge bellowing crowd, elephants and hippopotami and crocodiles and giraffes, many of them holding up wounded limbs to be healed. Lakwena asked them who was responsible for the civil war in Uganda, in which the Acholi rebels of the north were fighting the troops of Yoweri Museveni's National Resistance Army. They replied that "the people with two legs" were the violators of peace and Nature. A waterfall and a mountain were interrogated too. They gave back the same answer.

Thus began Alice's mission to purify first her native Acholi, then Uganda, then the world. Lakwena gave her stones and water, with which she went back to Opit and began to heal people. Beside the railway station she built a temple of mud-blocks and thatch in which, as Lakwena, she would sit on a throne and give instructions. When the men muttered that she was only a woman, Lakwena would announce in his commanding voice that he had possessed her precisely because she was a woman and a sinner, who had never got beyond seventh year in primary school; he was making an example of a hard case, saving her first, before he saved the wicked Acholi in general.

Lakwena also offered, in August 1986, to conduct the war for them. And when the rebel commanders ignored him, he and Alice formed their own army. The Holy Spirit Mobile Forces (HSMF) numbered at their peak around 10,000 souls, not a few of them abducted children; and for a brief spell they were the most successful of all the groups fighting the NRA, which was now the Ugandan government.

Their methods were unorthodox. Lakwena, giving orders that his soldiers wrote down neatly in school exercise books, forbade them to use weapons. They did not need to, because they were pure. Each man had burned his witchcraft charms, and had appeased the spirit of anyone he had killed previously; and as the army marched into battle, singing Catholic hymns and with their bare torsos smothered in shea-nut oil, the bullets of the enemy would bounce right off them. Nature, too, was on their side. Water, if they were polite to it and "bought" each river they crossed with coins and shells, would block the enemy or drown him. Stones, if they threw them, would explode like grenades.

Avoiding anthills

Lakwena expressed these war-rules through Alice twice a day, at seven in the morning and seven at night, as she sat in a white robe on a fold-up chair in the middle of the camp. He made her repeat the 20 Holy Spirit Safety Precautions: no walking-sticks on the battlefield, no hiding behind anthills, no smoking, and each man to have "two testicles, neither more nor less". Round Alice stood three

charcoal stoves on which little wire replicas of enemy weapons were heated until they glowed and then waved above the soldiers' heads to immunise them. Something worked, for in several encounters the NRA soldiers, faced by rampant hymn-singers, dropped their weapons and ran away.

Alice revealed a little about Lakwena. He was an Italian army captain, drowned in the Nile in the first world war, who spoke 74 languages, including Latin. He had taken possession of her so violently in January 1985 that she ran amok and could not hear or speak. Sometimes, to discipline her, he would make her ill or order that she should be beaten six times with a stick. But he shared her body with other spirits: Wrong Element, a loud-mouthed American; Franko from Zaire; several Koreans and Arabs; and an Acholi nurse, Nyaker, whose voice was so thin that the soldiers could not understand it. They never knew, they said, whether Alice was a spirit or a person from one day to the next.

Gradually, however, she seemed to resolve into an ordinary wilful woman. As the HSMF marched south towards Kampala in the late summer of 1987, the influence of the spirits and Alice's own power seemed alike to be fading. The bullets no longer bounced off, and the enemy didn't run away. At Jinja, not far from the capital, the HSMF was smashed by artillery fire, and Alice fled on a bicycle.

The remnants of her soldiers – mustered under Joseph Kony, an ex-altar boy who claimed to be her cousin – metamorphosed into the horrifyingly violent Lord's Resistance Army, which continues to kill, rape, pillage and abduct children in today's Uganda. Alice settled in a refugee camp in Kenya, a greying barfly drinking gin and Coke. Lakwena returned to the Nile, and the Nile flows on. ∎

Hedy Lamarr

Hedy Lamarr, a brain as well as a body, died on January 19th 2000, aged 86

WHEN HEDY Lamarr arrived in Hollywood she was seen as a rare and desirable acquisition: a genuine decadent, a temptress to send male pulses racing, and create envy in women's hearts. Home-grown temptresses had been tried with only varying success. An American houri is a contradiction. In the 1920s Theda Bara (an anagram of Arab Death) had done her vampish best to sully the minds of clean-living Americans, and had been much attacked from the pulpits of the mid-west, but her seductive powers had diminished when it emerged that her real name was Goodman and she had been born in Cincinnati. Miss Lamarr, though, was from deepest Europe, from Vienna. Not only was she disturbingly beautiful, but in a European film, "Ecstasy", she had appeared in the nude. She was the real thing.

Sadly, none of her American films turned out to be memorable. She was starred with many of the biggest names in the Hollywood repertory company, Clark Gable, Spencer Tracey, Victor Mature, John Garfield, and so on. All her films made money, some a lot. Women were sufficiently envious of her to copy her hairstyle, with its central parting. But male pulses remained normal. Men left the cinema no more discontented with their women than they previously were. Hollywood was careless of her talent. Once she was put in a comedy, as a foil to Bob Hope, another time in a western. Yet, although her last forgettable film was made back in the 1950s, Hedy Lamarr's name has retained a lingering association with the timeless idea of the femme fatale, a reason for writing about her.

Sexual attraction was not just a matter of looks, Miss Lamarr said. "Any girl can be glamorous – all you have to do is stand still and look stupid." You should have a brain as well as a body, she said. She was an admirer of Mata Hari, a spy in the first world war, who was both a seductress and a military expert. Louis B. Mayer, a Hollywood boss, was charmed by Miss Lamarr's talk as well as her looks when he first met her in London. He got her to change her name from Hedy Kiesler, and gave her a seven-year contract to work for MGM. But on the way to Hollywood some of her allure was seemingly mislaid.

A new habitat
Moving from her native environment was probably what went wrong for Miss Lamarr, as it can do for any animal. Even Marlene Dietrich, for all of her success in America, never repeated the sensuality she brought to "The Blue Angel", made in Germany in 1930. Greta Garbo retained the persona she had brought from Sweden, but it was her air of mystery that made her so watchable, rather than her sexuality. Sex was Hollywood's main product, but the movie bosses decreed, confusingly, that it should be wholesome. The film community might live in a sink of waywardness, but none of that got on to the screen. In "White Cargo", made in 1942, Miss Lamarr gamely said she set out to be "a memorable nymphomaniac". But there was no

running naked through a wood, swimming in a pool and seemingly enjoying making love. Miss Lamarr easily fell in love. Like Miss Dietrich she said, "I can't help it." Granting her a divorce from one of her husbands, the judge advised her that she should spend more than a month getting to know a future spouse.

She was defensive about all her marriages, and her affairs. "I did what I did for love," she said. "I'm a hell of a nice dame." She sued a writer who, she said, had written about her in "an obscene, shocking, scandalous, naughty, wanton" way, but the case went against her.

sympathy for five-syllable words in MGM, and the sexiest thing about "White Cargo" was its title.

She often thought of returning to her native Austria, but never did. In 1938 the Germans had taken over Austria and her father, a doctor, and her mother, a pianist, had left the country. "Ecstasy", made in 1932 when she was 18, remains the film she is most remembered by. Today it seems inoffensive, but it was condemned by the pope and banned in a number of countries, including the United States. Miss Lamarr's fans have traced a number of earlier films she made in Berlin.

Fritz Mandl, a Viennese arms maker who became the first of her six husbands, tried, fortunately without success, to buy up all copies of "Ecstasy". He objected to all the world seeing his wife

As a result of this and other litigation, the millions of dollars she had earned in Hollywood were dissipated as lawyers' fees, and in later years she had little money.

As it happens, Miss Lamarr might have made a second fortune out of an idea she developed with George Antheil, a composer she met in 1940 at a party in Hollywood. Applying their knowledge of musical harmony they devised a technology for military communications. In 1942 they were granted an American patent for the invention. The army was not interested, the patent eventually expired and the couple never profited. Today, though, a development of the invention, known as spread-spectrum technology, is being used in a wide range of electronic products, including mobile phones. Engineers reckon the concept is, so to speak, just beautiful. ∎

Morris Lapidus

Morris Lapidus, architect of make-believe, died on January 18th 2001, aged 98

WHEN THE Fontainebleau was opened in Miami, its architect, Morris Lapidus, proudly spoke of it as "the world's most pretentious hotel". Pretentious? He quickly corrected the slip of the tongue: "flamboyant" was what he meant, of course. Yet a lexicographer might note that in its original Anglo-French meaning, of make-believe, pretentious was the precise word to describe Mr Lapidus's style. He wanted the mostly ordinary holidaymakers who stepped into his hotels to feel that they were entering a wonderland. "I wanted people to walk in and drop dead," he said. "I wanted them to say, 'My God, this is luxury.'" Until Mr Lapidus built the Fontainebleau and other baroque hotels in Miami Beach in the 1950s, "luxury" had implied a quiet understatement.

If the hotel were modern it would tend to reflect the minimalist movement in architecture. To Mies van der Rohe's dictum, "less is more", Morris Lapidus responded, "Too much is never enough", which became the title of his autobiography. He believed in the virtues of vulgarity: lots of colour, lots of curves, lots of surprises. He put live alligators in a pool in the lobby of one hotel, so that guests would "know they were in Florida". He thought about having monkeys swinging from trapezes, but decided they might damage the chandeliers. There were jokes, some of them witty: replicas of classical statues playing golf, or using the phone. Laughter is a background noise in a Lapidus foyer. He saw his hotels as theatres with the guests taking on roles as actors. You could pretend to be famous. Some guests were. Some scenes in the James Bond movie *Goldfinger* were filmed in the Fontainebleau.

Extravagance is now so commonplace that Mr Lapidus's wild designs may no longer seem extreme. But they predated the Disney theme parks and the follies of Las Vegas. The guests at his hotels had seen such glamour only in films; and, like the old movie palaces, with their deep carpets and plastic finery, they provided a brief escape from the humdrum realities of everyday life. Showy Miami, best viewed through rhinestone sunglasses, was right for him. Others soon played his tune. Go there now and even the motels, with such names as Tangiers and Suez, seem exotic.

His critics

Morris Lapidus's hotels were loved by, or at least charmed, almost everyone except writers on architecture, who saw them as a blasphemous assault on the holy writ of austere functionality. "Pornography of architecture," was one of the milder comments. Mr Lapidus said that during much of his long career his work was never published in an architectural journal, except to abuse it. "I was anathema," he said. No one, though, doubted his acumen. He had a resemblance to another memorable American character, Sam Goldwyn, whose solecisms ("Never make predictions, especially about the future") concealed a brilliant Hollywood film-maker. Both men were born in eastern Europe, Goldwyn in Poland, Lapidus in Russia.

Growing up in Brooklyn, the big treat

for Morris was a trip to Coney Island. What he called the "whirling, twisting, colourful" lights were to reappear in Miami Beach. But contracts to design hotels do not come to young architects just out of college. Mr Lapidus spent some 20 years designing shops, small and big, attracting customers by using colour, light and "sweeping, curving" interiors. In the Fontainebleau, the first of several hundred hotels he designed, he incorporated "all the things I had learned from my store work. When I got into hotels, I had to think, what am I selling now? I was selling a good time."

Mr Lapidus was sometimes asked who were his own favourite architects. He would surprise questioners by mentioning Frank Lloyd Wright, an American traditionalist, and Le Corbusier, a Swiss-born architect famous for his massive box-like blocks of flats. But Mr Lapidus admired workmanship, whatever the architectural genre, just as a fashion designer such as John Galliano is praised for his painstaking craftsmanship however you view his crazy clothes. Mr Lapidus was a craftsman. One contribution he made to architecture that hotel users are grateful for is the short corridor. He recalled that when he was a young architect travelling a lot from town to town, at the end of a weary day he always seemed to have a long walk to find his hotel room. The hotels he designed are shaped to end those long walks.

In 1990, when Morris Lapidus was 88 and thinking of retiring, and a bit depressed that his life's work had gone unnoticed, he was suddenly discovered in Europe. His work, a critic noted, expressed the spirit of Main Street America. A Swiss publisher produced a tome entitled *Morris Lapidus: The Architect of the American Dream.* Mr Lapidus was invited to the Netherlands for an exhibition about his work. American critics swallowed their pride and conceded that he had indeed had an influence. Last year he was named an "American original" at a ceremony at the White House in Washington. Some architects, Mr Lapidus noted, were starting to round the corners of their buildings. It was all quite pretentious, in a make-believe sort of way. ■

Alan de Lastic

Alan Basil de Lastic, India's "conscience", died on June 20th 2000, aged 70

THE CHRISTIAN missionaries who accompanied European armies to India were largely unsuccessful in converting the multitudes to the teachings of Jesus. The Portuguese in Goa, the French in Pondicherry and the British all over the subcontinent found that Hindus and Muslims and other adherents to strong religions were mostly content with their own perceived paths to the Divine. Today, nearly 500 years after the first missionaries arrived, Christians account for fewer than 3% of India's one billion people. Nevertheless, some Indians, Hindus especially, are displeased that there are any Christians in the country at all. Last November, during Pope Paul II's visit to India, he was asked by a Hindu group to apologise for the atrocities committed by early Roman Catholic priests who, it is now conceded, were overzealous in their proselytising methods.

The pope on his trips abroad does not submit himself to rude questions by reporters. It fell to Alan de Lastic, archbishop of Delhi, and India's leading Catholic, to make it clear that there would be no apology. "How far back in history are you going?" he demanded. Mr de Lastic said he was more concerned about atrocities being committed against Christians in India now. Over the past two years there have been more than 200 reports of attacks on Christians. Thirty churches have been bombed or otherwise damaged. Priests and nuns have been murdered. An Australian missionary and his two young sons were burned to death in his car in Orissa.

Mr de Lastic said the government was not doing its duty to bring peace and justice to India. "We are told to fight against Pakistan and be careful about China," he said, while the evils at home were being neglected. This was fierce stuff from a senior cleric of a conservative church. But Mr de Lastic was concerned with the earthly problems of his flock, as well as its spiritual needs. India is often lauded as the world's largest democracy, but that grand description flatters a society that tolerates corruption and where life is cheap. Mr de Lastic founded a human rights group, the United Christian Forum, and, to the irritation of non-Christians, saw it as the conscience of the nation.

Journey of an archbishop
Alan de Lastic was born in Burma when it was part of British India. He was partly Burmese, partly Irish and partly French: his paternal grandparents came from Bourg-Lastic, a town in central France. But he was, he said, wholly Indian. He studied marine engineering, and worked for a time in the shipyards of Calcutta. As mystics do, he felt a call to the priesthood. He was spotted as a potential star, and sent to Rome and Dublin for polish. Thereafter he rose rapidly in India's Catholic hierarchy. Mother Teresa (Obituary, September 13th 1997) was a close friend. He was made bishop of Lucknow and, in 1990, archbishop of Delhi.

The community he led, though relatively small, has been remarkably influential. India's armed forces have had dozens of Christian generals, admirals and air marshals, members either of the Catholic church, or of the 40 or so other Christian denominations in India. Christian groups run thousands of schools and hospitals as well as business enterprises such as rural banks. Missionaries run most leper colonies: many Hindus regard the disease as a punishment for wrongdoing. One way and another, millions of non-Christians benefit from the work of the churches. Why are they being attacked in a country that claims to be tolerant of all religious belief?

The attacks are usually blamed on members of a militant Hindu group known as Sangh Parivar, or United Family. The group warns Indians of the "sweet poison" of Christianity. It complains that Hindus are being converted against their will. Mr de

Lastic said that what militant Hindus particularly objected to were Christian schools, especially those in rural areas. Many Hindus acknowledge that they are well run; so much so that they send their own children to them. But by accepting the poorest children as pupils, the Christians are seen as undermining India's Hindu caste system, which remains rigid in many areas. The upper-caste feudal lords fear that, once educated, the previously docile local people would demand new rights and could no longer be treated as near-slave labour.

The Indian prime minister, Atal Behari Vajpayee, told Mr de Lastic that "only lunatics can indulge in such acts". But the government has been reluctant to condemn the lunatics publicly, dismissing the attacks as "isolated

incidents" Mr Vajpayee is regarded as a moderate, but his government includes fervent Hindu nationalists. Some have links with the Sangh Parivar, whose members may be influential in constituencies the government needs to nurse.

Mr de Lastic died in a car crash in Poland. The vast congregation at his funeral in Delhi last week included representatives from just about every faith practised in the country. The president and a number of government ministers paid their respects. One said Alan de Lastic was "a great saint". For a few hours India experienced religious harmony. ■

Estée Lauder

Estée Lauder, queen of cosmetics, died on April 24th 2004, at a mature age

A NUMBER of newspapers thought Estée Lauder was 97 when she died. Others averred that she was 95. Most agreed that, until a broken hip slowed her down in 1994, she did not look her age, whatever that was. If anything, the hair had grown blonder and the skin tighter. Outrageous purple outfits, topped by natty hats, reproduced something of the glow of youth.

Subservience to hard facts, such as time and decay, seldom held Mrs Lauder back. Her own background was a study in selective self-improvement. By changing her name, acquiring that dainty little lift of an *accent aigu*, she suggested to customers that her background might be aristocratic and even European. French and Italian blood was hinted at, as well as a convent education. Her father, a monarchist by her telling, felt undressed in the street on Sundays without a cane and gloves.

These details were sprung on the world in 1985, in a book that accompanied the launch of a new perfume, "Beautiful". For the promotion in Paris, Mrs Lauder had bought up all the pinks in the city to match both the perfume boxes and the book's cover. This sensory extravaganza was designed to eclipse an unauthorised "inside story" of her life. Under covers of cream and blue (so tastelessly passé!) her rival revealed that Mrs Lauder's parents, Hungarian Jews, had run a seed and hardware store in Queens, a run-down borough of New York. The young Estée had probably not finished her studies at Newtown High School. Her first jars of face cream had been cooked up not just in a kitchen over a gas stove, but also in a makeshift lab in a stable, and by an uncle whose chemical experiments stretched not only to "Viennese Cream" but to lice-killer and embalming fluid.

These revelations, about a woman who now counted among her friends Princess Diana, Nancy Reagan, the Gorbachevs and the Begum Aga Khan, were somewhat irritating. Yet it was scarcely a tale to be ashamed of. Young Josephine Esther Mentzer, as she began, was convinced from childhood that women should be beautiful. She also hoped to make a fortune by persuading them that, if they bought her creams, their beauty would last for ever. It is a story, after all, that women tend to need to believe.

With tireless energy, she devoted her life to both causes. She began in the 1930s in the beauty salons of Queens, finding an audience held captive under hairdryers and dabbing their hot cheeks with her uncle's inventions. In 1948, Saks Fifth Avenue took a consignment; it sold out in two days. Steadily, Mrs Lauder acquired shiny counters in more and more department stores. With the help of a friend she branched out in 1953 from creams into Youth-Dew, a bestselling bath oil and perfume combined, and became the doyenne of all beauty.

Tactility was her byword. She loved to plunge her fingers in her own gently simmering creations, palpating and inhaling them. Her creams came in heavy jars, her lipsticks in cool metal sheaths, to advertise their quality. Whenever she could she smoothed them on customers herself, achieving a "gentle glow" that was immediate and miraculous. For a time, Fifth Avenue was not safe from her. Sales staff at Estée Lauder counters were trained by her to get similarly intimate with customers. Free gifts, then an innovation, were handed out with every purchase, and free samples were sent to aristocrats in Europe. The distinctive Estée Lauder blue-green was devised to harmonise with most rich people's bathrooms. By 2000, more than half of all cosmetics sold in America were hers.

Whether women actually became more beautiful by applying Body Performance Anti-Cellulite Visible Contouring Serum, or whether they would have done as well with a quick douse in cold water, is impossible to say. Clearly, many felt better for it. The very names of these products, energetic and pseudo-scientific, implied that the limits of knowledge had been searched. Mrs Lauder could have cut prices, but refused. Her Crème de la Mer, developed by a NASA scientist, cost $110 for an ounce of vitamins pulped with seaweed. But cheapness, she said, would shake her customers' faith.

Over the decades she became very rich. By this year, her personal fortune stood at $233m and the worth of her company at $5.4 billion, with annual sales of $5 billion in 130 countries. Mrs Lauder was asked to be ambassador to Luxembourg, but declined when her husband said he did not want to carry her bags. Fabulous dinners were arranged, with gifts of Cartier silverware and with the candles set low on the tables to cast a flattering upward light on the *assistance*. The New York gossip columns trailed her obsessively, and still could not find out how old she was.

Time, however, also trailed her, with his ghastly wrinkled face and his sallow hue that co-ordinated with no bathrooms. In 1988 she asked her elder son Leonard, then CEO of the company, to start dyeing his hair, as he was making her look old. That year the company brought in bleached wood and etched glass for its counters, a new blue for its packaging and more androgynous models who glowed with energy and health. Long before the death of the matriarch, Estée Lauder Companies Inc had been gently, but necessarily, moving out of her ageing shadow. ■

Frank Launder

Frank Launder, master of British humour, died on February 23rd 1997, aged 89

A S A footnote to the Ten Commandments, Hilaire Belloc suggested:
"Candidates should not attempt more
than six of these." If this sounds funny, it
may be that you appreciate that quirky
thing called British humour. If not, best
not to bother. Belloc took more than 30
years to become British, overcoming the
handicap of being born in France. The
British Council teaches "British humour"
to foreigners, but some believe this is
itself an example of British humour.

The Britishness of Frank Launder's
humour was the main reason why most
of his films never travelled well. In the
1950s British audiences from Newcastle
to Newport were in fits over the goings
on in an unruly girls' school called St
Trinian's, but in New York, let alone
Little Rock, these scenes were received
with bafflement. American family values
at the time owed much to 15 years of
sentimental Andy Hardy films, in which
Mickey Rooney's adolescence had
been phenomenally extended. In Mr
Launder's films, by contrast, there were
wild schoolgirls showing a shameful
amount of leg in their black stockings
and gymslips, and, most oddly, their
school was in the charge of a man
dressed as a woman.

The *New Yorker* and other classy
magazines praised Mr Launder's films.
Comics who wore women's clothes,
they explained, were continuing
a tradition of the dame in English
pantomime. They deplored the
prudishness of American censors who
had got Mr Launder to reshoot a scene
in another film of his, "The Rake's
Progress", in which Rex Harrison climbs

an Oxford steeple to crown it with a
potty. In the American version of the
film, renamed "Notorious Gentleman",
a top hat is used. But Mr Launder's
American friends were addressing a
relatively tiny audience. His productions
were dismissed by Hollywood as cult
films, the polite term for turkeys.

Into Wonderland
In Britain Frank Launder's films are
still regarded as very watchable, to
the extent that they are given good
slots on television. More important,
perhaps, they are seen as a link in a
long chain of British humour. In the
beginning, inevitably, was Lewis Carroll.
Innumerable references to "Alice"
turn up all the time in speeches and
journalism. A smattering of scholarship
underpins much of British humour.
ITMA, the most famous of the British
radio comedies in the second world war,
and the brilliantly awful "Carry On"
films have occasional literary jokes, as
do Mr Launder's films. "The Goons", on
the radio, and "Monty Python's Flying
Circus", on television, which later gave a
new thrust to British humour, are loaded
with artful literary references. Often the
references are missed, but get a laugh
anyway.

Frank Launder's literary scholarship
seems to have been picked up as he
went along. He had, he said, little
education, but was a compulsive reader.
When he started in films in 1928 they
were still silent. He wrote the captions,
and was paid £4 a week (about $16 in
those days).

In 1936 he gained attention and some

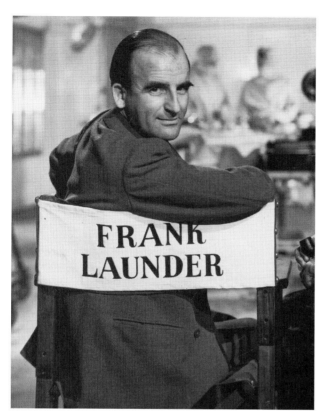

war. Class is an inviting battleground for satirists. The "idiotic and splendidly senseless" St Trinian's girls, as an admiring critic called them, were obviously from privileged homes. The staff at the terrible school were played by Alastair Sim and Joyce Grenfell, issuing their pointless orders in stately accents.

During the war Mr Launder made "Millions Like Us", about women factory workers. It is warm rather than funny. Mr Launder never made political statements, but it seems likely that his sympathies were with what is now called the disadvantaged. His film that he liked best was "Geordie", about a poor boy who has success as

more pay when he wrote the script of "The Lady Vanishes" in collaboration with Sidney Gilliat (his partner in many subsequent films).

"The Lady Vanishes", directed by Alfred Hitchcock, has something of the endurance of "Casablanca". Both are daft stories, quickly and cheaply made, but have the fascination of antiques that mirror an era. "The Lady Vanishes" is a melodrama, but for it Mr Launder invented two comic characters, Charters and Caldicott (Basil Radford and Naunton Wayne). Although Mr Launder said his films were solely to entertain, part of the entertainment was to show the British class system in its more absurd forms. Charters and Caldicott are upper-class buffoons, more interested in cricket scores than the imminent

an athlete. The director he most admired was René Clair, who like Mr Launder had a talent for fantastic satire, but also, as in "Sous les Toits de Paris", saw value in ordinary people.

Frank Launder's good fortune was to be a film-maker when the industry was presided over by a rich and generous patron. This was Arthur Rank, who had made millions as a miller, producing the flour for much of Britain's rather awful bread, and then became infatuated with the glamour of films. "We would go to Mr Rank," Mr Launder recalled, "and tell him we have a story. He says, 'How much?' We tell him. He hands it over and that's that. We then go about our business." The miller's tale. Quite amusing really, in a British sort of way. ■

Laurie Lee

Laurie Lee, explorer of a lost rural England, died on May 13th 1997, aged 82

THE ENGLAND that Laurie Lee wrote about so evocatively no longer exists. Perhaps it never existed, except in his imagination. In "Cider with Rosie", his best-known book, there is, for example, a certain scrumpy haziness about this temptress of the haystacks, who "baptised me with her cidrous kisses". The Rosie of the book shyly identified herself after it became a bestseller. They were marvellous days, Rosie recalled, but she dismissed the idea that she and Laurie had been "sweethearts or anything". Neither had she drunk cider with him, or anyone else. "I suppose all writers exaggerate," she said. Still, admirers of Laurie Lee's writing have never been put off by mere realities. He thought of himself primarily as a poet. Facts should not get in the way of the words.

In his next memoir, "As I Walked Out One Midsummer Morning", Mr Lee is off to Spain. As in England, the roads are "innocent of oil and petrol" but, even better, there is an abundance of generous Rosies. Mr Lee started out with no Spanish other than the words for "May I have a glass of water, please?" But this, together with scraping a tune on his violin, seemingly provided for his needs. Merrie old England and funny foreigners: a reader was blissfully comfortable with Laurie Lee.

Artfully, though, he wove into his memoirs the exemplar of the lad from a humble background who made good. The Anglo-Saxon virtues of "hard work and necessary patience" saw him through. His father had two wives who between them produced 12 children,

eight of whom survived. Lee senior abandoned the crowded Cotswold cottage and ran away to London where he became a civil servant, sending home £1 a week. Laurie left school at 14 and took a number of undemanding jobs. Then he, too, left "the honeyed squalor of home" in the village where "everyone minded everybody else's business", and did not see it again for 20 years.

His poetry

Fame did not come quickly, and almost did not come at all. During the second world war Mr Lee wrote government pamphlets and helped to make propaganda films, and published several books of poems, which were well regarded at the time. Cyril Connolly, the most influential literary critic of his day, encouraged him. Mr Lee considered his poems his best work, but this view is not now widely shared. Nothing of his was thought by Philip Larkin to be worth including in his "Oxford Book of Twentieth Century Verse".

The publisher of "Cider with Rosie" in 1959 was at first reluctant to take it on, doubting that it would sell well, despite the blurb Mr Lee wrote for its dustjacket: "Should become a classic". Even the critics who gave it good reviews could not have predicted that it would sell more than 6m copies around the world (in America, rather less invitingly, as "The Edge of Day: A Boyhood in the West of England").

Here on offer was a lost rural world, but one that seemingly could still be reached by using the most primitive of transport, your legs. When Laurie Lee

had left his village he had walked to London. He walked through Spain and a dozen other countries. Every born-again walker owes something to Mr Lee. Not surprisingly, the rosie hue of his writing has been welcomed by the tourist industry, which thrives on nostalgia. "Cider with Rosie" made Slad, Laurie Lee's Cotswold village, world-famous. Mr Lee is among those, such as Hardy, Hemingway and the Brontës, who have established literary landmarks. After visiting Slad and popping into the Woolpack inn for a Rosie special, a Lee pilgrim might nip over to Almuñecar, a fishing village and the scene of an episode in his Spanish book, to look at the statue put up in his honour.

This remarkable achievement came from a modest oeuvre: mainly three bits of biography (the third was "A Moment of War", about his experiences in the Spanish civil war, when he fought briefly against the Franco forces) and his poems. Laurie Lee was not contrite about writing slowly (with a 4B pencil). Barbara Cartland and Compton Mackenzie had written hundreds of books which had been forgotten, he said. His few were remembered. Nevertheless, he took his success without fuss. The main gain, he said, was that he could now afford whisky.

After becoming famous, Mr Lee returned to Slad and bought the cottage of his childhood. But he kept a flat in London. It was hard to write in the country, he said. If it was a nice day you would lie in the long grass or some friends would arrive and you would go to the pub for a chat. "And that's the day gone." But although an urbanite by adoption, Mr Lee liked to have reassurance that the country, his country, awaited him when he needed it. He joined with other villagers of Slad to oppose, successfully, a proposal to build a housing development on a meadow near the village. In such places, he said, the young decayed, "imprisoned by videos and computer games". They did not have the feeling of community he had known. No, he did not think Rosie would have cared to curl up in front of the telly. ■

James Lees-Milne

James Lees-Milne, who saved the country house, died on December 28th 1997, aged 89

THE OLD houses of England, James Lees-Milne once wrote, meant for him "far more than human lives". In the 1930s, when Mr Lees-Milne began his mission of mercy to save what he could of "the England that mattered", the old houses were falling like a property Passchendaele. The owners could no longer afford to run their vast estates, many of which had been designed for feudal economies. Some owners seemed themselves in a state of decay. Mr Lees-Milne recalled going to a party at a stately home where the owner entertained his guests by slashing at paintings with a whip and shooting the heads off statues in the garden. He was appalled. It brought home to him how he cared for "the continuity of history". It was, he said, a turning point.

Mr Lees-Milne's task was to persuade the owners of great homes deemed worthy of preservation to give them to the National Trust, a body that had been set up in 1895 by Victorians anxious about the spread of industrialisation. Up to 1936, when Mr Lees-Milne joined the trust, it had mainly acquired endangered land. Now it was after property as well.

It was difficult to persuade an owner of a property that had been in his family since Elizabethan times to hand it over, for nothing. Assurances that the nation would be grateful did not carry much weight with a lord of all he surveyed. Mr Lees-Milne's main carrot in his negotiations was the promise that, when the owner died, his heirs would not have to pay the huge death duties that had crippled many families. The heirs could, in some cases, stay in residence in part of the property. A series of acts of Parliament made the scheme law.

This redistribution of property was seen by some as secret socialism, although not by the conservative-minded trust, and certainly not by Mr Lees-Milne. The trust is independent of government and is supported mainly by members' fees and legacies. All the same, the 11.7m people who in 1996 happily tramped around the trust's 263 houses, castles and other once-forbidden premises must have included a fair number of Mr Lees-Milne's despised "lower classes".

Jam on the sofa

James Lees-Milne's parents were Worcestershire "gentry", which made them, in class terms, just below nobility. He paints a picture of a slightly dotty household, with a father deeply suspicious of young James's interest in art. Calling anyone "artistic" denoted "decadence, disloyalty to the Crown and unnatural vice", he noted in his memoirs. Mr Lees-Milne was notoriously disloyal in his gossipy memoirs. The stories he tells of the then famous are amusing in a schoolboyish sort of way. Of Ivy Compton-Burnett, he noted that the writer "ate half a pot of raspberry jam, and I was shocked to see her surreptitiously wipe her sticky fingers upon the cover of my sofa". He favoured the exotic. He had stories of Robert Byron, another writer, swimming in the Bay of Naples while being fed with chocolates from a boat and of Rosamond Lehmann, yet another, at a seance, apparently talking with the dead.

Although he had a wide circle

he did as much as anyone to save the country house. Others took up the cause, but Mr Lees-Milne, single-minded in this at least, pushed it forward.

He had his critics. A book on the trust by an American, Paula Weisdeger, criticised the amateurism of Mr Lees-Milne. Some critics agreed with her. But, as she put it, "several of the old boys took to spitting at me, in print. How dare I, an American, etc?" America's National Trust for Historic Preservation tends to look forward as much as back, perhaps because there is not all that much back to look at. It has just waged a campaign against "sprawl development" in Vermont, an echo of the anxieties felt by the Victorian founders of the British trust. France's *Demeures Historiques*, old houses where the family stays on but allows visitors (usually reluctantly) to look around, are closer to the British idea envisaged by Mr Lees-Milne.

The vision has become fuzzy, perhaps inevitably. James Lees-Milne regretted that some National Trust houses where the families had moved out now had the appearance of museums, with souvenir shops. Wandering around the rooms decorated and arranged with "suave good taste", it was difficult to imagine that anyone had once actually lived there. Reaching for his most devastating barb, he said it was "just very faintly suburban". ■

of acquaintances and admirers, Mr Lees-Milne regarded himself as an outsider. He was not sure whether to be a Roman Catholic or an Anglican, and tried both creeds. Politically, he was as right as you could get: he supported the Franco cause in the Spanish civil war. As well as his memoirs, he wrote a lot about architecture, published three novels and wrote some poetry, which he showed to friends but was otherwise unpublished. Probably he would have liked to be remembered chiefly as a writer. But the fashionable enthusiasm for conservation has provided him with his pedestal: during 30 years with the National Trust, as an official and later an adviser;

Roy Lichtenstein

Roy Lichtenstein, who turned comics into art, died on September 29th 1997, aged 73

THE FIRST of Roy Lichtenstein's comic-book paintings were produced to please his children. Or so he said. But he also said on another occasion, "I wouldn't believe anything I tell you." He, in common with many artists, would have preferred not to have talked much about his work. The language was all in the painting. But when he became famous there were interviews to give. "So what started you into this comic-book theme, Mr Lichtenstein?" "It was my children." It might even have been true. At least the story offered a clue to a vast American middle-class audience eager to understand the new pop art so as to discuss it in a seemingly informed and sympathetic way.

Unlike the abstract impressionists who had preceded pop art, it was clear that Mr Lichtenstein could draw. Not for him the abstractionists' random brush-strokes and drips; he had a meticulous line and a careful use of colour. Before he became a pop artist, he had an oeuvre of representational painting that anyone could appreciate. He was an artist to respect. You could warm to him. He had fought in the war. Then, in 1965, *Life* magazine asked: "Is he the worst artist in America?" The question was not so much a provocation as confirmation that he had become the most famous artist in America.

His name was made in two tumultuous years: from a show in the Leo Castelli Gallery in New York in 1962 to his public epiphany by *Life* and others. Critics at the Castelli show were both approving and hostile. But everyone agreed that marrying comic images to fine art was sensational. He had started something. A genre was born. Every artist seemed to turn to pop. Andy Warhol tried to rival him with his paintings of tins of soup, but Mr Lichtenstein was the pioneer. He was able to give up his part-time teaching jobs. In the next three decades he never stopped experimenting in various media, including sculpture, and became rich as his work sold for increasing, and eventually astronomical, prices. But it was for his work in the 1960s that he has a place, of whatever size, in the history of art.

America vs France

For most Americans the news that Roy Lichtenstein had died this week came in a tribute by President Clinton. America has been both proud and defensive about the flowering of its art in the post-war years. New York, it was said, had replaced Paris as the innovative centre of the art world. Plucking up its courage, America sent to Paris and other European cities a number of exhibitions of its best and brightest, taking the precaution of secretly bribing some critics and other influential people to give them a good reception. But for all this care, masterminded, it is said, by the CIA, Paris has mostly given American art the raspberry.

The likes of Jackson Pollock and Mark Rothko are seen as unworthy successors to Matisse and Braque. And Marcel Duchamp and other Dadaists had elevated the banal objects of everyday life to art back in the 1920s. The French view is not shared elsewhere in Europe. Mr Lichtenstein, particularly, is liked for his sense of fun. Sometimes he has seemed to be mocking the era of art in which he had been so successful. His father, a property dealer, had told him stories of the peculiarities of the marketplace, and no market is more peculiar than art.

Mr Lichtenstein reflected that you could hang a rag on the wall of a gallery and it would be taken seriously as a work of art. He seemed to be lampooning his success with his picture captioned, "Why, Brad darling, this painting is a masterpiece! My, soon you'll have all of New York clamouring for your work."

He once said that his own work was too despicable to hang. Who would want to have in their living room a huge comic picture of a fighter pilot saying "Whaam!" (one of Roy Lichtenstein's most famous pieces)?

His technique was certainly not despicable. His art school training, followed by experience as a draughtsman, was evident in the precision of his work. He started with small pencil sketches which he enlarged on to canvas with a projector and then filled in the colours. He used stencils and other mechanical aids to help with the shapes. Assistants helped with the boring bits. These are the techniques of commercial artists who produce magazine covers and advertisements. In this sense Mr Lichtenstein was the most successful commercial artist who ever lived.

Mere workers at the coal-face, the artists who laboured away on the comic books that Mr Lichtenstein copied, did not think much of his paintings. In enlarging them, some claimed, they became static. Some threatened to sue him. Whatever the justice of their complaints, in fact Mr Lichtenstein did them a sort of favour. Comic books these days are often taken seriously, the subject of theses (or a sign of growing illiteracy). But this is to miss the point of Roy Lichtenstein's achievement. His was the idea. The art of today, he told an interviewer, is all around us. It is not Impressionist painting. "It's really McDonald's." Of course, you don't have to believe everything he said. ∎

Walter Lini

Walter Hadye Lini, a voice of the Pacific, died on February 21st 1999, aged 56

ONE OF Walter Lini's minor pleasures was to get the better of the French. His country, Vanuatu, was for 74 years jointly run by Britain and France. It might have been thought that there were enough islands in the South Pacific for the colonial powers to take their pick without getting in each other's way. But both the British and the French fancied the New Hebrides, as Vanuatu was then called, and refused to budge. The two European administrations ran separate legal, educational and security systems in an atmosphere of mutual dislike, which persisted after the country's independence in 1980.

Mr Lini's first betterment of the French was in securing independence at all. France was reluctant to pull out and after Britain insisted gave covert support to a rebellion led by French settlers. Mr Lini put down the rebels in a skirmish, which briefly, if grandly, was called the "coconut war" by foreign newspapers.

Mr Lini could not afford to hold grudges: about a third of the population of 170,000 spoke pidgin French (and numerous local languages). All the same, he was one of the strongest voices in the Pacific region against French nuclear testing in Mururoa and against colonialism. From time to time Mr Lini expelled a French ambassador, seemingly just to remind Paris that he was keeping an eye on its artful ways. The French still remain in New Caledonia, French Polynesia and a number of other islands, the last of the European colonialists in the Pacific, and seemingly unshiftable. But, partly as a result of public opinion led by

Mr Lini and others, they have stopped testing their nuclear weapons there. In Vanuatu (Our Land Eternally) Mr Lini sought to integrate the British and French communities on the 83 islands and their ways of doing things, a process that is still going on. Parliament is largely based on the British model. Among the better-off in the capital, Vila, French cuisine is generally preferred.

The tide of ideas

Along with Bibles and hymn-books Christian missionaries carried to the Pacific European ideas about culture, property and politics. God set them a daunting task: even now some islanders still believe in the cargo cult dating from the second world war when American soldiers distributed goodies with divine abandon. But the missionaries were undeterred. The island where Walter Lini was born is called Pentecost, commemorating the missionaries' landing on Whit Sunday. Young Walter was a keen Christian. He was educated at a missionary school and sent to New Zealand to study for the priesthood. He was ordained in 1970. He returned with ideas about nationalism and joined an independence-minded party supported by the Anglican church. (The French-speaking Roman Catholics had a political party with similar aims.) Walter Lini was the obvious choice to lead the independent state's first government.

Belonging to a world-wide religion helped Mr Lini to overcome the sense of remoteness felt by Pacific islanders. Unlike the strident (though at present muted) countries of the Pacific rim, the

Lonely they may be, but the island-states are among the world's most peaceful places. Nothing much happens there. Even their occasional troubles – Bougainville's rebellion, Fiji's military coup – seem mere frolics in a world of Kosovos and Iraqs. Under Mr Lini, Vanuatu became one of the most desirable tourist destinations in the South Pacific, rivalled perhaps only by Tahiti. Rich Australians, especially, have villas there and pop over for the weekend.

Walter Lini gave an impression of modest confidence. There were no guards, not even a policeman, at his official residence when the writer of this article visited him. Yes, he believed in material progress, but it should be unhurried.

island-states are lonely specks in the ocean with few natural resources. Mr Lini appreciated that copra and cocoa, plus a dollop of international aid, were not going to do much to raise living standards. He turned to the dodges of the capitalist world. Vanuatu became a tax haven and a place to register a flag of convenience. In the 1980s Vanuatu sold licences to Russian fishing boats to trawl in its waters and there was talk of Soviet warships using its ports. America, which regarded the Pacific as its private pond, seemed about to offer tempting counterproposals when, sadly for Vanuatu, the Soviet Union collapsed.

He favoured small government, and not just for a small country. Any medium-sized nation, he said, could be run efficiently by a political leader and half a dozen able civil servants. Perhaps because of such views, his critics called him a dictator. But when his party was defeated in a general election in 1991, he stood down after 11 years as prime minister. Subsequent governments have been coalitions of parties linked to both the French-speaking and English-speaking communities. He served them as justice minister. The French were not at all bad, he said, those that had ethnic roots in Vanuatu. ■

Joan Littlewood

Joan Maud Littlewood, a theatrical prodigy, died on September 20th 2002, aged 87

MENTION JOAN Littlewood and those that still remember her may murmur, "Oh! What a Lovely War" and perhaps hum a few notes of its theme tune. The play was first put on in 1963 and some 40 years later remains a powerful snub to the propaganda of war. It has had a worldwide audience. Not only was it seen in theatres in London, elsewhere in Europe and in the United States, but it was made into a film that reached the millions who never go to a theatre.

Its strength was that it was hugely entertaining, featuring the immensely tuneful songs of the first world war. But just as a nostalgic number was captivating its audience, a news flash would read, "Battle of the Somme ends. Casualties, 1,332,000. Gain, nil." The play spared no one, especially those in command. A British general prays, "Well, God, the prospects for a successful attack are now ideal ... And I ask for victory, oh Lord, before the Americans arrive." The anti-war feeling of the 1960s that Miss Littlewood captured has endured, and the task of the war propagandist has never been harder.

"How I loathed those songs," Miss Littlewood said. They recalled a childhood of "photos of dead soldiers in silver frames, medals in a forgotten drawer". But she also loathed the commercial success of the play, and of other plays she conceived and produced that went on to make heaps of money. Many ordinary mortals would be delighted that a production that started life in a tiny theatre had gone on to do well. But Miss Littlewood was not ordinary and to her admirers there was something a bit immortal about her as well.

It wasn't the money she objected to: for much of her life she was hard up, and many of the plays she produced were put on with little money. What she feared was that her work would be tainted by its connection with conventional theatre. She once said that Laurence Olivier was "the most stupid ham that ever conned people into taking him for an actor". She dismissed a young Michael Caine with her gravest insult: "You will only ever be a star." Noel Coward's "Private Lives" was the sort of play she couldn't stand. Understandably, many in conventional theatre didn't much care for her either.

Street theatre
At the start of her autobiography, "Joan's Book", Miss Littlewood describes a childhood of poverty in London and how at the age of six she was a bridesmaid when her mother finally married. But prodigies have a way of surviving unpromising beginnings. A church school and the local public library provided her with the rudiments of education. At 16 she won a free place to Britain's leading acting school, the Royal Academy of Dramatic Art. In 1934, when she was 20, she joined a company called Theatre of Action, founded by Ewan MacColl, a folk singer she later married. It performed in the streets of Manchester and was one of several dozen such troupes in the north of England.

They modelled themselves on German theatrical troupes which were parodying the recently-installed Nazi government, and whose members would soon be rounded up and sent to concentration camps. Miss Littlewood's plans for a "people's theatre" stem from this time. Bertold Brecht, a German dramatist, was one of her heroes. In *Oh! What a Lovely War* there are echoes of Brecht's *The Threepenny Opera*, of 1928, with its film clips and messages on cards. But revolution had to be put on hold during the second world war, when Miss Littlewood worked for the BBC, making a soap for transmission to American listeners called "Front Line Family". It was about "everyday people" and at the BBC "I was the only one who'd had contact with such glamorous creatures."

After the war, bursting with ideas and with a new husband, Gerry Raffles, nine years her junior, whom she had met when he was a teenager, Miss Littlewood once again set out to show ordinary people the magic of theatre. The trouble was, ordinary people were not much interested. "There was an audience for us somewhere, but where?" she said indignantly. In 1953 she and Raffles rented and later bought a once-graceful but now dilapidated theatre in Stratford, not on Avon but in rundown east London. Surely the locals would support the revival of one of their old playhouses, proudly called the Theatre Royal? They did not.

But her company did become famous abroad. It toured throughout Europe. Three plays the company did at a Paris festival in 1955 won rave reviews in French newspapers. The Stratford theatre was "discovered" by London critics and its seats were soon filled by middle-class people. They tolerated the classics, such as Ben Jonson's "Volpone", and loved musical productions such as "Fings Ain't Wot They Used T'Be". Several were transferred to theatres in central London.

When Gerry Raffles died in 1974, Miss Littlewood gave up most of her theatre work. He had in many ways been her wife, taking on the domestic tasks she had no time for. For much of the rest of her life she lived in France, near Vienne, where he is buried. Joan Littlewood shook up British theatre, but only briefly. Seeing a play remains mostly a middle-class pleasure. "Private Lives" was recently revived with great success. ∎

Christopher Lloyd

Christopher Lloyd, an iconoclastic English gardener, died on January 27th 2006, aged 84

VISITORS TO Great Dixter, an old, rambling, timber-framed house among the steep woods and pastures of the High Weald, on the borders of Kent and Sussex in the south of England, would find it haunted by several tutelary spirits. One, with pipe in mouth and owlish mien, was the shade of Sir Edwin Lutyens, who after 1910 laid out the gardens in what had been a cattle yard. Another, with pebble-spectacles, trug and boots, was the ghost of Gertrude Jekyll, whose principles of gardening first informed the place. And then – short, stout, moustachioed, and looking at first sight as though he might empty a blunderbuss on you as soon as invite you to tea – was Christopher Lloyd. If he was not there, his familiar spirits Yucca, Canna and Dahlia, short-tempered dachshunds, kept guard over the turf.

Save for short spells at Rugby School and Cambridge, Mr Lloyd lived at Great Dixter all his life. He learned gardening there, helping his mother prick out seedlings as a child, and found he never wanted to do anything else. In a country devoted to gardening, Mr Lloyd thus became its best plantsman. With his invaluable head gardener, Fergus Garrett, he stomped round his five-acre domain, ceaselessly experimenting with trees, shrubs and flowers. Each plant would be inspected twice daily, and each experiment recorded in a weatherproof notebook. The fruits of his observations became columns in *Country Life*, *Gardens Illustrated* and the *Guardian*, and were turned into more than 20 books.

"Christo", as everyone called him,

was a great believer in such discipline, which he said he had learnt from the Japanese. But it was only half his philosophy, and not even the more important half. His strongest belief was in freedom and fun. He advised gardeners to plant what they liked, throw out what they didn't, discard all previous notions of colour, arrangement and taste, put up two fingers to horticultural rectitude and "Go for it".

In the staid, quiet world of English gardening, this was dynamite. Not so far from Great Dixter, at Sissinghurst Castle, lay the epitome of English taste in Vita Sackville-West's White Garden, surrounded by equally soothing beddings in blue, lilac and mauve. Mr Lloyd waved it aside. What about "Challenging Orange" or "Nothing to Fear Red"? What about a great big bush of mauve-pink *Daphne mezereum* underplanted with a carpet of *Crocus x luteus*, in bright orange-yellow? "The two colours may be shouting at each other," he wrote, "but they are shouting for joy."

Mr Lloyd believed in mixing up plants that had never been together before. His ambition was a closely-woven tapestry of colours and textures in which foliage – matt or shiny, grey or variegated, grass or coniferous – was as important as the flowers. In the borders at Great Dixter banana trees grew with verbena, and spiky agave with dahlias. Climbers, annuals, perennials and shrubs all clambered about, "helping each other", as Mr Lloyd liked to say, with their sheer differences of habit. His borders were a paean to desegregation. When he showed slides of them at his

lectures, audiences would sometimes gasp with horror.

His iconoclasm went beyond colour and arrangement. He believed that plants should go their own way in gardens. If a yellow spike of mullein decided to grow in a clump of bright pink phlox, he welcomed it. ("Hurrah for vulgarity!", as he wrote once.) He was delighted that lichens made patterns on his York stone paths, and that wild birds-foot trefoil colonised the Sunken Garden. These gave him ideas.

Two small lawns at the front of the house were always left unmown until the autumn. Mr Lloyd wanted orchids and fritillaries to grow there, but also hoped to enjoy the wind and light in the grass. Once he allowed a rambler rose to get so out of hand that it killed two holm oaks and made a gap in a hedge; but Mr Lloyd so liked what he saw through the gap, the twisted trunk of a crab-apple tree framed in ilex leaves, that he made a feature of it, underplanting the crab for good measure with bright yellow *Epimedium pinnatum*.

Certain flowers he loved especially. He would brake violently for poppies

seen at the roadside, and gloried in lupins and clematis. Hydrangeas, on the other hand, were "anaemic" and most salvias "rubbish". Roses and lavender he had little luck with; his clay soil was too heavy. He had a special fondness for the white Japanese anemones that backed, calmly and blankly, the psychedelic annuals he tried out in his beds.

His greatest appreciation, however, was for the hedges and trees that gave architectural structure to his garden, and held its history. The winding yew hedges at Great Dixter had been planted by his father, who had bought the house with his printing fortune. For Mr Lloyd they had "a presence", seeming to inhabit his garden rather than grow there. He treasured the fig trees introduced by Lutyens – their huge leaves so useful in his plantings – and the few pear trees left from the original farm orchard. On the western boundary stood a line of ash trees that he wished, in dictatorial moods, to cut down, because they filled his garden with seeds. But then freedom and joy prevailed: there was nothing quite like a sunset seen through their faint feathered leaves. ∎

Ronald Lockley

Ronald Mathias Lockley, a protector of nature, died on April 12th 2000, aged 96

THE DANGER of writing about Ronald Lockley is of presenting, probably unfairly, a portrait of an oddity. He believed he had a gift of communicating with animals. Writing in *The Economist* in 1979, an exasperated reviewer of one of Mr Lockley's books said he "should have kept off imaginary conversations with dying killer whales". But the old whale Mr Lockley befriended did have some strong points to make about polluted oceans. And if it was odd to talk with whales, and indeed with many other creatures, it was an affliction that Mr Lockley shared with Aristotle and Plutarch, to drop a name or two.

Anyway, Mr Lockley had pretty convincing proof that giving human characteristics to animals was fairly widespread. In 1964 he had published "The Private Life of the Rabbit". This study of the habits of the wild rabbit gathered by Mr Lockley persuaded Richard Adams to write "Watership Down", a kind of Disney story for adults, which became an immediate bestseller. Anthropomorphism, as it is bleakly known, was decreed to be free of health risks.

The two men became friends and went on an expedition together to the Antarctic. "I can't recollect that we ever had a disagreement," Mr Adams said last week. However, "Watership Down", which gave rabbits human characteristics and humanlike problems, was far removed from Mr Lockley's view of the animal world. "Watership Down" is a novel, a thriller set in the mean streets of the warren, requiring considerable suspension of belief. Mr

Lockley's request was more subtle: for a suspension of hostility by man towards nature. Like humans, he said, other creatures had "a measure of reasoning and individual action". A lecture Mr Lockley gave from time to time was entitled "The seabird as an individual". One of his books (he wrote about 40) was "Man against Nature", in which he chronicled the destruction of animals and plants in Australia and elsewhere in the South Pacific.

His dream island

Ronald Lockley felt most comfortable on an island. In 1927, when he was 24, he rented Skokholm, a small deserted island off Wales. It had few material comforts. The reason it was deserted was because the previous inhabitants could no longer stand the battering of Atlantic gales and the loneliness. Even fishing was hazardous off the rocky coast. But Mr Lockley and his wife repaired a farmhouse, using timber from a wrecked schooner, and coal from her cargo to keep warm. Fresh water was mostly provided by the relentless rain. Before coming to the island he had worked on a small farm, and was used to improvising.

He studied the real owners of the island, the seabirds, and wrote books about them. One was called "Dream Island". In 1933 he founded Britain's first bird observatory on the island, where migrating birds were trapped, ringed and released. Skokholm, and Mr Lockley, became mildly famous. Scientists arrived to peer at the shearwaters and puffins. A film was made about the life of the gannet and won an Oscar as

the year's best documentary. Princess Elizabeth, later to become the queen, thought she would like a pet razorbill. Mr Lockley brought one to Buckingham Palace, and on television was seen being attacked as he opened its basket. The king of Bulgaria turned up at the island, accompanied by a servant who carried a chair in case of royal exhaustion.

Mr Lockley inhabited his dream island until the second world war when he joined the navy and thought up ways to track submarines. After the war he bought a house on the mainland of Wales, where he did his study of wild rabbits. The problem was to get close to them. There had been rabbits on Skokholm, but they had resolutely kept their distance. Mr Lockley's solution was to fit glass panels to a warren, and for four years he studied such matters as overcrowding, the effects of myxomatosis and how the males defended the warren against stoats.

He thought he would like to live on an island again. But not Skokholm or any Welsh islands. Wales, where he was born, was, he judged, no longer protecting its environment. He tried to stop an oil refinery being built in western Wales, was unsuccessful, and that was that. He visited many islands that seemed interesting, from the Kuriles to French Polynesia. He settled in New Zealand. The country is overrun with rabbits, and the New Zealanders hopefully asked Mr Lockley if he could advise them how to get rid of the pests quickly. He could not. Rabbit-killing viruses were cruel and did not work, he said. Try to control the rabbits by traditional methods and be patient, he said.

Most New Zealanders are happy to be impatient and like to think that they are as modern as tomorrow, but outsiders insist that they are not, and that is their charm. Mr Lockley said that New Zealand was the last place of any size to be colonised by humans, and it was still in the happy position of having to catch up. "Go slow, New Zealand, go slow," Mr Lockley told his adopted country. It won't, not willingly. But New Zealanders liked Ronald Lockley, admired his reputation as a protector of nature, and would never laugh at him just because he talked to whales. ∎

Bernard Loiseau

Bernard Daniel Jacques Loiseau, a French chef, died on February 24th 2003, aged 52

DRIVING FROM Paris to Bernard Loiseau's restaurant, La Côte d'Or, in the Burgundy village of Saulieu, took about three hours, assuming no hold-ups. If it seemed a long way to go for a meal, the reward at the end was nothing as ordinary as the mere appeasement of hunger; it was to experience, Mr Loiseau said, "an explosion of taste in the mouth". His sauces were said to be among the finest in France, which for many serious eaters meant in the world.

France is fiercely proud of its restaurant and hotel industry. Bernard Loiseau's name "evokes all the perfection of the culinary art and the art of living", said France's culture minister. When he was president, François Mitterrand pinned the *légion d'honneur* on the overalls of Mr Loiseau, having first personally confirmed the quality of the chef's frog's legs in parsley juice and garlic purée.

As important to Mr Loiseau was being given a top rating of three stars by the Michelin guide, which has a reputation for honesty rare in the catering business. In Britain and the United States many guides carry reviews of restaurants and hotels that they pay for, while newspaper critics tend to be known among restaurateurs, who take care not to poison them. But Michelin, also a tyre manufacturer (19% of the world market), solemnly guards its godlike reputation as the bible of the catering business. The company insists that its 100 or so inspectors remain anonymous and that they are primarily interested in "what is on the plate".

Not long ago, according to a member of Mr Loiseau's staff, he anxiously asked Michelin if his restaurant was likely to keep his three stars. God declined to say but kindly advised him to "be careful and stay in your kitchen and don't do too much business". The restaurant kept its stars in the latest guide, but another French guide, GaultMillau, reduced its rating and has been blamed by some of Mr Loiseau's colleagues for driving him to suicide.

That is speculation, but what Mr Loiseau's sad death has made clear is that staying at the top in the restaurant business is cruelly demanding. "There is suffering and fatigue behind the façade," said a fellow chef.

Star struck

Bernard Loiseau's restaurant had started out as a coaching inn in the 19th century. In the 1930s under Alexandre Dumaine it became one of the best-known restaurants in France, gaining three Michelin stars, all of which were lost when he retired. Mr Loiseau arrived at the now rundown restaurant in Saulieu in 1975, aged 24, "with nothing but my toothbrush", having worked in various restaurant kitchens since he was a boy. To begin with he provided meals based on what Dumaine had called "the honest elements of French peasant cuisine". But he was drawn to *nouvelle cuisine*, favoured by GaultMillau (which may have made its recent criticism hard for him to take). He devised the sauces that helped to make him famous that were lighter than those made with butter and cream. Mr Loiseau's weightier customers were especially appreciative. In 1977 his restaurant gained its first Michelin star with Mr Loiseau as chef, in 1981 a second and in 1991 a third, putting him among the 20 or so top chefs in France.

By then Mr Loiseau had become the owner of La Côte d'Or and set about an ambitious transformation of what had been a fairly modest establishment, adding hotel suites, a pool and private dining rooms, and expanding his kitchen. At the end of a meal Mr Loiseau's guests could recall the pleasures of the tummy while strolling in an English-style garden. Before they left they were encouraged to browse in the restaurant shop, where food, wines, kitchen equipment and books of Mr Loiseau's recipes were on sale. At the time Mr Loiseau was said to have borrowed $5m to pay for the work.

He expanded further, buying three bistros in Paris. He licensed his name to mass-market frozen foods. He was, he said, like Yves Saint-Laurent: "I do both high fashion and ready-to-wear." He became a familiar face on television and on magazine covers. His culinary business traded on the French stock exchange, and its price has been sinking in line with other luxury businesses.

Was Mr Loiseau, so meticulous in the kitchen, an innocent at business? He told a reporter in 1997 that La Côte d'Or had to be full every night, in the restaurant and the hotel, to make any money. Since then luxury businesses have been hit by tighter purses. The current slanging match between America and France may raise a smile when French fries are renamed freedom fries. But it becomes serious when the American tourists who packed a Michelin guide in their luggage are less inclined to visit a country opposed to their government's policy on Iraq.

Yet to remain desirable, a top restaurant dare not be seen to economise. A Paris restaurateur remarked recently that his high fixed costs of maintaining an appealing establishment with a large staff meant that every customer costs him $70 before he eats or drinks anything. No wonder Mr Loiseau was worried about the possibility of losing one of his precious stars, and a consequent drop in custom. Stick to your kitchen, Michelin had told him. It wasn't bad advice. ∎

Cardinal Lustiger

Aaron Jean-Marie Lustiger, cardinal and archbishop, died on August 5th 2007, aged 80

AT THE funeral of Jean-Marie Lustiger, at Notre Dame de Paris on August 10th, his second cousin Jonas Moses-Lustiger read a psalm in Hebrew and placed on the coffin a jar of earth that had been gathered on the Mount of Olives. Then another cousin, Arno Lustiger, bent over the coffin to recite Kaddish. Only when those things were done was the body of Cardinal Lustiger carried inside the cathedral, where Catholic panoply took over.

There was no question of mixing the rites; the cardinal, said his staff, would not have liked that. Yet they were mixed in himself. He was a Jew by birth, instinct, emotion and devotion; he was a Catholic by conversion and conviction. He cracked Jewish jokes, and put on a suit and *kippa* to go to synagogue, although the evening would find him in his soutane again. For him, Christianity was simply the fruit of Judaism; his first religion came to completion in his second. Christ, in his eyes, was the Messiah of Israel, his cross worthy of a yellow star. And since the mission of Israel was "to bring light to the *goyim*", preaching the gospel became his own *mitzvah*.

The theology was complicated, despite the jut-jawed charm and aquiline intensity with which it was expressed. Many on both sides did not understand it. The Ashkenazi chief rabbi of Israel called Cardinal Lustiger a betrayer of his people; the *Jerusalem Post* denounced him as an apostate. On the Catholic side, arch-conservatives lamented that their archbishop was not "truly of French origin".

In one sense, this was correct. His father and mother were Polish-Jewish immigrants, keeping a hat-and-drapery shop in Montparnasse, in Paris. The young Aaron had been protected from Christianity, kept inside during Christian festivals and made aware that his grandfather had been a Yiddish-speaking rabbi in Silesia. But he had found a New Testament at his piano teacher's and discovered, as he read it, that he seemed to know this story already.

The moment of conversion came at 14, in Orléans, where his family had taken sporadic shelter in a Catholic household during the war. On Holy Thursday he stole into Orléans cathedral to find it blazing with candles and flowers. The next day, Good Friday, he found the church stripped as a sign of desolation. Christ's presence, followed by Christ's absence, impressed him so deeply that he asked to be baptised. Explaining to his parents was "unbearably painful"; outraged, they called in a rabbi, but the rabbi seemed to think their boy was either deluded, or sensible. Fourteen years later he was ordained a priest.

The future cardinal was convinced, even then, that he had not abandoned one iota of his Jewishness. To say he had, he once explained, "is like denying my father and mother, my grandfathers and grandmothers". He had kept the name Aaron as his first name at baptism, only adding Christian ones. At the same time, those who thought this a conversion of convenience, to save his hide, were wrong. He had not wanted to save his hide. Like most

survivors, he constantly mourned the members of his family who had died in the camps, especially his mother, who was transported to Auschwitz in 1942. He would say Kaddish for her on her death day, and on his first visit to Auschwitz, in 1983, he slipped away to kneel in the grass among the barracks, in his archiepiscopal robes with his scarlet skull-cap, and cry.

Motorbike and bulldozer

Possibly because that wound had never healed, possibly because melancholy kept dogging him, he pursued his career as a priest with a wild, frenetic energy. As a chaplain in the Paris universities, a post he held from 1954–69, "Lulu" was remembered in sharp black corduroys and black loafers, tearing round the Latin Quarter on a motorbike. As Archbishop of Paris, in 1984, he led a demonstration of a million people to protest against François Mitterrand's attempt to secularise Catholic schools. He set up Radio Notre Dame and a Catholic TV station; in his 70s, in 1997 and 2000, he organised joyous World Youth Days in Paris and in Rome. Fervent for evangelisation, "the Bulldozer" gingered up all his 106 parishes in Paris, summarily shifted clergy who failed to perform, and founded his own seminary, which eventually provided about 15% of the city's priests.

Though a new broom and a gale of fresh air, unafraid to shout "Merde!" if a crucifix fell over, he was intellectually conservative. Most of the world's wrongs, including fascism, communism and anti-Semitism, he traced to the Enlightenment and the cult of reason. Relativism and the collapse of moral values he blamed on the student riots of 1968, "this bedlam", in which he had refused to take the students' side. All his instincts and emotions, as well as his Polish background, endeared him to John Paul II, and it was under the mantle of that friendship that he rose first to bishop of Orléans, then to archbishop, and finally to cardinal, all within five years.

But he never forgot. He taught himself Hebrew in readiness for his *aliyah*, or formal return to Israel. Every detail of his funeral, with its two rites, he carefully arranged himself. Then he wrote his epitaph:

I was born Jewish. I received the name of my paternal grandfather, Aaron. Having become Christian by faith and baptism, I have remained Jewish. As did the Apostles. ■

Lillian Lux

Lillian Lux, star of the Yiddish theatre, died on June 11th 2005, aged 86

FOR HOMESICK Jewish immigrants in New York in the early decades of the 20th century, there were few better places than the theatre. There, in a small closed space, in the dark, they could recreate the neurotic, loving, oppressive atmosphere of the *shtetlekh* they had left behind. In that world, lost in the steppes of Russia or the forests of Poland, the fathers were tragic and the mothers scheming; the daughters were pretty and dangerously marriageable; their suitors were Talmudic scholars; and after an hour or so of singing, dancing and fallings-out, it would all end in hugs and tears under the wedding-canopy.

The Lower East Side once boasted 14 Yiddish theatres, with five on Second Avenue alone. They boasted a huge repertory of plays and operettas both classical and folkloric, but the folk plays were the most popular. Lillian Lux made her name with almost continuous performances, from the 1940s onwards, of "A Khasene in Shtetl" ("A Village Wedding"), in which she played the bride. Her husband, Pesach'ke Burstein, played opposite her. Burstein, 22 years her senior, was a Second Avenue matinee idol, able not only to foot it like Fred Astaire in a top hat and tails and to sing Al Jolson's "Sonny Boy" (in Yiddish), but also to whistle like a bird. Whistling, like *klezmer* music, was a *shtetl* thing to do.

Ms Lux and Burstein had met in 1938, when Ms Lux, trained since the age of six at the Yiddish Art Theatre, auditioned for Burstein's tour of Latin America. A *shtetl* scene followed, while her parents appraised whether he was good enough for her; he was, she went, and they were married in Montevideo. Just before the war the couple also toured the remaining, increasingly terrorised, Jewish enclaves in Poland. (Yiddish theatre had always been itinerant, and Burstein had in fact run away with a Polish troupe when he was 15, destroying his family's dreams of the rabbinate for him.) On this occasion, the Bursteins were lucky to catch the last ship out.

Ms Lux wrote plays and operettas for them and, when her twins were born, they eventually joined the act too. It became "The Four Bursteins". They played Second Avenue and, in summer, did the rounds of resorts in the Catskills where middle-class Jews took their holidays. Increasingly, though – tracking the scattered remnants of European Jewry – they went abroad. Ms Lux took to the boards in Buenos Aires, Johannesburg, Melbourne, Tel Aviv and any number of small towns en route. Wherever there were Yiddish-speakers, and memories of the *shtetl* longing to be resurrected, she would play the crucial, central role of the blushing village bride. Her blonde hair, only so slightly aided by the peroxide bottle, earned her the name of "the Jewish *shiksa*".

There was little glamour in these journeys. The family went mostly by bus, their costumes and props stuffed into suitcases, seeking the next little pocket of *Yiddishkeit* in exile. They stayed in cheap hotels. Ms Lux made her children perform even when they had the measles, just as she had performed, when pregnant, under heavy disguise of ostrich feathers. Her daughter found

in the early 1950s. Zionist hooligans broke the theatre windows, and the government imposed a special tax on their show, because it was in Yiddish and not in Hebrew, the proper language of the new state.

A need for roots

Ms Lux's devotion to her enterprise was complete. Travelling and performing were the only life she wanted. Even her children's bar- and bat-mitzvahs were staged as ticket-only events. When, as teenagers, they both left the act, she felt betrayed. Why, she asked, did they want to destroy her livelihood? One reason was that both could see that Yiddish, and its theatre, was a dead end. Another was the feeling that they had missed out on family life.

many of the audiences frightening: camp survivors, disfigured, with numbers tattooed on their arms. On one bus trip in Europe they visited a camp, looking at the gas chambers. It was said that people had sometimes gone to their deaths singing tunes from "A Khasene in Shtetl".

Their audiences, however, were fading away. By the 1950s, Jews in America and elsewhere had largely assimilated. The theatres on Second Avenue emptied, then closed; by the 1990s, only one was left. In the Catskills, the very old crept around the shells of the hotels where Ms Lux, a pretty chorus-girl, had once danced opposite Danny Kaye.

Many Jews, in any case, had always found Yiddish theatre vulgar and the language an embarrassing hybrid. This had been made shockingly obvious when the Four Bursteins toured Israel

Night after night, they had sung and danced as an ideal family troupe. But their way of life had guaranteed no neighbours and few friends. They had always moved on too fast to put down roots. Finding the perfect boyfriend or girlfriend was impossible. They had hardly known the rhythm even of regular meals. It was all quite unlike the close, settled, *shtetl* world of Ms Lux's operettas and the Yiddish stage.

She herself, however, did not seem to mind the discrepancy. Well into her 80s, she continued to perform. She was engaged in the business of evoking deep memories of a vanished home: so engaged, it was no wonder she did not have time to make a home herself. ∎

Maharishi Mahesh Yogi

Maharishi Mahesh Yogi, guru and tycoon, died on February 5th 2008, aged 91 (probably)

VISITORS ENTERING the World Bank in Washington one sweaty day in 1987 might have been surprised to come upon a team of smiling young men, legs neatly folded into the lotus position, hopping like frogs. In fact, most visitors were probably not surprised at all. Like many happenings connected with Maharishi Mahesh Yogi, this display of "yogic flying" had been well advertised. The only surprise was that the bank, usually cast as a bastion of hard-headed rationality, should provide such a ready audience for an event whose aim was not physical fitness but world peace.

Thirty years earlier the maharishi, who had studied maths and physics at Allahabad University, had calculated that one person practising the transcendental meditation he promoted could induce virtuous behaviour among 99 non-meditators. He had already, in 1944, helped to get 2,000 Vedic pandits, learned followers of one of the four holy books of the Hindus, to chant mantras in an effort to bring the second world war to an end. He had again assembled meditators in 1962 to solve the Cuban missile crisis. But his ambitions were bigger – world peace, no less – and by the 1980s he had come to realise that to bring harmony to a world of 5 billion people, he would need 50m meditators.

Undaunted, he did the arithmetic again, this time factoring in meditation of deep purity and concentration (including yogic flying), and happily found he needed a number no greater than the square root of 1% – a mere 7,000 or so. Accordingly, 7,000 flyers were assembled during the Taste of Utopia conference in Fairfield, Iowa, in 1984. Annoyingly, though, the "wide range of positive effects worldwide" ended with the conference. Something similar happened after 7,000 students gathered for yogic flying and Vedic chanting near Delhi in 1988. The Berlin Wall came down all right and the cold war ended, but the money needed to keep the group airborne ran out and, dammit, "new tensions" started to arise in the world.

If only the maharishi had had the necessary funds. Actually, he had. He may not have known how to make peace, but he certainly knew how to make money. After years studying under a Hindu divine in the late 1950s, he had pronounced himself a maharishi (great seer) and set up the Spiritual Regeneration Movement. This took transcendental meditation, which he had trademarked, to the world, with Hollywood one of the first stops. Disciples paid $2,500 for a five-day course, learning how to reach a "deeper level" of consciousness by inwardly repeating a mantra twice a day for 20 minutes.

Real fame came when the Beatles beat a path to his door, seeking enlightenment and spirituality through good vibrations. George Harrison had already fallen under the spell of the sitar and the maharishi's message appealed to John Lennon's angry pacifism. Before long the Fab Four were ensconced in the maharishi's ashram in the foothills of the Himalayas. Their stay was only a modified success, though, with Lennon and Ringo Starr complaining about the food, and all of them,

perhaps, beginning to resent their host's transcendental interest in using them for publicity, if not an outright percentage of their earnings.

No matter. Plenty of others were ready to step forward for a dose of spiritual bliss, and not all were celebrities. In America meditation was judged to be just the tonic for a variety of people ranging from underperforming executives to recidivist prisoners. An army general even joined the board of Maharishi International University, set up in Fairfield in 1974. All in all, some 5m people are said to have been taught the maharishi's techniques since 1955.

His other ventures blossomed, too. A property empire was valued at over $3 billion ten years ago. A television station offered meditation courses to subscribers in 144 countries. Companies sold unguents, books, videos and Ayurvedic treatment. His political movement, the Natural Law Party, which in the 1990s pursued the goal of world government by fighting elections in America, Britain and several other countries, was less successful, and eventually folded. This, however, did not stop the maharishi then launching the raam, a global currency intended to foster development.

Imagine (all the things he didn't do)

Crank? Crackpot? Charlatan? Maybe all three. Yet the maharishi was generally benign. He did not use his money for sinister ends. He neither drank, nor smoked, nor took drugs. Indeed, he is credited with weaning the Beatles off dope (for a while). He did not accumulate scores of Rolls-Royces, like Bhagwan Shree Rajneesh; his biggest self-indulgence was a helicopter. Nor was he ever accused of molesting choirboys; his greatest sexual impropriety, it was said, was to make a pass at Mia Farrow. He giggled a lot, and plainly had no lack of self-esteem. But his egotism did not mean he was always wringing his hands at pop concerts or blethering at Davos; after the 1960s he seldom appeared in public.

Moreover, his message was entirely laudable. He did not promote a cult or even a mainstream religion preaching original sin, purgatory and the likelihood of eternal damnation. He just wanted to end poverty, teach people how to achieve personal fulfilment and help them to discover "Heaven on Earth in this generation". And yogic flying, of course. ■

Norman Mailer

Norman Mailer, pugilist of American letters, died on November 10th 2007, aged 84

IT WAS on the Dick Cavett show in 1971 that Mailer (always "Mailer" in his writings; "Mister" was needless polish and priming), three-tumblers drunk, angry, little eyes blue as a touchpaper, was needled by Gore Vidal into saying this:

> In Hemingway's time there were great writers ... Our time has been much more complicated and there hasn't been that many really extraordinary writers around, and I have presumed with all my extraordinary arrogance and loutishness and crudeness to step forth and say, "I'm going to be the champ until one of you knocks me off." Well, fine, but, you know, they don't knock you off because they're too damned simply yellow, and they kick me in the nuts, and I don't like it.

He had only half got going, but then the commercial came in. Much more could have been said. How Mailer had written what George Orwell called the best-ever book about the second world war, "The Naked and the Dead". How he had won a Pulitzer for "The Armies of the Night", the story of the 1968 anti-war march on the Pentagon, and every other book prize going except the Nobel. How, despite the critical bile spewed over much of his fiction, he still had germinating in him the Great American Novel that would out-Tolstoy Tolstoy and out-Dickens Dickens. How he had invented, with a nod to Truman Capote, the non-fiction novel and the novelised news report, through both of which strolled his best character, Mailer, with his crinkly electrified hair and his maudlin writer's hang-ups, continually "in an intimate dialogue, a veritable dialectic with the swoops, spooks, starts, the masks and snarls, the calm lucid abilities of sin ... his tonic, his jailer, his horse, his sword".

Mailer was brave. That was his virtue of virtues. In the 1950s he disdained "the stench of fear that has come out of every pore of American life ... a collective failure of nerve". He smelled fear in the dark, rotting jungle mud where he had fought as a soldier in the Philippines, in the blood, shit and slobber of the Chicago stockyards, but also at Washington parties, among his own stupid bouts of tongue-tiedness and circumlocution, as "the hard gemlike flame of bourbon" burned through him. At such points he would be rescued by the wild man Mailer, a creature "who would have been admirable, except that he was an absolute egomaniac, a Beast".

Gristle and gravel

He talked and wrote of fighting more than he did it. Short and stocky, he was liable to be upended pretty fast. But he boxed a bit, and proudly jogged once with Muhammad Ali until his breath gave out. Instinctively, he put up his fists. In 1957, in an essay called "The White Negro", he recommended that white Americans should live like inner-city blacks, hip and cool as cats on the edge of violence, rather than fall into the deadness of post-war conformity.

The shock tactics sometimes misfired badly. He stuck a kitchen knife (or a pair of scissors, or a "three-inch dirty penknife") into the neck of his second wife, the second of six, all of whom loved and forgave him as long as their alimony was paid. He acted as literary

sponsor to a talented murderer, Jack Abbott, who murdered again when Mailer had helped to get him out of jail. He revelled in gross, boastful or mechanical descriptions of sex ("a hard punishing session with pulley weights, stationary bicycle and ten breath-seared laps round the track"), not least because this outraged the women's libbers with whom, in the 1970s, he was permanently at war. Once Mailer, with a sparkle in his eye that was maybe aggression, maybe fun, acting his usual part of the hollering Jewish leprechaun, proclaimed that all women should be locked in cages.

On form (as in "Miami and the Siege of Chicago", about the 1968 political conventions, or "Of a Fire on the Moon", about the first moon landing) he was a gloriously evocative, generous, sprawling writer, worthy of the scale of his country and his subjects. But Mailer dismissed these books as journalism, that ceaseless scavenging for "tidbits, gristle, gravel, garbage cans, charlotte russe, old rubber tyres, T-bone steaks" that went to feed "that old American goat, our newspapers". Despite his founder-role on the radical *Village Voice*, he took little

pride in that craft. The Great Novel was his quest: a quest that became weirder and more abstruse over time, taking him to Pharaoic Egypt and the corridors of the CIA and inserting Mailer (sometimes the very Son of God, sometimes the Devil) into the made-up lives of Jesus and Hitler.

By general consent, though not by Mailer's, his best book was "The Executioner's Song" of 1979. It won him his second Pulitzer. In it he told the story of Gary Gilmore, the first man to be executed after the ending of the moratorium on the death penalty, in sentences as spare and unadorned as the Utah desert in which it was set. The style was almost reminiscent of his great hero, Hemingway. Those short, declarative sentences, he wrote once, had a suicide's dread in their silences: dread that "at any instant, by any failure in magic, by a mean defeat, or by a moment of cowardice, Hemingway could be thrust back again into the agonising demands of his courage." Mailer's short sentences carried a more pugnacious message: he was the champ, and would be until someone braver and better knocked him off. ∎

Tommy Makem

Tommy Makem, an Irish folk-singer, died on August 1st 2007, aged 74

IT ALL began in the kitchen of a house in Keady, County Armagh, in Northern Ireland, where Tommy Makem's mother Sarah, as she stirred a pan on the hob or filled the kettle, would sing of morning dew and magpies' nests, Barney Mavourneen and Mary of Kilmore, ships and red roses:

> Red is the rose that in yonder garden grows
> Fair is the lily of the valley
> Clear is the water that flows from the Boyne
> But my love is fairer than any.

Mrs Green from along the street would join in too, until the house became a regular ceilidh at times and collectors would come, even from America, to write the songs down. Tommy said he could sing before he could speak; and not long after he could play piccolo, fiddle, tin whistle and the five-string banjo. He would stand up in the church hall, no taller than a chair,

and sing "The Little Beggarman":

> I am a little beggarman, a begging I have been
> For three score years in this little isle of green.

Music and tales filled not only his home but the rolling fields and hills of South Armagh itself. The heart of Ireland seemed to beat there beneath Slieve Gullion, the mystical mountain where the hero Cuchullain had learned his warrior skills and where the hunter Finn MacCumhail, bewitched and curious, had tracked a white doe to the summit. Tommy Makem picked up those legends too and, in 1955, took them to America, together with his bagpipes and a suitcase patched up with tape.

In an Aran sweater
He meant to work in a cotton mill and do a bit of acting, but one St Patrick's night he was paid $30 for singing two

songs in a club: "and I thought, by God, this is the land all right. Gold growing in the streets." By 1958 he had teamed up with his friend Liam Clancy and Liam's brothers Paddy and Tom, who had come from Tipperary to America before him, and the gold continued to accrue. The Clancy Brothers and Tommy Makem, all kitted out in Aran sweaters knitted by Mrs Clancy, triumphantly rode the wave of a folk revival that was turning Pete Seeger and Woody Guthrie into stars. Adapting to the new world, they added tin whistle and banjo to the old songs and quickened the pace, because, as Tommy said, "The heartbeat of America is so much faster than the old country." They did "The Morning Show" and "The Tonight Show", Ed Sullivan and Carnegie Hall, landed a $100,000 contract with Columbia and ended up singing "We Want no Irish Here" in front of Jack Kennedy at the White House, while Kennedy flashed his white teeth and rocked with laughter.

Tommy Makem was always the key man, with a baritone sweet as buttermilk or sharp as salt, nipping effortlessly over his "hi the dithery idle lum, dithery oodle idle loos" and his "roo run rye, fa the diddle dye, hey the O the diddle derry Os". And for a lifelong teetotaller no man had more feeling when he sang of hoppy beer or dark-frothing porter or devilish golden whiskey, or almost anything at all served up in a jug in a bar:

When I am in my grave and dead
And all my sorrows are past and fled
Transport me then into a fish
And let me swim in a jug of this.

The songs he wrote himself he dismissed as "garbage altogether", never to be compared to the old words and melodies he wanted to preserve in live performance. But a few he was proud of, and none more so than "Four Green Fields", in which "a fine old woman" – Ireland – sang of her fourth field, Ulster, that was still "in bondage/ In strangers' hands, that tried to take it from me". In America his audiences, largely third-generation Irish of the diaspora, would weep and sing along until, according to the *New York Times* man, they were "ready to go out and die for Ireland".

All told, Tommy Makem's choice of songs was fervently nationalistic: children's rhymes about "King Billy", or rebel songs such as "The Wind that Shakes the Barley", in which the hero's sweetheart is killed, as they caress in a glen, by a British bullet. And most stirring of all, in a voice with an edge like a knife, he would sing "The Patriot Game":

Come all you young rebels, and list while I
    sing,
For the love of one's country is a terrible
    thing.
It banishes fear with the speed of a flame,
And it makes us all part of the patriot game.

Bob Dylan adapted this for his great anti-war song "With God on Our Side". But Tommy Makem tried always to separate his love of country from the horrors of sectarianism. As Northern Ireland slid into the Troubles after 1969, he kept away from politics – a task made somewhat easier by staying in America, where he went on singing to the end of his days. In the dark low-ceilinged bar he bought in New York in the early 1980s, the rule of the house was tolerance and good fellowship. And the slow dawning of peace in Northern Ireland was celebrated by the founding in 2000 in South Armagh of his International Festival of Song, a deliberate declaration that singing could lead men out of darkness, just as Finn MacCumhail at the top of Slieve Gullion found the doe he was following transformed into a beautiful young woman, who smiled at him. ■

Michael Manley

Michael Norman Manley, an islander with a world stage, died on March 6th 1997, aged 72

THE MICHAEL Manley who visited the United States in 1990 had cast aside his Che Guevara bush jacket in favour of a suit. The free market had replaced his party's "ten steps to socialism". President Bush was happy to bless a sinner who had apparently repented and he went out of his way to praise the "first-class job" that Mr Manley was doing as prime minister of Jamaica. It takes style and gall to change sides successfully, and Mr Manley had plenty of both. He turned on a reporter who seemed puzzled that the old leftie had become a free marketeer, and said: "Is your outlook on everything the same as it was ten years ago?"

The conversion of Michael Manley meant more to the Americans than the simple falling into line of a politician from a small neighbouring island. Mr Manley sought to be an international figure. In the non-aligned movement and the United Nations he could rise above the little politics of Jamaica and use his accomplished oratory on a world-class audience: Indira Gandhi of India, Nyerere of Tanzania, Kaunda of Zambia, but also Canada's Trudeau and Germany's Brandt. He talked of a "new international economic order" with a redistribution of the world's wealth. Capitalism had to be demolished "brick by brick". Fidel Castro's Cuba was an "interesting experiment".

With stuff like this, whether he actually believed it or was just appeasing Marxists in his party, it was inevitable that opponents called Mr Manley a communist. But his inclination was more towards the democratic socialism invented in Britain called Fabianism. His teacher at the London School of Economics was Harold Laski, the mentor, for better or worse, of numerous students who became politicians in Britain's former colonies. Mr Manley called himself "the most privileged man in Jamaica", and there was some truth in this throwaway phrase.

The spur of a famous father

He was born into Jamaica's mixed-race elite. His father, Norman Manley, a barrister, piloted Jamaica to independence in 1962. His mother, born in Yorkshire, was a sculptor. The need to outdo his dad may have been a spur. And, in his day, Mr Manley commanded the sort of attention accorded to Lee Kuan Yew, another visionary politician from a small island. Sadly for Mr Manley, Jamaica, unlike Singapore, could not be held up as an example of a well-run and prospering nation.

Not all of Jamaica's poverty was Mr Manley's fault. Oil prices jumped, sugar prices did not. But he deserved much of the blame. In 1980, at the end of Mr Manley's first eight years as prime minister, the tourist hotels were almost empty, and so were the supermarket shelves. Much of the middle class had moved to Miami or Toronto. Almost 900 people had been killed in the run-up to the election, partly as a result of warfare between gangs allied to political parties.

Mr Manley's party was decisively beaten by that of Edward Seaga, a conservative. The foreign aid that had been cut off was resumed, but the economy still did not prosper. In 1989 Mr

to the United States, got into university, supported himself with part-time jobs and graduated as a dentist. Back home he founded a political party, which had huge success in elections under the colonial regime.

Dr Jagan seemed the likely leader after independence. But the Americans feared that he was a communist. Recently disclosed documents show that America fostered race riots in the country aimed at discrediting Dr Jagan and persuaded Britain to delay independence until voting arrangements could be fixed in favour of his opponent, Forbes Burnham. However, Mr Burnham turned out to be a nasty: an authoritarian with links to the Soviet Union. In retrospect, it seems likely that Dr Jagan would have been a far more desirable national leader. Mr Burnham died in 1985. After holding his party together in opposition for 28 years, Dr Jagan became president in 1992 in the country's first fair election since independence. Yes, he said, he had been a Marxist but "I was a Gorbachev even before Gorbachev". His politically-active wife Janet, an energetic 76, may stand for president in the election likely to be held this year.

With the deaths of Mr Manley and Dr Jagan, the Caribbean will seem a duller place. Only Fidel Castro remains to give the American State Department an occasional sleepless night. ∎

Manley was back in office but without his old ideology. He did as the IMF told him, liberalised foreign exchange and speeded up the privatisation of state enterprises. He stepped down in 1992 with failing health, and grew roses and orchids and watched cricket.

By one of the coincidences of history, another Caribbean politician who once worried the Americans, Cheddi Jagan, president of Guyana, died on the same day as Mr Manley, March 6th. He was 78.

Cheddi Jagan was not "privileged". His parents had come to what was British Guiana as indentured labourers from India. But young Cheddi, the eldest of 11 children, did well. With a few dollars in his pocket he made his way

Esther Manz

Esther Schuland Manz, American pioneer in the slimming industry, died on February 26th 1996, aged 88

SUCCESS FOR Esther Manz could be measured in human flesh. In 1995, it was claimed, the members of her organisation in America had collectively shed some 740 tons. Slimmers tend to be desperately optimistic. What comes off may quite quickly go back on, with a few pounds added. Mrs Manz agreed with St Matthew that the flesh is weak even if the spirit is willing. But tackling obesity was a battle, she said, that could last a lifetime.

This never-ending battle is the basis of a rich industry. In America alone it is estimated that about $30 billion a year is spent on slimming. Europe is catching up. In Britain, where, according to one study, about a third of the population over 15 wants to slim, the figure is $225m a year and growing. Diet books (more than 300 in print in America and Europe), videos, magazines, drugs, health farms, the surgeon's knife – all seek to combat the nutritional temptations of the rich world.The clothing industry sees that joggers dispense their sweat in expensive style, and that yoga slimmers contemplate the infinite with elegance. In the anxiety business, diet consultants are a profession rivalling that of psychiatrists.

Mrs Manz might be blamed (though, her supporters would say, unfairly) for having given a push to all this back in 1948, when she founded what was probably the first of the weight-watching organisations, called TOPS (Take Off Pounds Sensibly). She did not invent dieting. Discontent with the human body probably started in Eden. In the 19th century an overweight London undertaker, William Bunting, slimmed down on lean meat and dry toast, a diet that still has advocates today, and published a highly popular book about it. In the 1930s, Gayelord Hauser made a fortune from ten-day diets based on his "wonder foods", helpfully promoted by the bone-thin Greta Garbo.

The no-nonsense Mrs Manz saw obesity as a disease. Its sufferers should not have to face their malady alone, she said. Mrs Manz conceived the idea of fatties forming mutually-helpful groups, just as drunks gain support in the meetings of Alcoholics Anonymous. A "weight goal" would be set by a member's doctor. Esther Manz established a new approach for those who seriously wanted to be thin.

Now confess

The story that Mrs Manz's colleagues like to tell is that the first meeting of the organisation, consisting of the founder and three friends, took place around her kitchen table. Mrs Manz, a former teacher in a rural school, was pregnant with her fifth child and, in her view, noticeably overweight. The "confessional" system used by alcoholics was adopted at that meeting. Mrs Manz confessed that as a child she pleased her mother by eating up any piece of pie or cake left, so the dish could be washed. She continued to be a human waste-bin into adult life. By the second meeting of the group the four reformed women had between them lost 28lb.

As the movement grew, various incentives were devised. Those who lose weight are, in Mrs Manz's words, "treated like royalty". Those who do specially well are crowned "kings" or "queens" at well-publicised ceremonies. A bad offender in one group was called "Queen Pig". It may sound yucky, but the system of praise (and withdrawal of praise) has been widely copied or adapted by other slimming groups with apparent success. The most famous is Weight Watchers, founded in 1963. With its diet foods, cookery books and other products, Weight Watchers is a highly profitable business. For the past 18 years it has been owned by Heinz, a food firm. It sounds like a perfect business partnership. But any back-sliders tempted to nibble tasty titbits (a process that the food industry happily calls "grazing") are no doubt sternly rebuked at the next meeting. TOPS people say they feel "nothing negative" about Weight Watchers. But they note that their organisation was first and that, unlike Weight Watchers, it is not run for a profit. TOPS does not sell or endorse diet products. Any money left over from the modest dues of its 300,000 members around the world is used for research into the causes of obesity. So far, the group says, $4.5m has been contributed to obesity research, much of it to a medical college in Milwaukee, the town where Mrs Manz founded the movement.

One of the research projects TOPS is supporting is into the role of genetics in obesity. Mrs Manz hoped to find a "cure" for obesity. However, opponents of dieting believe that genetic research will eventually torpedo many widespread beliefs about fatness. Being heavier than the average should not be a problem, they say, any more than being above average height is a problem. You are born that way. Dieting, they claim, can actually make you fatter, because the body reacts against this assault. Stop fussing and get on with your life.

This argument is political as much as medical. Anti-dieters say that ordinary women (and men, too) should not be bullied into looking like fashion models with anorexia, just because the skinny look is the vogue of the moment. The robustness of this view would no doubt have appealed to the sensible Esther Manz. But, as one of her equally robust colleagues argues, the lifestyle of the rich world is on a collision course with our genetic make-up. Look at the growth of heart disease. But look at the growth of anorexia, say the anti-dieters. The debate continues. ■

Stanley Marcus

Stanley Marcus, purveyor of extravagance, died on January 22nd 2001, aged 96

THERE COMES a time in the life of the average billionaire when money ceases to be important. Suddenly it no longer seems to make the world go round; it has become quite boring. Stanley Marcus was sympathetic to the problem and sought to rekindle interest in possessions among those who wanted for nothing. "The people who come here actually need very little," he said with the air of a kindly doctor dealing with a particularly difficult patient. What Mr Marcus set out to do at his shop Neiman Marcus was to turn the sufferer into a "wanter".

Sometimes there was a quick success, especially if the patient were male, and billionaires usually are. "I've never found a man who *needs* a necktie," said Mr Marcus. "But he may be fascinated with the colour, or the design, and he *wants* it." But few cases were that simple. What about private aircraft? Got one, got several. But Mr Marcus was offering his and her matching aircraft. They would be the talk of the billionaire set. His wife would be charmed and especially attentive. They could keep boredom at bay for a week.

His and her aircraft, introduced in 1960, were followed by his and her miniature submarines, hot-air balloons and matching camels. Mr Marcus acquired two Egyptian mummies, established that they were male and female, and they too were resurrected into modern commerce. He sold Chinese junks and solid gold needles whose eyes no rich man could enter. His barbecues were silver plated and came with a live bull. His bathrobes were made of ermine. He is said to have discovered the shahtoosh, a sublimely soft scarf made in its original form from the neck hairs of Himalayan goats, and which in less exotic material has since become widely popular in high street shops. He never let up in his mission to save the very rich from the wasting disease of boredom.

The challenge of Dallas

The first Neiman Marcus shop was in Dallas, Texas. Cowboys and Indians were among the shop's first customers. From these rough beginnings Mr Marcus sought to make the firm an American symbol of luxury living.

His father, uncle and aunt, of German Jewish stock, had started the shop. Young Stanley went to Harvard and on his return at the age of 21 became bookkeeper, salesman and much else besides. In his autobiography *Minding the Store* Mr Marcus gives the impression that he was not all that keen to settle down in a hick town after having been given a glimpse of a wider world of books and ideas at Harvard. But having decided to be the dutiful eldest son he set about transforming the family business into something beyond the confines of 1920s Dallas.

He started with the considerable asset that Texas, a state of oil and cattle, was wealthy, and growing wealthier by the day. The scruffy girl in gingham could be the daughter of a suddenly wealthy oilman. Today she was buying another cotton dress. Tomorrow she would want fashion. In those days Mr Marcus's challenge was not to alleviate the boredom of the rich, but to keep up

Hawley Hale, sales were more than $62m a year (equivalent to $300m today) and there were Neiman Marcus stores in cities across the United States. Under the deal Mr Marcus ran the business until his retirement in 1975, and continued to be involved in it into his 90s.

In later years Stanley Marcus became a much-interviewed guru of retail selling. It was almost like being back in Harvard, but now he was a professor, dispensing erudition, occasionally raising a chuckle from an attentive audience. "I have the simplest taste: I am always satisfied with the best."

So where would you find the best, professor? Not, it seems, these days in department stores.

with the demands of Texans newly flush with money.

His weekly fashion shows were among the first in the United States. Eventually he introduced to Texas the great names of European fashion, Chanel, Courrèges, Balenciaga. The bookish Mr Marcus became an attentive pupil of the masters, particularly Balenciaga, the Spaniard who was himself the mentor of many famous designers. "He will enhance your beauty," Mr Marcus assured the matrons of Texas, "not dress you in ugly things, like some newer designers."

At the same time as promoting high fashion Neiman Marcus expanded from a speciality shop into an all-providing department store. When in 1969 the Marcus family sold a controlling interest in the company to a conglomerate, Carter

> Department stores have become cumbersome and dull. They have lost their sense of excitement, of adventure. If you blindfolded a woman and dropped her from a plane into a shopping centre in America she wouldn't know whether she was in Indianapolis or Minneapolis or wherever. She would see the same big stores, the same merchandise in the windows. A new fashion in Italy is faxed over from Milan to New York or Miami and it is knocked up and appears everywhere and becomes stale before it is even able to walk. Department stores are waiting to be re-invented. Starting out again, I'd learn from the boutiques, the small speciality shops that offer individuality.

It suddenly sounded as though Stanley Marcus was back in the 1920s, preparing to take on the world from Dallas. ∎

Princess Margaret

Princess Margaret Rose died on February 9th 2002, aged 71

IF THE life of the British royal family is the world's most brilliant soap opera, as some regard it, Princess Margaret was its most enduring and creative performer. In her prime she never failed to provide some new and intriguing twist in the script to beguile the less privileged millions as they faced another wearisome day. The competition was sometimes fierce. In the republics of Europe there are many who cling to their obsolete titles, countess this, marquise that. "First ladies" tend to adopt royal airs but their reigns abruptly end when their political husbands lose their jobs. For editors of newspapers and television, fierce guardians of the gates to fame, Princess Margaret was the real thing, an authentic living royal; moreover, and this was the important thing, she had a happily uninhibited streak. Our picture is of the princess at a London nightclub.

Margaret's Uncle Edward was really the founder of Britain's royal soap opera. He was the king who gave up his throne in 1936 so that he could marry Wallis Simpson, a twice-divorced American. Newspapers were more discreet then and television was in its infancy. But after the improbable story was made public, it ran and ran, became even more improbable when the couple were courted by Hitler, and never really faded until their deaths, of Edward in 1972 and Wallis in 1986.

The new king, George, seemed a dull stick. He was a disappointment after the lively Edward. However, George had two engaging daughters, Margaret, aged six, and her elder sister Elizabeth, ten. They were the first and second in line to the throne, and rapidly became the most famous children in the western world. Still, there is only a limited amount to say about children, however captivating, So, as is possible with soap operas, it is best to fast forward to a more interesting episode.

Behind palace walls

An American film called "Roman Holiday", first shown in 1953, starred Audrey Hepburn as a princess who runs away to Rome in rebellion against her stuffy life at home. It won numerous Oscars and started Belgian-born Miss Hepburn on a successful Hollywood career. The clever script was written under a false name by Dalton Trumbo, who had fallen foul of Joe McCarthy while he was hunting communists. But what mostly interested many filmgoers was that Miss Hepburn resembled Princess Margaret and it was assumed that Margaret was a rebel too.

The mixture of unverifiable fact wrapped in fiction that came to be written about Margaret seems to date from this time. What was known about life behind palace walls 50 years ago sounded pretty gloomy. When Elizabeth became queen on the death of her father in 1952, her grandmother, a previous queen, had curtsied to her. Did Margaret curtsy to her sister? Presumably. It seemed a rum way to run a family.

When Elizabeth was crowned the following year an alert photographer snapped Margaret removing what seemed to be a piece of fluff from the uniform of one Peter Townsend. Princesses are not expected to be valets. What was the meaning behind this extraordinarily unroyal act? There was much deliberation among the knowing. A long episode of the soap opera began to unfold. Townsend had been a fighter pilot in the second world war, the first in the RAF to shoot down a German bomber, and had later become an aide to the king, Margaret's father. Margaret, it

was said, had become fond of him. But he was 16 years older than the princess and, worse, had been divorced.

Margaretologists noted that Townsend looked a bit like Gregory Peck, who had starred with Audrey Hepburn. But in 1955 Margaret put an end to the guessing and said that she was not marrying him. She married Antony Armstrong-Jones, a photographer, in 1960. The 1960s seemed the decade she was born for. She was as much of the period as the Beatles, the mini-skirt and the joy of sex. *Time* magazine accorded London the adjective "swinging". Margaret and Tony (by now a lord) made it their playground.

The marriage broke up in 1978. The frolics of the period had long begun to pall. Gossips said Margaret had a number of affairs. Jean Cocteau said she told him that she loved disobedience: "I've always been the naughty one." Margaret became the princess who did not live happily ever after, which may or may not have been true. Royal despair may be different from the ordinary sort. For Margaret it was sitting next to a bore at a state dinner. However, thoughts she might have had about becoming queen had been put aside: she had fallen to 11th in line to the throne.

The guardians of true fame began to look elsewhere for interesting candidates. Margaret's two children have turned out to be unhelpfully normal. However, in the late 1970s the guardians' patience was rewarded by the emergence of Princess Diana, whose every public moment they diligently recorded until her death in 1997. In Diana's time the palace walls had become more transparent, but it was Margaret who had first let in a little light. Those who were not alive when Margaret was in the spotlight may have been surprised by the vast amount of newspaper space and airtime that followed her death. But it was the media's way of saying thank you. ∎

Marie-José

Marie-José, the last queen of Italy, died on January 27th 2001, aged 94

HER CORONATION, Marie-José said later, was rather a fussy affair. Her dresser had recalled that at Marie-José's wedding years earlier (pictured) her veil had come adrift three times while she was walking down the aisle. Madam would not want that to happen again, would she? Probably Madam did not care. She gave the impression of being indifferent to ceremony. But she submitted to the nagging of her attendant and everyone at the coronation said that no one in the history of Italy had looked more queenly. Marie-José and her husband Umberto were crowned on May 9th 1946. On June 2nd, Italy voted in a referendum to become a republic. The couple stood down after reigning for 27 days, Italy's last king and queen.

Like much that happens in Italy, the events of that early summer in Rome were political. The previous Italian king, Victor Emmanuel III, who had co-operated with the dictator Benito Mussolini, had abdicated, hoping to save the monarchy. His son Umberto and Marie-José would, he said, provide a fresh start.

But the Italians wanted a fresher start. They were tired of being the despised underdogs of Europe. In the second world war, while the Germans had easy victories in western Europe, Italian armies were defeated in North Africa and Greece. When Italy surrendered to Britain and the United States in 1943, Germany took over much of the country until its own defeat in 1945.

The monarchy could not be blamed for Italy's military incompetence, but it was associated with a discredited era. Umberto himself did not look all that fresh: he had been an army general. The monarchists' hopes had really rested on the popularity of Marie-José Charlotte Sophie Amélie Henriette Gabrielle of Saxony-Coburg, a royal name if ever there was one. It could not be said that they liked her: she was a rarity among the royals of Europe, politically of the left. But ordinary Italians loved the stories that were told of her rebellious ways.

Her meeting with Hitler
Admirers of Marie-José tend to portray her as a resistance heroine standing up to the iniquities of Mussolini. It is an understandable sentiment in a country seeking to atone for inventing fascism. *La Repubblica*, a newspaper not known for monarchist sympathies, gave three pages this week to the death of "the rebel queen". Marie-José's parents were the king and queen of Belgium, regarded as a liberal-minded couple for their time. Her mother Elisabeth was, at the age of 82, the first European royal to visit the Soviet Union, an enterprise that earned her the nickname the Red Queen.

With Marie-José's native Belgium swiftly annexed in 1940 (as it had been in the first world war), she had good reason to loathe the Germans, whom she called pigs and liars. She went to see Hitler at his retreat in Berchtesgaden to plead, without success, for food for starving Belgium. Her main recollection was that he ate chocolate throughout the interview.

Count Ciano, Mussolini's foreign

minister, noted in his diary that Marie-José asked him to use his influence to try to stop Italy entering the war on Germany's side, but it is unclear whether he followed it up. The king, her father-in-law, told her to keep her "nose out of family politics".

She had her little victories. She refused Mussolini's request to Italianise her name to Maria Giuseppina. But it is unlikely that Mussolini saw her as a threat. He valued her as the head of the Italian Red Cross. She accompanied the Italian army on its invasion of Abyssinia (later Ethiopia) in 1935 and was said to have "healing hands". The picture that emerges of her in the troubled 1930s and 1940s is of a divided personality, loyal to her husband's country but disturbed by a Europe run by tyrants. When she saw Allied bombers over Rome, she wrote of them as "white liberating birds".

She had talent with words. After the war, when she chose to live apart from her husband, she made her home in Geneva and built a career as a writer. Exile, she remarked, was one of the many inconveniences of royal life, and it had to be endured with dignity. One of her books is a history of Italian royalty. Republican Italy continues to be fascinated with monarchy. The popular picture weeklies rely on stories of royal escapades.

Should Italy decide to have a monarch again, Victor Emmanuel, aged 63, one of Marie-José's four children, or Emmanuel Filiberto, a grandson, would have claims. But neither has even been allowed back to Italy. When Romano Prodi became prime minister in 1996, he was inclined to allow them to come home but his government fell before he could get parliament to agree. Mr Prodi is now president of the European Commission, but not even Brussels has divine right over royal matters.

Marie-José saw little likelihood of a royal rebirth in Italy, or indeed anywhere else that had banished monarchy. When she was a child Europe was awash with kings and queens. Her mother's native Germany had some 20 principalities in the 19th century, each with its monarch. Marie-José thought that her father had got it about right in a changing Europe: "There will be many more unemployed in our trade." ∎

Albert Marshall

Albert ("Smiler") Marshall, the last British cavalryman of the first world war, died on May 16th 2005, aged 108

WHEN ALBERT Marshall was asked about the first world war, he sometimes thought it odd that so much was made of the Somme. For him the worst moment came the next year, in 1917. He was 20, and serving with the Essex Yeomanry in his third year at the front. A new regiment, the Oxfordshire and Buckinghamshire Light Infantry, had just come out from England to join up with his. The men were mustard-keen, in fresh-pressed uniforms that had not yet seen a shell-hole or a trench.

Eighty years later, Mr Marshall found it hard to remember whether the Ox and Bucks was sent "over the top" in the morning or the evening. What he never forgot was going into no-man's-land a few hours later, following an officer with a white flag, to bury their bodies. There were hundreds of them; all but a handful had been killed immediately. The mud was too compacted to dig down far. As his unit marched back, he trod under his boots the corpses of the men with whom, that morning, he had eaten breakfast.

Very few men – perhaps a dozen now in Britain – survive from the conflict that marked modern history, and seared the modern conscience, more than any other. Mr Marshall was the last representative of perhaps the most quixotic part of that doomed enterprise, the cavalry units of the Western Front. Once he had joined up, enthusiastically lying that he was older than 17, he had his picture taken in uniform, proudly astride his horse. He had ridden since he was five, starting on a goat for a tuppenny dare, and was a natural in the saddle. In 1915, no boy looked happier to have left the Wivenhoe shipyards for adventure in the fields of Flanders.

Some commanding generals, Haig among them, believed in 1914 that cavalry would win the war. A mounted charge, with swords or lances, was swift and flexible and had shock value. Even in later years, as the war on the Western Front bogged down in mud and barbed wire, horses seemed to hold the key to making it mobile again. A quick cavalry break through entrenched infantry lines could shatter the stalemate, take the fighting on to new ground, and move it forward.

Just once or twice, Mr Marshall lived that dream. At Cambrai in 1917 he met German infantry advancing: "We drew our swords and cut them down. It was cut and thrust at the gallop. They stood no chance." For a moment then, his blade gleaming, he was in a direct line that went back to the squadrons of Xenophon. A few days after the burying expedition, when German foot-soldiers surprised the Essex as they saddled up, he watched in amazement as the Bengal Lancers leapt on to their horses bareback, plucked their lances out of the ground and routed the enemy. It was "a colossal sight".

For much of the time, however, horses did not help in close engagements. High-explosive shells terrified them, and chlorine gas blinded them as it blinded men. (Mr Marshall fought at Loos, where 140 tons of gas, released by the British over the battlefield, blew back into their own trenches.) Horses also made large targets,

especially when corralled in numbers behind the lines, and soon weakened when they could not be cared for. Of 800,000 horses used on the Western Front, mostly for transport and pulling artillery, only about half survived.

In winter, when fighting eased, the cavalry's job was to hold the front line: "three lines of trenches, mud and devastation", as Mr Marshall remembered it. On one spell of duty, out in the middle of no-man's-land, an exploding shrapnel shell half-buried him in mud and smothered two of his friends. Unable to move, he sang hymns to them until he was pulled out. They were past rescuing.

A shared cigarette

When Mr Marshall turned 100, historians and documentary-makers began to show up at his farm cottage in Surrey – where he had lived since 1940, working as a handyman on a nearby estate – to ask him for his memories. He had never spoken about the war before, nor revisited the battlefields. Remembrance was sharp enough.

Under questioning, he revealed a slyly insubordinate streak. He used to trade cigarettes for other men's rum rations and, when the orderly officer's back was turned, quickly whip off puttee, boot and sock to rub the rum between his toes. As a result, while other men's feet were slowly rotting from trench foot or gangrene, "[mine] were as good as anything". He recalled, too, offering a drag on a cigarette to a soldier who had been tied to the wheel of a cart, without food or water, for some misdemeanour. Years later they met by chance in Oxford Street, and shared memories of how good that smoke had been.

His nickname, "Smiler", stemmed from an incident, soon after joining up, when he had thrown a snowball at a drill-sergeant. ("Hey, Smiler, I'm talking to you!" the sergeant roared.) He sang on the boat that took him to France, sang as he returned, and sang when he was there: "If the sergeant's pinched your rum, never mind", and "Nearer my God to Thee". His smile was one of the last of that crowd of sunny recruits who look out of their fading photographs in blithe and cocky ignorance of the horror they were to see. No faces are more haunting. ■

Benito Martínez

Benito Martínez Abrogán, possibly the world's oldest man, died on October 11th 2006, aged around 120

AMONG THE attractions that led the conquistadors to hazard their lives on the Atlantic, alongside dreams of mountains of silver and men slicked head to foot in gold, lay the thought of a fountain of perpetual youth. Where this fountain was, no one could say exactly. They would know they had found it when, stumbling on some hidden valley, they would see centenarians tilling the fields and dancing with the energy of young men.

The New World was found; the fountain was not, though Ponce de León, sweating through Florida, surely had premonitions of geriatric aerobics to come. By the 20th century, the mythical source of youth had become politicised and had shifted continents. Stalin placed it in the Caucasus, in Georgia and Azerbaijan: for there men and women lived to extraordinary ages, preserved both by pure air and by communism.

The connection of long life with Marxist dialectic is not proven, but in Cuba it is assumed. There, at the International Conference on Satisfactory Longevity in May 2005, Mercedes Matilde Nuñez, aged 102, sang a popular song; Juana Hernández Fernández, 103, and Professor Eduardo, 104, waltzed round the room to the tune "Almendra"; and Amada Hernández Fernández, 102, announced that she should really be in the kitchen, cooking up a storm of rice, chicken and vegetables with plenty of garlic and coriander.

The star of the show, however, was Benito Martínez Abrogán. He was not there in person, because he preferred to stay 240 miles east in Ciego de Ávila, breeding fighting cocks, growing bananas and tripping the light fantastic with any young nurse he could grab at the senior citizens' centre. He had turned up there on June 19th 2005 looking impressively

dapper, in a woollen jacket and trilby hat and a freshly ironed shirt, to celebrate his 125th birthday.

His precise age was something of a mystery. According to his Cuban identity papers he had been in Cuba since 1925, but his age on arrival was uncertain. He had come from Haiti, and remembered just a little of it: a childhood spent near Cavaellon, a few words of Creole. The Cuban government sent officials to Haiti to check, but they turned up nothing. More officials talked to Mr Martínez's oldest neighbours; they attested that he had always been the most elderly person they knew. The man himself, beaming his huge toothless smile, declared that his year of birth was 1880. He could not tell the time, relying on the sun's angle and his own instincts to know when to eat or sleep. But that one date he knew. "I am", he would say proudly, "the oldest person in the world."

The regime of Fidel Castro concluded that Mr Martínez was perhaps 119; but that was good enough. Whether or not acknowledged by the "Guinness Book of Records", it beat Elizabeth Bolden of Tennessee, a mere 116, and thus trumped the United States. In terms of longevity Cubans already matched Americans, living on average for 77 years. The country had so many centenarians, 2,721 out of 11.2m people, that Mr Castro's own doctor founded a club for them; and this in a country that spent only $251 per head a year on free lifelong health care, against $5,711 for patchy, elitist cover in the United States. Cuba contained, officials said, all the factors for a happy and lively old age: a good genetic mix, a diet without junk food, exercise, motivation and socialist solidarity.

Mr Martínez, their poster-boy, certainly got exercise. He was a labourer all his life, cutting sugar cane (on Mr Castro's father's ranch, among others)

and helping build the Central Highway. He worked so fast with the *guataca*, a small hoe, that his friends called him "El Avión", the aeroplane. Like most Cubans, he had no car; he biked or walked barefoot, or waited for a fume-spilling bus with that patience and stoicism that calms down stress. Since food was rationed, he did not eat much except what he could grow.

Cassava and pork-fat

Apart from all that, his life was not exemplary. He smoked until the age of 108 or so, cigarettes being handed out cheap among his rations. He never married, but chased many women. His "fresh" diet was mostly starchy cassava and sweet potatoes cooked in pork fat. Asked the secret of his youthfulness, he said he had never cheated a man or said bad things of other people. And he had a good socialist motivation to survive: he wished, someday, to shake Fidel Castro's hand.

Cuba's cradle-to-grave health care had in fact done little for him. He did not consult a doctor until he was around 115, and never went to hospital until the last few days of his life. Had he needed care earlier it would have been astonishingly good for a developing country, but standards are lower now than in the past. Money has been siphoned elsewhere, to "health tourism"; ordinary patients must bring their own lightbulbs and bedsheets. Cuba's best levels of health care, like its centenarians, are put on display mostly to show the world what it can do.

And what of that other elderly man, bearded and now frail, recovering slowly from "intestinal bleeding", but still the longest-serving ruler in the world? Why, says his optimistic doctor, he may still survive to 125; for he is lucky enough to live in Cuba, the site of the Fountain of Youth. ■

Eugene McCarthy

Eugene Joseph McCarthy, a maverick presidential candidate, died on December 10th 2005, aged 89

WHEN EUGENE McCarthy was making his first and most famous attempt on the presidency, in 1968, he was often asked why he was running. It was a good question. And he had a good answer:

> Nor law, nor duty bade me fight,
> Nor public men, nor cheering crowds:
> A lonely impulse of delight
> Drove to this tumult in the clouds.

This fragment of Yeats seemed to epitomise the man who quoted it. Irishness, daring, puckish humour, wilful solitariness, a sense of the pervading importance of higher things, were all delivered with professorial elegance by a man once described as "Thomas Aquinas in a suit". Two criticisms only could be made. First, that it was delivered in the white heat of one of America's nastiest election campaigns, to crowds chafing for more solid fare. And, second, that it was not true.

Mr McCarthy's peculiar political career was driven not by the impulse of delight but, in fairly equal measure, by principle and pique. His model of political behaviour was Thomas More, a witty but pig-headed martyr for his beliefs in Tudor England; his training ground was the hockey field at the various Catholic institutions at which he was educated, on which his desire to win could be shockingly intense. In political life, he kept his ambition well buried under layers of diffidence and urbanity. But he had some, and when he was slighted he did not forget.

His decision to oppose Lyndon Johnson in 1968 was a case in point. Mr McCarthy had come ardently to oppose the Vietnam war. He also could not help remembering that Johnson had humiliated him at the 1964 Democratic convention, choosing Hubert Humphrey, rather than him, as his running-mate at the last minute. He thought Johnson "a barbarian", determined to barge his way through any kind of checks and balances to prosecute the war. But the Senate had no desire to curb him. Someone, therefore, had to take the debate to the public. That someone (no one else being brave enough) would have to be Eugene McCarthy.

His campaign was odd in the extreme. He did not call himself a candidate, but an "accidental instrument" to express the will of the country. He knew he could not win. By challenging Johnson, he simply hoped to force the convention open for someone else. In fact, he came so close to Johnson in the New Hampshire primary that the president realised he was doomed, and soon quit the race. The nomination went eventually to Humphrey, no improvement in Mr McCarthy's view. But he had managed to shake his party to its foundations.

He had also mobilised the young, inspiring them to shave off their beards and get knocking on doors in a way not seen again until Howard Dean's insurgency in 2004. The radicals of the anti-war movement did not take to him, however, nor he to them. As riots raged in the streets of Chicago at the 1968 Democratic convention, Mr McCarthy, watching from the windows of the Hilton hotel, said the scene below reminded him of the Battle of Lake Trasimeno in the Punic Wars.

Politics as football

He was a politician, yet he despised politics. In the House, where he sat for Minnesota's Fourth District from 1949 to 1959, he would pointedly read books in committee meetings. In the Senate, where he served from 1959 to 1971, he seemed bored, and was often absent. Instinctively shy, he hated pressing the flesh or canvassing for money. He once compared politics to being a football

coach: "You have to be smart enough to know the game and dumb enough to think it's important."

Was it important to him? His opinions could be hard to sift, sometimes far to the left of his party, sometimes conservative. He believed in "redistributive justice", a relic of his youthful days in the Catholic Worker movement, but endorsed Ronald Reagan. He also opposed all limits on political donations as crimps on freedom of speech. That freedom was his passion in politics. Accordingly he hated the stale old bunfight between Republicans and Democrats, and left the Democrats in 1972 to become an independent.

His three later forays into presidential politics were embarrassing and looked self-indulgent. But Mr McCarthy believed he could still shake Americans out of their political torpor. The irony was that the Democrats, responding in part to the shock he had administered, became increasingly a party of the elite and intellectual rather than the working man.

He might never have entered politics at all. As a young man, he almost became a monk. In his home town, a small German-Catholic community lost in the Minnesota prairie, to take orders was the highest career. He tried the novitiate for a year, but was thrown out for intellectual pride.

The same pride tortured him in politics. His mind was too acute and freewheeling to suffer its restrictions. Norman Mailer, meeting him in 1968 at a fundraiser in Harvard, found him drooping and baggy-eyed, longing to be rescued. Some weeks later, he saw him in Chicago. He had just definitively abandoned the race, and was dining and joking with friends. He was free. And Mr Mailer suddenly glimpsed in him then the perfect president, "harder than the hardest alloys of steel". ∎

Malcolm McLean

Malcolm Purcell McLean, pioneer of container ships, died on May 25th 2001, aged 87

THE FIRST container ship was an elderly oil tanker, the *Ideal X*, whose deck had been strengthened to accommodate 58 well-filled boxes each some 30ft (9 metres) long. Malcolm McLean, normally an unemotional man, as befitted his Scottish ancestry, watched with a twinge of anxiety as the ship left Port Newark in New Jersey. Would the boxes survive the long journey down the east coast, into the Gulf of Mexico and on to Houston? Or might some of the boxes, or all of them, be swept unrecoverably into the sea, as some doubters had predicted? Would the valuable cargoes themselves arrive undamaged after the *Ideal X*, described by a reporter as an "old bucket of bolts", had been buffeted by Atlantic gales?

They seemed reasonable worries at the time, but even had the *Ideal X* sunk, the probability is that containerisation would have only been delayed for a year or two. Trade was ready for it. Mr McLean had the determination to push aside the initial obstacles. In fact the first voyage went without a hitch. Mr McLean's pioneer clients were delighted with the savings made by moving their freight from roads to sea. April 26th 1956, the day the *Ideal X* sailed, is seen as a marker in maritime history. On the 40th anniversary in 1996, by which time around 90% of world trade was moving in containers on specially designed ships, New York threw a party for Mr McLean, variously described as shipping's "man of the century" and the inventor of "the greatest advance in packaging since the paper bag". Bill Clinton simply said, accurately, that containerisation had helped to "fuel the world's economy".

Mr McLean disliked fuss. He was polite to reporters but avoided publicity. He hated the telephone, preferring to conduct a business discussion face to face. He liked, he said "to look someone in the eye". You could have a frank talk. That was how they did business in Maxton, North Carolina, where he was brought up.

Birth of an idea

He was a farmer's son, one of seven children. His first business transaction was selling eggs for his mother, taking a small commission. But in the 1930s, the time of the Great Depression, farming was one of the worst-hit industries. Mr McLean got a job at a petrol station and saved enough money to buy a secondhand lorry, calling himself, grandly, the McLean Trucking Company. He did well enough to buy five more lorries, hired drivers for them, but continued to drive himself.

He said the idea that gave birth to containerisation came to him one day in 1937. He had delivered a load of cotton bales to the port of Hoboken, for shipment abroad. In later life Mr McLean recalled the moment to *American Skipper*, a magazine:

> I had to wait most of the day to deliver the bales, sitting there in my truck, watching stevedores load other cargo. It struck me that I was looking at a lot of wasted time and money. I watched them take each crate off a truck and slip it into a sling, which would then lift the crate into the hold of the ship. Once there, every sling had to be unloaded, and the cargo stowed properly.

The thought occurred to me, as I waited around that day, that it would be easier to lift my trailer up and, without any of its contents being touched, put it on the ship.

Mr McLean did not rush to pursue the idea. First, he set out to become rich. By 1940 he had 30 lorries. In 1955, when he had decided that containerisation was the future, he sold his trucking business for $6m, equivalent to $40m today.

It seems unlikely that Mr McLean was the first to notice that the "break-bulk" shipping of goods, as it was called, could be improved on. There used to be a rather romantic train called the Golden Arrow which each evening travelled from London to Paris, the coaches crossing the English Channel by ship without the passengers having to get out. No doubt there are other examples. Perhaps the Romans thought of it. All the idea needed was an enthusiast.

But for centuries the trade of the world had depended on there being a vast labour force at every port to handle goods in manageable quantities. So why change? For Mr McLean the lure was lower costs. Moving a shipload of containers from the north to the south of the United States, as happened in the voyage of the *Ideal X*, was itself cheaper than trucking the containers individually. As the cost of dock labour was reduced, savings of as much as 25% could be passed onto the shippers. As containerisation spread around the world, ships were turned round more quickly with more savings.

In 1969, when Mr McLean sold for $160m his share in Sea-Land, the business he had created, it was the world's biggest container carrier. He guessed, correctly, that container ships would grow and grow. The latest are over 1,000ft in length, as fast as speedboats, accommodating hundreds of containers, and with small crews. Mr McLean said approvingly, "People are never going to pay a lot of money just to move things." He never really retired. He devised a way of moving a patient from a stretcher to a hospital bed with the minimum of discomfort. He started a pig farm, which had the reputation of being one of the cleanest in the United States. In Maxton, he said, the farmers always treated their pigs decently. ■

George Melly

Alan George Heywood Melly, jazzman and writer, died on July 5th 2007, aged 80

AMONG HIS many guilty pleasures – Marlboro Lights, Irish whiskey, bacon and eggs, blue jokes, smoke-filled dives where the music wandered on till four in the morning, voracious sex with good-looking men and women – George Melly especially liked to fish. The man famous for red, green and cream striped suits, red fedoras and a huge, rude, laughing mouth could often be found quite still, thigh-deep in the Usk or the Teifi, preparing to cast as soon as a bold trout tickled the surface of the water. And the singer whose party piece, when touring with John Chilton and the Feetwarmers, was to scamper round the stage and groom the clarinettist's head during his rendition of "Organ Grinder Blues", would admit that his thoughts on the river bank were of poppies, midges, Magritte and clouds.

And sex. This had been his driving force since his first schoolboy fumbles at Stowe, first rampantly homosexual, then generously heterosexual, among anchor chains and on Hampstead Heath, in the backs of vans and in glorious pulsating piles on the floors of stately homes. And there was, he confessed (being the most shockingly confessional of writers), sheer orgiastic pleasure in the tug of a bloody great fish, the line screaming off the reel, the catch leaping from the water in a shower of diamonds, the net sliding under it and the fish laid, beautifully marked, on the grass. Phew! Time for a ciggie.

But Mr Melly liked fishing for another reason. As a lifelong Surrealist, he was sure that the bizarre and marvellous lay in wait for him everywhere, and carried in his head a Surrealist motto,

"the certainty of chance". Chance might give him a fish with the next cast; and chance shaped his drifting, exuberant, deep-drinking life, from Stowe to the wartime navy to art-dealing to journalism on the *Observer*, through a rich cast of queens, hoodlums, sailors, old trouts, whores and martinets, until in 1974 the career of a risqué jazz singer finally hooked him for good.

He sang for 30 years, stoutly and louchely fronting the Feetwarmers at Ronnie Scott's and round the country, until he had to growl his Hoagy Carmichael numbers from a wheelchair. Mr Melly was possibly the most popular jazzman in Britain, and certainly the most outrageous.

Like all the addictions of his life, jazz burst on him at school. A friend's study; a gramophone; an old 78, and the voice of Bessie Smith, straight out of Harlem.

> Gimme a pigfoot and a bottle of beer
> Send me again. I don't care.

Mr Melly sang Bessie, "Empress of the Blues", more than anyone else. He would entreat her to possess him before a performance. But the Bessie that emerged from that quivering, beer-wet throat was partly a white, English, middle-class creature, drawn from music-hall turns and end-of-the-pier shows, dressed in bowlers and blazers, and with the plunk-plunk of a banjo never far away. Trad jazz, in the person of Mr Melly, Humphrey Lyttelton and a few others, limped through the 1960s and 1970s until out of sheer graft, longevity and good humour it came back into favour. He helped it survive.

ever since his inclusion as a wide-eyed *petit marin* in the Surrealist circle round E.L.T. Mesens in Soho in the 1950s. On impulse he made surreal objects himself (a dead starfish caught in a mousetrap, a nude with Carnation Milk tins as her breasts), but he also learned to buy cleverly in a difficult market. One train trip back to Liverpool from London was spent in silent adoration of two new acquisitions by Max Ernst, propped on the opposite seat.

As old age advanced, Surrealism became an increasing comfort to him. It gave an aesthetic purpose to his multicoloured lines of pills, and to the hours

Starfish in mousetrap

Classlessness and anarchism drew him to jazz also. Though his background was wealthy Liverpudlian, his inter-war fling with left-wing politics stayed with him for life. So, too, did other flirtations. On shore leave from the navy in "amusing" bell-bottoms in his roaring homosexual years, he admired a pimp encountered in Leeds in a mauve silk shirt and kipper tie, and the way Quentin Crisp's painted toenails accessorised his golden sandals. The gay fetishes faded, though as "an old tart" he could always have his head turned by pretty boys; but sharp tailoring in eye-watering colours became his stock in trade.

This aesthetic streak pointed to yet another side of his sprawling personality. He knew about art, and had an eye for it,

spent in limbo in the scanner. Deafness reminded him of Surrealist word-games in which question and answer were unrelated, or only incidentally and wonderfully so:

> What is reason?
> A cloud eaten by the moon.

Fishing, too, was still a comfort. He imagined his cancer – for which he refused all treatment so that he could go on performing – as a tiny fish dangling at the end of his lung, wrinkling its whiskers, ready perhaps to be caught. And he often said that his favourite end, other than collapsing in the wings of a theatre with wild applause still ringing in his ears, would be to be discovered smiling on a riverbank with a big beautifully marked trout beside him, death and sex together. ∎

Erich Mielke

Erich Mielke, East Germany's secret police chief, died on May 22nd 2000, aged 92

AFTER THE East German state collapsed in 1989, revenge was in the air. At the top of many people's lists for retribution, if not lynching, was Erich Mielke, the head of the Stasi, East Germany's secret police. He was put on trial for being jointly responsible, with the East German leader Erich Honecker, for the deaths of 49 people trying to escape to West Berlin over the Berlin Wall. The trial was abandoned, partly because the killings were proving hard to pin on those at the top, and partly because Honecker was dying, while Erich Mielke complained that he could not follow the proceedings.

Mr Mielke was put on trial again, this time, to many people's astonishment, for murders he had been involved in back in 1931, in the days before Hitler came to power. On the orders of the Communist Party, he and a colleague had shot dead two policemen who had incensed the party by breaking up its demonstrations. Young Mielke had escaped, but the German police had never forgotten the murders of their finest. This time there was no problem of providing proof of his misdeed, and in 1993 he was sentenced to six years in prison; not enough, said some, but at least he had not eluded justice entirely.

Perhaps Erich Mielke was himself impressed that his police file had survived through more than 60 years of war and peace, passed on from regime to regime. It was a tribute to the thoroughness of German bureaucracy. Mr Mielke was an obsessive bureaucrat. His speciality was collecting personal data. Of course, all governments do this,

democratic ones as well as dictatorships, as do commercial organisations; and laws are made to try to restrain their enthusiasm for intruding on the privacy of individuals.

Mr Mielke operated with few restraints. In 1957, when he became head of the Stasi, an abbreviation of *Staats* (state) and *Sicherheit* (security), it was just one of a number of bodies designed to protect East Germany against the western "imperialists". Mr Mielke so expanded the Stasi that, by the time he was toppled some 30 years later, he was the most powerful man in East Germany after the party leader: "the master of fear", as West German popular newspapers liked to call him.

Family treacheries

Erich Mielke scrutinised the lives of East Germany's 17m people with a thoroughness that probably even exceeded the Gestapo's. No detail was too minor to be noted on the Stasi files. Political views of course, but also reading tastes and sexual inclinations, even a preferred drink. From a dossier, a decision might be made about a citizen considered a threat to the security of the state, and consequently jailed, or shot. When the Berlin Wall was built in 1961, as a result of Mr Mielke's urging, the entire population became prisoners of the state.

It is estimated that some 2m people were informants for the Stasi at one time or another. Most of the files kept in the Stasi's vast complex in Berlin's Normannenstrasse have become accessible to those deemed entitled to view them. As a result people are distressed to find that close friends provided information about them; that there were treacheries even within families. Mr Mielke's own reflections to his subordinates are there. One is, "All this twaddle about no executions and no death sentences, it's all junk, comrades." Sometimes he would leave his desk and conduct his own interrogations. "I'll chop your head off" was one of his customary threats to anyone he suspected of betraying the party.

The Stasi tentacles extended into West Germany, where Mr Mielke had informants in many government ministries, among opposition groups, in NATO, American military bases, even in the churches. In 1974, the then chancellor, Willy Brandt, resigned after a Stasi spy was found to be working in his office. The East Germans knew about Helmut Kohl's misdemeanours long before they were revealed to the world. Even those who loathed Erich Mielke acknowledged that he ran an extremely well-informed service. As more Stasi files are made public it may turn out that the East Germans were also privy to intrigues in other European countries whose participants would prefer to remain secret.

Yet there was a sort of innocence about Erich Mielke. He seemed unable to comprehend why anyone should want to be other than a communist. The party had always looked after him, recognising that there was talent in the poor boy from a Berlin tenement; giving him an education in Russia, followed by experience among the comrades in Spain and France. In East Germany after the war he rose swiftly in the Stasi until he was allowed to fashion it his own way. Wanting "to know everything, everywhere", as he put it, seemed the only way to protect the state. When an angry crowd confronted him after he was deposed, he shouted back, "But I love you all."

In prison the unloved Erich Mielke was said to be cheered up when he was provided with a disconnected red telephone with which he could talk to imaginary agents. It was assumed that he was going mad, although sceptics, suspicious to the last, said that he was just feigning madness to avoid facing new trials. ■

Arthur Miller

Arthur Miller, playwright, died on February 10th 2005, aged 89

FOR MOST of his life, Arthur Miller was a carpenter. At 14, with the money made from delivering bagels on his bike round Harlem, he bought enough wood to build a back porch on the family house. In his old age, living on 360 acres in Connecticut, he made tables, chairs, a bed, a cabinet. To make extra-sure the angles were right, he once consulted a mathematician.

He loved making plays – which he did better than any other American of the 20th century, with the possible exception only of Tennessee Williams – for much the same reason. They gave him "an architectural pleasure". He tried novels occasionally and wrote, in "Timebends" in 1987, a chaotic autobiography. But he revelled in the structure of the drama. He thought of Ibsen and Sophocles, his early influences, as master-carpenters, and of his own best plays as careful constructions of "hard actions, facts, the geometry of relationships". It was no accident that his male characters were often skilful with their hands, even if they were good at little else.

Yet Mr Miller's plays were not conceived as simple artefacts. He meant them to move minds. If they could not do so, there was no point in writing them. His intention was to show the audience, in ordinary characters they might see every day, truths about themselves that they half-knew but would not acknowledge. Realising they were not alone in whatever they foolishly feared or unwisely hoped for, they might find the courage to change.

In "Death of a Salesman" (1949), the play that brought him global fame, he displayed in Willy Loman the futility of a salesman's life, the fragility of his dreams, his longing to leave a lasting mark on the world – and also, though Willy could not see it, the persistent strength of his family's love for him. In "A View from the

Bridge" (1955) he anatomised, in Eddie Carbone, the unacknowledged terrors of incestuous passion. In several plays, the last written only a year before his death, he tried to unravel his own relationship with Marilyn Monroe, his wife for almost five years. She remained surrounded, however, by "a darkness that perplexed me".

He also plunged into the past in order to illuminate the present. His account of the 17th-century Salem witch trials in "The Crucible" (1953) gave him the metaphor he needed to describe McCarthyism, a plague that touched him directly when he was called before the House UnAmerican Activities Committee in 1956 for attending meetings of communist writers. (He refused to name names, was held in contempt of Congress, fined, and had his passport withdrawn.) His play "Broken Glass" (1994), ostensibly about the 1930s, was intended as a commentary on public indifference to the Yugoslav wars of the 1990s. His audiences did not always notice these parallels, but they were always meant to.

Fixing on a star

Throughout his work, his message was consistent. Actions had consequences, and the individual was responsible not only for his own acts, but for what he knew others were doing. In "All My Sons" (1947), his clearest statement of this philosophy, a father had secured the future of his family by shipping defective aircraft parts that had caused pilots to die; eventually, his own son reported him. There were moments, Mr Miller wrote, "when an individual conscience was all that could keep a world from falling."

On the other hand, his characters were seldom that strong. Outside forces – destiny, law, political authority, sudden catastrophe – often overwhelmed them.

As a child during the Depression, he had seen his father's coat-making business destroyed and his mother, whom he remembered in fox-fur and diamonds, reduced to eking out shovelfuls of coal. His father and his colleagues, he noticed, never blamed anyone but themselves for what had happened. Mr Miller, already imbued with his lifelong socialism, tried to persuade his shellshocked father to blame the capitalist system too, and accept that profit was wrong. His father, naturally, could not begin to understand him.

His career was not all adulation. He had a dry patch in the 1960s, when he felt he did not speak with the accent of the time, and by the 1980s the all-powerful New York critics (whom he loathed) seemed to be tired of him. Constantly, critics objected to his blatant stage moralising: "like neon signs", one wrote, "in a diner window."

Mr Miller was unapologetic. He had a purpose, he confessed, even beyond teaching. Though he seemed to be didactic, he was in fact asking questions: "How can we be useful?" "Why do we live?" He was, he once admitted, "in love with wonder ... the wonder of how things and people got to be what they are." The aim of each of his plays was to discover which commitment or challenge his main character would accept, and which he would walk away from: "that moment when out of a sky full of stars he fixes on one star."

He remembered his own such moment, when he decided to be a writer. It came when, reading Dostoevsky's "The Brothers Karamazov" as a teenager, he discovered that among the most breathtaking passages were accumulations of hard, simple fact: "the kind of bark on the moonlit trees, the way a window is hinged". As well as the playwright, it was the carpenter speaking. ■

Théodore Monod

Théodore André Monod, a naturalist sage, died on November 22nd 2000, aged 98

LONG AGO, long before the earth had acquired its hordes of friends, long before nations were blaming each other for destroying the environment, Théodore Monod was giving warnings about the growing menace of pollution. An odd man, some said. And indeed there was something mildly alarming about his passion for what he considered the pure life. The problem for purists in an impure world is that they are necessarily against many things. Mr Monod had a long list. He was against the personal pollutants of tobacco and alcohol and never touched either. He was against eating meat; animals had to be respected, he said. Hunting should be banned. Bull-fighting was simply appalling.

He was a foe of nuclear power, which his native France uses to produce three-quarters of its electricity, and inevitably of France's nuclear-weapons tests in the South Pacific. He fasted each year on August 6th, the anniversary of the atom bombing of Hiroshima, a day he said marked the end of the Christian era. Christianity, of a fairly individual sort, guided Mr Monod's long life, and he could defend his intolerance of the world's waywardness by pointing out that eight of the Ten Commandments are in fact prohibitions.

His father was a priest, but a Protestant one in mainly Roman Catholic France, and an outsider even within his own minority dogma. He told his son he could, if he wished, choose Islam or Buddhism rather than Christianity. Young Théodore emerged from this confusing instruction with a notion of a world with one composite religion whose adherents would protect the earth and, he hoped, be vegetarians.

It cannot be said that much of this agenda has caught on. President Jacques Chirac praised Mr Monod this week as "a guide and a sage", but the French themselves remain enthusiastic carnivores and Europe's keenest hunters. Mr Monod was listened to, if not heeded, because he was one of the world's most eminent naturalists, following perhaps the least blameworthy of scientific occupations. And he did much of his work in that most intriguing of places, the Sahara, the world's largest desert.

Through life on a camel

Théodore Monod first glimpsed the Sahara when he was 20. He joined a team of researchers sent to Mauritania by the Museum of Natural History in Paris, an institution he was to be associated with all his life. After a year most of the team returned home, but Mr Monod stayed on. He acquired a camel and started on the first of his many safaris looking for interesting things.

He was hooked, as many Europeans have been. But, being a Monod, his view of the Sahara was different from that of his celebrated compatriot Antoine de Saint-Exupéry or of László Almásy, the Hungarian portrayed in the novel and film "The English Patient". Saint-Exupéry wrote evocatively about the Saharan wilderness as seen from an aeroplane. Both he and Almásy were as fascinated by the mechanics of exploring a

Germans and Italians in North Africa. He loathed the fascists even more than he did the car. Otherwise, he believed that the only transport compatible with desert life was the camel, travelling at three miles an hour. He saw himself as a kind of white Bedouin. He was married in the traditional costume of a camel-rider (although his bride preferred white). He said that if you could survive in the desert, as he did, it proved that you did not need meat for stamina.

In the course of more than 70 years of active adult life, Mr Monod covered many thousands of miles, even at camel speed. He found hundreds of previously unknown plants and animals, about 80 of which are named after him. He dabbled in the associated discipline of archaeology and discovered a series of rock drawings. He wrote numerous books and scientific papers, and collected just about every honour in his field of study.

In French newspapers Théodore Monod was sometimes called the Methuselah of the desert. If only he were, he said. Late in life, he felt that he was only just beginning to get to know the Sahara, and needed a few hundred years more of study. "The desert is beautiful because it is clean and never dies," he said. But it needed to be watched. Humans had been rather careless about living things. But were they perhaps more caring these days? "Probably not," he said gloomily. ■

previously almost impenetrable territory as they were by the territory itself.

Théodore Monod's explorations were more in the style of those of a British archaeologist, Sir Wilfred Thesiger, who in the 1940s went on foot and by camel across the "empty quarter" of the Arabian desert. Mr Monod loathed the petrol engine. He once came across the tracks in the sand of a model T Ford that had crossed the Egyptian desert in 1911, the first car to do so, and was most displeased. He was equally unhappy about the annual Paris–Dakar motor rally in which dozens of rugged vehicles roar through the Sahara, churning up the sands.

He set aside his prejudice only during the second world war when his knowledge of the desert was put at the disposal of the British fighting the

Akio Morita

Akio Kyuzaemon Morita, the man who made Sony, died on October 3rd 1999, aged 78

AT A restaurant in Düsseldorf in the 1950s Akio Morita was served with a bowl of ice-cream decorated with a miniature parasol. The friendly German waiter pointed out that the paper bauble was made in Japan. For Mr Morita it was a disheartening experience, that the world associated "made in Japan" with trinkets and cheap imitations. For the rest of his working life he sought to prove to foreigners that "made in Japan" meant originality, quality and value for money. Keizo Obuchi, the Japanese prime minister, got it right when he said this week that Mr Morita was "the engine that pulled the Japanese economy".

At heart, the man who made Sony a worldwide name was a tinkerer. He retained a childlike curiosity in pulling things apart to see how they worked. Even back in the 1930s his wealthy parents had many of the trappings of western life: a car plus all the electrical appliances of the day. The teenage Akio spent hours dismantling the family record-player and rebuilding it. His other passions were physics and mathematics. In the second world war, while serving in the Japanese navy, he met a fellow enthusiast for technology, Masaru Ibuka. In 1946, the two started a telecommunications company called Tokyo Tsushin Kogyo, with 20 employees, the precursor of Sony.

As things turned out, Mr Ibuka looked after research and product development while Mr Morita went out to raise the money and sell the goods. Mr Morita's great early coup was to persuade America's giant Western Electric to license its transistor know-how to his tiny firm (a move that infuriated Japan's powerful trade ministry, which was by-passed). After his chastening experience in Düsseldorf, Mr Morita journeyed on to Eindhoven in the Netherlands where the great Dutch electrical group, Philips, had its headquarters. Here was a company in a small country that had created a global brand. "If Philips can do it," he wrote home to Mr Ibuka, "perhaps we can also manage."

A star is born

Clearly, the tongue-twister, Tokyo Tsushin Kogyo, had to go. Mr Morita combined the Latin word for sound, *sonus*, with the English expression "sonny-boy" to give an impression of a company that was full of energy and youthful exuberance. Keeping things to essentials underlay many of Mr Morita's creative decisions. In the late 1970s he asked the engineers at Sony to build a miniature stereo sound system. People could listen to music while exercising, he said. The Walkman has become synonymous with Sony, and immensely profitable. Sony charges a hefty premium for the creative content its brand name implies.

There were disasters too. The Betamax video recorder was one. Though considered marginally better than the VHS recorder launched a year later in 1975 by the Japan Victor Company (both were based on an American design), the Sony version left little room for future improvement. Worse, Mr Morita upset manufacturers who wanted to make the Betamax recorder by driving too hard a bargain. The VHS design prospered and

Mr Morita's Betamax lay dead in the water. A foray into Hollywood in 1989 also turned out to be an ill-judged, costly adventure. With that, the man who built up Sony as a global enterprise almost brought it to its knees.

Mr Morita gave the impression of being a contradiction. Those close to him speak of the two sides to his personality. There was the strict Japanese traditionalist, the eldest son of a 300-year-old sake-brewing family in Nagoya who disinherited his own eldest son, Hideo Morita, for marrying without his consent. To the outside world he was a jovial, talkative and incandescent personality who illuminated a room and fired imaginations. It was an act Mr Morita worked hard to perfect. With his tanned skin from skiing and tennis, bluish eyes, rare among Japanese, and mane of white hair parted in the middle, he looked the dandy. Hideo Morita called his father a "consummate performer" whom no one outside the inner family ever saw unmasked. "He had to act as the most international-understanding businessman in Japan," was how the son described him to John Nathan for his book "Sony: The Private Life", published in September. Like Soichiro Honda and other entrepreneurs of his generation, Mr Morita embraced the outside world, America especially, because there was so little to be exploited in post-war Japan. The domestic market was sewn up by

pre-war giants such as Toshiba, Hitachi, Mitsubishi and relative newcomers like Matsushita. But embracing the outside world did not mean that Mr Morita enjoyed it.

He had to subjugate his traditional sense of decorum; he had to learn not only to speak English but also to think English; he had to learn to say yes or no when the weight of a dozen generations of family tradition pressed him to be ambivalent. On occasion, he misread foreign sensitivities. He tried to prevent the English translation of a book, "A Japan that Can Say No", of which he was co-author with a right-wing politician, Shintaro Ishihara, and subsequently distanced himself from it. Mr Morita's lifelong campaign to embed Sony in the hearts and minds of foreigners seems to have been a painful struggle. He bore the pain well. ■

Kathryn Murray

Kathryn Murray, America's dancing partner, died on August 6th 1999, aged 92

THE WAY to put "a little fun in your life", Kathryn Murray would say, and say it quite often, was to learn to dance. Over the years millions were persuaded. Learning to dance in the chain of the 500 or so studios of Kathryn and Arthur Murray seemed as properly American as drinking Coca-Cola or buying a Ford car. Like the drink that was "it" and the car that gave you freedom, learning to dance tapped into a social need, expressed in an early advertisement, written by Arthur Murray, headlined "How I Became Popular Overnight".

Men, perhaps lonely or simply shy, could break the ice by asking a woman to dance. Or so it was said. And the woman need never again be a wallflower. There is probably no better excuse for two people to touch each other, without any suggestion of impropriety, than to take to the dance floor. George Bernard Shaw put it quite brutally: "Dancing is a perpendicular expression of a horizontal desire."

Sex, though, while implicit in the Murray message, was never stressed. The 1940s and 1950s, when the Murrays were at their most successful, seem in retrospect wonderfully innocent. Carnal contact in the movies rarely progressed beyond a kiss. Love songs were restricted to yearning. Arthur Murray was happy to think of himself as a traditionalist. He had been born at the end of the 19th century. The favoured dances of his youth were waltzes and polkas. Ragtime was for riffraff. He most enjoyed the dancing of Vernon and Irene Castle, then the king and queen of America's ballrooms. He was a good enough dancer to give lessons to pay for his way through college, where he studied business administration. Combining the two disciplines, he set up a business that taught dancing by mail. In 1925, he married Kathryn, a schoolteacher and dancing enthusiast. At 17 she was 12 years younger than Arthur and became the driving force behind the business. A wag remarked, perhaps cruelly, that Arthur Murray became rich "by the sweat of his frau".

One two three, one two three ...
No doubt many Americans were so keen to learn to dance that they were willing to toil through the outlines of shoes and the arrows on the diagrams of Arthur Murray's original correspondence course. But it was no way to become the star of the dance floor. Kathryn and Arthur decided to teach dancing personally in a studio they set up in New York. It did so well that they started to sell franchises of the Murray method of teaching dancing in only six easy lessons.

Then television came along. Kathryn recalled that, now forty-something, she was reluctant to be the hostess of their show, "The Arthur Murray Party". Arthur, practical, if not always polite, said she did not have to be beautiful to be on television. People had such small sets and the reception was so poor that they wouldn't be able to tell.

Kathryn turned out to be a winner as a presenter. She realised that demonstrating the waltz could not alone keep viewers' attention for half an hour, and discovered a talent for comedy. "I've danced with bears and danced on

the more complicated geometry of the dance floor. They would watch, say, Latin American dancers to see if their talents, and passions, could be simplified for their novices.

Kathryn wrote the training manuals for teachers in the franchises. Well into middle age she was an enthusiastic explorer of new dance steps, and could perform the open swivel or the flirtation scallop like a teenager. She declined to criticise the style of dancing to rock music that became popular in the 1960s. You had to keep an open mind, she said, otherwise the young would think you were past it. But for Arthur there seemed no

roller skates as part of the show," she said. The show was, in essence, a sales pitch. Fast learning was as tempting as fast food. During the 11 years the show ran from 1950, the Arthur Murray dance empire spread in America and to a dozen other countries. A sardonic song by Johnny Mercer did the business no harm:

> Arthur Murray taught me dancing in a hurry.
> I had a week to spare.
> He showed me the groundwork, the walkin'
>   around work,
> And told me to take it from there.

The quality of your walkin' around work after six lessons no doubt depended on the tolerance of your partner. The Murrays encouraged pupils to take further lessons to master

business future in a dance, such as the twist, that needed no tuition, and where you did not even need a partner.

Demand for the Murray way on the dance floor did fall off. The couple gave up management of the business in 1964, sold most of their interest and went to live in Hawaii. Arthur died in 1991. Kathryn, though, lived to see a big revival in formal dancing. The Australian film "Strictly Ballroom" has been a runaway success, and not only among those old enough to remember the foxtrot. Ballroom is advertised these days as a way to lose weight and to stay young for ever, although making you instantly popular remains its greatest appeal. "Learn to dance tonight," says an Arthur Murray studio on the internet. Tonight? Is that a promise? ∎

Kiharu Nakamura

Kiharu Nakamura, a geisha, died on January 5th 2004, aged 90

THE QUESTION was one familiar to Kiharu Nakamura: what exactly was a geisha? In television interviews, at lectures and in her books she would explain that the word was composed of two Japanese characters, *sha* meaning entertainer and *gei* meaning artistic. Artistic entertainer: was that all? All? Miss Nakamura would list the accomplishments of a successful geisha: she would have to play musical instruments with feeling, usually the *shamisen*, a type of guitar, and the *tuzumi*, a small drum; she would have to sing and dance well and, most important, be a good conversationalist, with a ready flow of stimulating repartee.

What about sex? Miss Nakamura considered the word carefully. Perhaps, she said, the questioner was thinking of the *oiran*? Like a geisha, an *oiran* was a cultured woman but would be available to spend the night with a man for a high fee. The two professions were often confused by westerners. That said, it would be misleading to suggest that a geisha never had sex. She might form a relationship with a client and sex would follow naturally. But the distinguished men Miss Nakamura entertained, many of them important politicians and industrialists, were often too tired for sex or too old to bother with it. What they wanted was for their cares to be lifted for a few hours, to be soothed and perhaps gently amused. A geisha, she said, "knew how to handle men". They might boast to their friends that they were real dogs, but Miss Nakamura knew different. And of course she would never betray a confidence.

The idea that geishas were tarts seems to have been spread by soldiers from America and other victorious countries who occupied Japan after it was defeated in 1945. The girls who serviced the soldiers were happy to call themselves geishas and often wore geisha costumes, as many still do today. Geisha culture continues to be studied by Japanese historians. But for Miss Nakamura the war had ended a profession that dated back hundreds of years to a time when only men were considered to have the accomplishment to be geishas (just as today men still play the female roles in *kabuki* theatre). In old age she saw herself as one of the few surviving classical geishas, perhaps the last one.

The rebel

She must have been a handful as a daughter. Her parents had assumed that she would have an arranged marriage: that was the way things were in the Ginza district of Tokyo, where her father was a doctor. But the teenager had other ideas. She was fascinated by Tokyo's apprentice geishas as they paraded around town, and she copied their fancy costumes and heavy make-up. She stamped her little clogs and eventually her parents gave way.

At 15 she entered a school for geishas run by teachers who were honoured as "living national treasures". She in turn became the treasure of the school. Her teachers were charmed by the quavers she put into her voice and her ability to walk with her feet together. She tolerated subjects she found boring, such as flower arranging. The name she had been born with, Kazuko, was changed to Kiharu, which means happy spring. She says she managed to avoid the ceremony of *mizuage* (deflowering) by conversing with the guest who had paid for the privilege until he fell asleep.

She was one of the few geishas to learn English. Visitors to Japan who were curious about geishas were brought to see her. Most are now forgotten, but they were famous at the time: baseball's Babe Ruth, William Randolph Hearst, the model for "Citizen Kane", and Jean Cocteau, a French writer and artist who was smitten and wrote a poem about Kiharu.

Japan's secret service, perhaps influenced by stories of Mata Hari, a dancer who became a spy in the first world war, asked Miss Nakamura to spy on a foreign client. Understandably, she was a reluctant agent: Mata Hari had been shot at dawn. But no doubt she did her patriotic duty. When Japan went to war in 1941 she travelled to India, carrying a message from the Japanese government of support for an anti-British movement.

At the end of the war, Miss Nakamura felt that the geisha profession, like Tokyo itself, had been destroyed. She was 32, she had some savings and a baby son from a brief marriage. She worked for several years as a translator in Japan, but the future, she decided, was America. Her new life there was, in its way, a typical immigrant's success story. She had something to sell, her experience as a geisha and of Japanese culture, and she worked hard to market it. When the Metropolitan Opera did "Madame Butterfly" they employed Miss Nakamura as an adviser. Puccini's story might be ridiculous, but at least she could ensure that the costumes were correct.

Her ten books, memoirs and novels brought her into contact with universities. Perhaps her best known work, "The Memoir of a Tokyo-born Geisha", has been translated into eight languages. Miss Nakamura's lectures at Princeton, Columbia and other institutions were packed out. She would entrance her audience with the same verve she had shown when she entertained her clients as a geisha. "Now, another question, please, preferably not about sex." ■

Eric Newby

Eric Newby, travel writer and fashion buyer, died on October 20th 2006, aged 86

BY THE standards of many British explorers, Eric Newby was not particularly intrepid. He could not bear the thought of pain, and would faint away in any film that featured an operating theatre. Horses terrified him, especially when, in Italy, a reluctant mare he was riding was persuaded to clear a ditch by having a lighted cigarette inserted up its backside. Forced to sleep on rocks – to Wilfred Thesiger's huge disdain – he would blow up an air-bed to cushion the ordeal.

But then Mr Newby did not see himself as an explorer in the Thesiger mould. He was a traveller to whom things happened, and he would set off in that inquiring, ill-prepared, innocent way that has characterised Englishmen abroad from Chaucer to Evelyn Waugh. He was an amateur whose 25 travel books – most famously "A Short Walk in the Hindu Kush" (1958) and "Love and War in the Apennines" (1971) – were full of serendipity and surprise. A sudden view of a ravine with a grey heron winging across it; the moon rising "like a huge rusty coin"; Parmesan cheese, eaten after days of hunger, with "hard, salty nodules" of curd in it; the shock of blue and green phosphorescence dripping from his oar. Possibly only Mr Newby could notice, while treading water off the east coast of Sicily in 1942 and trying to avoid being shot at by Germans, that the plume of smoke over Etna looked like the quill of a pen stuck in a pewter ink-pot.

Well-equipped he may seldom have been, but he was usually well-dressed. For Mr Newby had another life. For 20 years, to finance his travelling and writing, he worked in the garment trade. After helping run the family firm of Lane and Newby Ltd, Wholesale Costumiers and Mantle Manufacturers, he joined the John Lewis Partnership in the Intelligence Department, meaning that he checked whether trousers fitted or not. After this, he was promoted to "Model Gown Buyer". If this life of pins and patterns seemed a come-down to a man dreaming of the Ganges or the Sahara, he certainly did not admit to it. To make "The Journey" as a sales rep through industrial Britain, rattling north overnight unsleeping in a third-class seat and then staggering up the back stairs of department stores with wicker baskets full of suits, was every bit as exciting.

Besides, he loved clothes. He had been drawn to travel in the first place, as a restless child growing up in suburban south-west London, by the pictures of foreign boys in petticoats in Arthur Mee's "Children's Colour Book of Lands and Peoples". His first unaccompanied journey, following a Devon stream down to the sea through nettles and cowpats at the age of five, was made in brown lace-up shoes and "a hideous red and green striped blazer with brass buttons". Apprenticed at 18 on a four-masted barque that ran the last great Grain Race from South Australia to Ireland, he first ran up the oily rigging, teetering 160 feet above Belfast, in grey flannel trousers and a Harris tweed jacket.

Melons and Sancerre
All this sounded rather upper class. And Mr Newby cut such a figure, handsome

in immaculate safari suits and, in London, a trilby hat. He had a gentleman's cavalier attitude to expenses when, from 1964–73, he was the travel editor on the *Observer*, and a gourmet's approach to his later journeys. ("Had a delicious mini-picnic under a tree," he noted during a bicycle ride through France in 1971; "small, ripe, melons and a bottle of cold Sancerre.")

Yet he himself was "middle-middle class". He had been to St Paul's, not Eton, and had left school at 16 because his family could no longer afford it. His time as a prisoner-of-war, from 1942 onwards, was diverting to him not only because it led him to his future wife (a tall, blonde, determined Slovenian girl who came to visit him when he was transferred to an outside hospital) but also because he could observe those strange creatures, the English upper classes, up close. Before that he had mostly met them in Harrods, small boys like him braving the "unending, snowy-white wastes" of the Linen Hall and the "savannahs" of Model Gowns, "endless expanses of carpet with here and there a solitary creation on a stand rising above it, like lone trees in a wilderness."

In his travelling life he had many a narrow escape. On the great Grain Race, he was almost washed away in a hurricane. Hunting with princes in Andhra Pradesh he was charged by a bear, but failed to shoot it because he dared not use a rifle (a .465 Holland & Holland India Royal) that had cost £800. In Italy during the war, a fugitive prisoner, he woke from a sleep on a mountainside to find a German officer standing over him. But the officer wanted merely to chat and catch butterflies. "The last I saw of him", he wrote, "was running across the open downs with his net unfurled ... making curious little sweeps and lunges as he pursued his prey."

Mr Newby was often asked why he loved to travel. It was, he said, to do with being free. But his attitude to freedom could be ambivalent. Twice, when he had got out of prisoner-of-war camps, he found himself musing that "real freedom" lay back inside the fence. There was no need, he wrote, to worry about anything there: no need to work, to earn money, or to think about what to eat. Or, indeed, what to wear. ∎

Stavros Niarchos

Stavros Spyros Niarchos, master of the high seas, died on April 16th 1996, aged 86

TYCOON, A word of Japanese origin meaning great prince, was often applied to Stavros Niarchos. The description was almost accurate. Mr Niarchos had a touch of greatness and lived in a style that few real princes can afford. There was, though, an amorality in his business dealings that a Japanese *taikun* might have thought not quite honourable. In 1970, when Greece was under a military dictatorship, Mr Niarchos, by then a major industrialist and the owner of the world's largest merchant fleet, gave public support to the junta and was rewarded with control of a state-owned oil refinery. Nothing exceptional in such a deal, perhaps, for a conservative and a Greek patriot, except that, at the height of the cold war, the Niarchos shipping fleet was also distributing Russian oil around the world.

Mr Niarchos took the view that, as an international businessman, he had the right to trade freely. America, a citadel of free trade, could hardly disagree, but it frowned on a Niarchos deal that allowed Russian oil to be shipped to Cuba. Mr Niarchos had an equivocal relationship with America. His parents were naturalised Americans, but he was born in Athens, and stayed Greek. Much of his early business was done in America, but his ships were registered in Panama to avoid paying American taxes. In 1953, when he was accused of breaking an American law by getting control of ships prohibited to foreigners, he moved his American business to Europe. He kept a house in New York, one of several around the world, but his palatial home was in Greece, on an island he owned in the Aegean. His preferred company was titled Europeans.

Against the grain

Stavros Niarchos's first job was as a clerk in a firm owned by his uncles, who were grain dealers. According to family legend, young Stavros persuaded his uncles to buy their own ships, making a big saving on grain imports. In 1939 he was given, or acquired, his own ship. In the second world war the ship was sunk in Antwerp harbour by a German bomber. Several other ships he later acquired were bombed, or sunk by submarines. The insurance money was the foundation of Mr Niarchos's fortune.

After the war Mr Niarchos came by a number of Liberty ships, which America had mass-produced in great numbers and was selling cheaply or giving away. But many of the Liberty ships were worn out. They were welded together (rather than riveted) for speed of manufacture, and the welds sometimes came apart, sending the ship to the bottom. Mr Niarchos started to order his own ships, usually from Asian yards, where costs were kept down through government subsidies. He is sometimes credited with inventing the supertanker: of hitting on the idea that a ship with twice the capacity did not cost twice as much to build and operate. But it had long been realised in every area of manufacturing that fixed costs, particularly labour, do not necessarily scale up to the size of the product. What Mr Niarchos did was to apply this truism to transporting oil, which he was sure would overtake coal

One of his soundest investments was in paintings. Like other self-made tycoons, Andrew Mellon for instance, Mr Niarchos liked to load up with blue-chip art. He owned Manets, Cézannes, Picassos, Renoirs, and numerous others, modern but not too modern, that filled a warehouse. These expensive tokens of graciousness will now move to other owners until, to the dismay of dealers, they end up in museums, as the Mellon collection did. He had the other toys of the rich: a private jet, several yachts, one of them said to be the most beautiful in the world, and numerous racehorses. He was

as the chief fuel in the rich economies. That was his vision. In 1956 he launched a ship (named after himself) of more than 47,000 tons, then the largest tanker afloat. This was the forerunner of tankers of up to 500,000 tons. Shipping oil became one of the fastest ways to make money. After a few voyages the ship had paid for itself.

Although the Niarchos name is identified with ships (and, as it happens, his name means "master of ships") much of his fortune was later diversified into property and elsewhere. At the time of his death the man who had once owned some 80 tankers, more than anyone else, was reckoned to have no more than Greece's 15th largest merchant fleet. Because of his canniness he was able to survive the shipping slump in the 1980s.

an impressive host: he introduced pheasants into his Greek island so that guests could have something to shoot at. He was married five times. The competition on the high seas that existed between Mr Niarchos and another Greek shipowner, Aristotle Onassis, seems to have extended into their private life. His fourth wife, at 56, was Charlotte Ford, aged 24, of the motor family. Shortly afterwards Mr Onassis was deemed to have outshone him by marrying Jacqueline Kennedy.

He will be missed, by a vast audience perhaps not much interested in tankers, even supertankers, but which was fascinated by this man who went shopping on a princely scale. Rich people, captains of industry, are commonplace. Tycoons are rarer. ∎

Duke of Norfolk

The duke of Norfolk, an English survivor, died on June 24th 2002, aged 86

MANY THOUSANDS of words have been written during the past couple of weeks about a soldier who inherited the title of the duke of Norfolk and with it the duties of earl marshal and chief butler of England. Readers of *The Times* were offered some 2,200 words. Newspapers catering for less patient readers made do with snappy accounts of the duke's soldierly habit of cleaning his own shoes. Perhaps that was enough to make a point. The more distant you were from the world in which the duke moved, the more peculiar it seemed.

The duke himself seemed aware of his title's growing irrelevance. He was perhaps the least ducal of the 17 holders of the title created by Richard III in 1483 (or possibly only 16; there is some dispute among the archivists). Succeeding by death, the duke said, was "a poor way of getting on" and he was prouder to have made his way to become a general. The duke upset some fellow members of the House of Lords by agreeing that those with inherited seats should no longer be involved in lawmaking, although he retained his own seat, as did the member who had the duties of the Lord Great Chamberlain.

His rebelliousness had its limits. Like many associated with archaic institutions, the duke was a charming contradiction. He epitomised old values, country, family, faith, without being stuffy about it. Tradition, he said, was one of the reasons that the country had not had a revolution since 1688 and had not been successfully invaded since 1066. That was a very British thing to say. Whatever its merits as an argument, it expressed a sentiment that drives the enormously popular history programmes on British television and perhaps also drove the royal feeling that unexpectedly swept the country when the Queen Mother died in March, moving those of a republican mind to silence. For anyone seeking to explore, if not to understand, the appeal of "this sceptred isle" – a long-running programme on BBC radio – the career of the country's premier duke was at least worth a look.

Into battle

At birth he was merely the Honourable Miles Francis Fitzalan-Howard, "honourable" being a politeness conferred on the child of a lord. In what he called the "wavy line of the succession" he later became Lord Beaumont, then Lord Howard, and finally, when a distant cousin died, found that he had become the duke of Norfolk. "I was never sure what I would be called next," he said. "Miles" usually sufficed.

At the age of 22 he joined the Grenadier Guards (raised in 1656). Two years later, at the start of the second world war, his mother made the sign of the cross on his forehead and he went off to France in command of an anti-tank platoon. He had an exemplary war, serving on the battlefields of Europe and North Africa. He gained a reputation for, in Hemingway's phrase for bravery, showing grace under fire. He stayed on in the army after the war until 1967 when he worked part time for Robert Fleming, a merchant bank with family connections.

In his army days he had bought a house in Oxfordshire, and preferred it to the edifices he eventually inherited in 1975 as duke of Norfolk, particularly Arundel Castle in Sussex, the ducal seat, nearly 1,000 years old, brimming with history, but mostly comfortless. More agreeable was his duty as earl marshal, choreographing the annual opening of Parliament by the monarch, a ceremony largely unchanged since medieval times.

Everyone agreed that he brought a soldierly efficiency to the event, in which he had to walk backwards before the queen without tripping. When his scarlet uniform became a bit tatty he asked Denis Healey, the chancellor of the exchequer in the then Labour government, if it would pay for a replacement. Mr Healey nodded through the expense. The two men had first met fighting in Italy in the war.

He possessed robes that had been made for his great-great-grandfather when a ban was lifted in 1829 on Roman Catholics sitting in Parliament. The survival of the Howard family in Protestant England dating from Henry VIII is regarded by historians as an example of tenacity and by many Catholics as miraculous. Some ancestors went under the axe, including Henry Howard, a Tudor poet much admired by the duke. Philip Howard was believed to have been poisoned and was made a saint. The duke was said to keep a book of prayers in his jacket. "We are like the British infantry in defence," he said. "We never give in."

These days the politics of Christianity arouse little general interest in Britain. "We are all so ecumenical and love each other," the duke said. "I am terribly ecumenical myself." He disagreed with the Vatican's opposition to birth control, but so do many Catholics. "Has every wife got to have eight children like my mother?" he said, and his listeners agreed. He enjoyed an argument but didn't much care for parties. What he mostly liked was working in the open, repairing walls, managing woodland. "I wish I was thinning trees," he was heard to say at a dinner party. He told of a party he had given for European royals who stayed on until three in the morning. "You might have thought some people hadn't got palaces to go to," he said. ■

Patrick O'Brian

Patrick O'Brian, captain of the sea story, died on January 2nd 2000, aged 85

YOU ARE, perhaps, trying to pass on to a friend your enthusiasm for the stories of Patrick O'Brian. So what are they about? They are sea stories, you say, set at the time of Britain's wars with Napoleonic France. But more than that, much more. Umm. Well, at least you tried. It may be that one day your friend, finding himself desperate for something to read, will pick up "Master and Commander", the opening book of Mr O'Brian's sea saga, and find himself enveloped in the story of Jack Aubrey as he sets sail in his first command, the tiny warship *Sophie*. The danger is that your friend will become an addict, devouring one after another all the 20 Aubrey novels with a fanaticism that excludes work, family life and other such humdrum matters, and then reading through the whole lot again. Why on earth did no one mention Patrick O'Brian before?

Under the O'Brian spell you move into an unfamiliar but entirely convincing world. Quite likely you start with no special interest in the British navy in the age of sail. But who could have predicted the appeal of Tolkien's fantasies? How many Londoners were lured to the first night of a play about a Dane who could not make up his mind? Mr O'Brian was among the illustrious line of writers who turned words into the nearest thing we have to a time machine.

The reader shares what Mr O'Brian called "the closed environment of a ship at sea, at sail, proceeding for months, perhaps for years, and its magnifying effect upon human relations". Such ships were the deadly machines that made Britain the master of much of the world in the 19th century, but they were also complex societies whose smooth functioning depended on civility and friendship, and, an unlikely ingredient in adventure stories, music. Starling Lawrence, a writer who did much to introduce the stories to American readers, sees in Mr O'Brian's world an element of wish-fulfilment. Despite the hardship of navy life, you are in a place "where the sails are white and the air is clean". Another writer, Amanda Foreman, one of the many women in thrall to the stories, says that in them, not far away from the fears in men's hearts, "is the vision of an ideal existence".

An innocent deception
Patrick O'Brian not only re-created another time; he re-created himself. For years his acquaintances had no reason to doubt that he was what he said he was: an Irishman, born in Galway to a Roman Catholic family; educated at home by a governess; fluent in Irish and other languages, among them Latin. But when he became famous it emerged that his real name was Richard Patrick Russ, the son of an English doctor who specialised in the treatment of gonorrhoea; and who was the son of a successful Jewish furrier who had emigrated to England from Germany. Richard Russ had been educated at a minor boarding school in Devon.

If there was deception, it was of the most innocent kind. It is clear from his novels that Mr O'Brian was half in

Napoleon's plan to invade India. The raw vividness of the Aubrey novels owes much to Mr O'Brian's sources, the logbooks and other contemporary accounts of navy life that fired his imagination. He said that in writing about that time "it is difficult to avoid understatement". Nelson, when the young captain of a small ship, boarded and captured two far more powerful enemy ships. "So very often the improbable reality outruns fiction."

He denied he was a romantic, an unbelievable claim for a novelist to make. Still, in the routine of his life he was a realist. He lived

love with Ireland. He provided Captain Aubrey with a seagoing companion called Stephen Maturin, a partly Irish surgeon every bit as interesting as Aubrey himself. Maturin is an intellectual, a linguist, a graduate of Trinity College, Dublin, which, late in his life, gave Mr O'Brian an honorary degree. O'Brianologists, of which there are many, are convinced that, deep in his imaginings, Mr O'Brian saw himself as Maturin. They point to Maturin's real job as a spy; Mr O'Brian was said to have worked for British intelligence, although the details are obscure.

Like Maturin, he was interested in how battles, especially sea battles, had shaped history. Lepanto, in 1571, ended the Turkish threat to the West; the defeat of the Spanish Armada in 1588 permanently damaged Spain's moral influence; Britain's victory over the French fleet on the Nile in 1798 ended

for most of his working life in Collioure, in southern France, because it was cheap, at least in the early days when he was poor. Several pre-Aubrey novels sank without trace, and Mr O'Brian and his wife Mary lived on his earnings as a translator; he may not have known much Irish, but he had far more useful French.

The Aubrey novels were not immediate bestsellers. That most enduring source of publicity, personal recommendation, gave them a fair wind. The publication of each new story became an event. Well into his 80s Mr O'Brian was content to continue to be the obedient recorder, in fine handwriting, of the exploits of Aubrey, by now an admiral. He thought he had another 20 years or so of useful life, and was working on the 21st Aubrey novel. His death means that the saga is not finished. But no work of art ever is. ∎

Sir Mark Oliphant

Marcus Laurence Elwin Oliphant, scientist, died on July 14th 2000, aged 98

LIKE MANY of the scientists who helped to make the atomic bomb, Mark Oliphant expressed dismay when it was used to destroy Hiroshima and Nagasaki. During the cold war years he was labelled a "peacenik", the contemptuous term used to describe those who questioned the morality of using nuclear weapons. In 1951 the United States refused to give the Australian a visa to attend a nuclear physics conference in Chicago. When the British tested 12 nuclear weapons in 1952-57 in the Australian outback, he was the most qualified Australian to join the team monitoring safeguards at the tests, but he was not invited.

He was never a security risk, and his brilliance as a scientist was never in question: he was knighted in 1959, when Australia still had such honours. What mostly annoyed the politicians and soldiers who constituted the nuclear establishment was Sir Mark's outspokenness. He scoffed at the American obsession with security. He recalled that when the bomb was being developed in the 1940s, the Americans gave false names to the eminent scientists being gathered from abroad, in case the enemy got wind of the project. "I became Michael Oliver, Niels Bohr became Nicholas Baker. We kept the same initials. It was so silly." In fact, the general principles of the atom bomb were already well known in the scientific community, and Klaus Fuchs, a German refugee working on the project, was passing on the finer details of its manufacture to the Russians.

Mark Oliphant was popular with ordinary Australians. He was the underdog standing up for what he believed. His avuncular manner and unpredictable chuckle made him the antithesis of an aloof scientist. At the age of 95 he turned up at his old university in Canberra to protest against the federal government's meanness to academe. Anyway, few Australians wanted nuclear bombs on their territory. They cast a wary eye across the Pacific where the French were doing their best to blow up the island of Mururoa with their own bombs. "The French are like a bandit with a sawn-off shotgun," said Sir Mark. That's telling them, Olly.

Why they did it
It has to be said that Mark Oliphant and his like-minded colleagues seemed to be content to work on the bomb, knowing that it would be capable of mass destruction. It was only later that they publicly expressed misgivings. In the chilling words of Robert Oppenheimer, the atom scientists' leader, "The physicists have known sin." Sir Mark said it was necessary to build the bomb before the Germans did, a justification also offered by Albert Einstein, who helped to persuade America to make the bomb. But Sir Mark added this candid observation: "I learned during the war that if you pay people well and the work's exciting they'll work on anything. There's no difficulty getting doctors to work on biological warfare, chemists to work on chemical warfare and physicists to work on nuclear warfare."

For Mark Oliphant, the most exciting time of his early career was when he won a scholarship to Cambridge to work with Ernest Rutherford, a New Zealand-born physicist, in whose Cavendish laboratory British scientists first split the atom. This was a golden period for Cambridge. At one time in the 1930s eight Nobel prize-winners were working in the Cavendish, then the world's leading centre for experimental nuclear physics. Sir Mark later became professor of physics at the University of Birmingham. His laboratory produced the magnetron, an invention that greatly improved the efficiency of radar. The magnetron helped Britain to track and sink German submarines in the Atlantic; and the

Americans used it decisively against the Japanese fleet.

Back home in Australia after his wartime adventures, Mark Oliphant turned his mind to creating a scientific elite in a country more famous for its fine wool and champion cricketers. In the fledgling capital, Canberra, he founded the Research School of Physical Sciences at the new Australian National University and helped to establish the Australian Academy of Science. Both institutions are now world-class.

He said the country should develop an atomic energy programme to develop its vast open spaces as a hedge against the day when fuels like coal and oil, which Australia has in abundance, would run out. He believed that nuclear power, driving desalination plants, could transform deserts into farmland. It hasn't happened. Australian lethargy defeated Sir Mark's enthusiasm. Nor did he have much luck with his plan to build the world's most powerful accelerator for nuclear research. The project ran out of money and was mocked as a "white Oliphant".

After Sir Mark retired from science he was appointed governor of South Australia, his home state, in 1971. No figurehead, during his five-year term he spoke out on the issues that worried him: the environment, racism, the importance of the family, themes that stayed with him for the rest of his life. One of his last pieces of writing was a reflective pamphlet, which he distributed to friends. He wrote, "Lord, let now thy servant depart in peace." ∎

Harry Oppenheimer

Harry Frederick Oppenheimer, voice of reason, died on August 19th 2000, aged 91

VISITORS FROM democracies to white-ruled South Africa would, if they were important enough, usually be received by the prime minister and then, to protect their reputation for fair-mindedness, meet Harry Oppenheimer. In 1960, Harold Macmillan, Britain's prime minister, had a talk with Mr Oppenheimer on the eve of his speech to a dismayed South African parliament: "The wind of change is blowing through this continent." In 1982, Mr Oppenheimer's guest was Henry Kissinger, America's ever-travelling fixer, then in South Africa to observe that the wind was gathering strength.

The Macmillans and the Kissingers of the world felt at ease with Harry Oppenheimer. After enduring a government lecture on white supremacism, it was comforting to dine with Mr Oppenheimer in his splendid home in Johannesburg with its Goyas and Degas and other emblems of good taste; and hear his liberal-minded views delivered in quiet Oxford English. The answer to racial oppression, he said, lay in financial prosperity. In a growth economy, new, well-paid jobs would be open to blacks, who would join the middle class. Apartheid would hinder such a development. It had to go.

Mr Oppenheimer of course spoke with authority. His knowledge of economics had been honed in Oxford under Roy Harrod, a pioneer in the study of growth. He had succeeded his father as head of the Anglo American Corporation, vastly expanding its assets. It now had a stake in almost every large business in South Africa, and a very large stake in some, namely diamonds, gold and other desirable minerals.

In South African terms, Mr Oppenheimer was a humane employer. He built decent housing for many of the blacks he employed; he encouraged the creation of black trade unions and provided advanced education for blacks, some of whom gained important jobs in his companies. He liked to quote Thomas Jefferson's dictum that it was impossible to have democracy in an uneducated country. Still, Mr Oppenheimer had his critics. His sentiments were fine, but, with such a hold on the South African economy, could he not have hastened reform?

His years as outsider
The answer is perhaps he could have; but probably not. Some liberals may have chided Harry Oppenheimer for his too-quiet opposition, and complained that his miners were often brutally treated by their unliberal overseers. But many Afrikaner whites simply loathed him. Politicians such as Jaap Marais (Obituary, August 19th) feared that even talk about reform would undermine white rule, just as in China today the communist leaders fiercely refuse to acknowledge the possibility of any alternative form of government. Mr Marais believed that Harry Oppenheimer's industrial power would have to be broken if white supremacy were to survive. His views were too extreme for even the Nationalist government; nevertheless, during the first 34 years after the National Party took power in 1948, Mr Oppenheimer, the country's foremost businessman, was never asked to dine with the prime minister. Mr Kissinger persuaded the reformist P. W. Botha to break bread, albeit reluctantly, with the outsider in 1982. Mr Botha's theme was "adapt or die". Mr Oppenheimer praised him for his bravery and subsequently he had meetings with Mr Botha's successor, F. W.

de Klerk. He was no longer the outsider.

In an interview a few years ago Harry Oppenheimer said he had tried to build a "better sort of society and a better sort of country". At a personal level he had tried to keep alive "what I considered a voice of common sense and humanity". It was the sort of summing up that a politician might offer. Mr Oppenheimer was for ten years a member of parliament for the United Party, which disintegrated when defeated by the Nationalists. Had it retained power, he would probably have become finance minister, and possibly prime minister. The subsequent history of South Africa would have been different, but not all that much. Mr Oppenheimer would have introduced democracy gradually over a period. The National Party held things up because they did not accept what "had to happen".

After taking over Anglo American Mr Oppenheimer was content to keep politics as a hobby, supporting the Progressive Party and its sole member of parliament, Helen Suzman. In the wider world he became known, through his chairmanship of De Beers, as the king of diamonds, and was a presence on lists of the richest people. He had 25 years as chairman, but for years after his retirement he would turn up at the company's offices at 44 Main Street, Johannesburg, "to talk to my friends – they even ask my views from time to time". He acknowledged that making money was the measure of success in business, but "one seeks success more than money after a certain point". As for diamonds, they were bought out of vanity. What about gold, another great source of wealth for Anglo American? People bought gold, he said, because they were "too stupid to think of any other monetary system that will work". Harry Oppenheimer had never forgotten his economics. ■

Henri d'Orléans

Henri d'Orléans, would-be king of France, died on June 19th 1999, aged 90

THE FRENCH are, it sometimes seems, reluctant republicans. The revolutionaries who sent Louis XVI to the guillotine hesitated for more than three years before doing so in 1793; and the "national convention" that passed the death sentence managed a far from unanimous vote of 387-334. Henri d'Orléans, a French duke and count of Paris, who sought to restore the French monarchy, took comfort from opinion polls that said a fifth of the French liked the idea of a monarchy, or at least were not opposed to the proposal. It was, he said, a good base to build on.

Henri was unusual among claimants to discarded thrones, the so-called "pretenders", in proposing that a modern king should be elected and was convinced that a vigorous and well-argued campaign would give him the crown. In 1964 he believed that his

moment had come. Charles de Gaulle, then president and regarded by many in France as their saviour, was thinking of retiring. He had taken a liking to Henri d'Orléans and sent him on a number of diplomatic missions to North Africa, a region on which Henri was an expert.

De Gaulle seemed to be uncharacteristically humble towards Henri, whose royal inheritance, he said, made him "eternal", while the general was just a man. Henri gives the impression in his autobiography that De Gaulle listened sympathetically to his proposals: to stand as a non-political candidate "concerned only with the general interests of France" and, when elected, to restore the monarchy. He would become Henry VI. He felt that he would have appeal as a family man: his long marriage had produced 11 children. (Large families were a feature of Henri's ancestors: one ancestor, though a homosexual, dutifully fathered six children, helped, it is said, by "holy medals".)

Henri had a good record as a patriot, joining the Foreign Legion in the second world war after the army had turned him down because of a law that then banned the descendants of former kings from living in France. A son had been killed in the Algerian war. An elected king, he argued, would be a truly French idea: the first French king, Hugh Capet, had been elected in 987, albeit by his nobles rather than by universal suffrage.

The president as monarch

Henri's campaign would undoubtedly have been a fascinating one, much enjoyed by connoisseurs of the by-ways of democracy. "The general wanted to re-establish the monarchy," Henri recalled later, "and I think he was sincere when he talked to me about it." However, De Gaulle decided after all to stand for re-election and, even as just a man, was unbeatable.

One of the obvious obstacles to Henri's ambition to become king was that France already has a sort of monarch, although he is called a president. From De Gaulle to Chirac, French presidents, enjoying powers that far exceed those of most of the world's 20 or so real monarchs, have rapidly assumed custodianship of *la gloire*. Appropriately, the president's home in Paris is a palace. In 1982, François Mitterrand, then France's newly elected president, entertained the world's leaders at Versailles, the elaborate palace and gardens built for Louis XIV. For the occasion he had the taps in the palace bathrooms replated in gold.

Henri regarded Mitterrand as the most monarchic of French presidents. As De Gaulle had done, Mitterrand was content to accept Henri into his circle

of admirers. Henri's intimacy with the French leaders probably did no harm to his application for government money to keep his château at Amboise, on the Loire, in royal condition. Henri and Mitterrand were, in an odd way, two of a kind: Mitterrand the socialist monarchist and Henri the royal democrat. Both had for a time supported Henri Pétain's collaborationist government after the French had been defeated in 1940. Mitterrand had worked for it; Henri had been offered the job of food minister but had declined.

Henri's support for Mitterrand was not shared by his wife, granddaughter of the last empress of Brazil, who said the president was a bandit. However, the couple tolerated each other for 52 years before they separated. The real opposition to Henri came from another branch of the royal family, the Bourbons. They had their own claimant to the French throne. Henri's claim, they considered, was dishonoured because one of his ancestors had been a member of the convention that had sent Louis XVI to the guillotine. The proper politics of royalty was on the right, the Bourbons said, and they objected to the liberalism of Henri, whom they called "the red prince".

He may not have been that liberal. He publicly rebuked his daughter Chantal for criticising the National Front, a right-wing party. It was not that he disagreed with her views, but she should not have spoken without his permission. Chantal was then aged 45, the mother of three children. Henri's successor as count of Paris, his eldest son, also called Henri, appears to be more easygoing. He is the author of a cookbook and markets a perfume called Royalissime. It is unclear whether he will pick up his father's hopeful sceptre. But among the 41 grandchildren left by the fecund Henri, it seems likely that someone will. ∎

Maureen O'Sullivan

Maureen O'Sullivan, queen of the jungle, died on June 22nd 1998, aged 87

FOR TRUE devotees, "Tarzan and His Mate", made in 1934, is the one to see, and see again. This is the "Hamlet", the Fifth Symphony of the genre. A critic wrote of the film's "sweet paganism" as expressed by Maureen O'Sullivan and Johnny Weissmuller as Jane and Tarzan. Jane's outfit is determinedly pagan, and Tarzan paganly appears to undress her as the couple dive into a jungle pool, where the girl swims in the nude. An increasingly puritanical Hollywood deleted the seven-minute sequence, fearing that suburban America might believe it approved of such goings-on. (It has since been restored in the video version.) In subsequent Tarzan films Miss O'Sullivan would wear more and more clothing. "In those days," she recalled, "they took these things seriously."

So, in a sense, this was the end of innocence. A cloud had appeared over Paradise. Or so it would seem from the many thousands of words that have been written about the Tarzan films and the books by Edgar Rice Burroughs (1875-1950) from which they are derived. Tarzan is the noble savage, the simple lifer whose habitat seems so much more desirable than the urban jungle. Some have seen him as an early environmentalist. According to Gore Vidal, Tarzan created a generation of American men who "tried to master the victory cry of the great ape", which, as every Tarzan expert knows, is a jungle-piercing "Ungawa". In one day, a collector of useless information noted, 15 children in Kansas City were taken to hospital after falling from trees imitating Tarzan.

Damsel in distress

"Tarzan and His Mate" is one of those modest films produced in the Hollywood factory that have curiously refused to go away. "King Kong", made in 1933, is another. They have something in common. Maureen O'Sullivan and Fay Wray, the heroine of "King Kong", are at the mercy of wild creatures, but tame them with their womanly ways. It is a classic tale, the damsel in distress. Its classicism, though, did not impress Miss O'Sullivan. She was in some 60 films and was understandably cross that people mostly remembered her in the six she had made as Tarzan's mate. But in later life she expressed a fondness for them. The Tarzan films are said to be the most lucrative and longest-running series ever made. "It's nice to be immortal," she said, not entirely jokingly.

When Miss O'Sullivan first came to Hollywood the publicists said she was born in a thatched cottage in Ireland and spoke Gaelic. In her biography she says her father was a British army officer and she went to a finishing school in France. One of the problems of writing about showbiz people is finding the real person behind the make-up. At least Miss O'Sullivan's biography is amusing, and takes a pleasantly sceptical view of Hollywood. The studio she first worked for told her she was a failure. Miss O'Sullivan blamed the studio for putting her in musicals although she could not sing. "I realised that what really counted in Hollywood was looks rather than talent," she said. If you were pretty, photogenic and did what the director told you to, you were made. She had

at wrestling alligators and a marvellous swimmer (a former Olympics champion). Miss O'Sullivan's swimming was a gentle breaststroke, so a double did the nude scene.

Burroughs turned up at the studio one day to see what sort of a mess it was making of his masterpieces, but was polite to the couple. "He said we were perfect," Miss O'Sullivan recalled. Many would agree, among them Stalin, who would put on a show of Tarzan films for favoured visitors. They were more fun than "Battleship Potemkin".

It would be unfair to Maureen O'Sullivan not to say more about a career that stretched over 50 years. But what? Most of her pictures were second features; or if they were first

some alluring photos taken, was given a film test and became Tarzan's Jane.

The alluring Miss O'Sullivan nicely matched the Jane of the Burroughs books. Tarzan took her into his arms "and smothered her upturned panting lips with kisses". Johnny Weissmuller, though, was hardly the Tarzan of the books, described as an English lord fluent in six languages. The scriptwriters gave him a more limited vocabulary, usually remembered as "Me Tarzan, you Jane" (although there is some argument among Tarzan experts over whether he ever used these words). Weissmuller, though, was good

features she had small parts. Some critics remember her fondly in "The Big Clock", a much-praised thriller directed by her husband, John Farrow, in 1948. This is a cue to say that they had seven children, one of them Mia Farrow. Mother of Mia? "That's me," Miss O'Sullivan would say. Girlfriend of Tarzan? "That's me, too." It is a fame not to be sniffed at. Many other Tarzan films have been made besides the O'Sullivan six. None though has a Jane like hers, as Burroughs describes her, "lithe and young, her eyes wide with mingled horror and admiration for the primeval man who had fought for her and won her". ■

David Packard

David Packard, the inspiration of Silicon Valley, died on March 26th 1996, aged 83

AT A memorial service for David Packard at Stanford, the university he credited for his start, more than 1,000 mourners showed up. It seems a lot of people credited him for their start, too. Mr Packard founded, along with Bill Hewlett, one of the most successful high-tech firms in history, Hewlett-Packard. (The order of names was chosen by the toss of a coin, but, as it turned out, in reverse order of influence.) More importantly, in a small garage in Addison Avenue in Palo Alto, California, the two men started what would become Silicon Valley.

It is hard, on reviewing Mr Packard's life, to understand how this boy from Pueblo, Colorado, who liked to be in the open air and would spend some of his happiest moments driving a bulldozer on his ranch, could have inspired such digital-age icons as Microsoft's Bill Gates, Intel's Andy Grove, and Steve Jobs, Apple Computer's co-founder. Mr Packard was always a gentleman, who insisted that his employees respect their competitors and never criticise them in front of customers. Today the business is full of predators, publicly contemptuous of their rivals, who preach such battlefield exhortations as "Eat lunch or be lunch" and "Only the paranoid survive".

As a child, Mr Packard wished he had been born in an earlier day, when America's west was still a frontier and its people pioneers. He proved that the same spirit, channelled into technology and business rather than land and conquest, could create and cross new frontiers.

Birth of the brightest

Mr Packard and Mr Hewlett started HP in 1939 as a west coast firm in an industry dominated by east coast firms such as General Electric and Westinghouse. Their first sale was an audio oscillator used in a Disney film, "Fantasia". HP built up ties with Stanford: an engineering professor named Fred Terman tutored many of those who would become Silicon Valley's early stars. HP was one of the first firms to move into Stanford's business park, ground zero of the Valley's industrial explosion. It was an innovator and nimble in entering new business, traits that today define the region's firms. And it made heaps of money: more than $30 billion in annual sales today, not terribly far behind IBM. It is the Valley's largest company and biggest employer. Some 25 of the Valley's top executives are HP alumni.

No doubt there would have been a computer industry in California without HP. It was just one of several electronics firms that were starting up on the west coast in the late 1930s, a trend that accelerated during the second world war. But HP is the only one from those early days to have survived as a force in the industry. The fact that HP started with two guys in a garage, and took off, was an inspiration. It wasn't quite log cabin to White House – it was better.

But, the lack of courtesy apart, there is much that Mr Packard would have disapproved of in today's Valley. Growing up in the depression, and seeing what banks could do to companies, he swore never to take on long-term debt. The firm grew on profits

alone, and did not even go public until nearly its 20th year. Today's computer industry start-ups often go public before they are two, and will beg and borrow whatever it takes to keep up with the industry's skyrocketing growth. Compaq reached $1 billion in annual sales in less than a decade, something it took HP 40 years to achieve.

The firm practises pragmatic benevolence. It has never had a lay-off, and was one of the first firms to offer share options and profit-related pay. It has trusted employees, leaving equipment rooms unlocked (and believing that access to equipment might encourage employees to tinker in their off hours, perhaps inventing some new product).

At 6ft 5in, Mr Packard had an imposing presence, and he relished face-to-face contact with his employees. When he worked at General Electric after leaving university, he spent a day on a factory line and cracked the problem behind its failure rate with vacuum tubes. From then on, when things went wrong at HP, he would head for the shop floor. This "management by walking around" (later dignified by management theorists as MBWA)

reflected Mr Packard's low tolerance for boardroom decision-making, business schools and professional managers (although the firm would have to embrace all three as it grew larger). In 1969 he was asked by the Nixon administration to become assistant secretary of defence. He found the three years he spent in the job frustrating. The defence procurement system ran counter to the principles of efficiency HP held dear. He said the Pentagon would do as well picking names from a hat.

He was generous with his wealth. With his death the Packard Foundation's endowment will grow to $6.6 billion, making it America's third largest charity. He and Mr Hewlett gave Stanford more than $300m. Sharing his wealth with the region that made him great may partially account for his revered status with even the most jaundiced young Silicon Valley entrepreneurs. But there is more to it than that. The days of civility and organic growth may be gone in the industry hothouse, but the geeks still know solid technology, well made. David Packard set the tone of Silicon Valley by valuing nothing higher than a good machine. ■

Kerry Packer

Kerry Francis Bullmore Packer, tycoon and transformer of cricket, died on December 26th 2005, aged 68

BEFORE 1977, the words "cricket" and "commerce" had never been put together. The game belonged to gentlemen and players; sponsorship and long-term contracts were unheard of; the pay was poor. When a young man donned his whites, he was expected to symbolise fair play and national glory, not to earn a decent living. As for the game itself, though it had excitements, the pace of five-day matches could be glacial. The sight of small white figures endlessly regrouping, wandering about, pondering the light, all seen from one fixed angle, made poor spectator sport and even worse television.

So thought Kerry Packer. He was no expert; a huge, brawling, bull-shouldered man, he had been a heavyweight boxer at school and preferred a good game of polo, when he could find a pony strong enough to take him. But as the owner of Channel Nine, Australia's biggest and most successful commercial television network, he wanted to broadcast cricket to the nation, and make it lively. In 1976 he offered the Australian Cricket Board A$1.5m ($1.8m), seven times the usual fee, for exclusive rights to national and international games ("There's a little bit of the whore in all of us, gentlemen. What's your price?"). Astonishingly, they turned him down. So off strode Mr Packer to redesign cricket as he thought it should be.

In World Series Cricket, which ran for two seasons before the ACB caved in, the players wore pink and yellow, and the ball was white. Matches were sometimes played by floodlights at night, to get world audiences. They were often also finished in a day, compressing the action to unbelievable heights of tension and speed. Cameras were put at both ends of the pitch, so that with each ball the batsman could be seen reacting; microphones were fitted on the stumps, to catch the sweet thwack of leather on willow and the thunder of the bowler's feet. Top-rank players, including Tony Greig, then captain of England, and various South Africans, banned from the world game during apartheid, were poached for Mr Packer's teams, where they were treated to good pay and proper contracts. Mr Packer also took the cricketing authorities to court for restraint of trade. The game, though shellshocked, was modernised and professionalised, and has never looked back.

Swashbuckling ruthlessness typified Mr Packer's life. He was an iconoclast, a playboy and a man with an impressive instinct for when to buy, when to sell and when to get nasty. His father, Sir Frank Packer, had amassed an empire that included two TV stations, five radio stations, the *Sydney Daily Telegraph*, nine provincial papers and 60% of the country's magazines. The son, shrewdly building on that basis, rapidly came to dominate Australia physically, financially and commercially.

In 1972, two years before he became chairman, Mr Packer persuaded his father to sell the *Telegraph* to the family's great rival, Rupert Murdoch. He himself, convinced that the future lay with television, not newspapers, pumped the money into Channel Nine. In 1987, at the top of the market, he sold the network to Alan Bond, a financier, for an unheard-of

Queensland and New South Wales. Millions were given, sometimes secretly, to charity; millions were also spread over gambling tables in London and Las Vegas. (Though Mr Packer preferred to stay at home, no Australian casino could handle his wagers.) A three-week losing streak in London was said to have cost him A$28m but, overall, he came up lucky. Life was one big gamble, and a massive heart attack in 1990 had convinced him that "fucking nothing" lay on the other side.

Questions were often asked about the small amounts of tax his companies paid. Mr Packer brushed that off. Canberra was already spending his money so badly that it deserved to get no more. One government commission strayed close to linking him to organised crime, but the attorney-general cleared him. Politicians on both left and right were afraid of him and gave him what he wanted. A rare rebuff, when media cross-ownership laws blocked his designs on the rival Fairfax newspaper empire in 1991, left him furious.

Yet he was not particularly interventionist. His most brutal moment probably came in 1962, when he was sent by his father, with a few mates, to rough up the owner of a Sydney publishing house who was refusing to sell. He was busy trashing the office when Rupert Murdoch, also with a few mates, turned up to fight him. Almost as good as cricket, Packer-style. ∎

A$1 billion; three years later, he bought it back for a quarter of the price. "You only get one Alan Bond in your life," he said happily. But 1987 had been a great year; that October, Mr Packer had liquidated his stock holdings just before the market crashed.

A gambling man

He died Australia's richest man, with a fortune of A$7 billion. This was not bad going for a second son with no obvious ability, publicly called "Boofhead" by his father, who had lost two years' schooling with polio and whose first job in the firm had been to shovel newspapers on to the loading machine.

His money was funnelled into ski resorts, casinos, polo ponies, diamond mines, cattle stations, oil, engineering works and vast tracts of land in

Maurice Papon

Maurice Papon, collaborator, died on February 17th 2007, aged 96

AMONG THE ranks of the French civil service, it would be hard to find a more perfect example than Maurice Papon. Well informed, elegant yet self-effacing, he had the confidence of a man who had passed with smooth diligence through some of the best *lycées* in Paris. In his prefectures, with the tricolour furled behind his desk, instructions were carried out to the letter and correct form was followed. *Un fonctionnaire*, as the tag went, *est fait pour fonctionner*: the purpose of a bureaucrat is simply to do his job.

The Germans who occupied Bordeaux found Mr Papon easy to work with. The secretary-general of the prefecture of the Gironde, as he became in 1942, proved courteous and pleasant, an admirable officer of the Vichy regime that had been set up, in ostensible neutrality, to govern France alongside the Nazis. Occasionally, on delicate issues, he would hide behind his boss, the prefect; but in general he was dependable and "correct". He could be relied on not merely to do what Vichy and Berlin asked, but even to go further.

And he was a busy man, in charge of traffic, petrol rationing, requisitions and Jewish questions. These were two: status (identity, parentage, whether baptised) and Aryanisation (transfer of their property to non-Jews). Mr Papon had to arrange the seizure of Jewish shops, lands and jewellery across the whole region, their valuation and their sale by auction. In July 1942, in a first report, he noted that he had "dejudaised" 204 businesses, while 493 others were "in the process of dejudaisation".

That summer he also received other orders. He was to round up a "sufficient number" of Jews and send them to a staging camp at Drancy, in northern France. And he was to make such convoys regular. This meant ordering arrests, arranging police escorts and organising express trains that would not stop at stations. He managed it with his usual competence. Between 1942 and 1944 1,690 Jews were shipped out of Bordeaux, including 223 children. Most ended up in Auschwitz.

Had he known they would? No, he insisted later, nor did he have any inkling of the Nazis' broader plans. He had certain fears about Drancy. But people had to understand that he was not a free agent. There was a German *imperium* in force; Vichy was subject to it and he, after 1940, obedient to Vichy. With the coming of the Nazis numbers of civil servants had been sidelined or silenced, but he had a job to do, and "desertion was not in his ideology". There was a duty to survive, to keep things running, to avoid gratuitous provocation that might make a bad case worse. In Bordeaux he resisted in his own way, he said: taking names off arrest-lists, tipping off families in advance, sheltering a rabbi in his house. Why, he even chartered the city trams to spare the very young or old the walk to the station, and booked passenger trains, not goods wagons, to make their journey comfortable.

A code of silence

These self-justifications came out at Mr Papon's trial, one of only two of French

officials who collaborated with the Nazis in their crimes against humanity. Hundreds more might have been charged, including all those who worked for him. But once the Vichy leaders had been executed for treason after the Liberation, a different imperative prevailed: to keep France united, to avoid recriminations and to draw a veil over the past. In this new version of history all Frenchmen had resisted, including those who were now intent on quietly protecting each other. In his mind Mr Papon, too, had spent the Occupation fighting.

For almost four decades after the war he continued his steady upwards climb. He was prefect in Corsica, in Morocco and in Algeria; after 1958 he assumed charge of the Paris police, under orders from de Gaulle to "hold the city" against rioting Algerian nationalists. Those orders, as usual, were carried out with maximum efficiency; in one operation in 1961 up to 200 Algerians were killed, their bodies for days afterwards dragged out of the Seine. He had done his duty, Mr Papon said later. He had kept order. The Légion d'honneur was conferred on him, joining his treasured medal of the Resistance.

By 1981, now deputy for Cher, he had reached the cabinet as budget minister. Punctiliously, he was going after the rich who were evading taxes. But at the same time the families of the Jews he had deported were going after him. Lists and reports, carefully filed away, were discovered in corners of the town hall in Bordeaux. An article in *Le Canard Enchaîné*, a satirical weekly, forced his resignation from government; 16 years of languid inquiries and technical hitches followed. His eventual trial, in 1997–98, was the longest in French history. It ended with a sentence of ten years in prison, of which he served three until ill health excused him.

In court, assured as ever, he played the scapegoat. He felt no remorse, had no regrets. He had done his job. Most days, a walking affront to the self-delusion of France, he would appear with his yellow dossier underneath his arm. He would lay the papers out neatly before him, making constant notes. At one point, when a psychiatrist was called, he objected. He was not insane. Though perhaps, he added bitterly, he was mad to have stayed so long in the service of the state. ■

Rosa Parks

Rosa Parks, a pioneer of civil rights, died on October 24th 2005, aged 92

AS THE bus approached, she knew this particular driver was trouble. He had turned her off once before because, after paying her fare, she had refused to walk round the bus to get in by the back door. Rosa Parks knew better than to do that. While you walked round, the driver was quite capable of shutting the doors and driving off, leaving you stranded. So she had got in at the front and walked through to the back, like anybody else.

Or not quite like anybody else. In Montgomery, Alabama in the 1950s, as in much of the South, the first four rows of seats were for whites only. No more than four rows were needed, since few whites, and those poor ones, took the bus anyway. But whether they were filled or not, no black could sit there. Blacks sat at the back, in "Coloured", where they belonged.

Between the two worlds was a middle section. Blacks could sit there, but if a white needed their seat they were expected to vacate not one seat, but the whole row, in order to spare the white the embarrassment of sitting by a nigger. On December 1st 1955, Mrs Parks sat in that section. After three stops, a white needed a seat. The three other blacks in the row stood up meekly, but when the driver ordered Mrs Parks out, she said, firmly, "No".

In the mythology that came to gild this scene, Mrs Parks, who was 42, was said to have complained that her feet were tired. She herself denied it. Her job, as a seamstress in a department store, did not involve much standing. What had wearied her was drinking from black-only water-fountains, using black-only elevators, going to the back, standing aside, being demeaned in a hundred ways. She wanted no more of it. On December 5th, on the day she was convicted of violating a city ordinance and behaving in a disorderly manner, the young minister of the Dexter Street Baptist church in Montgomery, Martin Luther King, summed it up: "We are tired, tired of being segregated and humiliated, tired of being kicked about by the brutal feet of oppression."

Mrs Parks had meant to do no more, she said, than show one rude bus-driver that blacks were being treated unfairly. She was not the first black ever to refuse to give up her seat. But her action had unprecedented consequences. King and other black leaders started a boycott of Montgomery's buses; it lasted for 382 days, with blacks walking, cycling or going by mule instead. Other cities followed suit. Mrs Parks's case went to the Supreme Court, which ruled that bus segregation was illegal. Most important, a movement of non-violent protest had begun, with King as its extraordinary spokesman, which eventually recruited the courts, the president and Congress to the cause of equal rights. And Mrs Parks, small, pretty, bespectacled and soft-spoken, was seen as its instigator.

The Klansmen riding
Racism had tainted her life from the beginning. On her grandparents' farm at Pine Level, in the Alabama wilds, she attended for a while a one-room school for blacks only; classes lasted only five months, to release the children for work in the fields. At night she sometimes heard lynchings, and the Klansmen riding. Once the body of a young black was found in the woods; no one knew who had killed him.

Her later schooling was cut short by the need to care for her sick grandmother. She took in sewing, learned typing, married young, but also got involved in black politics. In the Montgomery Voters' League, she helped would-be voters weave their way through the Jim Crow tests designed to keep them from the ballot, and tried

several times to register to vote herself. She also joined the National Association for the Advancement of Coloured People (NAACP), becoming secretary of the Montgomery chapter in 1943. Long preparation, therefore, preceded her act of defiance.

Yet life in the South became too hard for her after the boycott. Fired from her job, she left for Detroit in 1957, the destination in those days of thousands of other poor blacks. She was still no celebrity, and continued to take in sewing. Eventually, a local black congressman, John Conyers, hired her to manage his office. She raised funds for the NAACP, appeared at events alongside King, and slowly came to realise that she was an inspiration. In 1999 she was given a Congressional Gold Medal of Honour, the highest honour possible for an American civilian.

As she grew older she was asked, often and almost obsessively, how much race relations had truly improved in America since the passing of the civil-rights laws. She thought there was still far to go. In 1994 she was beaten and robbed by a young black high on drugs and alcohol and fuelled, she supposed, by frustrations much like her own. Although he knew who she was, he said it made no difference to him.

In 1987 she had founded the Rosa and Raymond Parks Institute for Self-Development which, as one of its programmes, took children of different races round the country to learn about the civil-rights movement. They travelled by bus, naturally, sitting where they pleased. By this time, the famous green, white and yellow bus on which she herself had sat, unmoving, had become an exhibit at the Henry Ford Museum in Dearborn, Michigan. But Mrs Parks was well aware that the journey she had started that day was unfinished. ■

Luciano Pavarotti

Luciano Pavarotti, the world's favourite tenor, died on September 6th 2007, aged 71

H E REMEMBERED the moment it began, at four years old: jumping on the kitchen table, setting the lamp swinging, singing "La donna è mobile" to an audience of adoring women. His father sang, beautifully, as a tenor in the church in Modena; the soaring voices of Gigli and Caruso filled the house from the crackling gramophone; at the cinema Mario Lanza sang and young Luciano Pavarotti copied him, warbling and gesturing into the mirror. To sing was to be loved.

Football was still his chief obsession. Yet as his musical career unfolded, it crossed paths with the Beautiful Game. He performed in stadiums, in front of thousands. The final of the 1990 World Cup in Rome was marked by a concert with Plácido Domingo and José Carreras, "The Three Tenors", who then sang together for 13 years. Pavarotti's version of "Nessun dorma" from Puccini's "Turandot", the anthem of that World Cup, came to epitomise all the drama, glory and pain of football, with his three climactic "vinceros" at the end of the aria like a perfect free kick, rising, arching, landing sweetly on the very note, safe in the corner of the net.

Pavarotti made it seem so easy. "Natural" and "effortless" were the words most often applied to that smooth, honeyed, gorgeous voice, which made skin break out in goose-bumps and raised the hairs on the back of the neck. *Lasciare andare*, pouring it forth. No matter that the singer was huge and almost immobile, his beard blackened with burnt cork and his face running with sweat mopped away with an enormous white handkerchief; the smile was ecstatic, and the voice was from heaven. His biggest break had come, in 1972, when he hit nine high Cs in Donizetti's "La Fille du Régiment"; he was dressed then like a fat toy soldier, patently unable to act, but the crowd adored him. He took 17 curtain calls and, by his death, held the world record for them.

The easiness and naturalness were deceptive. He was terrified of the high notes, full of the usual performer's superstitions: a bent nail kept in his pocket, and a quick cry of "Malocchio!" if anyone mentioned bad luck. Though his voice showed no strain, he could be seen rising on the balls of his feet in recital, using every sinew and nerve to produce the sound. Wherever he went, he made sure to surround himself with home comforts: espresso machines, prosciutto-slicers, bottles of Lambrusco, his blotter and pens laid out exactly as they would be on his desk in Modena, and a secretary – nubile, pretty, obliging – who would hold up cue cards for him in the wings and who, when needed, would warm his extra-marital bed.

Critics and other singers often called him lazy. He seemed as undisciplined in singing as he was about food, abandoning diet after diet in favour of porterhouse steaks or caviar scooped up with a tablespoon. Certainly he was unintellectual, without conservatory training and barely able to read music. Learning from a score, he once said, was "like making love by mail". Words – even those of "O sole mio", every tenor's meal-ticket – were hard to drum in; in

opera or recital he almost never ventured out of his crisp, supple Italian. Narrow as his repertoire was, he was choosy in it: "Tosca", "Rigoletto", "Un Ballo in Maschera". His tendency to cancel got him banned from several houses and soured his farewell at the New York Met.

Macaroni for the masses

Yet Pavarotti knew what he was doing. He took things easy, hid throat lozenges in his handkerchief, and looked after his instrument. His voice was "gifted from God"; he sang purely by instinct, aware of "how it should go", and trusting that a good conductor could follow after him. The sheer beauty of his sound, without acting and without musicianship, could bring the audience to its feet, and he would earn the hard-negotiated money that made him the highest-paid singer in opera.

He was also a natural populist in a field that was sniffy and exclusive, bringing to the Met and Covent Garden a sense of opera as Italian peasant fare, "macaroni" for the masses. Larry King once asked him about singing for the elite. "Why should be elite, music?" came the reply. Pavarotti went on "The Tonight Show" and "Saturday Night Live"; in his charity concerts he performed with Elton John and the Spice Girls. When critics sniffed about "popera", he fought back stoutly: "If you call pop singer, you can sell the ticket." The numbers backed him up: live audiences in the hundreds of thousands, TV audiences in the millions, more than 50m albums sold, five Grammys. "The word 'commercial' is exactly what we want," said the maestro, who also starred in TV ads for American Express. "If you want to use ... something more derogatory, we don't care."

To the frustration of his rivals, though they were gentlemanly about it, Pavarotti became the world's favourite tenor. He was the first opera star to be imitated, drunkenly, by legions of joyful or heartbroken football fans. Still crazy for football himself, he never minded. For all his frustrations, sulks and cancellations, a life spent bringing music to mankind was the greatest joy imaginable: singing, and then the crowd's adoration for his singing, as he jumped from the kitchen table and the cheese, the wine, the pasta and the sausages were lavishly spread before him. ■

John Peel

John Peel, born John Ravenscroft, music lover, died on October 26th 2004, aged 65

THE MODERN world of music offers an embarrassment of riches. Faced with shops full of compact discs, records and tapes, the ordinary listener hardly knows where to start. With popular music, in particular, there is now an almost inverse relationship between the popularity of a song and its quality. The best new film or book usually gets noticed; the best new popular song is undoubtedly one that few people have heard of and that fewer still will have the patience, or the funds, to find.

What is the popular-music lover to do? For the past 37 years, in Britain at least, the answer has been clear: listen to John Peel. From 1967 onwards, Mr Peel broadcast a music show on the BBC's Radio 1 where he played records he liked. In his eyes, he was no more responsible for the music than a newspaper editor is for the day's events. He did not, after all, create anything. The music was all there already.

Yet selection is creating, after a fashion. A sculptor picks which bits of marble to include and which to chisel away. Mr Peel's medium was larger than that of any of the bands he championed: the whole of popular music, which was shaped, at least to some degree, according to his taste. The number of acts he raised from obscurity to fame (David Bowie, Marc Bolan, Captain Beefheart, the Undertones, the Smiths) is large; the number of bands he raised from obscurity to semi-obscurity is even larger. Happily, though, he never saw promotion as his task. His demeanour on the radio was one of pure delight: delight in the new, the unexpected and the good. Listening to him, it was difficult to avoid the conclusion that the listener was at some level irrelevant – the point was for Mr Peel himself to revel in the music.

That is not to say he avoided the usual formalities: "I hope you enjoy this one", and the like. He said such things, and meant them. But they were secondary. He never pandered to the audience. A catchy, addictive tune might be followed by a few minutes of sheer noise. What he most liked, he once said, was not only music he had never heard before, but music he could relate to nothing else.

Mr Peel's show was quite unpredictable, save, in later years, for one fixture: "Pig's Big 78", halfway through. This was a 78 rpm record chosen by his wife, affectionately nicknamed Pig. The sound quality would be terrible, as no one had made such records since the late 1950s, and the ones Mr Peel played often came from much earlier than that. But the 78s were no exception to his passion for novelty. They were old enough to be new again.

Radio shows are by nature ephemeral. But from his early days on the BBC, Mr Peel had invited musicians to come into the studio and perform for him and his audience. These "Peel Sessions", as they came to be known, were a sort of shadow Greatest Hits of popular music of the past 30 years. Bands liked coming on his show as much as he liked having them. The publicity, of course, did not hurt, and Mr Peel's own enthusiasm seemed to lend the music vitality. For all that, he rarely formed close relationships with musicians. It was the end product that mattered to him, not the process of creation.

Crashing the car
Mr Peel lived in Suffolk, a gently undulating county two hours away from London, in a house he dubbed "Peel Acres". He kept chickens there, like a country yeoman. On the long drive home from the studio after recording his show, he would listen to demo tapes that unknown bands had sent him, throwing the ones he didn't like on the floor and the ones he did on the back seat. One

day, he supposed, he would be squinting to discern a good new band's name and would kill himself by crashing the car. It was probably, he said, how people imagined he would like to go.

Yet Mr Peel always seemed too young to be considering how he would like to die. And there was too much music to be listened to. Although it was not work to him, but sheer pleasure, he nonetheless spent hours every day listening to music he had never heard before. By the time he died – suddenly, of a heart attack in Peru – he had possibly listened to more music than anyone else alive. And though studios had become as computerised as the rest of the world, he continued to prefer playing vinyls on turntables. They sounded better.

He did not start his radio career at the BBC, but at WRR, in Dallas, Texas. He had been in America for two years, working as a crop-insurance agent, when the Beatles started sweeping America. His scouse accent was suddenly marketable, even if he hammed it up a bit. Although he was born just outside Liverpool, the son of a cotton broker, he went to Shrewsbury, a mid-ranking public school. He once said that his life was changed, and set on course, at Shrewsbury when he first heard Elvis Presley singing "Heartbreak Hotel". If it had not been Elvis, it would have been some other song.

He also credited his time at Shrewsbury with sustaining his BBC career. The toffs at the corporation figured that an old boy couldn't be all that bad, even if he played music no one else on the station knew. But he remained a slightly dangerous outlier. When he first returned to England in 1967, he spent six months working for a pirate radio station on a ship in the North Sea. He never lost that pirate streak. ∎

Alejo Peralta

Alejo Peralta y Diaz Ceballos, Mexican industrial pioneer and government collaborator, died on April 8th 1997, aged 80

THE INDUSTRIAL revolution came late to Mexico, perhaps because it was held back by other less beneficial revolutions. Alejo Peralta, who as much as anyone fostered industrialisation in Mexico, set up in business in 1939. By then, Britain's industrial revolution, founded on James Watt's steam engine, had been pounding away for some 170 years, and Henry Ford, the pioneer of assembly-line production, was an old man. Anything on sale in Mexico that was made in a factory quite likely came from America or Britain. "I was the beginning of Mexican industrialisation," Mr Peralta liked to say. It was not wholly true, but he was enough of an innovator for the claim, made with his usual forcefulness, to go unchallenged.

In setting out to change things, Mr Peralta had, as it happened, the same obsessive interest in how things worked that had motivated Watt and Ford. His father had sold and serviced sewing machines (American ones) and Alejo recalled playing with spindles and other bits of discarded machinery. After getting some training as an engineer, Mr Peralta set up his first enterprise with a capital of 650 pesos (about $1,400 today) and a staff of two. He made candles from waste material he obtained free. Using Bakelite, an early plastic, he turned to making buttons for industrial clothing. By 1943 he had 200 employees producing conductors and other electrical goods. At his death his Industrias Unidas Sociedad Anonima, known as IUSA, was a conglomerate of more than 100 companies, producing a range of goods from ballpoint pens

to cellular telephones. Last year, *Forbes* magazine reckoned the Peralta family was worth $2.5 billion.

The darkest hour

It has to be said, though, that Mr Peralta's rise to riches was not entirely a triumph of selfless individualism. It owed a lot to his successful cultivation of leaders of the Institutional Revolutionary Party, or PRI. The party set out in the 1920s with the admirable aim of building a free and progressive society after a century of revolutions, civil war and fights with the United States. But in 70 years of power, the PRI has turned Mexico, although formally a democracy, into an authoritarian one-party state. Mr Peralta went along with the policies of the party, cultivating its leaders. He was an adviser to President Gustavo Diaz Ordaz during modern Mexico's darkest hour, when the army, acting under government orders, calculatedly opened fire with machineguns on a demonstration in Mexico City's Tlatelolco Plaza in 1968, killing hundreds of people.

In an interview in 1992 Mr Peralta defended the massacre, claiming that the stability of the country was under threat. At the time, he said, "you feel bad that there were so many victims, but over time you understand that this was necessary". Stalin could not have put it better, but other Mexican businessmen who have done well under the government's patronage share his view. Indeed, perhaps the main interest in Mr Peralta's life is that it was an archetype of the relationship between tycoon and government which has become commonplace, not only in Mexico but elsewhere; for example, in South Korea.

But whereas ordinary Koreans have done well from the unholy alliance, Mexico remains distressingly poor. In a couple of generations, South Korea, once a country of peasants, has developed a large middle class. In Mexico, according to a United Nations report published last year, 43% of the rural population and 23% of those in towns live in poverty. Mr Peralta reckoned that his companies provided work that supported more than 13,000 families. Other Mexican industrial firms could proudly produce comparable figures. But these firms are oases in a desert of the unemployed and underemployed.

If the inequities of Mexican society bothered Mr Peralta, he had the consolation of baseball, for which he had a passion. In the 1930s he played professionally for a time, and when he became rich he founded a baseball team, the Mexico City Tigres. His death was mostly written about in the sports pages of Mexican newspapers, and the Mexican Baseball League called for a period of mourning. Mr Peralta liked to dash about, in sports cars, his helicopter and a private jet. He underwent heart surgery four times. "I've lived as I wanted to live," he said.

But to younger industrialists in Mexico Mr Peralta and his like are dinosaurs who have outlived their time. They fear more decades of underdevelopment and human misery unless Mexico throws off its old ways. Mexico is changing, they say. The PRI is losing elections. Television reporting is less biased towards the government. The sons of the old guard tend to be well educated, often in the United States. They like to paint a picture of peaceful democratic modernisation. The congressional and other elections due in July will, it is claimed, be cleaner than before. Not difficult, perhaps, but already there are doubts. The PRI, fearing electoral disaster, is expected to spend more than it is legally entitled to in a bid to buy votes. Mexico may be changing, but hardly at a revolutionary pace. ∎

Max Perutz

Max Ferdinand Perutz, scientist, died on February 6th 2002, aged 87

A FAVOURITE word of Max Perutz, if perhaps an unscientific one, was "Fantastic!", with the exclamation mark given its full value. In the spring of 1953 at the Cavendish Laboratory in Cambridge he was using the word quite frequently. Francis Crick and James Watson were solving the structure of DNA. Mr Perutz and his colleague John Kendrew were advancing the knowledge of molecular biology. All four men were to be awarded Nobel prizes as a result of their work in that spring. Since the 1950s the laboratory and its successors have been home to the winners of nine Nobel prizes.

If you can say that the spirit of a place can inspire people to do, well, fantastic things, the Cavendish is a telling example. This homely building was a birthplace of nuclear physics and other earth-moving developments. As a chemistry student working for a doctorate Max Perutz came under its spell. His native Austria was absorbed by Germany in 1938. Cambridge, he said, was where he wanted to spend his life. In Cambridge Lawrence Bragg was working on a method of examining the molecular structure in a crystal by shining x-rays through it (for which he had got a Nobel at the age of 25, still the youngest recipient). Some molecules, such as those of salt, had been found to have simple atomic structures. Young Max boldly suggested that x-ray crystallography might be used to examine more complex molecules, such as proteins, which make up organisms.

A friend proposed haemoglobin, whose large oxygen-carrying protein molecules make red blood cells red. Haemoglobin carries oxygen and carbon dioxide through the bloodstream with great efficiency, essential to life. How it did this was a mystery, although it was evident that the molecules changed shape during their journey.

An obliging physiologist grew Mr Perutz some crystals of haemoglobin of horse. Bragg saw at once the attraction and immensity of dealing with so large a structure. "Haemoglobin of horse!" Mr Perutz was to exclaim. Sometimes, he said, the difficult choice for his experiments "seemed like a curse". In 1939 Mr Perutz encountered a different sort of curse. His experiments were delayed with the outbreak of the second world war and Mr Perutz was interned as an enemy alien.

The ice aerodrome

Max Perutz came from a moneyed family of textile manufacturers who moved to Britain when their business was confiscated. Max had been expected to study law but at university in Vienna had found science vastly more attractive. As happened to many scientists who found freedom in Britain, he was first detained and then released to resume his scientific work. In one of the odder exploits of the war Mr Perutz was asked to examine the mechanical properties of ice, with a view to creating an aerodrome of ice in the middle of the Atlantic. Someone high up in the government had discovered that before the war Mr Perutz had published a paper on the science of glaciers (in order, he sometimes said, to justify

began to yield. What was true of haemoglobin proved to be true about scores of other proteins. A colleague at the Cavendish said last week that Mr Perutz's work on protein structure had become especially relevant as scientists sought to make sense of the human genome and the mechanisms of disease.

Max Perutz wrote many essays and reviews. One of his collections is typically called *Is Science Necessary?* He had a happy facility

skiing holidays). The project was named Habakkuk, after a Jewish prophet who foretold beastly punishments on the wicked. It was abandoned when military aircraft were developed with enough range to make a mid-ocean stop unnecessary.

In Cambridge after the war, Mr Perutz became chairman of the Medical Research Council Laboratory, a unit at the Cavendish, where the tools of physics were applied to biological problems. He kept the administration minimal and informal, qualities that helped to make the laboratory a magnet to attract other gifted researchers. "Mountains of futile paperwork" can kill creativity, he said.

In his own tenacious pursuit of a scientific goal he was what a colleague said was "a force of nature". In a series of experiments during the 1950s and 1960s by Mr Perutz the mystery of the haemoglobin molecule's efficiency

at explaining science vividly, whatever his audience, school children, prime ministers, journalists or other scientists. If Mr Perutz was seen to have an eccentricity, it was perhaps about food. He could not digest anything made with flour, nor onions, pepper or most spices. He liked soft foods, such as ripe bananas, or cold boiled potatoes with butter. He stepped down as chairman of the Cambridge laboratory at 65, but never really retired. Over the past 22 years he published more than 100 papers.

Mr Perutz turned down the offer of a knighthood. He said that at the laboratory the most junior member could talk science with anyone: a handle to the chairman's name could only get in the way. Anyway, his wife Gisela didn't want to be Lady Perutz. He was made a Companion of Honour and was awarded the Order of Merit, both of which are far rarer than knighthoods. Fantastic! ■

Pham Van Dong

Pham Van Dong, Vietnam's chief in war and peace, died on April 29th 2000, aged 94

OF THE Vietnamese who became world celebrities, the best known were no doubt Ho Chi Minh, Uncle Ho to his admirers, and Vo Nguyen Giap, still alert at 88 and happy to reminisce about how he beat the French at Dien Bien Phu, the fortress they believed was impregnable. Quite likely, Pham Van Dong was envious of both men. Both had retained their colourful reputations. Ho had died in 1969, at a time when the war was moving Vietnam's way. Giap was an unbeaten general, a name for the military history books.

Mr Dong, prime minister from 1955 to 1986, saw his own reputation decline once peace came to Vietnam in 1975. It is not only in the West that political careers tend to end in failure. Mr Dong told visiting westerners that running Vietnam in peacetime was far more difficult than waging a war. Of course it was. The old unity had gone, and had been replaced by people's expectations. Mr Dong longed to return to the simplicities of wartime when a Vietnamese was grateful for a pair of sandals, and a straw mat to sleep on; and a bicycle was a luxury. Now the same Vietnamese wanted a television and a car, and had developed a taste for Coke. Vietnam made a nod, if not a bow, to market forces. "Produce and make a profit" was an approved slogan. But the country's flirtation with capitalism was blamed for corruption, never a problem during the war.

Worse, Vietnam had become unimportant. Mr Dong wrote many essays about Vietnam's 2,000 years of struggle against invaders from the north, principally China. He was an authority on two sisters named Trung who had led a rebellion against the Chinese invaders. In modern times the Vietnamese had fought the Japanese when many Asians had collaborated. Since beating the French and the Americans, the Vietnamese had chased Pol Pot out of Phnom Penh in 1979, and had repulsed China when it had come to Pol Pot's aid. These days Vietnam was merely a statistic in charts that compared its dismal performance with the likes of Algeria and Cuba. It occasionally turned up in stories about claims for the Spratly islands, a group of extremely boring rocks in the South China Sea. You could not get more unimportant than that.

On stage in Geneva
If Pham Van Dong had to pick a moment in his life when he felt he had stepped on to the world stage it would probably be in the Geneva peace talks of 1954. These took place in the aftermath of the French defeat. Back in 1945, after the end of the second world war, the French had returned to their former colony and refused it independence. Now their chief concern was to save what face they could. Mr Dong, representing the victors, was far removed from the Vietnamese peasant the French expected. His father had been secretary to one of Vietnam's last emperors, and Mr Dong had received a good education in Hue, the old imperial capital, and at Hanoi University. As a young man he was also rather good at football.

Although America sent only an observer to the talks, Mr Dong was aware that President Eisenhower loathed French colonialism. He thus felt he was in the strongest of positions. But at Geneva he let the French off lightly, allowing them to run the south of the country under a puppet Vietnamese government.

The communists believed that their chief weapon was patience. They would first establish their northern state, then tackle the problem of the south. Mr Dong told an American reporter in 1966, "How long do you Americans want to fight? One year? Five years? Twenty years? We will be glad to accommodate you." That sort of talk caused a chill in Washington as American casualties mounted. Even Henry Kissinger, Mr Dong's adversary after the Americans replaced the French as the enemy, lost his customary urbanity when discussing the North Vietnamese. "Just a bunch of shits; tawdry, filthy shits," he said in one of his high-level briefings for Richard Nixon. They were incapable of negotiating in a decent and responsible way. Pham Van Dong, he said on another occasion, was "wily and insolent". The angrier the Americans got, the cooler was Mr Dong's response. When the Americans leave, he said, "we will strew the path of your departure with flowers".

This past week the Vietnamese have been celebrating the 25th anniversary of their capture of Saigon, now Ho Chi Minh City. As the Americans are reminded of the only war they lost, the debate has been rekindled about whether Pham Van Dong and his comrades were more nationalist than communist; and if they were, was too much made at the time of their supposed threat to the rest of South-East Asia?

For all his sophistication, Mr Dong did play the part of the party heavy. He never budged from his belief that Vietnam should remain a one-party state, although quite likely the communists could have won, or at least done well, in multi-party elections, as other communists have done in the former Soviet Union and eastern Europe. He insisted, though, that he was a patriot. "The Communist is the most genuine patriot," he said, leaving others to puzzle out quite what that meant. ■

Abbé Pierre

Henry Groüès ("Abbé Pierre"), champion of the homeless, died on January 22nd 2007, aged 94

TRADITIONALLY MOST saints are gentle creatures. Those enshrined in French homes, or on prayer-cards stuffed into the missals of elderly churchgoers, are usually St Anthony carrying the child Jesus, or smiling St Thérèse of Lisieux with a bouquet of flesh-tinted roses. Odd, then, that the nearest modern France has come to a saint was a man fuelled and driven by unceasing anger: anger that the poor should suffer and that the rich did not care.

For any man in authority, clerical or lay, a visit from Abbé Pierre was an unsettling experience. First there was the look of him: the *coupe zéro* haircut under a black beret, the straggling beard, the black cape thrown dramatically across the shoulders, the belted soutane and muddy boots from tramping through slums. Then came the disquieting blue stare, and the surprisingly loud, ringing voice. He was not a large man or a strong one: lung trouble had disrupted his studies as a boy, and he had been advised at 26 to give up the monastic life for his health's sake. His anger surprised even himself; it did not seem in character. But it made him a giant.

Charles de Gaulle summoned him in 1945, after giving him the Croix de Guerre for a brave, clandestine war, to have an appreciative word; Abbé Pierre lectured him on the lack of milk for babies. Almost 50 years later, the elderly priest refused to wear his Légion d'honneur until a crowd of 300 poor African families, sleeping rough on the esplanade de Vincennes in Paris, was given lodging. When Jacques Chirac, hoping to score electoral points, offered to open up empty buildings for the homeless, Abbé Pierre berated him for hypocrisy. With "measured insolence", he scolded John Paul II for not allowing married priests and for refusing to retire. He would bite people's ears like a flea, he said, and yell, "Wake up!"

France first heard that voice at lunchtime on February 1st 1954. The napkins were tucked in, the spoons poised over the soup, when Abbé Pierre, having seized the microphone at Radio Luxembourg, told his listeners that a woman had frozen to death that night on the boulevard Sebastopol. She had been clutching an eviction notice, served to her the day before. The weather was grim; all over France, thousands more were dying. Abbé Pierre appealed for blankets, food, stoves and money to be brought to his temporary headquarters at the Hotel Rochester. The response was so enormous that not only the hotel lobby, but the disused Gare d'Orsay nearby, were filled to the roof with donations. Army lorries helped distribute them, and the National Assembly voted 10 billion francs for housing for the poor.

The organisation to which the rich brought their jewellery, and ordinary people packets of rice and jars of jam, was still a strangely fluid affair. It was run from a large ramshackle house in Neuilly-Plaisance, a Paris suburb, where Abbé Pierre in 1949 had started taking in the homeless, first in rooms and then, as numbers grew, in shacks in the garden. He had no idea what this project would become. Perhaps it would be no more than a kindly bourgeois gesture, the sort his own wealthy father had made when

he went, each Sunday, to wash and shave the poor in the shelters of Lyon.

His colleagues were a strange, quarrelsome band, ex-cons and ex-legionnaires, some of whom had been homeless themselves. To raise funds they picked rags and salvaged furniture, or begged with laundry baskets in the Paris streets. Abbé Pierre called his project "Emmaus", after the place where two disciples had given shelter to the risen but unrecognised Christ.

Love human, love divine

Emmaus communities caught on and thrived; by 2006 there were 350 of them in nearly 40 countries, 110 in France itself. Abbé Pierre became a thorn in the side of successive French governments, and a year before he died was still lobbying for a law establishing the right to lodging. Yet he did not relish publicity on his own account. After regularly topping the annual poll of best-loved figures in France, in 2004 he asked to be removed from it. Celebrity helped the cause, but it appalled him.

He had little enough to hide: a clutch of Utopian left-wing views, and one

dismaying brush with Holocaust denial which seemed the mere misjudgment of old age. In 2005 he also admitted, in a memoir, that chastity was too hard for him. He had decided to become a monk at 15, and had joined the Capuchins at 19; from then on, the pain of living without sexual love was constant. Indeed, he did not always live without it. He occasionally slept with women and would sometimes, wistfully and innocently, fall into discussions of sex with women who scarcely knew him.

Yet those who imagined him deprived of love were wrong. Abbé Pierre was possessed by it. Priest though he was, he rarely preached or mentioned God by name, a fact that only added to his popularity in proudly secular France. The force he invoked was different. "Despite all the evil that men and women suffer", he said once, "I believe that the Eternal is Love all the same, and we are loved all the same, and we are free all the same." Love would absorb him in the end, when his "Sister Death" came, as tenderly as any woman, to embrace him. And it was Love, he said, that made him so angry. ■

Gene Pitney

Gene Pitney, singer and songwriter, died on April 5th 2006, aged 65

AGEING POP-SINGERS are not meant to die. The waist thickens and the lush dark hair turns white; the tan grows more improbable, the trouser legs more short; yet the voice, given a bit of a run at them, can still reach those high notes, and the warbling now comes smoky with experience. There may be no hopes left of chart appearances, but an audience can still be found, climbing slowly out of the tour buses into one or another sherbet-coloured theatre in Branson, Missouri.

Gene Pitney never inhabited one of Branson's living mausoleums. Well past middle age he trod the boards in Europe, mostly in Britain, taking his ancient hits to the likes of Peterborough, Birmingham and Glasgow. He died unexpectedly in Cardiff, of heart disease, after another sell-out show.

Why Mr Pitney, an all-American boy, was so much more popular in Britain than in America is difficult to say. Sheer contrast had something to do with it. Mr Pitney hit the pop-music scene at the same glorious moment as the Beatles and the Rolling Stones; but where the Beatles were all Mersey jauntiness and the Stones strutting London rudeness, Mr Pitney offered the wailing of disappointed teenage love from a strange, distant land.

"Twenty Four Hours from Tulsa" (1963), his greatest hit in Britain, fell on ears that had no very clear idea where Tulsa was. As in "Wichita Lineman" and "Do you Know the Way to San José?", half the song's drama came from its evocation of America as a land of highways, plains and (broken) dreams.

The lyrics, too, painted a picture worthy of a James Dean movie, and sung like one.

> I saw a welcoming light
> And stopped to rest for the night
> And that is when I
> saw her
> As I pulled in outside of a small motel,
> She was there
> and so I walked up
> to her
> Asked where I could get something to eat
> and she showed me
> Where

Mr Pitney's appearance gave credibility to the poor traveller's tale. He was improbably clean-cut and besuited even for the time, with brooding brows and a pained, naive expression. You could well believe that he had been born in Hartford, Connecticut, the home of insurance, had studied electrical engineering and, in his spare time, had painstakingly trapped and stuffed racoons. He had also sung in the church choir. Clearly he was shy and good, and the world was hell to him.

But he was not as shy as all that. He was writing songs and singing them from an early age, and hawking them where he could. Some say he was spotted by an agent at a seminal concert by Gene and the Genials in Rockville, Connecticut, in 1959 or so. Others remember him going, with a greased-up pompadour and a bag of demo tapes, to knock on doors on Broadway, where Burt Bacharach and Hal David eventually adopted him. "Tulsa" was one of their songs, as was "Only Love can Break a Heart", Mr

the model for David Bowie's odd sounds and manners as Ziggy Stardust.

He had some claim to have done all this. Most remarkably, he moved at the highest levels of the pop charts in the 1960s without melting down, by the end of the decade, in a blur of LSD and flowers. Mick Jagger, Keith Richards and Marianne Faithfull were his friends, and his recording of the Jagger/Richards song "That Girl Belongs to Yesterday" helped to get the Stones known in the States; but in that maelstrom Mr Pitney remained his small-town self. He provided some frenzied maracas for the Stones' cover of "Not Fade Away" and some company for Ms Faithfull, but (it was said) of a gentlemanly kind.

Pitney's biggest hit in the United States. The combination of Mr David's dramatic words, Mr Bacharach's wistful melodies and Mr Pitney's tear-filled tremolos was powerful stuff.

Unlike a Rolling Stone

Asked to sum up Mr Pitney, critics found it difficult. His music ranged all over rock, pop and country, and merged them together. His voice, though pretty good, was also "heart-stopping", "panic-stricken" or "like a kid pulling a wagon across a gravel road". He was as famous for writing songs for others ("Rubber Ball" for Bobby Vee, "He's a Rebel" for the Crystals) as for recording them himself. His admirers credited him with large influence, from bringing Indian music to the notice of the Beatles, to encouraging Phil Spector towards his "Wall of Sound" period, to providing

This was rather typical. Away from the stage he liked to fish, or just look at water. As a teenager he would drive out of Rockville five miles to Walkers Reservoir, sit there for hours in his candy-apple red Ford coupé, and write songs. In later years he disappeared so frequently from the American scene that he was often assumed to be dead, or living as a recluse in the woods somewhere. In Glasgow, Peterborough and Cardiff they knew different: Mr Pitney's voice, one of the stranger instruments ever heard in pop music, swooping and aching through three octaves, was still ringing round them.

Oh I was only 24 hours from Tulsa
Ah, only one day away from your arms ∎

George Plimpton

George Ames Plimpton, writer and madcap, died on September 25th 2003, aged 76

PERHAPS ERNEST Hemingway started it. In the 1920s he was a hungry young writer in Paris, inventing a new way of putting words together that was to make him the world's best-known novelist. "Happiness", Hemingway wrote much later, "is a moveable feast", and "A Moveable Feast" was the title he gave to a nostalgic memoir of his life in Paris at that time. In the 1950s a new generation of young Americans felt the allure of Paris. Like Hemingway, they had been in a war. They were not especially hungry. Some were rich. All had dollars in their pockets. America had treated them generously for their wartime services. Still, "they seemed endlessly delighted in posing as paupers and dodging the bill collectors", wrote Gay Talese in an essay called "Looking for Hemingway". They lived "in happy squalor on the Left Bank for two or three years amid the whores, jazz musicians

and pederast poets". In the summer they drove down to Pamplona to run from the bulls, as Hemingway had done. In the winter, like him, they skied in the Alps.

George Plimpton was probably the most interesting of the young Americans. He was working on his first novel and one of the walks that he liked to take in Paris was in Montparnasse, along the streets that Jake Barnes takes after leaving Lady Brett in Hemingway's "The Sun Also Rises". Then he would go into a bar and have a drink, as Hemingway would have done. Some friends of Mr Plimpton persuaded him to take over as publisher and editor of a little magazine called the *Paris Review*. The *Review* was one of many literary magazines of the time that would be started, with great hopes, and die after a few issues when the printer could not be paid. The *Review* survived. It was also extraordinarily good. It published much early work by gifted writers, among them Philip Roth and Italo Calvino. Its interviews with established writers, among them, naturally, Hemingway, remain important pieces of biography. Mr Plimpton was to go on to do many amazing things, but keeping the *Review* going and maintaining its quality was his best achievement. He put the 50th anniversary edition to bed the night before he died.

With the Kennedys

George Plimpton was born into what is regarded as aristocracy in the United States. His father was a wealthy lawyer who later became a diplomat. At Harvard he became chums with many of the people who were part of America's privileged circle of influence. He was close to the Kennedys and was one of the team that helped to get John Kennedy elected president. After Kennedy was murdered he joined Kennedy's brother Bobby in his bid in 1968 to become president and was with him when he too was shot dead.

Mr Plimpton was not by nature a name dropper. Being with the Kennedys, playing tennis with the elder George Bush, travelling with Bill Clinton, knowing movie stars: what was exceptional about that? Doesn't everybody? He wanted to be known as a writer, and wrote a couple of dozen books, more than his hero Hemingway did. But although in 2002 the American Academy of Arts and Letters graciously named Mr Plimpton as a "central figure in American letters", it is difficult to think of a title of his that will endure. Possibly "Paper Lion". It is a funny account of his disastrous experience playing football with the Detroit Lions. He was applauded as he hobbled from the field "in appreciation of the lunacy of my participation".

There were other lunatic moments in Mr Plimpton's experiences in what he called participation. In tennis, Pancho Gonzalez beat him easily. In golf, he lost badly to Arnold Palmer. He climbed from the boxing ring with his face blooded by Archie Moore; never mind, hadn't Hemingway once been floored by Morley Callaghan, a Canadian writer then in Paris?

It wasn't a bad journalistic idea: the outsider taking on the professional, and showing that being a pro takes more skill than is often realised. Other writers have done the same. But the public, uninterested that Mr Plimpton might have a serious motive for his jaunts, took the view that he was simply a moneyed idiot looking for ways to pass the time. He persuaded Leonard Bernstein to let him join an orchestra he was conducting, and was allowed to help out with the percussion. But even playing the triangle is a skill. He missed his cue in a Mahler symphony. Determined not to miss out next time, he prepared to strike the gong softly in a Tchaikovsky piece. But, in a state of nerves, he bashed it with all his strength, bringing the performance abruptly to a premature end. Mr Plimpton's oeuvre includes a number of movies, but his parts tended to be brief. He was an Arab in "Lawrence of Arabia" and was beaten to the draw by John Wayne in a western.

He was much liked by those who knew him well. "Friends were almost always happy to see him because you knew he was bound to improve your mood," said Norman Mailer. "Few could tell a story with equal humour." Cheered-up friends seemed always ready to chip in to keep the *Paris Review* going. George Plimpton said that some people called him a dilettante who was "having too much fun". But there was nothing "inherently wrong in having fun". And he gave a lot of people fun too. ■

Anna Politkovskaya

Anna Politkovskaya, a Russian journalist, was shot dead on October 7th 2006, aged 48

SHE WAS brave beyond belief, reporting a gruesome war and a creeping dictatorship with a sharp pen and steel nerves. It may be a chilling coincidence that Anna Politkovskaya was murdered on Vladimir Putin's birthday, but her friends and supporters are in little doubt that her dogged, gloomy reporting of the sinister turn Russia has taken under what she called his "bloody" leadership was what led to her body being dumped in the lift of her Moscow apartment block.

Miss Politkovskaya's journalism was distinctive. Not for her the waffly, fawning and self-satisfied essays of the Moscow commentariat, nor the pervasive well-paid advertorials. Austere and a touch obsessive, she reported from the wrecked villages and shattered towns of Chechnya, talking to those on all sides and none, with endless patience and gritty determination.

She neither sentimentalised the Chechen rebels nor demonised the Russian conscripts – ill-armed, ill-fed and ill-led – who have crushed the Chechens' half-baked independence. She talked to soldiers' mothers trying to find their sons' corpses in military morgues where mangled bodies lay unnamed and unclaimed – the result of the Russian army's unique mixture of callousness and incompetence. And she talked to Chechens whose friends and relatives had disappeared into the notorious "filtration camps" to suffer torture, mutilation, rape and death.

Few journalists, from any country, did that. The second Chechen war, which started in 1999 and still fizzles on now, made that mountainous sliver of territory in the northern Caucasus the most dangerous place on the planet for a journalist. Most Moscow-based reporters went seldom, if at all, and then only in daylight and well-guarded. Ms Politkovskaya was unfazed, making around 50 trips there, often for days at a time.

Ordinary Chechens, and many Russians, adored her. Piles of post and incessant phone calls came, some offering information, more often wanting her help. Could she intercede with a kidnapper? Trace a loved one? She always tried, she said, to do what she could.

She loathed the warlords who had misruled Chechnya during its brief spells of semi-independence; the Islamic extremists who exploited the conflict; the Russian goons and generals, and their local collaborators. She despised the Chechen leaders installed by Russia: they looted reconstruction money, she said, using torture and kidnapping as a weapon. She was due to file a story on this the day she died.

The worst effect of the Chechen wars, she reckoned, was on Russia itself. Her reporting from all over her native country made her see it in what many regarded as an unfairly bleak light. Mr Putin's regime was utterly brutal and corrupt, she would say in her soft, matter-of-fact voice. He represented the worst demons of the Soviet past, revived in modern form. Hundreds had died to bring him to power, and that was just a foretaste of the fascism and war that was to come. Now her pessimism seems less extreme.

A duty to tell

Mr Putin, condemning her murder four days late, said she had "minimal influence". Yet Miss Politkovskaya was often threatened with death. Once Russian special forces held her captive and threatened to leave her dead body in a ditch. She talked them out of it. In 2001, she fled briefly to Austria after a particularly vivid death threat scared not her, but her editors at *Novaya Gazeta*, one of Russia's few remaining independent papers. In 2004, on her way to the siege of a school in the North Ossetian town of Beslan, where she hoped to mediate between the Chechen hostage-takers and the Russian army, she was poisoned and nearly died.

This time there was no mistake. She was shot in the body and the head. A pistol was left by her side – the blatant hallmark of a contract killing. She was well aware that the authorities might have her murdered, but in conversation she would brush this aside, saying that her sources were in much more danger than she was. Journalists had a duty to report on the subject that mattered, she said, just as singers had to sing and doctors had to heal.

Much of her life mirrored the changes in her country. She was born in New York, the child of Soviet diplomats. That gilded upbringing gave her access to a world of ideas and knowledge denied to most Soviet citizens. Her university dissertation was on Marina Tsvetaeva, a poet then in deep official disfavour. She had good jobs too, first on *Izvestia*, the government paper, then on Aeroflot's in-flight magazine.

Having discovered democracy and the free press as Soviet power collapsed, her faith was uncompromising and sometimes uncomfortable. Nor was she always easy company. A fondness for both sweeping statements and intricate details sometimes made conversation heavy-going. She was both disorganised and single-minded; that could be unnerving, too. But she enjoyed life. She often said that with a KGB officer as president, the least you could do was to smile sometimes, to show the difference between him and you.

It would be nice to think that Russians will find her example inspiring. Sadly, they may conclude that brave work on hot topics is a bad idea. ■

Lazare Ponticelli

Lazare Ponticelli, the last French foot-soldier of the first world war, died on March 12th 2008, aged 110

THE BUSINESS of memory is a solid and solemn thing. Plaques are unveiled on the wall; stone memorials are built in the square; the domed mausoleum rises brick by brick over the city. But the business of memory is also as elusive as water or mist. The yellowing photographs slide to the back of the drawer; the voices fade; and the last rememberers of the dead die in their turn, leaving only what Thomas Hardy called "oblivion's swallowing sea".

The approach of the death of Lazare Ponticelli therefore caused something of a panic in France. This *derdesders*, "the last of the last", was for a while the only man in the country who remembered the first world war because he had fought in it. The suburb of Kremlin-Bicetre, where he lived, had like most other communities in France a memorial to the war dead. But, more important, it had Mr Ponticelli, who up to his 111th

year appeared every November 11th in his flat cap and brown coat, lean and bright-eyed, gamely managing the few steps required to lay his small bunch of carnations there. The most astonished and serious observers were always children, to whom – if they wanted – he would tell his stories.

Successive presidents of France strove to honour Mr Ponticelli. It was a way of detaining all the other shadows he represented: the 8.4m workmen, peasants and common folk who, in pointed steel helmets and flapping greatcoats, had gloriously defended the fatherland as *poilus*, or foot-soldiers, between 1914 and 1918. Jacques Chirac suggested a state funeral for him and perhaps interment in the Panthéon, alongside Rousseau and Voltaire. Nicolas Sarkozy proposed a mass at Les Invalides. Mr Ponticelli wanted none of that: no procession, no racket, *pas de tapage important*. He was grateful for his belated Légion d'Honneur, which he kept with his other medals in a shoe-box. But he was keenly aware that he drew such attention only because he was the last.

What had become of the others? The stretcher-bearers in the Argonne, for example, who had told him they didn't dare leave the trench for fear of German fire. The man he had heard from no-man's land, caught in the barbed wire and with his leg severed, screaming to be rescued, until Mr Ponticelli ran out to him with wire-cutters and dragged him back to the lines. The German soldier he tripped over in the dark, already wounded and expecting to be killed, who mutely held up his fingers to show him that he had two children. The comrades who helped him, because he could not read or write, to keep in touch by letter with the milkmaid he had met before the war. Or the four colleagues who held him down when, after the battle of Pal Piccolo, the army surgeon gouged out of his cheek a piece of shrapnel already lodged in gangrene.

With each new round of shelling, he said, they all expected the worst. They would reassure each other by saying, "If I die, you'll remember me, won't you?" Mr Ponticelli felt he had a duty to try, but struggled. These were *mes camarades, les gars, un type*: faces, not names. And as he faded, even those faces lost their last hold on the living.

Bread for tobacco

In many ways Mr Ponticelli was not typical of the *poilus*. He was an Italian, from dirt-poor Emilia-Romagna, who followed his family to France to find work. Some of his childhood, peacetime memories were perhaps as rare as his wartime ones: catching thrushes by hand in the rocky fields, hand-stitching his own shoes, setting up a chimney-sweep business in Nogent-sur-Marne. He thought France "paradise", and enlisted in the Foreign Legion at 16, under-age, by way of thanks. When Italy joined the war in 1915 he switched to an Italian Alpine regiment, but only because two policemen marched him bodily to Turin; and he kept his French military passbook carefully on him through three years as a machine-gunner, until he was able to return to paradise again. In 1939 he became a French citizen, and the rest of his life was spent setting up Ponticelli *frères*, a company that still builds and takes down chimneys and makes industrial piping.

Increasingly, however, people wanted to talk to him about the war. He always courteously obliged them, though by the end his thin, scratchy voice came out in gasps. It was as important to him as it was to them to underscore the horror and futility of it. More than anything, he was appalled that he had been made to fire on people he didn't know and to whom he, too, was a stranger. These were fathers of children. He had no quarrel with them. *C'est complètement idiot la guerre.* His Italian Alpine regiment had once stopped firing for three weeks on the Austrians, whose language many of them spoke; they had swapped loaves of bread for tobacco and taken pictures of each other. To the end of his life, Mr Ponticelli showed no interest in labelling anyone his enemy. He said he did not understand why on earth he, or they, had been fighting.

On March 17th he had his wish, or most of it: a state funeral for all the *poilus* at Les Invalides, and then a simple family burial. The government badly wanted this last foot-soldier to be memorialised; but he preferred to be uncelebrated and ordinary, even in some sense forgotten, and thus the more symbolic of all the rest. ■

Anthony Powell

Anthony Dymoke Powell, English satirist, died on March 28th 2000, aged 94

WHEN ANTHONY Powell was the literary editor of a magazine, he told his book reviewers to write concisely, "say what it's about, what you think of it", and perhaps make a joke. This admirable instruction naturally warms The Economist to Mr Powell, as it is not very different from that given to its own writers. He was also clearly his own man, undaunted by the corruption of friendship or popular taste. W. H. Auden, he said, was overrated, Graham Greene "absurdly overrated", Laurie Lee "utterly unreadable". Vladimir Nabokov writes "third-rate tinsel stuff'; Gabriel Garcia Marquez writes "pretentious middlebrow verbiage of the worst kind". You might not agree with his judgments, but they were distinctive.

However, it is not as a literary critic that Mr Powell may be remembered. The yards and yards of obsequies that followed his death last week sought to honour him as one of the great novelists of the 20th century, a match for Marcel Proust. He certainly had admiration for Proust, who he considered not at all like those nonentities Greene and Nabokov. It is understandable to see similarities between "A Dance to the Music of Time", Mr Powell's sequence of 12 novels, and "Remembrance of Things Past". Both are concerned with exotic upper middle-class behaviour, and both novelists wrote at great length, but that's about all they have in common. One reason why Mr Powell's admirers sought to place him among the elect may be that he had endured in the literary life more than any other writer. At Eton he was a fellow pupil with George Orwell.

At Oxford he knew Evelyn Waugh. In Hollywood in the 1930s he had lunch with Scott Fitzgerald. And so on. He was still crafting words in his 90s, beginning, as he put it, with a paragraph of 30 words, turning them into 50, then 80, and revising all the time. Best to forget about Proust, and Dostoevsky, also sometimes linked to Anthony Powell, and appreciate him for what he was: a clever story-teller, with a quiet turn of wit.

The American view

In his writing style, Mr Powell was closer to Ernest Hemingway than Proust. A lot of his dialogue echoes Hemingway's stripped-down mannerisms. Many Americans were among his fans. Just as they sought to master the language of the sea in the novels of Patrick O'Brian (Obituary, January 15th), so they patiently deciphered the fantastic world of Mr Powell's England. (An American newspaper thoughtfully explained that he preferred to have his name pronounced to rhyme with Lowell.) Perhaps they took it seriously.

This was the England of which there will always be one: class obsessed, snobby but, in its way, endearing. In his personal life, Mr Powell encouraged this misleading view. He was married to an aristocrat and much concerned with genealogy. He claimed to have discovered a 12th-century ancestor called Rhys the Hoarse. In his memoirs he describes a life not far removed from the fantasies of his novels, peopled by friends called Fluff, Bumble, Hilly, Fram, Monkey, Liddie, Pansy and a dentist called Sussman, who is for ever fixing Mr Powell's teeth. His father was a professional soldier, and when Mr Powell was called up in the second world war he naturally joined his father's regiment. He was, of course, a Tory. He declined a knighthood, but was happy to be made a Companion of Honour, a rarer distinction.

Probably it is useful to be English to appreciate that much in Mr Powell's writing is satire. But while the humour is a treat, it is the story that really matters. Anthony Powell was kind to his readers. In the 1m words or so in "A Dance to the Music of Time", published between 1951 and 1975, several hundred characters make their distinctive entrances and exits. Some have walk-on parts, some disappear and then turn up surprisingly in later books in what he called "the inexorable law of coincidence". A few dominate the action. Kenneth Widmerpool is present from his emergence in the first volume out of the mist on a school run to his bizarre death in the last volume. In between he serves a sinister capitalist, does well out of the war, marries a nymphomaniac and is made a lord. Widmerpool is always on the make, always pretending to be sympathetic to the latest political fad, the antithesis to the hopeless, if charming, losers of the upper class.

It is tempting to say that Anthony Powell despised the upper class. Perhaps he did, in the sense that in every satirist there is a bit of loathing. But he saw himself simply as an observer. His writing, he said, "dealt with things as they are". Nick Jenkins, his narrator in "Dance", seeks to be coldly objective. Although Mr Powell's upbringing was on upper class lines, he never had the prospect of being one of the idle rich. For years he worked as a hack in a publishing office. As a literary editor, he had "to read some frightfully boring book every fortnight". In the early years his novels sold modestly. No wonder he was vitriolic about authors he considered had easy success. His urbane manner may have concealed an angry man. He grumbled about the "really terrible rubbish written about people", including himself. He would have hated his obituaries, picking over his life. Even this kindly article? Probably. ■

Kukrit Pramoj

Kukrit Pramoj, wit, aristocrat, actor, and fighter for democracy in Thailand, died on October 9th 1995, aged 84

BEING CALLED Thailand's "pillar of democracy" did not much appeal to Kukrit Pramoj. Not only was the title "boring", there were times when, as Mr Kukrit put it, he began "to think that democracy is not suited for this country". But "nor is dictatorship for that matter".

Stability or the people's choice? In the West, where democracy was invented, the two are regarded as inseparable. In Asia, where democracy is a (sometimes unwelcome) newcomer, there may be a difficult choice to be made or, more commonly, a compromise to be reached. No government in Asia is wholly democratic in the western sense. Thailand comes as close as any to providing personal freedom. There is a civilian government, albeit one that came to power in July in an election marred by corruption. The army, the villain of numerous coups or attempted coups, the most recent in 1991, is at present keeping its distance. The newspapers are pleasantly unthreatened. Mr Kukrit, whatever his vacillations, has probably done more than any other politician to promote these blessings.

Thais like to point out that, unlike the other countries of South-East Asia, theirs was never colonised. "And it only has itself to blame," remarked Kukrit Pramoj. When he was born in 1911 Thailand was still an absolute monarchy. "The secret life of the court", as described by Anna Loenowens, an English governess of the king's children in the 1860s, was little changed. Indeed, to this day the king remains a power: "The King and I", a film based on Anna's experiences, is not shown in Thailand, where *lèse-majesté* is a crime.

Scourge of the generals

Mr Kukrit was related to the royal family. He had a title, Mon Rajawong, abbreviated to M.R., which he jokingly dismissed as standing for minor royalty. He might have spent his life as a courtier, dispensing wit and wisdom. However, as a young man, he was sent to Britain to discover the world outside. When he returned to Thailand in 1934 after a spell at Oxford, a constitutional government had taken over. "As a true aristocrat," he recalled, he was overjoyed at the end of absolute monarchy.

He had jobs in banking and the civil service. But the true aristocrat needed a stage. Mr Kukrit entered parliament in 1946 and started a newspaper. He gained fame as a scathing opponent of the military dictators who ruled the country for many years after the second world war. Once, he sent out his reporters to count the number of windows in the interior ministry. It was, he said, a pointless exercise, but it would baffle the censors. He was a hero to the students who waged sometimes bloody battles against governments run by the army.

In 1963 Mr Kukrit caught the eye of Hollywood. In "The Ugly American", a film occasionally still seen on late-night television, he plays (see picture, right) the prime minister of a tottering Asian country threatened by Vietnam. Marlon Brando plays the American.

Mr Kukrit became a real prime minister in 1975, when the army gave way, briefly, to civilian rule. For 13 months he led a fractious coalition. As in the film, Vietnam was a menace. Mr Kukrit feared that, having beaten America, the Vietnamese would invade Thailand. There was already a communist insurgency in the country. Mr Kukrit swallowed his loathing for communism and went to see the Chinese leader Mao Zedong. This finished the communists in Thailand, and the Vietnamese held off.

There was a price to pay. Mr Kukrit closed the American bases in Thailand. The country's defences were weakened, but Mr Kukrit told himself that at least

Thai culture was being spared further western influence. One of his dogs, he liked to say, only bit foreigners. However, the brothel industry that had grown up to serve the Americans continues to thrive on tourism.

Mr Kukrit never held office again. Such has been the fickle nature of Thai politics that, to date, it has produced 21 prime ministers. Mr Kukrit settled into the role of an influential elder statesman. This, after all, was the man who had haggled with Mao, stood up to the generals and spoken firmly to America.

Mr Pramoj was admired by Thais, not only as an emblem of democracy, but of the best of Thailand itself: a Buddhist (and briefly a monk) but mischievous; pluralist but monarchist. But he had his weaknesses, at least for those who prefer single-mindedness in a leader. Kukrit Pramoj had many distractions. He was a novelist, he taught classical Thai dance. In his Bangkok house there were 2,000 fish, all of which, he said, had names. The Thai ideal, he wrote, was "an elegant sort of life, with adaptable morals and a serene detachment to the more serious problems of life". This attitude informed Mr Kukrit's politics, which were those of a gifted amateur. The problem in Thai politics is the machinations of the professionals, particularly in the army. ∎

Rama Rao

Nandamuri Taraka Rama Rao, Indian politician and film actor, died on January 18th 1996, aged 72

WHEN RAMA Rao died, four of the many Indians who worshipped him committed suicide. Others, no less devoted, stoned some of his political rivals. Worshipped, devoted? The words are not inappropriate. As a film actor Mr Rama Rao was often cast as a Hindu god, and this role seemed to stay with him during his later career as a politician. The attention accorded to him sometimes bordered on religious ecstasy. Admirers lined up in postures of prayer outside his house daily.

It would be misleading, though, to assume that they were fools ignorant of the difference between a god and an actor. Many other actors in India have played the role of god but none has excited such popular frenzy as Mr Rama Rao.

The Rama Rao phenomenon has been much discussed by political observers. They noted that he was the hero in more than 300 films, about one a month over three decades, an astonishing number even for India's relentlessly productive world of dreams. As well as playing god, Mr Rama Rao portrayed rural underdogs fighting against and triumphing over feudal exploiters. A plausible view was that, as an opponent of villains and tyranny, he was a drug that eased the harsh life of ordinary Indians. But his acolytes dismissed such intellectualising, and claimed simply that Mr Rama Rao's concern for humanity was so transparent that people were instinctively drawn to him.

The god of the hustings

In 1982 Mr Rama Rao stepped from the screen to test this appeal in the real world. He founded a party called Telegu Desam (Land of the Telegus). Telegu is the language of the state of Andhra Pradesh, where Mr Rama Rao was born. He decided to fight the Andhra Pradesh state assembly election called for 1983. Many of his admirers felt he was making a mistake. The Congress party, which then, as now, ruled nationally, controlled the state, one of India's largest with a population of 70m. The prime minister, Indira Gandhi, had shifted her parliamentary constituency to Andhra Pradesh. But Mr Rama Rao saw the Congress party as a corrupt monster that needed to be challenged where it appeared strongest. It was a shrewd decision. Enormous crowds responded to his appeal to Telegu pride, which he said had been hurt by the contempt with which the Gandhi family treated local politicians. At campaign meetings he would dress in the robes he wore in films where he played god, and spoke from a pick-up truck made to resemble, as he put it, a "chariot of valour". His party won with a massive majority, and Mr Rama Rao became chief minister of the state.

The poor of Andhra Pradesh were rewarded with cheap, subsidised, rice. As a result of Mr Rama Rao's generosity the state's finances began a long slide that has not ended even today. The Congress party set out to bribe assembly members of Mr Rama Rao's party to defect, a common practice in India. The governor of the state, a Congress party man, dismissed him as chief minister, claiming he had lost his majority. Mr Rama Rao rallied his forces, fought a fresh election and again won resoundingly.

But he was more popular with voters than with his own colleagues. Gods do not look kindly on dissent. The autocratic Mr Rama Rao humiliated even his ministers in public, making it clear he regarded them as minions who must obey orders. He stuffed the state government with relations. There was no shortage: he had 11 children.

He spent long hours with astrologers and mendicants, and on their advice was said to wear saris and earrings in bed in the hope that such rituals would help him to become prime minister of India. Meanwhile, the corruption he had accused the Congress party of began to permeate his own party. Though his personal reputation remained untarnished, that of some of his relations did not. To nobody's surprise, his party was thrashed in the general election of 1989 and the subsequent state election. But the indefatigable Mr Rama Rao refused to give up. He made a few more films, which no doubt added to his appeal, and in 1994 he again won a crushing victory in Andhra Pradesh, his third. Some observers believed that, as leader of a coalition with other parties, he could win the Indian general election due this April, and national power would be his.

It was not to happen. Some of his relations holding top positions in the Telegu Desam decided that Mr Rama Rao's ambitious second wife, Lakshmi Parvathi, was beginning to dominate the government. Led by Mr Rama Rao's son-in-law, they staged a palace coup and formed a new government without him. The old man swore revenge. He toured the state condemning as traitors those who had flung him out. He might have triumphed again, but a heart attack did for him. It was a dramatic ending, even though Mr Rama Rao, the eternal hero, would have written it differently. ∎

Allen Read

Allen Walker Read, etymologist, died on October 16th 2002, aged 96

FOR MUCH of his long career studying language Allen Read sought the origin of OK, perhaps the most useful expression of universal communication yet devised. You can use OK not simply to indicate agreement but, with appropriate facial expressions, shades of agreement, even disagreement. It is a vocabulary in itself. No wonder that OK has found its way into nearly every language in every country, and beyond. It was the fourth word, if you can call it that, heard on the moon, spoken by Buzz Aldrin. For etymologists, establishing the origin of OK became something of an obsession, equivalent to mathematicians' long quest for the proof to Fermat's last theorem.

For years Americans assumed that OK must be of American origin, if only because it was so successful. Some doubt about this claim arose in the second world war when American soldiers discovered that OK was already familiar in other countries; in Britain, of course, but in Japan and even (according to H. L. Mencken, an American writer on language) among the Bedouin in the Sahara.

Some linguists suggested that OK was of European origin. After all, the Europeans had been knocking around the world long before Americans got on to the scene. Germans said it was the initials of the fiercely-sounding rank of Oberst Kommandant. The French put in a claim for Aux Cayes, a town they had established in Haiti that produced superior rum. A British scholar said the use of OK in Britain predated any American influence and had probably come from Elizabethan English. Things were getting serious in the world of etymology. Step forward the Americans' champion, Allen Walker Read.

Racy words

As early as he could remember Mr Read was interested in the origin of words. In Minnesota, where he was born, he sought the source of local place names, and wrote a paper on the subject while studying at Iowa University. He had a spell in England as a Rhodes scholar and returned to teach English at various universities in the midwest. He sought words that he said had "a racy, human quality", and there were none racier than the graffiti collected by Mr Read during a trip of several months through the western United States and Canada in the summer of 1928.

He put together the results of his trip in a book entitled "Lexical Evidence from Epigraphy in Western North America: a Glossarial Study of the Low Element in the English Vocabulary". Notwithstanding the academic title, the book contained material unacceptable for publication at the time in America. One of the milder entries, found by Mr Read on a monument, reads: "When you want to shit in ease / Place your elbows on your knees / Put your hands against your chin / Let a fart and then begin". Mr Read had the book printed in Paris in 1935, perhaps encouraged that James Joyce had first published "Ulysses" there in the 1920s. Even so, only 75 copies of "Lexical Evidence" were printed and issued privately to "students of linguistics, folklore, abnormal psychology and allied branches of social sciences". The book was published in the United States in 1977 as "Classic American Graffiti".

Mr Read, who was professor of English at Columbia University in New York for nearly 30 years from 1945, published several other books and hundreds of papers, mainly on American English. Discovering the origin of OK was, he said, no more than an agreeable diversion from his main work. It was fun to do the research, helped by his wife Charlotte, a scholar in semantics. But for envious fellow etymologists it was the pinnacle of his career.

In his hunt for the origin of OK he was offered dozens of theories. The first to go were the European ones. They were appealing: Mr Read liked what he called "frolicsome" ideas. But they had no substance, he said. He was convinced that OK was American. He warmed to the idea that the popularity of Orrin Kendall biscuits, supplied to soldiers on the Union side in the civil war, had lived on as OK. He noted there was a telegraph term known as Open Key. But OK proved to have been used much earlier. Writing in *American Speech* in 1963, Mr Read said that he had come across it in the *Boston Morning Post* in 1839. In what was apparently a satirical article about bad spelling it stood for "Oll Korrect". The next stage in OK's popularity was when it was adopted by followers of Martin Van Buren, who in 1836 became the eighth president of the

United States, and unsuccessfully stood for re-election in 1840, by which time he was widely known as Old Kinderhook, a nickname he derived from his home town. "Vote for OK" was snappier than using his Dutch name.

Mr Read showed how, stage by stage, OK was spread throughout North America and the world to the moon, and then took on its new form AOK, first used by space people and frowned on by purists. This being an exercise in the academic world, there remain some doubters. Some believe that the Boston newspaper's reference to OK may not be the earliest. Some are attracted to the claim that it is of American Indian origin. There is an Indian word, *okeh*, used as an affirmative reply to a question. Mr Read treated such doubting calmly. "Nothing is absolute," he once wrote, "nothing is forever." ■

Robert Rich

Robert Rich, inventor of frozen non-dairy topping, died on February 15th 2006, aged 92

AS SALES presentations go, the one Robert Rich gave in Long Island, New York, in the summer of 1945 was one of the more nerve-wracking. Eighteen sales reps faced him. Mr Rich had brought along some samples of his new invention, a concoction of soy-oil shortening, isolated soya protein, corn syrup and water, in the hopes of persuading them that this could taste as yummy, and whip as lightly, as heavy cream. To keep them from the heat, on the long train journey from his home in Buffalo, he had wrapped the samples stoutly in dry ice and newspaper. Now they hit the table with a thud, frozen solid.

Mr Rich kept talking. As the words flowed, he took a knife surreptitiously to the chunks of "cream", trying to soften them. When words ran out, he turned the hand-beater on them; and they whipped like a dream. White, unctuous,

splendid stuff rose up in mounds, as in the picture above, where Mr Rich holds the bowl.

Few revolutions have been made with a hand-beater. But Mr Rich's was one. Before he began to experiment with flaking and precipitating soyabeans, whipped cream was a hit-or-miss affair. It would not keep, especially in the humid South. Nor would it freeze. Over-beating produced a buttery mess, and ambitious decorations sank gradually into gloop. To top it all, in wartime, heavy whipping cream was a banned substance. All available milk was needed fresh for the people, or dried and condensed for the troops. To dream of an éclair or a cream puff, even of a modest dollop nestling a cherry or topping off a sundae, was close to a traitorous act.

Mr Rich, however, dreamed often of whipped cream. His boyhood had been spent in and out of his father's ice-cream plant, and in 1935 he started such a plant himself, the Wilber Farms Dairy in Buffalo. He should have been fat, but he was a fine and fit sportsman, captain of both football and wrestling at university. Possibly he might have gone into sports professionally. But Mr Rich became fascinated with the process by which, through a series of vats and pipes and settling beds, the humble and ubiquitous soyabean could be made to do the work of a cow.

Henry Ford, as it happened, was then attempting the same thing. When Mr Rich went to Michigan as the government's local administrator of milk orders, in 1943, he inspected Ford's soya-milk-making machinery and was offered a licence to the process for a dollar a year. That offer was later withdrawn (Ford officials telling him, with attractive candour, that they sold a lot of tractors to dairy farmers). Mr Rich therefore devised his own in the garage of his dairy, adjusting it to turn out cream. As his chemists laboured to find the best emulsifiers and flavourings, the world's first non-dairy topping, Delsoy, was creeping from rival nozzles elsewhere in the state. But since Delsoy could not be frozen, it never got beyond Detroit.

Mr Rich's topping did. Before his trip to Long Island he had promoted it rather diffidently to customers on his milk round. Afterwards, knowing that his invention both froze and could be whipped from frozen to three or four times its volume in minutes, he began to sell it everywhere. His topping could be kept, without spoiling, for six months; it kept a hard, neat edge in decoration; it was twice as nourishing as cream, but cheaper and non-fattening. The taste, especially once he had added corn syrup and coconut oil, was plausibly that of cream. His name did it no harm either. "Whip Topping" was bland; but "Rich's Whip Topping" hinted effortlessly at an experience that was thick, indulgent, faintly golden and utterly unwarlike.

A quart of trouble

Utterly uncreamlike, too, cried the dairy trade, and raced to court to stop him. On 42 separate occasions from 1949 onwards, Mr Rich had to defend his topping and, later, his non-dairy Coffee Rich whitener from furious milk men. He was not imitating cream, he argued, but replacing it with something better, as the car had replaced the horse. Mr Rich became a leading light in the new National Association for Advanced Foods, with other soyabean experimenters, and let the red-faced representatives of unadvanced foods impound his coffee whitener if they felt like it. He won every case.

Meanwhile, he had also diversified into éclairs, cake frosting and (less successfully) Chil-Zert, a soya-based ice cream. He began to bake dough for pizza companies and supermarkets, and to make desserts for schools. His topping spread across America. Today's Rich Products Corporation website shows desserts almost unimaginable before his revolution: a world of pies topped with white peaks, swirls, whirls and swags, of multicoloured doughnuts and flawless, thick-frosted cakes. One sequence shows a strawberry milkshake with a perfect red rose, but still missing something. Smoothly, Rich's Whip Topping morphs on.

Eventually, Mr Rich's business became, as it remains, the biggest family owned food-service company in America, with 2,300 products, sales of $2.5 billion last year and plants all over the world. In 1990 Mr Rich was among the first four people inducted into the Frozen Food Hall of Fame. He joined Clarence Birdseye and his fish fingers; but, unlike Birdseye, he had not really meant to freeze his "cream" at all. ■

Bobby Riggs

Robert Larimore Riggs, American tennis champion and braggart male chauvinist, died on October 25th 1995, aged 77

WHEN BOBBY Riggs was 55 he said, in a remark mischievously designed to upset feminists, "Even an old man like me, with one foot in the grave, could beat any woman player." Margaret Court, an Australian aged 29 and the world's best woman player, took him on. And was beaten. Billie Jean King, an American amazon of the tennis court, and the world's number two woman player, stepped forward. This was serious. The honour of women was at stake, and perhaps democracy, freedom, the whole damn thing.

In the run-up to the Riggs–King game in 1973 America appeared to lose interest in anything else. If the Russians had invaded no one would have noticed. This was the Battle of the Sexes. Mr Riggs arrived at the court in a rickshaw drawn by six women. "When I get through with Billie she might just go home and start raising a family," he said. "That's where women should be, barefoot and pregnant. Then they can't get out."

The game was watched at a Houston stadium by more than 30,000 people, a gate for a tennis match that has never been surpassed, and by millions on television. Miss King won. Women rejoiced, bras were burnt. It was that sort of time.

Some say Mr Riggs lost deliberately. He did not dislike women; rather he may have been too fond of them. He may have regarded the whole battle of the sexes as a joke. He denied this, although in his denial – "the most disheartening experience of my life" – he may have been protesting too much. Whatever the truth, the professed anti-feminist had

actually done feminism a good turn. The much-publicised match "was such madness", said Miss King, but it "helped put women's tennis on the map". It "slew the beast of male chauvinism", she claimed, perhaps optimistically. As for Bobby Riggs, he had gained far more fame from the match than he had simply as a tennis star.

First-time winner

Bobby Riggs first came to prominence when he won the Wimbledon crown in 1939. He arrived as an outsider and won not only the men's singles, but added the men's doubles and the mixed doubles as well. To this day no one else has won the triple title on a first visit to the world's supreme festival of tennis. Mr Riggs never returned to Wimbledon. During the second world war Wimbledon was suspended, and, anyway, Mr Riggs was in the American navy. Later he turned professional, while Wimbledon was (for a time) open only to amateurs. He became professional champion in America three times.

He continued to play tennis until shortly before he died. His claim, which no one disputed, was that he was always the best player in the world against anyone his own age, from his teens to his 70s. If he seemed to be a braggart, he was of a variety that might have been played by Woody Allen; slightly undersized at 1.65 metres (5ft 5in) and having occasional trouble with his toupee. Like Mr Allen, he was a recognisable American symbol, the little guy who astonished everyone by taking on the big guy. In a famous match he beat Don Budge, then the biggest guy, certainly physically, in American tennis. "No one could believe a little runt like me had a chance," said Bobby Riggs. Some of his fancy for ballyhoo he probably owed to his father, a preacher who delivered a message of fire and brimstone to congregations in the American South. If Mr Riggs had a sin it was a love of gambling. When he arrived at Wimbledon he had the audacity to make a 200–1 bet on himself to win the triple. Later, he would upset traditionalists by taking bets on himself while handicapped in various bizarre ways: wearing handcuffs, carrying an umbrella or wearing wellington boots. In one doubles game his partner was a donkey. He always won these stunts and enriched himself considerably.

"Millionaires are the salt of the earth," he remarked.

He was simply an excellent player, although, compared with today's stylists, an old-fashioned one. Not for him the power smash of a Sampras. His favourite shot was the lob, sent high across the net to land with cruise-missile-like precision just short of the baseline, and often unplayable. His casualness was, of course, deceptive. He took pleasure from scoffing at those who took tennis over-seriously. It was, after all, no more than a game of bat and ball. But his

manner hid a zealot. He had been playing tennis since he was 12. In his autobiography he wrote, "Nobody gets to the top who has not played for at least ten years, 300 days a year, six hours a day." But he was a prodigy as well. When playing golf, for which he had no special training, he successfully called on the inborn sense of judgment, or whatever, that lifts an athlete into greatness. "I want to be remembered as a winner," he said. More likely, he will be remembered, though mostly affection-ately, for the match he lost. ■

Amalia Rodrigues

Amalia Rodrigues, Portugal's queen of fado, died on October 6th 1999, aged 79

WHEN AMALIA Rodrigues died last week, the government of Portugal declared three days of national mourning. Political activity in the country's general election campaign came to a halt. The president was the chief mourner at the singer's state funeral. It was a singular expression of national grief and in some ways a peculiar one.

Entertainers, however famous, rarely, if ever, depart in such ceremony. It did not happen to Maria Callas, perhaps the most celebrated opera singer of recent times, when she died in 1977; or to Frank Sinatra, who died in 1998. There was some sadness, certainly; a lot of reminiscences, of course; but life went on largely uninterrupted in Greece and America. The sanctifying of Amalia Rodrigues may say something about the nature of the Portuguese as well as about what the prime minister called "the voice of the country's soul".

She was known simply as Amalia. The diminution of her name was itself a reflection of her fame (as was Britain's Diana, or Di, whose death in 1997 also briefly interrupted the life of her country). Her style of singing is called fado, the Portuguese word for fate. "I have so much sadness in me," Amalia said. "I am a pessimist, a nihilist. Everything that fado demands in a singer I have in me."

Amalia's message of fatalism seems to have echoed a mood among her admirers. Portugal is still among the least modern of European countries, though it has been modernising rapidly of late. It expects its economy to grow by about 3% this year, compared with an average of only 1.9% growth for the rest of the euro area. But GDP does not change a country's sentiment overnight. Portugal was the first European country in modern times to carve out a great trading empire. Go almost anywhere in the world and you find traces of Portuguese architecture, language and genes. Generation by generation, the once-rich Portuguese have seen their empire slowly vanish, and not very gracefully. East Timor is still formally Portuguese. "I sing of tragedy," Amalia said, "of things past."

The politics of song

Amalia Rodrigues was never sure of her exact birthday. Her grandmother said it was in the cherry season, so she assumed she was born in early summer. Other details of her childhood were also obscure. Some accounts said her father was a shoemaker; others that he was a musician. The story that as a teenager she sold fruit on the docks of Lisbon, capturing the hearts of her customers with her singing, was willingly believed by those who adored her. The adoration was put to the test in 1974 when Portugal emerged from half a century of dictatorship. Amalia's critics said she had benefited from the patronage of the most enduring of Europe's fascist regimes.

"I always sang fado without thinking of politics," Amalia responded angrily. It was a claim impossible to contradict. Yet fado, with its melancholy fatalism, was an appropriate accompaniment to the thinking of the Portuguese leader, António de Oliveira Salazar. Not for

him the ruthless urgency of Hitler. Rather, in his corporate state he wanted to preserve Portugal as a rural and religious society where industrialisation and other modernising influences would be excluded. He kept Portugal out of the second world war. It was too wearisome.

Fado was the music of Portuguese tradition. If it had any foreign ingredients they were from Africa, but these were acceptable: huge areas of Africa had been Portuguese. And here was Amalia, the queen of fado, clad all in black, her throbbing voice accompanied by two guitarists, her head thrown back, her eyes closed. She was the essence of sadness, bearing the memories of two marriages; both unhappy. When Salazar heard "O Grito" ("The Cry") he allowed himself a tear.

Unsurprisingly, the Portugal that followed the dictatorship wanted cheering up, as well as modernising. The question of whether Amalia had been a supporter of the old regime became irrelevant. Fado itself fell out of fashion. Rock was the music of democracy.

Amalia, however, had built up other audiences abroad. The Brazilians, whose language is Portuguese, flocked to see her dozen or so films. A six-week tour to Rio and other cities had to be expanded to three months. In the United States record collectors said that her songs, with their four-line stanzas, were like the blues, and she did indeed make some recordings with a jazz saxophonist, Don Byas. Italians claimed to see links between fado and opera. The French said Amalia reminded them of Edith Piaf, who sang nostalgically of the tragedies in her life. A fado song given the English title "April in Portugal" became a hit in several countries.

In Portugal fado and Amalia gradually made a comeback. Amalia showed that she was really a democrat at heart by recording "Grandola Vila Morena", the song that had swept the country when the dictatorship ended. The socialist government presented her with the country's highest decoration, the Order of Santiago. She was giving concerts up to a year ago, and every one was sold out. "The sadder the song, the more the Portuguese like it," she said. In this new time of change, pessimism was back in fashion. For Amalia, it was the happiest of endings. ■

Andres Rodriguez

Andres Rodriguez, Paraguay's unexpected liberator, died on April 21st 1997, aged 73

OF THE countries of Latin America none has had a more melancholy history than Paraguay. For nearly 180 years from 1811, when the country became independent from Spain, it had a succession of dictators, some bad, some very bad. One allowed no newspapers or schools. Another confiscated half the country. When Alfredo Stroessner was overthrown in 1989 it was assumed that Andres Rodriguez, the general who organised the coup against his old master, would be a dictator too. To many people's astonishment, in Paraguay and abroad, he freed political prisoners, ended the ban on opposition political parties, lifted newspaper censorship, reached an accord with his critics in the Roman Catholic church, and successfully stood for president in what was acclaimed as the cleanest dirty election in the country's history. What Mr Rodriguez started eight years ago is growing, albeit slowly, into a stable democracy.

It would be difficult to ascribe Mr Rodriguez's actions to a change of heart. In the view of many Paraguayans he had no heart. He had been the army's second in command, after Mr Stroessner, and an unswerving servant of the police state that crushed its critics and was a haven for all kinds of undesirables from Nazi fugitives to drug smugglers. Mr Rodriguez was even part of the Stroessner family: his daughter had married one of the dictator's sons.

But Mr Stroessner had been in power for 34 years and was thought to be ailing. His inner circle, which had taken on the character of a medieval court, was endlessly in dispute over who should succeed him. Mr Rodriguez set out to settle the matter. Putting family sentiment aside, he tried to arrest Mr Stroessner at the home of his mistress. But the dictator, getting wind of the coup, had abandoned that agreeable lodging for his palace stronghold in Asuncion, the capital. All through the night of February 3rd 1989 the Stroessner forces fought the Rodriguez forces tooth and claw. The palace guards were loyal, but Mr Rodriguez had tanks. Some 500 soldiers died before Mr Stroessner surrendered and was exiled to Brazil, where he still lives, aged 84.

A criminal economy

The country that Andres Rodriguez took over was a mess. Its largely criminal economy based on smuggling had benefited some individuals enormously but not the country. Discontent with Stronismo, as Paraguayans called it, was shared by groups as diverse as landless peasants and poorly-paid doctors. Some two-thirds of Paraguay's 4m people were said to be short of food.

The United States, ever scenting an opportunity in Latin America, whispered that perhaps dictatorship, with its corruption and all that, was going out of fashion. Dictator fatigue was setting in. Paraguay's neighbours, Argentina, Brazil, Chile and Uruguay, had all dumped their military leaders in recent years. Why not try democracy, Mr Rodriguez? Discover human rights. Get popular.

Mr Rodriguez stepped down as president in 1993 after piloting through a new constitution that looks impeccably

was $500 a month, managed to become one of the richest men in Paraguay, building a home that was modelled on a French château. There were persistent stories that he was involved in running cocaine from Bolivia to Europe. Mr Rodriguez took the precaution of becoming a senator, which gave him immunity from any legal proceedings.

No one doubts the fragility of the recently-won freedoms. Last year an army officers' revolt against their loss of political power was quashed, but only, apparently, by diplomatic pressure from America and Brazil. The main political force remains the Colorado Party, which sustained Mr Stroessner through seven rigged elections, sometimes giving his supporters more than 100% of the vote by including the dead. Many in the party still have a nostalgia for the Stroessner era. "Decades of great government," said a former minister without a trace of irony.

democratic. The current president, serving a five-year term, is Juan Carlos Wasmosy, a civil engineer. Paraguay is less of a smugglers' Shangri-la now that it is a member of Mercosur, a trading block that includes Argentina, Brazil and Uruguay. Public and private monopolies are being broken up and sold off. The contraband barons that thrived under Mr Stroessner's protection are turning to legitimate trade.

Mr Rodriguez long ago stepped out of his general's uniform and anyway had grown too fat for a soldier. The popularity he gained as a born-again democrat mostly stayed with him. As a politician he turned out to have a jovial streak. Paraguayans appreciated his weakness for horse racing. Only the ungrateful questioned how a farmer's son, whose top salary in the army

Paraguay's revitalised opposition parties believe that the Colorado Party's grip on power can at last be ended. This hope will be tested at the next presidential election, due in May 1998. Still, whatever the result, the reforms started by Andres Rodriguez have made Paraguay a better place. Better to be a tinpot democracy than a tinpot dictatorship. ■

Brother Roger

Roger Schutz, founder of Taizé, died on August 16th 2005, aged 90

DEEP QUIET was what first drew Roger Schutz to Taizé. The young Swiss theology student, climbing off his bicycle one summer day in 1940 after riding a strenuous 70 miles north from Geneva, found himself in the wooded hills and valleys of *la France profonde*. A few sandstone houses, some unlived in, made up the village. The road was unsurfaced, and there was no telephone; the world did not come through here. No priest had been resident since the Revolution. He might have pushed on, but an old woman offered him a meal and pressed him to stay with them. "We are lonely," she told him.

This lost corner had not always been so silent. Ten minutes away lay the ruins of the great Benedictine abbey of Cluny, which had once been full of melody and chant sung to the glory of God. Taizé, on that same "inspired hill", still echoed with what Shelley once called "the memory of music fled". It was the ideal place for Brother Roger, as he soon became, to found an order whose religious life was based profoundly on the principles of music and silence.

Establishing a monastic order is always a struggle, not least in the 20th century, and in wartime, and for a Protestant pastor's son whose knowledge of the subject had been gained from his theology studies in Lausanne. He meant, at first, to be a writer. But his father's mysticism infected him; he decided on the religious life, and burned his first published book in the fireplace of the broken-down house he bought in Taizé.

In its first years, the house was mostly a hostel where Jewish refugees were offered soup and a bed on their way through to safety. Brother Roger, a classically trained musician brought up in a household of singing and piano-playing, wanted music at its centre, but not yet. Out of respect for his guests, he would go away and sing Divine Office in the woods, restoring sacred music to the landscape again.

From these humble, almost naturalistic, beginnings sprang an extraordinary Christian revival. On the day Brother Roger died, 2,500 people were in the church in Taizé. More than 100,000 visitors now come each year, so many that they stay in tents on the surrounding slopes. The order itself has 120 monks, some in the monastery and some, as Brother Roger always wanted, living with the poor in the world, in the slums of Kolkata and Manila and New York. Taizé prayer-groups meet in every continent.

Leaders of the established Christian churches – popes, metropolitans, archbishops of Canterbury – would visit with amazement. They could not understand how, as the world turned unremittingly secular and their own churches dwindled down to congregations of old women, one monastery in France could be crammed with the noisy, enthusiastic, back-packing young. Pope John Paul II called Taizé "a spring of water". Little like it could be found in the Vatican's gilded halls.

A pillar of fire

Brother Roger, too, was perplexed by what had happened. His monastery had never recruited, advertised or sold itself.

It was never – he insisted it should never be – a "movement". He only knew that, from 1959 onwards, young people had started to come to Taizé, and the word had spread. Some said that he himself, a tiny man with a luminous, sweet smile, was the reason they came. He doubted it but, just in case it was true, granted few interviews and kept apart from the theological wranglings of the day. Taizé was, and always had been, resolutely ecumenical, taking brothers from all Christian sects and basing itself on love, reconciliation and forgiveness; there was much space for searching there, but none for dogmatism. Hence its attraction for the alienated souls of the modern age.

Brother Roger offered, to anyone who wanted it, a way to the spirit of the risen Christ through light, music and silence. The services he devised at Taizé were often held by candlelight. The music, based on ancient mantras but developed by him, was simple melodic phrases sung over and over again until they became a meditation, sometimes continuing under and through the prayers in what he called "a pillar of fire". In between these chants would come long spells of silence when, as Brother Roger put it, "with a childlike trust, we let Christ pray silently within us."

Listening, rather than preaching, was the essence of Taizé. Christian leaders would have done well to imitate that secret. As it was, churches all over the Christian world borrowed the Taizé songs. Fame forced Brother Roger to worry about copyright and piracy; it also gave him critics. For some he was too Catholic, allowing masses and observing the Marian feasts. For others he was too timid, championing the oppressed but disbanding branches of his order when they became politically violent. Brother Roger ignored all this. Moral and political reform, he believed, would come only when bitterness and resentment vanished from human hearts.

He was attending the evening service when a deranged woman cut his throat, killing him almost instantly. He died in the midst of the reviving music he had brought to Christianity. Had anyone asked why, he would have gently reminded them that he did not leave a silence that was empty. ∎

Mstislav Rostropovich

"Slava" Rostropovich, the world's greatest cellist, died on April 27th 2007, aged 80

MUSIC, UNDER totalitarianism, was one of the great escapes. The most vicious secret policeman could not wholly curb the human spirit once it moved into the world of sounds. "Slava" Rostropovich (the diminutive of his Christian name means "glory" in Russian) used to the utmost the freedom that music gave him inside the Soviet Union. When forced to move abroad, he became the ambassador of free Russian culture to the world, doing in music what Alexander Solzhenitsyn did, more gloomily, in words.

He was present at the two defining moments of the collapse of communism, the fall of the Berlin Wall in November 1989 (when he played Bach suites all night by a breach between the concrete blocks), and the attempted hardline putsch in Moscow in August 1991. On that occasion he talked his way into the Soviet Union without a visa to stand, rifle gingerly in hand, with Boris Yeltsin

in the besieged Russian parliament. Its defenders claimed his presence stopped the putschists storming the building. He would have been happy to die there, he said, on the "most important, dangerous and emotional day of my life".

In the 17 years before that, apart from one visit with the National Symphony Orchestra of Washington, DC, he had not set foot in his own country. His defiance began when his two greatest teachers, Sergei Prokofiev and, chiefly, Dmitri Shostakovich, fell out of official favour. A cannier Soviet citizen might have dumped or denounced them, but Mr Rostropovich refused to do so. For a time, his glittering musical talents protected him. Other artists and intellectuals, however, were silent in his defence, and his friendship with Mr Solzhenitsyn was the last straw. In 1969 the writer, persecuted by the authorities, had nowhere to live; Mr Rostropovich invited him to stay. Then he, his wife

Galina and some other brave souls wrote an open letter to the Soviet leader, Leonid Brezhnev, protesting at the regime's abuse of cultural freedom.

After that, Mr Rostropovich was on the blacklist. He became a prisoner in his own country, ignored by the state-controlled media, unable to play in public or make recordings. He was stripped of his musical awards, and his name was even removed from the many scores that had been dedicated to him. Though Russia was "in my heart – in my mind", and ever would be, in 1974 he asked to be allowed to leave. His citizenship was revoked four years later.

He had been adored in the West since his first visit in 1956, frequently performing at the Aldeburgh festival and becoming close friends with its towering talent, Benjamin Britten. The two communicated in broken German, which they called "Aldeburgh Deutsch"; Britten wrote cello suites, a sonata and a symphony for him. In exile Mr Rostropovich learnt English, or at least developed an idiosyncratic version of it. But he lost none of his Russianness, greeting friends with a massive bear hug. After Britten died, Mr Rostropovich would hug his tomb when visiting Aldeburgh.

Hearing his own voice

Off-duty, he was an assiduous socialite. In London, Washington or Paris he was glad to mix with the appreciative, anything in stockings and (especially, jealous critics said) the famous. But his main energies went to music. He would rise at five, study scores for three hours, relax after a concert with a four-hour practice session. Such discipline had been inculcated from childhood, when he had studied the cello with his father at their home in Baku, in Soviet Azerbaijan. At 13, he would hang flatbread from the ceiling-lamp so that he could snatch swaying mouthfuls as he played. And when, as a young man, he thought he might be allowed to premiere Shostakovich's first cello concerto, he practised for ten hours a day.

He played the piano too – his first instrument, on which he had been coached by his mother from the age of four – and was accomplished enough to accompany his wife, a soprano, in her recitals. He conducted, though his sessions had a mixed press: sometimes clumsy and lacking in fireworks, sometimes inspirational, with an unmatched ability to communicate his profound understanding of the music to the orchestra. When contemporary composers played through their pieces for him, he said, he would watch their faces, and try to pass their feelings on.

As a performer, he combined extraordinary technical virtuosity with a sublimely confident and passionate interpretation of the music's melodic line. His sound was as huge as his humanity. When his interpretations departed a bit from the printed score, few complained: the music was enriched, not merely transmitted, through his playing. He had fallen in love with the cello in the first place, he explained, because it seemed to be his own voice. But the music he heard in his head as he played was "symphonic", far surpassing even the sound of the instrument he embraced.

Perhaps his most memorable performance was of Dvorak's cello concerto, in London in September 1968, just after the Soviet-led invasion of Czechoslovakia that crushed the Prague Spring. Protesters outside the Royal Albert Hall were cross that a "Soviet" concert was going ahead. But Mr Rostropovich wept for his country's crimes and its captives' suffering, and so did those who heard him. ■

Miriam Rothschild

Dame Miriam Rothschild, a scientist of the old style, died on January 20th 2005, aged 96

IN A typically generous moment, Miriam Rothschild once named a flea after a writer on *The Economist*. He had fortuitously helped to discover a new one on a zoological expedition in Africa. The gesture was probably the highest honour she could bestow on anyone.

She thought fleas beautiful. Gazing at their stained sections through the microscope, she once said, gave her a feeling as ecstatic as smoking cannabis. In her bedroom she kept them in cellophane bags, in order not to miss a thing that they were doing. She had discovered, by watching thousands of them jump, that they were actually adapted for flight, and that the jumping flea developed an acceleration on take-off 20 times that of a moon rocket re-entering the Earth's atmosphere. A lifelong atheist, she admitted that she had been tempted to believe in a creator when she discovered that the flea had a penis.

Her fascination had begun young, on holiday in Transylvania, when her father had allowed her to help him catch fleas from a mouse. Already, in the sprawling Rothschild family seat where she was brought up and informally schooled, Miriam had a collection of ladybirds and butterflies, the butterflies pinned on card by herself. But her father was a flea man. He and her uncle Walter had already established, at Tring in Hertfordshire, the largest private natural history collection in Britain: 200,000 birds' eggs, 300,000 bird skins, 144 giant tortoises that wandered in the grounds, more than 2m butterflies, and plenty of fleas. These included 12 dressed fleas from Mexico, with a couple garbed like a bride and groom.

Her father's obsession with fleas, however, was not a dilettante enthusiasm, but a serious scientific interest. He had identified the flea that carries plague, *Xenopsylla cheopis Rothschild*, and had written more than 150 papers on the creatures. His daughter followed him into the depths of parasitology. It was not a glamorous field. As she noted ruefully in her book "Fleas, Flukes and Cuckoos", a popular study of parasitism, "Birds' fleas and feather lice do not sing. Nor do they fly about flashing brilliantly coloured wings in the sunshine ... The collectors of fleas and lice can be counted on the fingers of one hand!" Yet she loved them. Her life's work, which took 30 years and filled six volumes, was to catalogue her father's collection.

Nor did she stop there. As a passionate enthusiast for all living creatures (except some irritating humans), she produced more than 300 scientific papers over the years. She did special research into a parasite that lived only in the eyelashes of hippopotami. She studied the behaviour of black-headed gulls, buying gull-eggs in Leadenhall market in order to incubate them herself and put them in her aviary. During the second world war she tracked the role of wood pigeons in transmitting TB to cattle and, as she lurked in the fields with her crate of birds, was once taken for a German spy. She discovered that monarch butterflies absorbed toxins from milkweed in order to use them, as the plant did, for defence. She was most

fascinated by the role of pyrazines, or aromas, in the lives of insects, pointing out that each species of butterflies and moths had its own distinctive scent. The smell of a very gently squeezed ladybird, she once said, "will stay on your hands for days".

A natural philosopher
As the years passed, this passionate scientist, who had never taken a degree and lived most of the time on the farm where she had been born, accumulated eight honorary doctorates. She became a Fellow of the Royal Society and of St Hugh's College, Oxford. These honours were not always given without grumbles from the men in the labs. In an age of intense specialisation and professionalism in science, she appeared as a happy amateur and generalist. She was, in fact, a throwback to a different age, when gentlemen of means (and the Rothschilds had plenty of those) set up their own home laboratories and cabinets of curiosities, and pursued science for the sheer joy of it.

She also had a view of science that was unashamedly broad, taking in arts, literature and natural philosophy – much in the mould of Erasmus Darwin at the end of the 18th century, whose tomes on botany and zoology were written in enthusiastic verse. Very early, she was a part of the environmental movement and an exponent of the "web of life" theory, in which all species in an area depend on each other and on the preservation of habitat. Visitors to her farm in Northamptonshire found it a riot of weeds and wild flowers, a style she impressed on the Prince of Wales at Highgrove. She herself moved through the gardens like a ship in full sail, dressed in her favourite purple or sea-green gowns. Since she had eschewed leather on principle (together with meat and alcohol), she would sometimes wear white wellingtons for evening.

Perhaps the most pleasing image of her, though, was the one that appeared in the Latin citation for her honorary degree from Oxford in 1968. "She has come to this our Capitol", it read, "not by degrees, but by one leap as of her fleas, in a triumphal chariot ... drawn not by Venus's doves, Juno's peacocks, Alexander's gryphons or Pompey's elephants, but by her sixty-odd species of avian parasites." ■

Tiny Rowland

Roland Walter (Tiny) Rowland, capitalism's outsider, died on July 24th 1998, aged 80

HUNTING AROUND for something not too brutal to say about Tiny Rowland now that he is dead, those who knew him have remarked on his charm. The English language is helpful with the evasive word. So, he was charming, if you like, but was he not ruthless? Yes, comes the response, he could be. What about his private life? A long and happy marriage and a liking for Siamese cats. Was he a crook? Some have said he was. But much that has been written about his life is based on hearsay, has the feeling of myth and is uncheckable. Undoubtedly he cut corners, pushed to the limits of the law, but was not, probably, a crook.

Charming and ruthless men are a theme in British business: not enough of them, some would say. What was it about Mr Rowland that made him loathed by many in the community of commerce, that made him say, defensively, "You can never have enough enemies"?

In a sense he was a born outsider. His father was German, a trader working in British India. In 1917, when the first world war, and British patriotism, was at its height, father and mother were in a fairly disgusting detention camp in Simla. That was the birthplace of Tiny, the affectionate nickname given to the strapping baby and which he kept all his life: "Tiny" was the simple signature on his business letters.

After the war the family settled in Hamburg. Tiny was enrolled, like most German boys, as a member of the Hitler Youth. Although the tall, blond-haired, blue-eyed Tiny looked the perfect example of the master race, it seems unlikely that he had Nazi sympathies. Rather the opposite: in 1939 he was jailed for two months for befriending critics of Hitler. The family was allowed into Britain as refugees, but when war broke out Tiny's parents were again detained, this time in the Isle of Man.

Tiny changed his name from Fuhrhop to Rowland and joined the British army as a medical orderly. He was discharged after disclosing that a brother was in the German army. He got a job first as a porter then as a waiter. When peace came, he worked for a time, as far as is known, as a door to door salesman. This was his rock-bottom start as a businessman.

Into Africa

For a young man seeking his fortune after the war, Africa was the place to be. Much of it was still British, and pre-war British at that. Mr Rowland seems to have been welcomed in what was Southern Rhodesia as a fellow white who spoke with a decent upper-class accent. He did well, acquiring a farm, mining interests and the Mercedes dealership (helped by his fluent German). In 1963 he became head of Lonrho, short for the London and Rhodesian Gold Mining Company, a moribund firm he built into a major corporation with annual sales of around $8 billion. At its peak, by the late 1980s, Lonrho was running some 600 companies in 50 countries. It was Africa's largest food producer. Tiny Rowland got on well with Africans. His own humble beginnings may even

Tiny Rowland that upset other charming and ruthless tycoons who feared that he was giving money-making a bad name. He had an awesome temper and a waspish way with words. Calling non-executive directors "Christmas tree decorations" was impolite, even if true. His efforts to prise Harrods store from another less-than-popular tycoon, Mohamed al-Fayed, gave entertainment to millions but in the financial establishment was seen as an unseemly public brawl.

The City of London cheered in 1973 when eight directors of Lonrho tried to get rid of Tiny Rowland, saying he was unfit to run a public company. Mr Rowland survived but suffered a body blow when the then Conservative prime minister, Edward Heath, said that his activities were "the unpleasant and unacceptable face of capitalism". It was Mr Rowland's bad luck that he was the target of one of Sir Edward's few memorable phrases, and one that was continually used against him. Still, it was not personal attacks that scuppered Tiny Rowland, but the judgment of the market. In 1991 Lonrho hit a bad patch. A loan from Colonel Qaddafi of Libya was not much help (and did Tiny much personal harm). In 1995 he was removed from the company by his fellow directors. Had he been younger he might have outwitted the rebels, but at 78 some of the old fire had gone. He went home to play with his cats. ■

have given him a rapport with the dispossessed.

It also has to be said that, in furtherance of business, he dispensed generous bribes to leaders of newly independent black countries. Money, he believed, probably correctly, could buy almost anything. Donald Trelford, a former editor of the *Observer*, a venerable Sunday newspaper that Mr Rowland bought and used as his publicity sheet, wrote this week that he introduced the tycoon to Garry Kasparov, the Russian chess champion. Mr Rowland told him, "If you can introduce me to the man who makes all the decisions about plutonium in Russia, I'll transfer £1m to any bank you nominate."

Did he mean it? Was there such a plutonium king in Russia? It does not matter. There was a vulgar streak in

Herbert Simon

Herbert Simon, artificial intelligence pioneer, died on February 9th 2001, aged 84

THE STORY goes that one day Herbert Simon announced to a group of his students that he and some of his colleagues had invented a "thinking machine". He said it was equal, and perhaps superior, to the human brain.

The idea of such a marvellous machine had been around for centuries. René Descartes (1596–1650), whose philosophy was bound up with mathematics, wondered whether a machine could be made to think; but generally the notion was considered as unlikely as turning iron into gold, another fantasy that occupied great minds. Now here was Mr Simon disturbing his class on a sleepy afternoon in Chicago in 1957 with his improbable claim for computers.

At that time the computer was chiefly famous for having been invented by the British to decode enemy messages in the second world war. High-tech in the world at large was not much more than the electric typewriter. But for several years Mr Simon had been examining whether a computer could match the process of human thought. As a test, he showed that a computer could quickly provide a proof of theorems in *Principia Mathematica*, a key 20th-century work on logical theory. Bertrand Russell, one of the book's authors, said a trifle testily that he wished he had known what "can now be done by machinery" before he had "wasted ten years doing it by hand".

But can artificial intelligence, AI as insiders call it, really be dignified with, well, "intelligence"? Is this what Descartes had in mind when he wrote, "I think, therefore I am"? A machine will deliver a bar of chocolate in return for a coin, provided it is working, but not even a child believes it is a thinking instrument. A computer is a machine, however intricate. Is it no more than a number cruncher? For more than 40 years Mr Simon was regularly interrogated about his claim that there was little difference between a suitably programmed computer and the human brain's use of neurons. He usually answered questions with good grace, but he refused to give ground.

Obvious once you know

In 1978, Herbert Simon was awarded the Nobel prize for economics. What for many people would be regarded as the culmination of a life's work, Mr Simon took almost casually, a diversion. The Swedish judges at the presentation ceremony were a touch hurt to hear that artificial intelligence had been his central interest, rather than economics, although of course he was interested in that discipline too. But to those who knew him such versatility was no great surprise. He dabbled in many things, usually with great accomplishment. What he called "social science" took a hold on him, but he could probably have made a career as a pianist or a painter.

His parents were German immigrants who, like many before them, had settled in Milwaukee. While still at university he had a part-time job with Milwaukee's local authority and became interested in how the administration made budget decisions, or choices as Mr Simon preferred to call them. Years later "Administrative Behaviour" was the

describe it: "satisficing", a composition of the words satisfy and suffice. Not all economists agreed with Mr Simon, "But they are mistaken," he said.

His views on economics tied in with his ideas on artificial intelligence. Even a computer displayed its intelligence by making choices, he said. Like a human, a chess computer would analyse the consequences of a move, but it would do better than even a grandmaster, who would be unlikely to see beyond eight moves ahead. But what about insight? Or indeed wisdom and creativity? Mr Simon tended to be dismissive of such vague human terms. His computers had created drawings, which he was happy to display in his office, and music, which musicians said had aesthetic interest. They had made choices, as a human artist or musician would.

For many people, artificial intelligence suggests Hal, the worryingly clever human-like computer which rebelled in the film 2001. Although Mr Simon sometimes seemed to suggest that a Hal was just around the corner, he was not going to be drawn into comparisons with science fiction. His strictly scientific aims, he said, were limited to using computers to understand how humans think, and as an aid to human thinking. What about the soul? No one, he said, would tell him what the soul was. When someone did, he said thoughtfully, he would program one. ■

subject of his doctorate, and later still the dissertation was turned into a book of the same name, probably the best known of Mr Simon's 20 books. It was his ideas on decision-making, especially in business, that caught the eye of the Nobel judges.

Like many economic theories, Mr Simon's seems obvious once you know it. In taking a decision, he said, no business could process satisfactorily all the "zillion things" affecting the marketing of a product, in the hope that the right answer for maximising profit would pop out at the end.

That was classical economic theory, he said, but it was "a ridiculous view of what goes on". Rather, a business tried to make a decision that was "good enough". He called his theory "bounded rationality" and invented a name to

Frank Sinatra

Francis Albert Sinatra, the voice of an era, died on May 14th 1998, aged 82

THE STORY goes that Frank Sinatra asked John Paul II to hear his confession. The pope declined, despite Mr Sinatra's promise to see him right. The story may have been made up, perhaps by Mr Sinatra's own publicists; little that is reported about showbiz can be taken on trust. But it sounds right. Frank Sinatra liked to say he dealt only with the best, and the best could be bought or intimidated like anyone else. The great singer would give his greatest performance, this time to God, recounting how the ten commandments, the seven deadly sins, had been broken: his way.

Mr Sinatra did meet a predecessor of John Paul at a reception in Rome. This pope did not seem to have heard of him before and politely inquired what operas he had sung in. Such ignorance; but it has no doubt been shared this past week by many in the world's younger generations, baffled by the huge headlines and the yards of articles about Mr Sinatra in newspapers, and the hours about him on television. Who was this octogenarian getting all the attention? That was the immortal Ol' Blue Eyes, darling. Newspapers and television are mostly run by the middle-aged middle class, and Frank Sinatra was part of their youth.

Go back to the 1960s and 1970s. There were the Beatles and the Rolling Stones, of course, twanging their guitars and shouting themselves hoarse, and Elvis lewdly rotating his pelvis. But the Sinatra light baritone backed by a thousand strings was preferred by those who still liked to dance cheek to cheek. The words were often banal, but don't laugh; lose yourself; it's schmaltz that makes the world go round. Al Jolson produced the same effect, and in the 1920s was an idol too, down on his knees crying for "Mammy". It seems unlikely that Jolson and Sinatra were faking it. Much has been made of Frank Sinatra's short temper, his intolerance of criticism, his links with gangsters, but this may only prove a point. "Sentimentality is a superstructure covering brutality," wrote Carl Jung.

Romance was not enough

Was that then the secret of Frank Sinatra's success, a listenable voice and a reputation for roughness? His longevity must have helped. He was born in a slum district of New Jersey to Italian immigrants (father a fireman, mother a nurse) and had a first-generation American's determination to succeed. He never willingly retired and had to be carried off the stage in 1994 when he collapsed in the middle of singing "My Way".

Other singers had their moment of fame and were quickly gone, but he endured. When Mr Sinatra was making his first records with the swing bands of Harry James and Tommy Dorsey, the foremost pop singer in America was Bing Crosby. He seemed unsurpassable in popular esteem. He had an easy and wholesome style. Pope John Paul would have had no problem with Crosby. Frank Sinatra sang the same ballads, but made them sound sexier. Crosby, you felt, would be happy with a kiss; Sinatra sought possession of the whole body. Cole Porter demanded to know why he sang so many of his songs if he did not like the way they were written. But Frank Sinatra had captured the public's new mood for licentiousness rather than mere romance, and received the reward of fame and money.

You could not get away from him. There were dozens of films, most of them forgettable. According to Billy Wilder, a film director, Frank Sinatra had talent but did not have the discipline to be a great actor. He had a fleshy private life that was remarkable even for Hollywood. There were many affairs and four marriages. A reporter asked him what he looked for in a woman. "A sense of humour," he said. His fourth wife, Barbara, had been married to one of the Marx brothers.

It was not much fun for the reporters whose job it was to follow him around. They were, he said, "a bunch of hags", and the women were "hookers". Frank Sinatra needed continuous publicity to stay ahead, but loathed the stories he could not control. People were only mildly interested in accounts of his concerts for charity. They were absorbed by his appearance before a commission investigating his links with organised crime, which he denied. "Bugsy Siegel? He's a gangster?" They were incredulous about a report that he washed his hands obsessively, especially when an obliging newspaper pointed to a reference in *Macbeth*: "What, will these hands ne'er be clean?" After that he was called Lady Macbeth, at least behind his back.

There was an unpleasant side to Frank Sinatra, and more dirt will probably come out now that he is beyond the protection of libel laws and the mob. More important though, much more than this, may be that he characterised an era. It was a less gentle time than Crosby's, but not that different. Frank Sinatra sang about a mating game in which men and women played their timeless roles. Today's pop singers, with their hermaphrodite looks, their taste for drugs and violence, suggest a darker era. Or so it may seem to the middle-aged who write about them. ■

Anna Nicole Smith

Anna Nicole Smith, a peculiarly modern celebrity, died on February 8th 2007, aged 39

NAMES WERE a problem for Anna Nicole Smith. She was born Vickie Lynn Hogan, but never liked it. At high school, before she was kicked out for fighting, she went by Nikki Hart. As a model for Guess jeans in 1992 she was called "Anna Nicole", and settled for that; later she acquired the title "Gold-digger", though she indignantly rebuffed it. "Vickie always wanted a different name," her aunt said. The name she really wanted, from childhood onwards, was Marilyn Monroe.

Yet all this was somewhat beside the point; because what you saw first, on meeting Ms Smith, were the Breasts. There were only two of them, but they made a whole frontage: huge, compelling, pneumatic. They burst out of tight red dresses – preferably red – or teased among feather boas, or flanked a dizzying cleavage that plunged to tantalising depths. These were celebrated, American breasts, engineered by silicon to be as broad and bountiful as the prairie. With them, a girl from nowhere – or from Houston, Texas – could do anything. The body behind them waxed and waned, sometimes stout as a stevedore's and sometimes almost waif-like, matching the little-girl voice; but the Breasts remained. "Everything I have", Ms Smith admitted, "is because of them."

"Did you have breast augmentation?" asked Larry King redundantly, bow tie a-quiver, when she appeared on his show. "Up or down?" "Both." "Aren't there downsides to it?" Yes, Ms Smith said; they hurt her back. But, she might have added, it did no harm to flaunt them in gentleman's clubs in Houston in the half-dark, where ancient oil tycoons would try to grapple them. One such withered specimen, with a twinkle in his rheumy eye, made the attempt in October 1991; three years later, she married him.

J. Howard Marshall was not the first. That was Billy Wayne Smith, whom she married when she was 17 and he was 16, he the cook and she a waitress at Jim's Krispy Fried Chicken in Mexia, Texas. They had a son, but the marriage didn't last. To make ends meet, Ms Smith worked at Wal-Mart, danced topless and slipped naked photos of herself in the post to *Playboy*, hoping to be noticed. She was. By the time she and Marshall tied the knot at the White Dove drive-thru Wedding Chapel – he 89, she 26, the Breasts barely contained in white satin – Ms Smith had become *Playboy*'s Playmate of the Year 1993. In her questionnaire she confirmed she wanted to be the new Marilyn, and in a dozen ways, from the blonde curled hair to the bright red lips to the gorgeous pouts and poses, she was.

She acted too, though it was the Breasts that stole every scene, full in Leslie Nielsen's astonished face in "Naked Gun 33 1/3". The spotlight loved her, but unlike Marilyn she was not favoured by high-flying politicians; there was always too much of the tabloid queen about her, besides her tendency to start slurring and stumbling and writhing, as if on something illegal, in the presence of a microphone. Her fame came, in the end, from being in court.

Prozac and Sugar Pie

The case of *Marshall v Marshall*, a label suitably Dickensian, started almost as soon as Marshall died in 1995. It had been a brief, strange marriage, with Ms Smith hardly ever at home. Each evening she would telephone him after seven, his bedtime; he called her his "sleeping pill". Outsiders imagined that she was simply waiting for his money. But when his will was read, he had left her nothing.

She was sure this was wrong. While alive, he had given her cars, a little ranch and $50,000 a month; orally, she claimed, he had also promised her half of his estate of $1.6 billion. Without it, she was bankrupt. Over a decade various courts found for her, then against her. In 2004 an appeals court ruled that Ms Smith should get nothing. But in 2006 the Supreme Court, no less, said she could go on fighting.

By then her life revolved round the case. She told Larry King she did nothing else, and her reality TV show, which ran from 2002 to 2004, suggested the same. The show followed her to the dentist and to the lingerie shop; trailed Bobby Trendy, her decorator, as he continually redesigned her bedroom; and watched as she gave Prozac to her poodle, the oversexed Sugar Pie. Her lawyer, Howard Stern, was so constantly in the frame that in 2006 she married him, on the catamaran *Margaritaville* off the Bahamas, before tumbling fetchingly in her white veil into the surf.

Americans watched and enjoyed it all; and were also aware, like gawkers driving past the scene of an accident, that they might at any moment witness something awful. The story of poor-girl-makes-good was never quite straight, the fame never without its tawdry side, the money never reliably there, the behaviour rarely unembarrassing. In later years, Ms Smith was seen more and more in black. She often looked beautiful in it, but seldom happy.

Within three days last September she had a daughter, Dannielynn, by no certain father, and lost her son Daniel, at 20, to an accidental overdose of methadone and anti-depressants. Five months later she was dead herself, of causes still unknown, after collapsing in her hotel room at an Indian casino in Hollywood, Florida. She was far from the real Hollywood; yet not so far, in her young, lonely death, from the great name she had most longed to be. ∎

Marie Smith

Marie Smith, the last speaker of the Eyak language, died on January 21st 2008, aged 89

BEYOND THE town of Cordova, on Prince William Sound in south-eastern Alaska, the Copper River delta branches out in silt and swamp into the gulf. Marie Smith, growing up there, knew there was a particular word in Eyak, her language, for the silky, gummy mud that squished between her toes. It was *c'a*. The driftwood she found on the shore, *'u'l*, acquired a different name if it had a proper shape and was not a broken, tangled mass. If she got lost among the flat, winding creeks her panicky thoughts were not of north, south, east or west, but of "upriver", "downstream", and the tribes, Eskimo and Tlingit, who lived on either side. And if they asked her name it was not Marie but *Udachkuqax*a'a'ch*, "a sound that calls people from afar".

Upriver out of town stretched the taiga, rising steadily to the Chugach mountains and covered with black spruce. The spruce was an Eyak dictionary in itself, from *lis*, the neat, conical tree, to *Ge.c*, its wiry root, useful for baskets; from *Gahdg*, its blue-green, flattened needles, which could be brewed up for beer or tea, to *sihx*, its resin, from which came pitch to make canoes watertight. The Eyak were fishermen who, thousands of years before, were thought to have crossed the Bering Strait in their boats. Marie's father still fished for a living, as did most of the men in Cordova. Where the neighbouring Athapaskan tribes, who had crossed the strait on snowshoes, had dozens of terms for the condition of ice and snow, Eyak vocabulary was rich with particular words for black abalone, red abalone, ribbon weed and tubular kelp, drag nets and dipping nets and different sizes of rope. One word, *demexch*, meant a soft and treacherous spot in the ice over a body of water: a bad place to walk on, but possibly a good one to squat beside with a fishing line or a spear.

This universe of words and observations was already fading when Marie was young. In 1933 there were 38 Eyak-speakers left, and white people with their grim faces and intrusive microphones, as they always appeared to her, were already coming to sweep up the remnants of the language. At home her mother donned a *kushsl*, or apron, to make cakes in an *'isxah*, or round mixing bowl; but at school "barbarous" Eyak was forbidden. It went unheard, too, in the salmon factory where Marie worked after fourth grade, canning in industrial quantities the noble fish her people had hunted with respect, naming not only every part of it but the separate stems and shoots of the red salmonberries they ate with the dried roe.

As the spoken language died, so did the stories of tricky Creator-Raven and the magical loon, of giant animals and tiny homunculi with fish-spears no bigger than a matchstick. People forgot why "hat" was the same word as "hammer", or why the word for a leaf, *kultahl*, was also the word for a feather, as though deciduous trees and birds shared one organic life. They lost the sense that lumped apples, beads and pills together as round, foreign, possibly deceiving things. They neglected the taboo that kept fish and animals

separate, and would not let fish-skin and animal hide be sewn in the same coat; and they could not remember exactly why they built little wooden huts over gravestones, as if to give more comfortable shelter to the dead.

The end of the world

Mrs Smith herself seemed cavalier about the language for a time. She married a white Oregonian, William Smith, and brought up nine children, telling them odd Eyak words but finding they were not interested. Eyak became a language for talking to herself, or to God. Only when her last surviving older sister died, in the 1990s, did she realise that she was the last of the line. From that moment she became an activist, a tiny figure with a determined jaw and a colourful beaded hat, campaigning to stop clear-cutting in the forest (where Eyak split-log lodges decayed among the blueberries) and to get Eyak bones decently buried. She was the chief of her nation, as well as its only full-blooded member.

She drank too much, but gave it up; she smoked too much, coughing her way through interviews in a room full of statuettes of the Pillsbury Doughboy,

in which she said her spirit would live when she was dead. Most outsiders were told to buzz off. But one scholar, Michael Krauss of the University of Alaska at Fairbanks, showed such love for Eyak, painstakingly recording its every suffix and prefix and glottal stop and nasalisation, that she worked happily with him to compile a grammar and a dictionary; and Elizabeth Kolbert of the *New Yorker* was allowed to talk when she brought fresh halibut as a tribute. Without those two visitors, almost nothing would have been known of her.

As a child she had longed to be a pilot, flying boat-planes between the islands of the Sound. An impossible dream, she was told, because she was a girl. As an old woman, she said she believed that Eyak might be resurrected in future. Just as impossible, scoffed the experts: in an age where perhaps half the planet's languages will disappear over the next century, killed by urban migration or the internet or the triumphal march of English, Eyak has no chance. For Mrs Smith, however, the death of Eyak meant the not-to-be-imagined disappearance of the world. ∎

Reg Smythe

Reg Smythe, creator of Andy Capp, died on June 13th 1998, aged 80

ALTHOUGH THIS is an obituary of Reg Smythe, it may turn out to be more about Andy Capp, the cartoon character he created. For the benefit of anyone who has never noticed Andy Capp's appearance in some 700 newspapers around the world, it may be worth explaining that he is ... well, what exactly? When Hugh Cudlipp was editor of the *Daily Mirror*, a British tabloid which first published the cartoon in 1957, he said that Andy Capp was a "work-shy, beer-swilling, rent-dodging, wife-bashing, pigeon-fancying, soccer-playing, uncouth cadger, setting an appalling example to the youth of Britain".

He was, therefore, good for a smile among the beer swillers of Britain, but to the continuing surprise of Mr Smythe he crossed the English Channel and took up residence in France as André Chapeau and in Germany as Willi Wacker. America quickly fell to his charms. Pick up the *Denver Post* and a dozen other newspapers and there he is, Andy the pioneer male chauvinist pig.

What do the non-Brits make of him? For France and Germany Andy Capp is the Britain they can happily sneer at, just as British cartoonists waspishly portray the French as frog-eating wimps and the Germans as humourless automatons. Now, doubtless, he is welcomed as an antidote to "cool Britannia", a pose fostered by British government publicists that irritates its European partners as the old enemies and allies move inexorably and suspiciously closer together.

The hero of Hartlepool
America has no such fun with its neighbours. Perhaps, rather alarmingly, Andy Capp is sometimes seen by Americans as part of a real Britain. In this country of thatched cottages and Big Ben, there is a place called Hartlepool in the north of England where, according to an American guide, the people are friendly and "will reply to a 'good evening' or 'good afternoon' even if you don't know them". Among its famous people, the guide notes, are Ridley Scott, a film director (*Blade Runner*), and Andy Capp. He has been adopted by American academe. "Andy Capps", explains a sociologist on the internet, are "long-term unemployed males who are registered for unemployment compensation but not really willing to work at the going wage." Just fancy, his long-suffering wife Flo might have said, it makes him sound almost respectable.

Flo, short for Florence, was also the name of Reg Smythe's mother. "Flo's the sort of woman I admire," he said of the cartoon character. "Stalwart, sleeves rolled up, prepared to put up with her man and get on with what has to be done. She should have been in the title. Never mind, she knows she holds the cartoon together, and that's enough for her."

Various writers about the Andy Capp phenomenon have made the obvious link to Flo the mum, and Mr Smythe did not argue about it. In industrial Britain, the mother was often the real boss, managing the home, minding the money and sometimes having an outside job as well, just as Flo Capp does. Some students of the shirking-class hero (thanks, *Mirror*) believe he was based on Mr Smythe's father. Reg Smythe would not confirm this, but there have been dark rumours.

Like Andy Capp, Mr Smythe came from Hartlepool. He was born about the time the town was beginning to decline as a centre of shipbuilding and steel-making. In 1936, when Britain and much of the rest of the world were in depression, Mr Smythe joined the army in desperation. Three years later war broke out and he was stuck with soldiering until it ended in 1945. Then he had a number of dead-end jobs, drawing cartoons in his spare time and eventually making enough from them to live on.

Later, when the money rolled in, he, like Andy Capp, never had more than a pound or two in his pocket. During his 48-year marriage Mr Smythe was content for his wife Vera to handle the bills, getting pocket money as he needed it (but he had a Mercedes in the garage).

Reg Smythe never had any formal art training. His figures are crudely simple. But you could say the same about Peanuts and Garfield, two of his rivals for popularity. Character is what matters. Andy Capp is reassuringly unchanging, living in a grimy north of England that no longer exists, wearing the sort of flat hat that is no longer common. His only concession to social pressures is to give up smoking, at least in public. He is one of a number of outrageous fictional characters that Britain has let loose on the world during the past few decades. Another is Alf Garnett, a racist and general bigot who commanded huge audiences on television. Such characters are so appalling as to be beyond criticism. They are part of the grand march of British culture, of tatty fashions, improbable art, ear-damaging pop music, distrust of foreigners and politically-incorrect opinions. Reg Smythe worked to his dying day to keep it going and left behind a big pile of cartoons. He is gone, but Andy Capp has at least another year to live. ■

Helen Snow

Helen Foster Snow, a long marcher for China, died on January 11th 1997, aged 89

CLEVER WOMEN run the risk of being overshadowed by clever men who happen to be close to them. Zelda Fitzgerald comes to mind. A writer of talent, she had the misfortune, professionally, to be married to Scott Fitzgerald, perhaps the finest American writer of this century. Gwen John was probably a better artist than Augustus John, but her brother was the celebrity. However the coin spins, a woman may feel she is the loser. Helen Snow certainly felt that.

In 1938 her husband, Edgar Snow, made his name with "Red Star over China", the first substantial account of what the Chinese communists were up to. It brought Mao Zedong to the attention of the outside world. A year later Helen Snow published her own account of meetings with Mao, "Inside Red China". She had sought out Mao on her own in Hunan, his home province, after the communists had ended their extraordinary 6,000-mile "long march" for survival. She had spent four months with him, a whole summer, much longer than Edgar had managed. But her book was little noticed. Edgar had got the scoop. Just in case anyone linked his wife with him, he persuaded her to publish her book under a pseudonym, Nym (Greek for name) Wales (Utah-born Helen had Welsh relations).

Mrs Snow's book and the 40 or so other books and papers she wrote, mainly about China, are thought these days to be superior to her husband's work. Edgar Snow was a journalist. As journalists do, he endeavoured to write entertainingly, offering quick judgments that pass muster at the time but, in some cases, turn out to be facile, or indeed wrong. Mrs Snow declined simply to pick out the busy bits from the mound of original information she collected on the Chinese communists and their leaders, and throw the rest away. History was so important, she said, she could not trust herself to make selections. Her archive, in numerous boxes of documents which she "dragged halfway round the world", is now pored over by researchers at the Hoover Institution, a think-tank analysing the events of this century.

Steaming to Shanghai

The China where Helen arrived in 1931, aged 24, was attractive to adventurous young Americans. Europe, with Paris and all that, had been the place of the 1920s. China seemed new, and was cheap, for those with dollars. A bestseller in America was "The Good Earth", written by Pearl Buck, a missionary who was later to receive the Nobel prize for literature. Helen was going to become "a great author". She took a slow boat to China, steaming up the Whangpoo river to Shanghai. Her father, a lawyer with a mining company that had connections in China, had set up a secretarial job for her in Shanghai. In the evenings she met other Americans in a place called the Chocolate Shop, favoured for its ice-cream. One of them was Edgar Snow. They were married 18 months later. What Mrs Snow called "the boiler of marriage" multiplied "all their powers manyfold". The boiler blew up in 1949, when the Snows were divorced. Their experience was worthy of a better

never communists, but were content to be of the left. Joe McCarthy, the scourge of American radicals, never touched them. The Soviet Union was his black beast. The "loss" of China saddened and puzzled many Americans, but China, until recently, never seemed a threat, but more a part of the mystery of the East.

Just before she died, China named Helen Snow a "friendship ambassador", about the highest compliment it can pay to a foreigner. The Chinese had in mind her pioneering of the "gung-ho" movement. Gung-ho, from the Chinese *gonghe*, meaning working together, came to be shorthand for the industrial co-operatives set up in China to fight the Japanese invasion. A number of westerners in China pushed for the idea, which seems originally to have come from Sweden, and Mrs Snow was the most vigorous pusher.

The co-operatives were supported by Mao, and by Chiang Kai-shek when he joined with the communists to fight the Japanese. After the communists took power it was the communes that were gung-ho. The name was given to co-operative movements in Japan and elsewhere, most notably in India. And Helen Snow, the middle-class girl from America's west, took pleasure from the knowledge that gung-ho was the slogan of the marines in the second world war. ■

ending, she said, with its "struggle between good and evil" in China.

The evil was the Japanese invaders. By 1937, when Japan launched a full-scale attack on China, America was already anti-Japanese. The Flying Tigers, a squadron of American pilots, was fighting for China. Both the Snows forsook their neutrality and marched in patriotic parades mostly composed of students. Their home became a refuge for anyone hiding from not only the Japanese but also Chiang Kai-shek's Nationalists. And the "good"? Mrs Snow came to the conclusion that socialism offered a good future for China, guided by what she called "its historically high ethics". She and her husband were

Muriel Spark

Dame Muriel Spark, novelist, died on April 13th 2006, aged 88

A S SHE lay on the divan in her flat in Queen's Gate, Caroline Rose suddenly heard the sound of a typewriter. Tap-tappity-tap.

> It seemed to come through the wall on her left. It stopped, and was immediately followed by a voice remarking her own thoughts. It said: On the whole she did not think there would be any difficulty with Helena.

Caroline, on another plane of existence, was Muriel Spark. She was trying to scrape a living by writing in London in the mid-1950s, divorced, with a small son. Coffee and diet pills kept her going, but also gave her hallucinations. Because "if you're going to do a thing, you should do it thoroughly", she had converted in 1954 from vague Christianity to Roman Catholicism. In her first published novel, "The Comforters" (1957), she was both Caroline and God, or fate, or that ubiquitous typewriter, tapping out behind the wall page after page of Caroline's life.

God loomed large in Ms Spark's dark, biting, witty novels. In the early years of her career it was the vogue for Catholic converts to be obsessed with Him, sin, and themselves. But unlike Evelyn Waugh, who warmly praised her, or Graham Greene, who kept her going with a monthly allowance and cases of wine, Ms Spark preferred to leave aside the heavier, guilt-ridden aspects of the faith. Her newly-made Catholics were comic and somewhat tentative. They did not agonise much. But, like her, they were perplexed that a divine Creator should allow evil in the world, and especially intrigued by the permutations of free will and fate.

Fate had taken Ms Spark to Africa in 1937, to a miserable marriage from which she escaped six years later. But Africa also gave her the material for a short story, "The Seraph and the Zambesi", with which she won the *Observer*'s Christmas short story competition in 1951. After this, gradually, she became famous. She wrote 23 novels, mostly daring, usually surprising and impossible, as she proudly said, to classify. Anything, it seemed, might inspire a burst of that needle-sharp pen, from Watergate ("The Abbess of Crewe", 1974) to the disappearance of Lord Lucan ("Aiding and Abetting", 2000). Her works were short, tight and beautifully constructed, hinting perhaps at the poet she would slightly have preferred to be.

Dabblings on the dark side held a particular fascination. "The Ballad of Peckham Rye" (1960) satirised Satanism in south London, while "The Bachelors" (1960) anatomised spiritualism in Victoria. ("The Interior Spiral ... That's a make of mattress, isn't it?") Her light touch still managed to carry maximum disapproval. A phrase, too, could pin down more or less anything she spotted. "The evening paper rattle-snaked its way through the letter box and there was suddenly a six-o'clock feeling in the house." "She yawned with her mouth all over her face." Bathos was a speciality: "Human nature is apt to fail in spite of regular prayer and deep breathing".

The beginning and the end

By birth and childhood formation Ms

Spark was a Scottish writer, and always acknowledged it. Like freckles, as she said, her Scottishness could never be lost, though in her later Italian exile she revelled at being European. She wrote of Edinburgh with a child's intensity: the "amazingly terrible" smells of the Old Town, the sight of the unemployed fighting, spitting and cursing, but also the way it might become "a floating city when the light was a special pearly white".

Her own neighbourhood, Bruntsfield, was middle-class, and her parents Jewish-Episcopalian. But she became gradually aware of the Calvinism around her, symbolised by the frightening blackened stone of the city's churches. The God of Calvin, as she wrote in "The Prime of Miss Jean Brodie", her small autobiographical masterpiece of Edinburgh public-school life, "sees the beginning and the end".

As a writer, she could see it too. In "Brodie", which became both a play and a film, she ran dizzyingly forwards and backwards in time, revealing how her characters would turn out or how they would die. There was, it seemed, quite a streak of Ms Spark in the scatty, romantic Miss Brodie: "Safety does not come first. Goodness, Truth and Beauty come first." But Ms Spark painted herself as Sandy Stranger, a clever, ugly girl with "small, almost non-existent" eyes. Sandy was the sly onlooker and chief teller of the tale, as well as the puller of the strings. It was she, naturally, who betrayed Miss Brodie to the authorities and ended her teaching career. And Sandy, after one torrid affair and one acclaimed book on psychology, became an enclosed nun, Sister Helena of the Transfiguration.

Nunnishness, it might be thought, figured little in Ms Spark's real life. Instead there was fame, many prizes (though she missed out on the Booker, the biggest British fiction award), sleek clothes, and a fortune that drove her abroad to escape the taxman. Yet she lived for 27 years in a converted 13th-century church in Tuscany, happily eschewing the literary whirl, writing longhand in spiral-bound notebooks that were sent to her from Edinburgh. And she died in the Easter season, the best time for Catholics, in a way that might almost have been planned. Tap-tappity-tap. ■

Stephen Spender

Sir Stephen Harold Spender, British poet, novelist, playwright and critic, died on July 16th 1995, at the age of 86

IN 1933, when Stephen Spender was 24, he wrote the poem that came to be most closely associated with his name. In later life he confessed to worrying that he would be remembered, not by his numerous novels, plays, translations, essays and other poems, but by only this one poem with its first line, "I think continually of those who were truly great." His heart would have sunk had he read this week's voluminous words of praise, which were often accompanied, glutinously, by this work.

Still, even with his one remembered poem, Stephen Spender has done better in a bid for immortality than most of his contemporaries. Christopher Isherwood, who also died in his 80s with millions of words behind him, is remembered mainly as the creator of the minx Sally Bowles, and that because his story of pre-war Berlin was turned into a musical, *Cabaret*. Louis MacNeice and Cecil Day-Lewis, close friends of Spender, and themselves once famous poets, have sunk pretty well without trace.

But, most important, Stephen Spender stood for an era, as distinctive as that of Virginia Woolf's Bloomsberries or of Scott Fitzgerald's Jazz Age. Once it was royals who marked eras. Now it is writers. In the 1930s Spender, Isherwood and the others formed a circle of admiration around W. H. Auden, the 20th century poet most likely still to be read in 100 years' time. Spender and Auden met at Oxford. Auden, slightly older than Spender, was haughty and self-possessed. Spender was awkward and affected. He had gained some notoriety by sitting on a cushion in a college quadrangle reading poetry. When unpoetical hearties burst into his room he read aloud from Blake as they broke up his furniture.

A sort of club

Spender tentatively showed Auden some of his poems. Auden's cruel comment was, "You are infinitely capable of being humiliated. Art is born of humiliation." The unhumiliated Spender printed Auden's first collection of poems, and remained his champion. Being a young and noticed poet was fun in the 1930s, with plenty of travel and the patronage of the famous, although Auden called it, accurately, a "low, dishonest decade".

Like Auden, Spender had homosexual affairs, but later said he was "not really happy" living with another man. "It was a sort of club, and if you forsook the club they got very annoyed." His early homosexuality, he said, "just withered away". He was married twice, since 1941 to Natasha Litvin, a pianist, and fathered two children.

In company with many Oxbridge intellectuals, Spender flirted with communism. Some made a career of it and became Soviet spies. But Spender soon left the party. He decided that telling lies was incompatible with being an artist. He would have made a poor spy. Cyril Connolly called him "a great big silly goose". Along with a number of other former sympathisers, among them Arthur Koestler, he confessed his sins in a recantation in "The God that Failed", published in 1949. But unlike many who rejected that god, Spender never moved to the right. He resigned from the staff of

Encounter, which he had helped to found, when it turned out the magazine was getting money from the CIA.

Any youthful transgressions were eventually forgiven or forgotten. At the safe age of 74 the "grand old man of letters", as he had become, joined other entertainers who were by then being given knighthoods and he became Sir Stephen. Still, he never seemed entirely comfortable with the gifts of a middle-class life. In an interview in 1994 he agonised over a familiar moral dilemma: what to do if the television shows pictures of starving African children when the viewer is eating a meal. "Do you stop eating the lamb chop? Do you turn off the television?" he asked. "I think you somehow have to go on ... facing the lamb chop and thinking, well, this is my life."

Auden, Isherwood and Spender in 1938

If Spender fell a little short of greatness in his writing, he was a delightful and indulgent person. But in the last decade of his life he surprised many of his admirers by reacting furiously to two attempts by others to write about him. He dismissed one unofficial biography as rubbish, and filed a 40-page rebuttal of it in the British Library. He went to court to secure the banning in Britain of a novel called *While England Sleeps*, based on a homosexual relationship Spender had already written about. Many people thought Spender was acting out of character. He was, after all, a campaigner for freedom of speech, and a founder of a journal called *Index on Censorship*.

But one of the penalties of Spender's long life was his increasing concern with reputation. Last year he grumbled that obituaries about him were being prepared, and that they were "all about your sex life and things like that". And don't forget that poem. ∎

Dr Spock

Benjamin McLane Spock, family doctor to the world, died on March 15th 1998, aged 94

IT WAS, on the face of it, an odd book to have become one of the bestsellers of the century. The one endeavour the human race was used to, and indeed had become quite good at, was having babies and bringing them to adulthood. Benjamin Spock, who seemed continually to be surprised, and perhaps disturbed, by his success, acknowledged that parents already knew, if instinctively, much of what he set down in his handbook, first published in 1946 under the title *The Common Sense Book of Baby and Child Care*. Although the title was changed from time to time as the book went through numerous editions, and its contents were updated to take note of single-parent families and other social developments, he retained the sentence that was the key to his teaching: "Trust yourself – you know more than you think you do."

It is unlikely that many of the 50m copies said to have been sold around the world were ever read through from cover to cover. This was a book to be consulted if, say, Baby was reluctant to get to sleep or had kicked over its potty. The parent would consult the relevant page (helped by Dr Spock's very detailed index), and, reassured by his words, do what she thought best anyway. Many parents gained from the book the comfort once provided by the family Bible. It was a rock to lean on; far too much, said Dr Spock's critics.

In the late 1940s, the memories of the recent war, and the threat of an even worse one, may have made parents feel especially protective; or, as the doctor's critics put it, their children were indulged. "Spockmanship" was denounced by Spiro Agnew, vice-president from 1969 to 1973 (when he resigned over a corruption scandal). By then the post-war children had grown up and were credited, or discredited, with the permissive society. Blame the parents, said the Agnew camp, but particularly blame the sinister Dr Spock. The doctor insisted that his book, by then seen by some Americans as subversive as the works of Marx, had not encouraged permissiveness; it aimed rather to relax rigidity. But it wasn't the book alone that drew fire. Dr Spock himself was now a political figure, an opponent of the Vietnam war.

Sentenced to jail

In 1968, after being arrested at various anti-war demonstrations, Dr Spock appeared before a Boston court accused of helping Americans to dodge the draft. The government regarded him as a formidable nuisance. He shone on television: clearly middle-class, the son of a lawyer, educated at Yale, with the warmth that you expected from a children's doctor, and above all the author of this marvellous book. He could not even be called a coward: he had served in the American navy in the second world war, and had supported the Korean war. But the Vietnam war, he told the court, was "illegal, immoral" and "unwinnable". It was certainly unwinnable, as the generals later acknowledged. But the court was unimpressed by the doctor's words and gave him two years in prison, a sentence that was, however, quashed on appeal.

only a few remain in print. All are distinguished by the clear writing of the baby book, but these days probably no one cares to read *Dr Spock on Vietnam*, published in 1968.

It would be nice to say that domestically, anyway, Dr Spock's life went smoothly. But he dumped his first wife, Jane, after 49 years of marriage, and then married a woman 40 years his junior. Jane grumbled that she helped a lot with the baby book and should have been credited as co-author. They had two sons, who in Dr Spock's autobiography are rather shadowy figures, perhaps because, sensibly, he tried to keep them out of the limelight. But his stepdaughter, by his second wife, seems to have been a terror unresponsive to every trick in his book. "'Ginger,' I said one day, 'in my 75 years I've been acquainted with thousands of people, but not one of them has been as rude as you.' I thought I saw a faint smile of triumph."

Although the two made peace as Ginger grew up, Dr Spock never found an easy answer for society's increasing problem of what he called "naturally accursed, naturally poisonous" step relations. But in the vast child-care literature that has grown up since Dr Spock opened up this profitable marketplace, there is probably a book about it. Or if not, somebody no doubt will soon write one. ∎

In 1972 Dr Spock ran for president as candidate for the People's Party, a mildly socialist group more European than American in feeling. Even now its platform looks improbable: free medical care, legal abortion and marijuana, a guaranteed minimum income for a family, and the withdrawal of American troops from abroad. He received a pretty modest 75,000 votes. He seemed not to be discouraged. Into his 80s he was being arrested in anti-nuclear demos that stretched the limits of American tolerance. His view of nuclear war was simple, if conventional: "There's no point in raising children if they're going to be burned alive."

He wrote 13 books, some in collaboration with other writers, but

Irving Stevens

Irving Stevens, America's king of the hobos, died on May 4th 1999, aged 88

THE FIRST thing you should know about hobos, Irving Stevens would say, is that they are not tramps. If you are a tramp you are content to live by begging, with perhaps a bit of stealing to help things along. Hobos are wandering workers, prepared to go anywhere in search of a job, and when that job runs out to move on to somewhere else more promising. Being a hobo, self-sufficient, despising welfare, is thus acceptably American, and probably more than that.

When Mr Stevens was elected king of the hobos at the hobos' convention in Iowa in 1988 he became nationally famous. His homely wisdom dispensed on television programmes formed the subject of numerous newspaper articles extolling the merits of the hobo philosophy. Perhaps only a country as rich and secure as America could get irrepressibly sentimental about what is, in essence, casual labour. If there are hobos in Japan, they keep quiet about it. In Europe, the remaining gypsies have largely lost what romance they had and are mostly regarded as a nuisance.

American hobos, though, are associated with two powerful sources of myth: freight trains and cowboys. The great ranches of the west were a reliable source of seasonal work, either herding cattle or, less glamorously, doing farm work: hobo is probably a corruption of "hoe boy". Some hobos carried their personal hoes from job to job, like old-time shepherds with their crooks.

The railroads got you there. Many hobos were known by names derived from their prowess at riding the rails. Steamtrain Maury and Choo-Choo

Johnson were two of the most famous. Mr Stevens already had a nickname, Fishbones. "Everyone called him that, he was so thin," his sister recalled this week. "You could see his bones through his skin." It wasn't so much the romance that sent Fishbones in his early 20s on his travels from his home in Maine. He was simply poor and hungry and America was in depression. The story-telling came later.

His secret formula

Irving Stevens wrote two books about his experiences, "Dear Fishbones" and "Hoboing in the 1930s". His stories have charm, and usually end with a moral point. Kind reviewers have said that they are a bit like Aesop's fables. But distance may have lent enchantment to what must have been a life of hardship. Other hobos who have put their memories into words tell of the "bulls", the railway police who would beat up the boxcar riders, or shoot them; and of life in the "jungle", the name given to a community of hobos who had pooled their resources.

Mr Stevens was most famous for inventing a fly repellent that he refined, and seemingly perfected, over many years. It smelt abominably, but it kept the biting things away. "Well, I thought, if the stuff works so well, I can probably sell it." Mr Stevens enhanced his American credentials by becoming an entrepreneur, if in a small way. Irving's Fly Dope, bought by grateful fishermen and campers, provided Mr Stevens with a regular income in his later life, when he had given up hoboing. He kept the formula as secret as Coca-Cola's.

The second world war (in which Mr Stevens served in the air force) ended America's Great Depression, and ended the need to look far and wide for work. There was plenty nearer home. Mr Stevens settled down, got married and had six children. There were now fewer hobos trailing across America but the breed was not extinct. There was still casual work to be had, the amount influenced by the booms and busts of the American economy.

Even now, with the economy roaring ahead and seemingly unstoppable, some hobos still feel a need to

roam. "Hoboing gives you an absolute peace and freedom," recalled one addict. "There's nothing better than riding the rails in a clean boxcar and watching the world go by." This idyllic picture has helped to give birth to a new type of American hobo: young, often well-educated but not poor, not in need of work, unlikely to carry a hoe, and only a phone call away from anxious, supportive parents. The *Hobo Times* is full of fatherly advice to the innocent: don't travel alone; keep a supply of one dollar bills handy so you are not seen changing a big one; best to light a fire only in the daytime because at night it might attract unwelcome strangers; remember that there are serial murderers roaming the "high iron".

The railway companies have put up posters aimed at deterring hobos and others from riding freight trains. In 1997,

529 people died as a result of trespassing on the railways. Even experienced rail-riders find it difficult to get aboard modern trains driven by diesel engines which gather speed more rapidly than the steam trains of the old days.

The history of hoboing, ancient and modern, has become a respectable academic discipline. As his fame grew, Mr Stevens saw himself as the head of American hobos' first family. In 1993 he crowned one of his daughters, Connie Hall, queen of the hobos. They are together in our picture. More than 30,000 people watched the ceremony. Yes, Mr Stevens said, there were female hobos, like Boxcar Bertha of Iowa, who died about five years ago. They were treated as equals by the men and never harmed. Irving Stevens thought they might be called early feminists. But that's another story. ■

Chidambaram Subramaniam

Chidambaram Subramaniam, a "green" leader, died on November 7th 2000, aged 90

MOST OF the garden around Chidambaram Subramaniam's house in Delhi was taken up by a cricket pitch, where he entertained friends to a game at weekends. One day in 1966 he gave orders for the garden to be dug up, cricket pitch and all, and planted with wheat seed.

Mr Subramaniam, India's agriculture minister, believed that the seed, a new variety, would transform Indian farming. Not everyone was convinced. This imported seed, critics said, could introduce foreign pests and diseases, ruining the already impoverished Indian farmer. Nationalists noted that the seed had been developed by an American scientist, Norman Borlaug, and everyone knew that Americans were no friends of India.

Opposition politicians saw the issue as a way of getting at the Congress government. Bureaucrats gave them their tacit support, fearing that the dangerous Mr Subramaniam was pushing ahead too fast, undermining their authority.

The real fear for India, Mr Subramaniam said, was that it faced severe famine unless more grain was produced. Look, he would plant the seed in his own garden, on his cricket pitch. The dramatic gesture in cricket-mad India did not wholly end the opposition to the seed but it was dented. The seed was sown throughout India, in around 1,000 "demonstration" sites, as well as in the Delhi garden. The resulting wheat yield, double that of previous sowings, astonished even Mr Subramaniam.

The pariah seed was suddenly in demand. Some farmers who could not buy the seed stole it. The next year, 1967, India harvested 17m tons of wheat grain. Never before had the harvest been greater than 12m tons. Schools were closed and their classrooms were used to store the extra bounty. Its immediate effect was to have saved many thousands of Indians from starvation. Today India harvests about 70m tons of wheat grain a year, more than enough for self-sufficiency in an ever-expanding population, with some left over for export. This was what came to be called India's green revolution, a rare example of a discovery delivering even more than it had promised.

Who gets the credit?

Last year there was a lot of support for naming Mr Subramaniam India's man of the century, even of the millennium. He was too modest, and too wise, to allow himself to be given the laurel for a discovery for which many claimed credit. Norman Borlaug had got a Nobel in 1970 for developing the high yielding wheat at the international Maize and Wheat Improvement Centre in Mexico, and had been supported by the Rockefeller Foundation. Indian scientists adapted the seed to Indian conditions. Two of the prime ministers Mr Subramaniam had worked under, Lal Bahadur Shastri and Indira Gandhi, had defended him against all the flak from his critics.

All the same, it was Mr Subramaniam who got the wheat growing, skilfully guiding the project through India's political and bureaucratic fog, Monkombu Swaminathan, an agricultural scientist who worked with Mr Subramaniam, said this week that the politician had helped farmers to achieve in four years as much progress as they had managed in the preceding 4,000 years.

Perhaps because others sought to be acknowledged as "father" of the green revolution, India was slow to acknowledge officially what Mr Subramaniam had accomplished: he was awarded the country's highest civilian honour, the Bharat Ratna (Jewel of India), in 1998, only some 30 years after the new seed had proved itself.

Then, as in the obsequies since his death, much was said about his integrity. Nor was it flattery. Whatever the controversy over the seed, most people considered him a trustworthy minister, a quality not always evident in Indian politicians. He was born into a landowning family in what is now Tamil Nadu, in southern India. He practised law, but became increasingly involved with Mahatma Gandhi's independence movement. In 1941 he was imprisoned by the British, who were desperately holding the Japanese at bay and had no time for agitators. His term in jail was a useful credential when he made politics his career, first at local level and then in the national parliament. In various Congress governments he had a variety of jobs other than agriculture. He had a go at finance and defence and was reckoned to do them ably, if not spectacularly. He said you could not be a hero all the time.

His last job was as governor of the state of Maharashtra. He resigned in 1993 after some private remarks he had made criticising the Delhi government were printed in a newspaper. Perhaps by then, at 83, he was anyway tired of the political round. He gave his attention to the Tamil Nadu Cricket Association, where each year young cricketers compete for a cup donated by him. He had long forgiven the British for jailing him in the fight for independence. The British had given to India "the graces of a great game". Cricketers were a brotherhood of gentlemen sportsmen. "Do you remember," he would reminisce to gentlemen as old as he was, "that time I had to dig up my lawn ..." ∎

Sue Sumii

Sue Sumii, the champion of Japan's untouchables, died on June 16th 1997, aged 95

WHEN SUE Sumii was six, the Emperor Meiji visited the village where she lived, near Nara. After he left, the villagers scrabbled for souvenirs: cigarette butts adorned with the imperial seal, anything that the god-king might have touched. One farmer went into the lavatory the emperor had used and reverentially scraped out a sample of sacred stool. For the child the incident was a revelation. "If the emperor shits," Mrs Sumii wrote later, "it must mean he eats, too. In that case, he's no different at all from me." She spent most of her adult life exposing the idiocy of Japan's class system, and inspiring sympathy for its most despised victims: the untouchable caste known as *burakumin*.

The subject is avoided in polite society, but Japan has had untouchables – similar in some ways to the *harijan* of India or the *paekchong* of Korea – since at least the 13th century. Buddhism bars the killing of animals, and Japan's native Shinto creed rules that contact with dead flesh is defiling; so butchers, leatherworkers and gravediggers have traditionally been confined to ghettoes and shunned. In feudal times, the *eta* (much filth), as they were called, were banned from socialising with other Japanese and sometimes forced to wear leather patches on their sleeves to mark them out as unclean. In 1859, when an untouchable was murdered in a brawl, the judge ruled that the murderer could not be punished unless he was allowed to kill six more untouchables: an *eta* life was worth a seventh of that of an "ordinary" Japanese.

Although segregation was legally ended in 1871, discrimination persists. There are more than 1m *burakumin* (hamlet people) in Japan today, mostly concentrated in the Osaka region. They are distinguishable from other Japanese only as a result of where they (or their ancestors) live. Companies buy (illegal) lists of *buraku* addresses to avoid hiring them, and "respectable" families pay private detectives to check that potential in-laws do not come from untouchable stock. *Buraku* household income is perhaps 60% of the Japanese average.

Fiction and fact

Sue Sumii was not a *burakumin*. But she lived near a ghetto, and recorded and decried its residents' plight in speeches, articles, and in a series of novels collectively entitled "The River with No Bridge". This sad, tender saga, begun in Mrs Sumii's 50s, after her husband died, tells of the trials of a family of sandal-makers: the poverty, the taunts, the shame of trying to buy food when shopkeepers will not touch coins that have been handled by an outcast. When a fire breaks out in their village, the neighbours stand around remarking how an *eta* fire stinks, instead of helping. In a real-life reflection of Mrs Sumii's story, the areas worst hit by the fires that followed the Kobe earthquake of 1995 were the narrow streets and wooden shacks where the *burakumin* lived. Local people claimed that the fire brigade doused *buraku* flames last.

Extraordinarily, given Mrs Sumii's controversial subject matter and radical politics, the seven volumes of "The River with No Bridge" have sold more

in an article on private investigators.

Partly, the silence that enshrouds *buraku* affairs reflects editors' embarrassment at the existence of a tormented minority in their supposedly harmonious society. But, also, it is because campaigners for *buraku* rights have been known to fight prejudice with their boots and fists. Publishers of books considered offensive have had their offices invaded and their bookshops picketed by bellowing firebrands from the Buraku Liberation League. Since few papers or television companies can keep pace with the league's ever-shifting decrees about which words are acceptable when referring to *burakumin*, and which are not, most choose to avoid the subject entirely. Mrs Sumii's work was the only conspicuous exception to this rule.

than 8m copies, and been turned into two films. At no small risk to herself, Mrs Sumii made links between the imperial family's wealth and its subjects' wretchedness, and between the shared religious roots of emperor-worship and scorn for the *burakumin*.

For many Japanese, Mrs Sumii's writings were their sole window on the untouchables. The subject is almost never aired in the Japanese media, and foreign books that touch on the *buraku* problem have all references to it deleted when they are translated into Japanese. Japan Airlines once pulped an edition of its in-flight magazine because of a brief mention of the topic

It should be said in fairness that life for the *burakumin* has improved in the past two decades. Special grants have made the ghettoes less slummy, and three-quarters of *burakumin* now manage to marry non-*buraku* partners. Some achieve this by moving house, changing their names, and concealing their origins; but other "mixed" weddings reflect a waning of medieval prejudice. If anyone deserves the credit for this, it must surely be Sue Sumii. She was working on an eighth volume of her saga when she died. ∎

Sun Yaoting

Sun Yaoting, a eunuch serving China's last emperor, died on December 17th 1996, aged 93

THE MEN who run China were uncertain what to do with Sun Yaoting. Some were minded to condemn him to a gulag or simply to execute him. He was seen as a relic of life in old China. While a boy his genitals had been removed. As a eunuch he had been a servant in the court of China's last emperor. Clearly, it was argued, he was not fit to live among revolutionaries forging a new society. This feeling took hold during the cultural revolution of the 1960s, when he was attacked by the Red Guards, an organisation of young Communist Party toughs.

But some in the party were, and are, reluctant to dismiss all Chinese history before communism. It is instructive for a foreigner to be lectured by a senior party official about China's 3,500 years of continuous civilisation, sometimes enthusiastically expanded to 5,000 years. Mr Sun, for all his shortcomings, was a part of this history. This sentiment enabled him to survive China's random purges and live to a remarkable age.

A historically minded official might also point out that castration was an accepted practice in other advanced societies. The emasculation of boy singers in Europe in the 17th and 18th centuries enabled them to retain their higher range of voice, known as falsetto, into later life instead of allowing the voice to deepen. Some of Handel's operas contain leading roles for a eunuch. A castrato sang in the Sistine Chapel as recently as 1922. A technically brilliant castrato, Carlo Broschi (1705-82), had a tone which so enraptured Philip V of Spain that he consulted him on matters of state.

The Chinese eunuchs, though, were not primarily admired for their voices. They were servants in the Forbidden City, the palace in Beijing of the emperors of the Manchu dynasty, who had ruled China since the 17th century. At dusk all men, apart from the emperor, had to leave the palace. The women of the imperial family and the emperor's concubines were guarded by the eunuchs. It was into this society that Sun Yaoting entered at the age of eight.

Getting rich

It may be wondered why any parent would allow a child to undergo a crude operation (with, it was said, hot chili sauce as the only local anaesthetic), to be followed by a life of servitude. There was no compulsion. On the contrary, there was great competition among the poor for a son to be admitted to the sanctum of the Chinese ruler. Eunuchs, with their control of the royal household, became the conduit between the emperor, confined to his palace, and the civil service running China's vast bureaucracy. They often became rich through bribes, and their relations outside the palace benefited accordingly.

Mr Sun, though, did not become rich. A few months after he entered the emperor's service the Manchu dynasty was overthrown, and in 1912 China became a republic. The last of the emperors, Pu Yi, was allowed to go on living in the palace, and Mr Sun seems to have become a close friend. At any rate, they passed the time playing tennis in the palace courtyards.

Outside, the republic tore itself apart. The revolutionary leader, Sun Yat-sen, lost control and warlords took over the country. Civil war followed. The Japanese invaded in the 1930s and Pu Yi became their puppet. In 1940 he rode in state through Tokyo. He died in 1967. His ashes were lost for a time, but subsequently, as a result of the party's "rediscovery" of Chinese history that has also benefited Sun Yaoting, they were placed in Beijing's imperial cemetery. Young Chinese have given him a sort of accolade: Pu Yi sunglasses, like those in a film about the emperor, are selling well.

With his mentor gone, Mr Sun took refuge in various temples. According to a friend, he lamented the fall of the imperial system and longed for its return. However, no such counter-revolutionary ideas were publicly expressed by Mr Sun, described by the friend as "a man of rare intelligence". He was respected for his great age and in 1993 was invited to make a nostalgic visit to the Forbidden City. He wandered around his old haunts, now a museum, pointing out a number of inaccuracies in the displays, and these were courteously noted.

A more personal concern for Sun Yaoting was the whereabouts of his penis. A eunuch would take great care of his amputated genitals so that they could be united with the rest of his body at the time of death. This would ensure that he would be reincarnated, as taught by his religion, as a whole man. Mr Sun learnt that, during the cultural revolution, a relation had destroyed the penis, fearful that the Red Guards would find it. "When I die I will come back as a cat or dog," he lamented.

Was Mr Sun the last of the imperial eunuchs? In China's large population, most of it in rural areas, it is possible that a few eunuchs are living out the end of their lives, just as there are old women still alive whose feet were bound in childhood. But, one way or another, old China is passing unthreateningly into official history. ■

Robert Taylor

Robert Taylor, a possible victim of alien abduction, died on March 14th 2007, aged 88

WHAT WAS it about Bob Taylor? He was an unassuming man, steady, phlegmatic, with a thick brush of white hair and a craggy outdoorsman's face. He liked a pint, and a dram too, but not when he was working. He smoked, but not too many. In his house at the edge of Dechmont Woods near Livingston in West Lothian, where he had worked all his life as a forester, there were very few books. And certainly there was none that could explain what happened to him on November 9th 1979, and why his trousers, of thick navy serge like a policeman's and with useful pockets in the sides, should have ended up in the archives of the British UFO Research Association.

Mr Taylor set off that morning, with his red setter Lara, to check the woods on Dechmont Law for stray sheep and cattle. It was a damp day and, after he had parked the van and set off down the forest track, even the noise of the Edinburgh-Glasgow motorway was muffled by thick, dark fir trees. The dog ran, and Mr Taylor's trudging wellingtons made the only sound. Then he turned a corner into a clearing filled with light, and saw it.

It was a "flying dome", 20 feet wide, hovering above the grass. No sound came from the object, and it did not move. It seemed to be made of grey metal, shiny but rough, like emery paper. About half-way down it had a circular platform, like the brim of a hat, set with small propellers. There were darker areas on it that might have been portholes, but the strangest thing was that the dome would be solid one moment, transparent the next, so that Mr Taylor could see the fir trees through it, as if it was trying to camouflage itself.

Both he and the dog stood stock-still with surprise. But then, suddenly, two smaller spheres dropped out of the dome and came trundling across the grass, one to his right, one to his left. They were covered in long spikes, like navy mines, that made a ghastly sucking sound as they dug in and out of the mud. They grabbed his trousers, one on the right leg, one on the left, ripping right through to his winter long johns, and giving off a foul choking smell like burning brakes. Mr Taylor felt himself being pulled towards the craft; then he blacked out. When he came to, the visitors had gone.

So far, so impressive a story to explain a dishevelled homecoming on a Saturday night. But it was in mid-week and at midday that Mr Taylor crawled home, with the dog but without the van, with a graze on his chin and his trousers torn, covered in mud and with a thumping headache. His wife called a doctor and the police. Mr Taylor felt no need for the doctor, and after two days of a wild, craving thirst and the weird brake smell, he felt fine. But he took the police to the scene.

And there was the evidence. A large circle and inner "ladder" marks, which had flattened the grass but not dented the ground, as if a heavy craft had hovered but not landed. Forty little round holes, leaving the circle clockwise and anticlockwise, as if spiky "mines" had indeed rolled out of it. But no track entering or leaving the clearing, making

the machine's arrival impossible unless it was a helicopter or something dropped by a mobile crane; and nothing of that sort had been seen in the area that day or the day before.

Lights over Livingston

The detective sergeant in charge of the case did not believe in space visitors. Mr Taylor's boss at the Forestry Department did not believe either, and thought it was probably some secret device being tested by the government. UFO debunkers thought Mr Taylor might have seen a magnified image of Venus distorted by the earth's atmosphere, which had made him fall down in an epileptic fit. The press came; and by the time the story reached Edinburgh, it was "small furry creatures" that had poured from the spacecraft to attack him. "I know what I saw," said Mr Taylor. So doughtily and drily did he stick to his tale (and kept a camera with him ever after, to take the aliens' pictures if they ever came for him again) that the police opened a criminal investigation for assault, the only one in Britain to arise from a UFO "sighting". It remains open.

Mr Taylor's neighbours proving much more sceptical, he eventually moved away to an undisclosed address. But he also became the most famous "witness" to aliens in Britain. His trousers were taken to spiritualist meetings to be analysed by psychics ("I feel pain from these trousers"), and on anniversaries of the sighting UFO-spotters would gather in the clearing, just on the off-chance.

The aliens, meanwhile, did not give up. Since that November day they have filled the skies of West Lothian with glimmering discs, strange lights and bouncing balls of fire. The "Falkirk Triangle" now registers more UFO sightings, around 300 a year, than any other spot on Earth. A good many happen outside the Forge restaurant in Bonnybridge, where fireballs sail over the trees and "wingless planes" are seen in the fields. Some experts say West Lothian may be a "thin place", offering a window from the Earth into another dimension; others say the sightings are linked to the lack of jobs locally, and cheap liquor. But some know the aliens are just looking for Bob Taylor, or his dog, or his van, in the place where they last saw him, suddenly amazing them in a clearing among the trees. ■

René Thom

René Thom, inventor of catastrophe theory, died on October 25th 2002, aged 79

GREAT THINGS were expected from René Thom's catastrophe theory when it first emerged in the 1970s from the arcane deliberations of mathematicians into the everyday world of people who just hope for a more ordered life. Mr Thom did his best to make his theory sound simple. Take the example of a river, he said. It flows along smoothly and predictably until it turns suddenly into a catastrophic waterfall. Salvador Dali, in what he said was "homage" to Mr Thom, helpfully painted a picture of a landscape of smooth hills with a crack running through them, and added a formula for viewers with a mathematical turn of mind.

But slightly more technically, Mr Thom defined catastrophe as the loss of stability in a dynamic system. Catastrophes are inevitable, but obviously their damage could be lessened if they could be predicted. Could Mr Thom's theory be applied, say, to the safety of buildings or of ships at sea; to riots; to strikes; to when a tyrant leader would lose control and become vulnerable? The world of finance, alternately in a state of cockeyed optimism and deep gloom, was very interested in the theory. Mr Thom was slightly taken aback by being associated with astrologers, the apocalypse and UFOs, but he referred those interested to his book, "Structural Stability and Morphogenesis", which briefly became a bestseller.

It is full of ideas, many of which are only marginally related to mathematics. He claims, for example, that men are physically more fragile than women; women are more rounded, closer to the sphere, the strongest shape in the universe. Maths-type symbols, he said, are recognised by animals: a tiger could spot a gazelle's hoofprints. In this sense the animal could read.

Down in the forest

But the book was less an offering of easily digested novelties, than a mathematical treatise dealing with the seven ways in which things are likely to collapse suddenly. It is no reflection on the intelligence of many people who tackled the book that they found it baffling. In the 19th century, a mathematician such as Henri Poincaré, a compatriot of Mr Thom, could claim to understand all the important maths of his time. This would have been a rare claim in the 1970s, and rarer still today. Popular interest in catastrophe theory lasted for about 20 years; not bad as ideas go. It waned when it seemed to offer no obvious material gain, and returned to the specialised area from which it came. "All good minds", Mr Thom said, a touch bitterly, in later life, "decided that it was of no value."

One of the theory's few practical applications was to decide how to save forests from the catastrophic spruce budworm. The answer provided by Mr Thom's maths was to chop down old trees, which foresters said they knew anyway.

Mr Thom's theory may have been treated unfairly. It was philosophical as much as mathematical. The theory continues to be cited occasionally in discussions of how catastrophes have suddenly intervened to reshape history. Mr Thom was keen to explain how the theory worked in the history of his own country. The French revolution was the big bang of catastrophe theory, he said, and its effects had not yet been exhausted.

One of its effects, he said, was the second world war, a catastrophe for France, and for René's parents who ran a shop in Montbéliard in eastern France. In 1940, when the Germans invaded, René, then 16, joined the refugees fleeing south. Like many French of his generation he was appalled by France's quick defeat, but was equally defensive of France's greatness. Any criticism of his work he disparagingly called "Anglo-Saxon".

The young René made his way to Switzerland but then returned to France, settling for a time in Lyons, where he resumed his education. He gained entry to the Ecole Normale Supérieure, in Paris, which then as now sought only the most brilliant of students. After gaining a doctorate in mathematics Mr Thom taught at various universities in France. He was awarded grants to visit the United States in 1951, where he talked physics with the ageing Albert Einstein.

He won the applause of his peers with his work on cobordism, a branch of maths that involves algebra and geometry. In 1958 he was awarded the Fields medal, named after J.C. Fields, a Canadian mathematician, which has something of the standing of a Nobel. The judges spoke of "the grand simplicity" of Mr Thom's ideas. He published a paper on catastrophe theory in 1968, and his seminal book four years later.

What is a catastrophe? Some commentators on Mr Thom's work question whether the momentous events of history can really be called catastrophes, using the word in the sense that they were totally unexpected interruptions of an ordered existence. Even the supine French court sensed that something nasty was happening in Paris in the 1780s. Followers of Mr Thom claim that the fall of the Berlin Wall in 1989 was unexpected, although only the timing was a surprise. Such events did have unimagined consequences: the emergence of Napoleon; the sudden break-up of the Soviet Union. But they can be accounted for by chaos theory, which is another matter altogether. ∎

Graham Thomas

Graham Stuart Thomas, gardener, died on April 17th 2003, aged 94

IT MAY be some comfort to those who like gardens but find gardening a hard grind, that Graham Thomas was of the same view. Mr Thomas was irritated by programmes on television that instantly turned a wasteland into an Eden. "Good gardening is never easy," he said. Some people regarded Mr Thomas as the world's greatest gardener. He was certainly one of the most experienced. He reckoned that he first took an interest in gardening when he was six. His godfather gave him a fuchsia for his birthday, which, he said, "set me on my earthly career". It continued for more than 80 years.

Much of his career was spent as adviser to the National Trust, which has the richest collection of gardens in Britain, and probably in the world. The trust was founded in the late 19th century to rescue the great aristocratic estates from what Mr Thomas called their "uncontrolled destruction" as a result of the growth of population, the spread of industry and the lack of planning. In the early days of the trust, gardens were looked upon as mere extras to the grand houses. Gradually they became valued for themselves, and in many cases regarded as more interesting to visitors than the houses they were attached to. Mr Thomas took charge of the gardens when many had fallen into scruffy ways and re-stored them to their former glory. He started with four and gradually took over all the main ones. He was the commanding officer of the pastures, woods and lakes in the trust's keeping. The militaristic title is apt. Mr Thomas saw his task as "a battle against nature". He wrote,

> it is pleasant for a visitor to enter a garden and to find it in a good state of upkeep. But few … have any inkling of the ceaseless battle which goes on … against nature, a formidable adversary with arms of incalculable diversity and resource, on the one hand, and against the wear and tear of people on the other … On a glorious June day it is easy to be persuaded that we are holding the fort, even winning. At other times we feel unnerved by the never-ending combat.

Tea with Miss Jekyll

Graham Thomas was in a gardening tradition that stretches back to Theophrastus, the most influential botanist of antiquity. Rather more recently, Gertrude Jekyll was regarded as the most influential of gardeners. In the autumn of 1931, when Miss Jekyll was 88 and almost at the end of her life, she had a letter about gardening from Mr Thomas, then 22, and invited him to visit her. She said she was too old to walk around her garden with him, but he should pick a leaf of any plant that interested him and they could discuss it over a cup of tea. The story is told in "The Garden through the Year", published in 2002, and the most recent of Mr Thomas's 19 books. He was too modest to suggest that this was the moment when a great tradition passed to the next generation. But it is a pleasing assumption.

His parents were keen gardeners and amateur musicians. The two interests often go together. Mr Thomas had a pleasant tenor voice and for many years sang with an amateur group. His early

gardens were rather more sophisticated than those of most children. He recalled importing a seedling of a dwarf pine from Japan. It compared well, he noted, with a specimen in the botanic garden of Cambridge University. Cambridge was his home town and in his late teens he was taken on as a student in the 40-acre university garden, where Charles Darwin had once studied. After four years there he worked for a number of private nurseries, and started to build up a reputation as a writer on garden design and restoration. He reintroduced to English gardens many plants that had gone out of fashion, particularly roses.

He gained all the medals and other honours that horticulture can grant. In plant catalogues his name frequently comes up. There is a "Graham Thomas" honeysuckle here, a rhododendron there. The most popular English rose is named after him, a winner in cool climates.

The millions of people who hopefully potter about in their gardens may be intimidated by Mr Thomas's scholarly approach. The man who restored the ruined gardens of Moseley Old Hall in Staffordshire (soil neutral, altitude 250ft,

annual rainfall 27in) to their original state in the 17th century, when Charles II knew the place, did not seem the sort of expert you would ask about growing potatoes. Mr Thomas himself said that gardening was a "never-finished art" allied to craft. Yet he never forgot his earthy beginnings, digging and weeding. A lot of advice applicable to the humblest plot turns up in his 19 books. Avoid gimmicks such as painted fences, he said. They distract from the plants; stick to a well-placed urn. Anyone moving to a new house and garden should allow a growing season to pass, seeing what comes up before planting anything new. He was against plants that bloomed in vivid colours early in the season. Leave colour for later in the year. Design your garden yourself, and make it your own.

And although gardening involved physical work, it should be done thoroughly. In his last years Mr Thomas could no longer bend to dig in his own garden. He said he employed a man to dig and weed. "He does what I tell him," said the master, a bit gruffly, "but that's about all I can say for him." ■

Hunter S. Thompson

Hunter S. Thompson, doctor of gonzo journalism, died on February 20th 2005, aged 67

THERE WERE always way too many guns around at Hunter S. Thompson's farm in Woody Creek: .44 Magnums, 12-gauge shotguns, black snubnosed Colt Pythons with bevelled cylinders, .22 calibre mounted machineguns. He also kept explosives, to blow the legs off pool tables or to pack in a barrel for target practice. His quiet bourgeois neighbours near Aspen, Colorado, complained that he rocked the foundations of their houses.

Explosions were his speciality. Indeed, writing and shooting were much the same. His very first newspaper story, written when he was ten for a neighbourhood newsletter in Louisville, Kentucky, was headlined "WAR!" ("The Voits declared war on Hunter's gang on Oct. 1, 1947. At 3.00 Hunter's gang attacked the Voits"). Later, as a working journalist, he fired off reckless fusillades of words that were meant to shock and

entertain and wreak collateral damage.

He had always been a problem, kicked early out of high school (drinking, vandalism) and rapidly out of the air force, but his casual smashing of the rules of American journalism happened more or less by accident. Assigned to cover the Kentucky Derby in 1970, his mind was too blown with drugs, as usual, to write the story. One by one, with his trembling hands, he ripped the pages of whiskey-fuelled ramblings out of his notebook and sent them to the printer. The piece that resulted, "The Kentucky Derby is Decadent and Depraved", was a runaway success, though he had neither described the race nor mentioned the winner. And he was astonished: it was like "falling down an elevator shaft and landing in a pool of mermaids."

A friend called his style "totally gonzo". The name stuck, though, as he confessed, nobody knew what the hell it meant. For the literary, he could explain that it followed William Faulkner's dictum that "the best fiction is more true than any kind of journalism." Mr Thompson stalked, rifle in hand, cigarette (in holder) dangling, on the wild borderlands between fact and fiction, leaving readers to decide what was true and what was not.

Editors tried to control him, but failed. Journalistic objectivity was a nonsense to him; he threw it away, and turned his gaze on himself. He and his excursions into depravity became the central and only theme of every story he wrote. Sent to Puerto Rico for the *New York Herald Tribune*, in 1959, he shot rats at the San Juan city dump until he was arrested. Assigned in 1971 to write a 300-word caption on the Mint 400 motor-cycle race for *Sports Illustrated*, he wrote the 50,000 words of mayhem that became "Fear and Loathing in Las Vegas". It began: "We were somewhere around Barstow on the edge of the desert when the drugs began to take hold." Posted to Zaire in 1974 to cover the fight between George Foreman and Muhammad Ali, he never watched the boxing. Instead he floated naked in the hotel pool, into which he had thrown a pound and a half of marijuana, and let the green slick gather round him.

"Fear and Loathing" made him famous: so famous that the Republicans came courting him, although he was a Democrat. It was not just the guns, but the fact that he wore a twisted sort of patriotism on his sleeve. That journey through the Californian desert to find fame and fortune, stocked up with "two bags of grass, seventy-five pellets of mescaline, five sheets of high-powered blotter acid, a salt shaker half-full of cocaine, and a whole galaxy of multi-coloured uppers", was

also, Mr Thompson claimed, "a classic confirmation of everything right and true and decent in the national character." ("Jesus! Did I *say* that?")

Nixon's men wondered if this madman could be their bridge to the alienated, war-hating young. But they were playing with fire. Mr Thompson thought Nixon a liar and a bastard. He covered the 1972 election in typically take-no-prisoners style, producing what one campaign aide called "the least accurate and most factual" book about it; and when he toyed with politics it was on the Freak Power ticket, running for sheriff of Pitkin County, Colorado, where he could blow things away in the woods.

At Hemingway's grave

He did not give "a flying fuck" what he smoked, or ingested, or did, but there was a thoughtful side. Early in his career, in an obituary of a friend, he wrote of "the dead-end loneliness of a man who makes his own rules." He was often melancholy, and wild conviviality and celebrity made no difference to that. The epigram to "Fear and Loathing" quoted Dr Johnson: "He who makes a beast of himself gets rid of the pain of being a man." It was not thought surprising that his death was a suicide.

In 1964 he had made a long journey to Ketchum, Idaho, to the grave of Ernest Hemingway, one of his models and heroes. He wanted to understand why Hemingway had killed himself in his cabin in the woods, and concluded that he had lost his sense of control in a changing world:

> It is not just a writer's crisis, but they are the most obvious victims because the function of art is supposedly to bring order out of chaos, a tall order even when the chaos is static, and a superhuman task when chaos is multiplying ... So finally, and for what he must have thought the best of reasons, he ended it with a shotgun. ∎

Leonard Tose

Leonard Tose, a big spender, died on April 15th 2003, aged 88

AT A hearing by the United States Congress into gambling, the most compelling witness by far was Leonard Tose. He reckoned that he had lost about $40m through gambling, or it might have been as much as $50m. He couldn't be sure. The money had seeped away gradually though consistently, sometimes no more than $10,000 during a frugal night at a casino, sometimes as much as $1m. But he had vast winnings too. He recalled times when everything went his way. The dollars rolled in obediently. He felt he could not lose. Such moments kept Mr Tose going when fortune seemed to have deserted him. In one bleak run of ill-fortune he lost 72 nights in a row. A lesser man would have given up. A lesser man would probably have managed to hold on to at least some of his money.

There was nothing stupid about Leonard Tose. In many ways his was the classic American success story. His parents were immigrants from Russia who had settled in Philadelphia. Mr Tose told stories of his father selling goods from a pack on his back and saving up to buy a truck. From modest beginnings the son built up a business of 700 trucks whose logo became familiar throughout the United States.

The politicians who listened in fascination to Mr Tose's account of how to lose money quickly were trying to understand the nature of gambling, and whether it should, or could, be controlled. Mr Tose was asked if he had any advice for Congress. "Don't drink when you gamble," he said. It sounded obvious, but it drew attention to the practice of some casinos that provide big-spenders with an unlimited supply of drink.

In various countries in the rich world similar inquiries are going on. In America and other liberal societies, a strongly-held view is that if you want to gamble, it is no business of the government. However, the consensus is that gambling is increasing, helped on by the internet, but little can be done about it except to provide counselling for those unkindly called "pathological" gamblers. The good news for governments is that gambling, though routinely deplored, is easily taxable, like its sinful sisters drinking and smoking. State lotteries are promoted as a good thing. Britain's provides much of the money to nourish its much-praised culture.

His hobby

One of the lures of gambling is its simplicity. The apparatus of a casino, the roulette wheels, the slot machines, requires little technological skill. Mr Tose favoured blackjack, similar to pontoon, a children's game. The player has to be able to count up to 21 but it is otherwise undemanding. There are books that claim that a player with a prodigious memory for the sequence of cards can gain an advantage over the casino. But whether playing in Las Vegas or Atlantic City, Mr Tose never bothered with such affectations. What he liked was to play a number of games at once, often losing them all.

In a revealing moment he once said, "My hobby is spending money." Gambling was not all of his life, and perhaps not the most important part of it. After Mr Tose had made his pile, he gave generously to medical charities. He willingly subsidised local public services that were short of cash. He provided playing fields for schools. He bought the Philadelphia police their bulletproof jackets. When the Philadelphia Eagles, a football team, was struggling to survive, he bought it for $16m. Sportsmen should

stick together, Mr Tose said: as a student at Indiana's Notre Dame University, he had played for its noted football team.

He was in the tradition of American industrialists who, having made a fortune, seek to give it away. The collections of European paintings and sculpture of Henry Frick, Andrew Mellon and other pioneering tycoons, bought when they became rich, were the foundations of America's great national art galleries in New York and Washington. Leon Levy, an American financier who died on April 6th, aged 77, was a similar benefactor. He gave away $140m, including $20m to the Metropolitan Museum of Art.

Mr Tose did not see himself as that sort of philanthropist, assembling alms for oblivion. If he had a philosophy it was to use his money to provide entertainment for the public. He liked the company of reporters, a habit he formed in the second world war when he edited an army newspaper. He became a regular read in American newspapers. One of the serial stories was about his five marriages and their consequences. One wife asked a court to declare him incompetent to handle money. She lost. He was sued by a casino for a debt of $1.23m, and claimed that it had made him drunk. He lost.

In the end he lost pretty near everything: his football team, the control of his trucking business, his Rolls-Royce, a model that matched that of his fourth wife. On his 81st birthday he was evicted from his colonial-style home, and he moved into a modest hotel, where the rent was paid for by some of his remaining friends. Last year, at the age of 87, he declined to be sorry for himself. He thought he had done well to reach a great age. He occasionally took a holiday, he said, but nothing flamboyant. He had a car, albeit one eight years old. And he still had his spirit. ■

Gilbert Trigano

Gilbert Trigano, a founder of Club Med, died on February 3rd 2001, aged 80

A S OFTEN happens when a project turns out to be as successful as Club Med, there is some disagreement about who should have the credit. Some would give it to Gérard Blitz, a Belgian who in the 1920s and 1930s had won several Olympic medals for swimming and water polo. After the second world war he was running transit camps for Belgian soldiers returning home. He bought tarpaulins and other useful materials from a French factory owned by Gilbert Trigano's family. Gérard suggested to Gilbert (or it may have been the other way round) that, with Europe at peace, they should get into the holiday business. In 1950 they bought some American army surplus tents and camp beds, set them up in a pine wood on the Spanish island of Majorca and called the enterprise Club Méditerranée.

The idea was a success from the start. Holiday camps were not new. In Britain Billy Butlin's camps had provided cheap refuges from often rainy summers. But Club Med offered reliable sunshine and warm seas, along with what Gérard Blitz called "an antidote to civilisation". He saw no need for the holiday "villages" to make money, as long as they covered their costs. What mattered was that people could be liberated from their working lives for a week or two and live as the noble savage, do some cooking if they wanted to and help with the rudimentary washing-up. It was Mr Trigano who turned Club Med into a profitable business. Tents were soon replaced by thatched huts. During Mr Trigano's four decades with Club Med, bungalows and hotels were added with

the soft comforts of home. Staff were hired to do the chores. There were Club Med establishments throughout the world, from Tahiti to, ahem, Bulgaria.

Mr Trigano did not discard the romanticism that had made Club Med so appealing when he and his early partner had banged in the tent pegs in Majorca. Rather, he made Club Med's hint of a sensual paradise a key part of its sales appeal. The partly Belgian idea which had been launched in Spain became as French as Bardot. As a loyal Frenchman, Mr Trigano made Club Med a messenger of his country's superiority in food, wine, language and indeed in culture. Then, suddenly, it seemed that paradise was lost.

End of enchantment

After Club Med had showed losses for three successive years in the 1990s, Harvard Business School chillingly used the firm as a study to illustrate "the death of a brand". Club Med had become Club Red because the young people who were once its customers were now middle-aged and less thrilled by its offer of organised, communal living, however comfortable. The next generation saw Club Med as just another big hotel chain.

Gilbert Trigano seemed puzzled quite what to do. Before he became a joint founder of Club Med at the age of 30, he had had little business experience. He had worked briefly in the family firm, done some journalism and tried his hand as an actor. As a Jew in German-occupied France in the war, his chief occupation had been one of survival.

What he brought to Club Med was a seemingly boundless energy. Chain-smoking kept him going on 15-hour working days. His enthusiasm for making Club Med "the laboratory of the modern holiday" was its driving force. He was skilful at getting countries to surrender their finest beaches for new resorts in return for electricity and other infrastructure, and persuading bankers to finance them. He made the brand famous. According to a survey, 78% of Americans had heard of Club Med, and in Europe an astonishing 88%. He brought quality to the much-derided development of "mass tourism".

He was less at ease when asked by his critics about the morality of planting self-contained expensive "pleasure domes" in poor countries where the visitors never ventured out, not even to a local restaurant. When some wanted to see local ceremonies Mr Trigano would bring in actors to stage them. He believed his duty was to protect his *gentils membres* from possible local hostility, but for them it was not quite the same as seeing the country. A guest at even an ordinary local hotel might well feel more of a sense of adventure.

It may be that Mr Trigano eventually became bored with tourism. He was captivated by new developments in technology. Years ago, when computers were still a novelty, he installed them in some of his holiday villages, to the surprise of guests who still believed that Club Med meant the simple life. Mr Trigano claimed, not wholly convincingly, that the distinction between work and leisure was breaking down. He personally rarely took a holiday. He passed his enthusiasm for new technology to François Mitterrand. Back in the 1980s the French president got computers into every school in the country.

After a revolt by shareholders of Club Med in 1997 Mr Trigano and his son Serge, who had become chief executive, stood down from management. Philippe Bourgignon, who had revived Disney's sickly theme park near Paris, took over, with a promise to return Club Med to health. After all the problems there would be a happy ending. Spoken like a Disney. ■

Pierre Trudeau

Joseph Philippe Pierre Yves Elliott Trudeau died on September 28th 2000, aged 80

REMINISCING ABOUT his early life, Pierre Trudeau told of exploring in southern Iraq where, so it is believed, civilisation began. Three rather uncivilised Arabs waylaid him and demanded money. He pointed to his torn shirt and pleaded for money from them. They were startled at the reversal of roles; and were angered when he seized a dagger from one man's belt, pretending to examine it. As they began to haul him away, "I recited poetry, performed drama, started a speech." The robbers "feared madness", Mr Trudeau said, "and beat an anxious retreat."

For many Canadians, the story, although perhaps embellished in the telling, summed up their view of him: his daring, the power of his oratory, his originality in dealing with a problem. As the Arabs had soon decided, and the Canadians came to learn, he was an original. There was nothing more original than the simple facts of his political career. He became a member of parliament in 1965 and three years later he was prime minister.

He had some luck. More than half of Canada's population was under 30. In the 1960s, looking cool and toying with a red rose were political assets lacking in Mr Trudeau's rivals. Gays commended his argument for decriminalising homosexuality, that "the state has no place in the bedrooms of the nation". The 14 previous Canadian prime ministers had been worthy rather than hip. One of them criticised him publicly for wearing sandals in parliament. Commentators spoke of Trudeaumania, just as the pop world went dizzy with Beatlemania.

Even so, to rise so swiftly to the top job and then to keep it almost continuously for nearly 16 years required more than luck. Neither can his success be explained by saying he was an able politician. Aiming for "a just society", however sincerely expressed, is hardly original. Pierre Trudeau "overflowed his office", a commentator said. Whether he was arguing a case with passion, kissing beautiful women or canoeing some remote river, he was daring Canadians to be venturesome, to shed caution.

To exotic places

He was a rich man's son. His father owned a chain of petrol stations, and much else. Pierre was brought up fluent in both English and French, a big asset for a politician in bilingual Canada. But politics lay in the distant future. The Trudeau who became a visionary in his own country and a performer on the world stage seems to have been parochial as a young man. He dismissed the second world war as a squabble between the big powers, although he later regretted "missing one of the major events of the century". He gained a law degree and had a spell at Harvard. He travelled to Europe and to exotic places, such as southern Iraq. With his mind seemingly broadened, he returned to Canada appalled at the narrow nationalism in his native French-speaking Quebec, and the authoritarianism of the province's government.

It was Mr Trudeau's belief in a one-nation Canada, rejecting Quebec

Canadians, would do little to explain why Pierre Trudeau was seen as an exciting politician by the world at large. It can't just have been the gossip stuff, although his marriage, at 51, to a 22-year-old brightened a million television screens. His admirers shared his agony when she humiliated him by becoming a rock groupie; and a worse agony when one of his three sons died in an avalanche. His foreign policy adventures interested a specialised audience. He made friends with Fidel Castro, opposed the Vietnam war, sniped at NATO, and generally upset the United States. Living next door, he said, was like "sleeping with an elephant", affected by "every twitch and grunt".

separatism, that persuaded him to give up a career as a lawyer and enter Parliament. In 1970, two years after he became prime minister, Quebec separatists kidnapped a British diplomat and a Canadian politician, who was later found murdered. Mr Trudeau put tanks on the streets of Montreal to counter what seemed to be an insurrection. His reputation as a champion of civil liberties suffered, but no one doubted where he stood about keeping Canada unified. His view prevailed in subsequent referendums over the status of Quebec. He towered above the nationalists with speeches that drowned their bid for independence. Keeping the country together was among his most important achievements, although even now the separatists are far from extinct.

But a catalogue of his domestic reforms, however important to

What Mr Trudeau mostly gave to a grateful world was a certain style, all the more surprising coming from a Canadian, a species given to understatement. Canadians are urged by their present prime minister, Jean Chrétien, to be proud that the United Nations puts their country at the top of its "human development index", based on a mix of statistics such as adult literacy, life expectancy and purchasing power. "Canada," says Mr Chrétien, "is the best place in the world to live." Perhaps it is. But pride in being Canadian arose less artificially in the nearly 16 years of the Trudeau government, and from the confidence and vitality Canada's most unconventional prime minister spread about him. ■

Galina Ulanova

Galina Sergeyevna Ulanova, a Bolshoi legend, died on March 21st 1998, aged 88

IN HIS eulogy of Galina Ulanova, President Yeltsin said she had been a "symbol of conscience" for Russians. It is understandable that the head of state would wish to suggest that the Stalin period was redeemed a little by those with a conscience. And there were indeed a remarkable number of Russians who demonstrably stayed true to their beliefs despite the shadow of the gulag and judicial murder. Miss Ulanova does not appear to have been among this company. She was, though perhaps innocently, a redeemer of Stalinism.

Important foreign visitors to Moscow would be offered a special treat: a good seat at the Bolshoi, where Galina Ulanova, the prima ballerina, was performing, perhaps in *Swan Lake*. As Miss Ulanova floated on to the stage to Tchaikovsky's syrupy music, any misgivings the visitor might have felt about the regime would perhaps be appeased, at least for a time. Whatever you might say about communism, you had to give it full marks for culture, did you not? Would the visitor care to come back-stage after the performance? Miss Ulanova has always admired your country.

The state was suitably grateful. Miss Ulanova was named a Hero of Socialist Labour (twice) and received the Order of Lenin, the Soviet Union's highest honour. She gained the Stalin Prize on four occasions. Her tours abroad took on the appearances of state visits. Ecstatic reviews were expected, and when a New York writer made a minor criticism of one of her performances, *Pravda* accused him and his newspaper

of seeking to continue the cold war. She had an impregnable escort of minders, but there was never any suggestion that she would run away. In 1956 the aircraft bringing the Bolshoi troupe to Britain was diverted from Heathrow to an RAF station because of fog. Despite assurances from her minders that the capitalists were not trying to kidnap her, Miss Ulanova refused to leave the aircraft until she had received permission from high up in Moscow.

A family of dancers
For her devoted admirers it was enough that Galina Ulanova was among the greatest dancers of classical ballet this century. She had brilliantly sustained a tradition from the tsarist days, when Russian ballet became unequalled in the world. Her mother was a dancer, her father a choreographer, and as a child she was placed in a ballet school. Miss Ulanova was seven at the time of the Russian revolution. As she grew into adolescence, she, like many young people, was excited by what seemed the promise of a modern, vibrant Russia. The aristocracy was finished. "Our audiences," she was to say later, "are ordinary people." In 1928 she joined Leningrad's Mariinsky Theatre, where her mother had danced, and which was later to be called the Kirov (after Sergei Kirov, a popular communist leader much mourned by Stalin, but always thought to have been murdered on his orders).

Miss Ulanova had rather a stocky figure, but such was her talent that on stage she seemed to be transformed. "As soon as she dances, a metamorphosis

Two of the Kirov's greatest stars defected to the west, Rudolf Nureyev in 1961 and Mikhail Baryshnikov in 1974. Along with other discontents, they had become bored with the old ways. While Soviet ballet persisted, if brilliantly, with classical dance, in Europe and America dancers were finding new ways to tell stories, or even no stories at all, just abstractions, with new dance movements and modern music. In the Soviet Union experimental works by Shostakovich and Prokofiev were suppressed. Stalin seems to have liked only pretty music. Jazz, which plays a part in much modern ballet, was considered to be decadent. Tikhon Khrennikov, Stalin's musical controller and one of his most abject acolytes, now aged 84, recalls that "nobody could say no to Stalin". He draws a finger across his neck.

takes place," said a critic. "With each part she has a different body, a new personality." So in *Giselle*, her most famous role, she makes an idiotic story about a peasant girl who turns into a ghost seem entirely true.

In 1944, on Stalin's orders, she was brought to Moscow and to the Bolshoi. Although Leningrad was where the revolution started, Stalin never cared for it. He saw it as a rebellious city. In his great purges of the 1930s, members of the Leningrad party suffered most. Rebellion was in fact present in the Kirov, although it did not become evident until after Stalin's death in 1953, with the gradual easing of repression in the Soviet Union.

As for Miss Ulanova, she was getting rapturous applause into middle age. But at 50 she gave up public dancing and spent much of the rest of her life teaching. The Bolshoi she leaves is in a poor way. Ballet is costly. In the Soviet days, a former Bolshoi manager recalled, there was unlimited cheap labour to man the workings of the theatre. If money was requested it would be available immediately. Democratic Russia's struggling market economy has destroyed such uncommercial extravagance. The fabric of the theatre itself is crumbling. Well, you can't have everything. ■

Chiyo Uno

Chiyo Uno, a passionate Japanese, died on June 10th 1996, aged 98

THE SECRET of a good life, Chiyo Uno said, is to do exactly what you want. In these enlightened days that remark does not sound particularly radical; it is no more than the sort of thing that any independent-minded woman might come out with. But Miss Uno said it in the late 1930s, in a Japan that was becoming increasingly intolerant of civilians it believed were undermining the country's spirit in its war against China. Neither could she be dismissed contemptuously as a mere *moga*, or modem girl. Miss Uno had an audience. Her novel *Confessions of Love*, published in 1935, had been a popular success and had won the approval of intellectuals.

Tokyo between the two world wars had similarities with Berlin. Something like the notorious nightlife of Weimar Germany existed in the *ero-guro* (erotic-grotesque) haunts of Japan. Miss Uno lived in a writers' colony in Tokyo. Eventually, though, the pleasure domes gave way to the growing needs of war. In the 1940s, when Japan went to war with America and Britain, even Miss Uno abandoned her western-style dress, put on a kimono and allowed her bobbed hair to grow. Patriotism and the need to survive had by then engulfed every area of Japanese existence. But after the second world war she resumed what she called her "lust for life".

American ideas of individualism that arrived with the occupation forces made her feel less of an oddity. She founded a women's magazine and wrote more books, one, triumphantly entitled "I Will Go On Living", when she was 85. Her life story was serialised on television,

and movies were made from her books. The Japanese establishment came to accept her, if not to like her, and the emperor was persuaded to name her "a person of cultural merit".

The feminist question

Was Chiyo Uno a feminist? Some American feminists might have doubts. A true feminist, in their judgment, campaigns for the social and political reforms that give women equal rights with men. Shidzue Kato, a Japanese woman who was jailed in 1937 for subversion and later became the country's first female member of parliament, would be closer to their model. Miss Uno was not a politician, although she wrote what she called a "charter". It proclaimed that a woman should have economic and "emotional" independence, two ideals that any feminist would approve of. But, more important, perhaps, she set an example, a wild and enviable one for the millions of Japanese women brought up to believe that their first duty is to serve men; a bad and irresponsible example in the eyes of Japanese husbands and fathers.

Chiyo Uno had an early experience of what it meant to be brought up in a rigidly traditionalist society. While in her teens she was forced into an arranged marriage with a cousin. It lasted ten days. She was later married to Takeo Kitahara, a novelist. But it was her love affairs outside marriage that fascinated her public. Like Jean Rhys (1894-1979) and Anaïs Nin (1903-77) in Europe, she wrote of sex with candour and style.

Her most famous affair was with Seiji Togo, a painter. She went to see him, she wrote, after reading that he had tried to commit suicide with his mistress, an admiral's daughter. She thought he would make a character in a novel. The painter had a bloodstained bandage on his neck where he had tried to cut his throat. "It got me," Miss Uno recalled. She moved in with him the same day. They lived together for five years, but she eventually decided that he was an idiot rather than a hero. His attempt to kill himself is fictionalised in the novel "Confessions of Love". Chiyo Uno's story may be the only humorous account in literature of a bungled suicide.

This is a passage from the story: "When I decided to use the scalpels I had bought some popular medical books to make sure I did everything correctly. I was under the impression that I knew precisely where the artery was, but since I had been drinking to stir up my circulation I assumed that I only had to thrust the scalpel in where the blood was strong. But the place where the blood vessel was exposed and the blood pulsing was not the real carotid artery. The real artery, I was dumbfounded to discover later, was about an inch further in."[1]

Some critics, while admiring Miss

Uno's writing, frowned on an irreverent account of an attempted suicide. In Japan there is a culture of death. Yukio Mishima, a novelist who died in 1970, is respected, not so much these days for his writing, but because he committed ritual suicide. Television programmes about wartime suicide pilots compare them to cherry blossoms, beautiful but soon to die. Miss Uno would have none of this. Male fantasy, she said. "All deaths before the age of 100 are accidental," she said, "caused by carelessness or thoughtlessness." Chiyo Uno died 18 months short of her century, but close enough to have made her point. ∎

1 "Confessions of Love", by Chiyo Uno, translated by Phyllis Birnbaum. Peter Owen, 1990.

Leo Valiani

Leo Valiani, a maker of modern Italy, died on September 18th 1999, aged 90

ON THE evening of April 25th 1945, Leo Valiani gave the order that Benito Mussolini should be killed. It was *finito*, he said later. In 1943 Italy had surrendered to the Allies, but Germany had taken control of the north of the country, and had set up a separate state with Mussolini as its leader. Now the Allies were advancing rapidly northwards and much of Mussolini's "state" was controlled by the Italian resistance.

On this April evening, Mussolini met resistance leaders on neutral ground, the archbishop's palace in Milan. Mussolini wanted an agreement that would protect his followers and their families. Mr Valiani said that Mussolini was in no position to make terms, only to surrender, and the meeting would last one hour only. An angry Mussolini stormed out of the palace. Shortly afterwards he was shot dead while on his way to Switzerland.

Accounts of Mussolini's end are varied. In some stories, the resistance leaders prepared a death warrant signed by Mr Valiani and the sentence was duly carried out on the fleeing Mussolini. This would have given his execution a façade of legitimacy, but little that was lawful was happening in northern Italy in the last days of the second world war. What is clear is that, whether or not there was a formal death sentence, Mr Valiani brushed aside any talk among the resistance for clemency and insisted that Mussolini, having refused to surrender, should be executed without a trial. "Let's end it," he said.

The body of the inventor of modern fascism, and the early mentor of Hitler, was displayed, with that of his mistress, hanging upside down in a square in Milan. General Eisenhower, the Allied commander, said, "God, what an ignoble end." Leo Valiani was said by his friends to have disapproved of the displaying of the bodies, but otherwise seems to have had no regrets. He saw himself simply as a servant of history. He went on making history after the war. He helped to write the Italian constitution and was regarded as a founding father of the republic. But he declined to pursue a career in politics. History is what interested him more. Mr Valiani was that rarity, a historian who had made history.

Lessons of history

Leo Valiani was an old European, using the term in a respectful and slightly awed sense, like old money. One of his books was "The End of Austria-Hungary". Who now gets excited about the break-up of this once powerful empire whose origins date back to the 13th century? Perhaps only those, like Mr Valiani, who saw that history does repeat itself, albeit in new guises. The Austro-Hungarian empire was bedevilled by the constant demands of competing nationalities within the super-state, a problem that these days the European Union faces as it toys with federalism.

Mr Valiani had an additional interest in Austria-Hungary. He was born there, in the Adriatic seaport of Rijeka (now in Croatia), and took Italian nationality when the town was annexed by Mussolini's Italy in 1924 and renamed Fiume. As a Jew and a communist,

Mr Valiani had a natural antipathy to Europe's new caesar. Mussolini's only virtue, he said, was that he encouraged Italian football, which for Leo Valiani rivalled history as a worthwhile pursuit.

He was often in trouble as an agitator and had several spells in prison in the 1920s and 1930s. When Russia signed an agreement with Germany in 1939 to divide Poland he broke with communism. But new masters, the British, were waiting in the wings.

The British had given up trying to recruit resistance workers in Germany, where any dissent was efficiently crushed. But Italy seemed less brutal, or was simply inefficient. Resistance groups operated with some success, among them Leo Valiani's. In Mussolini's northern Italian "state" in 1943, Mr Valiani set up a "committee of national liberation", which claimed to be the next provisional government. It had the support of both Britain and America, whose Allen Dulles, later to be head of the CIA, was a spy operating in the region. With Mussolini dead and the Germans defeated, Mr Valiani's committee was in a strong position to help shape Italy's real government.

The constitution he helped to produce in 1948 runs to many thousands of words and, judged as a piece of democratic guidance, is a model of its kind. But, whatever its successes, it has not produced enduring governments. Since 1948 there have been more than 50, although their defenders point out that in many of them the members were simply reshuffled without any great change of political direction. Corruption became widespread.

The constitution's weakness, Mr Valiani later agreed, was that it had the effect of paralysing government. He wanted a stronger presidency, and in his books and articles in *Corriere della Sera* was fiercely critical of the politicians who held on to the old system. He thought Italians were a bit soft. Just as they had once accepted the abuses of fascism, they were lax in dealing with the Mafia. He once argued for the return of the death penalty. Parliament took his scoldings gracefully and made him a senator for life. He never took a job in government and said his great regret was that he had never written about football. ■

Cyrus Vance

Cyrus Roberts Vance, a principled statesman, died on January 12th 2002, aged 84

WHEN CYRUS Vance decided to resign in 1980 he sought to do it with a minimum of fuss, for that was his style. He wrote to his president, Jimmy Carter, that a plan to try to rescue by force 52 Americans held prisoner in the United States embassy in Tehran had been made against his judgment and that he was resigning as secretary of state, whether the mission succeeded or failed. Several days later, when the mission had failed, dismally, Mr Vance's resignation was made public. But he was not allowed to bow out quietly. No one could remember a secretary of state, the highest post in the cabinet, resigning on a matter of principle. It took some searching to find a single precedent, William Jennings Bryan, a pacifist who had resigned as secretary of state in 1915 because he believed American policy favoured joining the war in Europe.

Mr Vance was not a pacifist. He had served in the navy in the second world war, and saw action in the Pacific. He had no liking for the revolutionary government that had taken over Iran. But he believed that some of the American prisoners might die in an attack, and that even if the mission, called Eagle Claw, were successful it would disturb an already unstable region. He was doubtful about the ability of the army to cope with conditions in a land they had no knowledge of. He had no great faith in the marvels of military technology. In 1962, when he was secretary of the army, the walkie-talkies of soldiers guarding blacks from white supremacists in the southern states failed at crucial moments. His misgivings were justified. Eagle Claw never got near the prisoners. Helicopters that were the mainstay of the mission were disabled in an unanticipated sandstorm in the Iranian desert. Eight American servicemen died and eight aircraft were lost. The mission was judged a brave one, but stupid. The embassy Americans were eventually freed as a result of painstaking negotiation, a process Mr Vance had pressed for.

The president's ear

Cyrus Vance was aware that, despite his exalted job, others could have a say in making and carrying out American foreign policy, particularly at times of great national stress. (The present star in the war against terrorism is the defence secretary, Donald Rumsfeld, a man of strong words and once a champion wrestler.) At the time of Eagle Claw Mr Vance's rival for President Carter's ear was his hawkish national security adviser, Zbigniew Brzezinski.

For much of his three years as secretary of state Mr Vance was uneasy as he battled with Mr Brzezinski for influence over foreign policy. Mr Vance knew that the president backed him in many ways, particularly in the view that human rights should be a pillar of American foreign policy; that was one of the reasons he had been picked for the job. But in the run-up to an election against Ronald Reagan, Mr Carter wanted to show that he could be tough with the Iranians. Mr Vance was even bothered that his office in the State Department was a mile or so from the White House, whereas Mr Brzezinski's office was next door to the president's. Even the great and the good exhibit human fears.

Polish-born Mr Brzezinski, a naturalised American, was clever, ambitious and ten years younger than Mr Vance. He saw him, he wrote later, as a relic of "the once dominant WASP elite" whose "values and rules were of declining relevance". Mr Vance was indeed a WASP, born to a prosperous family in West Virginia and expensively educated. He had a successful career as a lawyer and seemingly was without political ambition. He once said,

> A lot of us were raised in families where we were taught that we were very fortunate, that we were going to have a good education, and that we had the responsibility to return to the community some of the benefits and blessings we had, and that there was an obligation to participate in government service at the local, state and national level.

For some 30 years various presidents, among them John Kennedy and Lyndon Johnson as well as Jimmy Carter, together with international organisations, valued his WASPish talents. His departure as secretary of state did not end his service to government and the United Nations. He would be lured away from his law practice, given a working title, special this or special that, and asked to take on problems that had no solutions but could perhaps be made less menacing. So he went off to the Middle East, to the Balkans, to the Koreas, to Cyprus, and, until it broke up and created a new set of problems, to the Soviet Union. He was sceptical of any proposed American "master plan" for the world. His method was to take each problem, look at it as a lawyer would a brief, judge what could be negotiated, and draw up a contract.

Mr Vance was sometimes compared with another indefatigable American traveller, Henry Kissinger. Philip Habib, an American career diplomat who worked with many negotiators, greatly admired Mr Kissinger. His capacity "to put things together, to move, to produce the precise word at the right time, and his wit, were marvellous things to behold". But Cyrus Vance's "absolute, total and complete honesty" made him "probably the finest public servant I ever worked with". Not bad for a WASP of declining relevance. ∎

Veerappan

Koose Muniswamy Veerappan, bandit, died on October 18th 2004, aged 52

"BANDIT", LIKE "brigand", has a romantic ring. To some ears it evokes fugitive outlaws – from Robin Hood to Jesse James – who have seemed nobler than the forces of law and order on their trail. It is probably how the man known throughout India simply as Veerappan would like to be remembered. That, however, would be an injustice to the 124 people he is said to have killed. Veerappan was a murderer, and a cruel one at that. An Osama-style old video shows him talking with relish of the pain inflicted on one victim before he blew his head off.

Veerappan was himself shot through the forehead when the police ambushed him and three henchmen. His proud killers posed around his corpse with broad smiles and their thumbs up, like tiger-hunters. But the applause for them was not universal. In the villages dotting the thick forest that was his stomping ground, some recalled Veerappan showering sweets on children and reports of his generosity to the poor. The families of the dozens he had killed as informers were incredulous. But some 20,000 packed the village where his funeral was held, drawn by his mystique and his fame. His distraught widow told journalists he was a good man, though her two daughters hardly knew him.

Already, treasure-hunters were scouring the forest for the fortune he was supposed to have buried in plastic bags under trees. In death as in life, Veerappan, a petty thug with a gift for public relations, spread a potent myth. In this his hunters abetted him. A 750-strong special task-force had spent 14 years and a fortune trying to catch him. To explain their failure, it helped to credit him with near-supernatural powers – "like a forest ghost", said one.

Veerappan started his career following in his father's footsteps as an ivory poacher in the thickly wooded hills between the Indian states of Karnataka and Tamil Nadu. He is said to have been 14 when he killed his first elephant, and to have slaughtered hundreds over the years.

As elephants became harder to find, he diversified into another endangered species: ancient sandal trees. Sandalwood, prized for its oil in soap, perfume and traditional ayurvedic medicine, is also, as incense, integral to Hindu religious ceremonies. Forty years ago the governments of Karnataka and Tamil Nadu imposed a monopoly on the ownership and felling of the trees. They restricted cultivation, trusting to their abundant wild crop.

As sandalwood prices rose, a black market flourished. Sandal trees, which take 25 to 40 years to reach maturity, were chopped down in private gardens and public parks. Veerappan was not the only bootlegger to turn abundance into shortage. But he was one of the most prolific. Eco-vandalism has a short-term commercial logic: scarcity inflates prices. In the long run, however, killing off your raw material is not a sustainable business model, and Veerappan branched out again.

His region had another money-spinning product: granite. Running a quarry was not Veerappan's style, but he

spotted a way into the business's profits. In 1990, one of the first of many people he kidnapped was a quarry owner. This was a line of work with an inexhaustible supply of victims, and only some had to be killed to ensure the flow of ransom money.

Hitting the big time

Veerappan's fame began to grow. So did his moustache and his ego. He would pose for photographs with his rifle and his luxuriant handlebar. He mocked the policemen and politicians who condemned him. His gang acquired more and better weapons and its numbers swelled to more than 100. He even began to present himself as some kind of freedom fighter, a Tamil nationalist – like the "Tigers" of Sri Lanka, whom he resembled only in his brutality.

His career as a kidnapper reached its zenith in 2000, when he seized Rajkumar, one of the biggest stars of the Kannada-language film industry of Karnataka. A policeman who was involved in the transaction says that Rajkumar's release after 108 days in captivity cost 200m rupees ($4.4m) in ransom from the Karnataka state

coffers. Two years later his victim was H. Nagappa, a former minister in that government, who had been one of his fiercest critics. This time the price paid was Mr Nagappa's life.

By the time he died, however, Veerappan was a diminished figure. His gang had dwindled to a handful, and had been infiltrated by the police. He was lured into a trap, leaving his forest hideout in a phoney ambulance on his way, he thought, to have a cataract operation. Even allowing for the punctured forehead, his corpse looked old and tired. Shockingly, his lush whiskers had been drastically trimmed. As vain as he was vicious, he would have been distressed that this was the last image he left his public.

Human-rights groups criticised the police for not nabbing him alive. Among Veerappan's boasts was that he had bribed powerful policemen and politicians in return for protection. Knowing the morals of their public servants and how long the hunt had taken, many Indians believed him, and suspected the police of deliberately silencing him. It is not just treasure-hunters who regret that he has taken his secrets to the grave. ■

Rosemary Verey

Rosemary Verey, an English gardener, died on May 31st 2001, aged 82

SHE WAS in the luxury goods market and her offering was English gardens. Rosemary Verey's own garden was in a 17th-century former rectory called Barnsley House in the Cotswolds. The English climate, warm but not too warm, wet but not too wet, was ideal for the sumptuous garden she created there. But for those who did not have the good fortune to live in England, she was prepared to do her best to create something similar in less blessed countries. Many Americans set their hearts on a Verey garden. It had the kind of cachet attached to, say, Harrods (despite the loss of royal patronage) or a Rolls-Royce (though the marque is now owned by Germans), survivors in the slow decline of England's reputation for quality merchandise. How do you make an English lawn? Sow, and mow for 500 years. Real luxury involved time and experience.

Mrs Verey spared her clients too much waiting. She said she envied perfect lawns but they were not her obsession. Her garden designs would begin to take shape in a few seasons. She created a feeling of timelessness by using styles from the past. So there were hedges of traditional roses, herbaceous borders, laburnum arches revealing statues, and formal areas of clipped boxwood. She helped to create three gardens for Prince Charles at his estate, Highgrove, not far from Barnsley House. One was a kitchen garden. Mrs Verey was particularly clever at making vegetable patches that looked far too pretty to crop. The prince said, "She makes gardening seem the easiest and most natural thing in the world."

It was a princely compliment: "naturalness" in the artificial world of gardening is difficult to pull off. Money helped: the Verey look was a rich person's indulgence. But that was not all. There is a bit of magic in gardening. The prince is said to talk to his plants. Mrs Verey said that plants "love to know they are being cared for". All the same, she gave the impression of demanding that her plants behave or be banished from her Eden. You were not surprised to learn that she was the daughter of a colonel. An American visitor said at the end of a conducted tour of Barnsley House, "She is the most refined lady. We all felt humbled in her presence."

The long tradition

Rosemary Verey was in the tradition of gifted women gardeners that stretches back to Bess of Hardwick, who in the 16th century created some of England's greatest estates. They have tended to be comfortably off (Bess was the richest woman in England after Queen Elizabeth, with ample leisure and a determination to shine in a world run by men. Although mere men could be drafted in to slave with the routine work, no true woman gardener surrenders the command of her territory. Vita Sackville-West (1892–1962), who created a splendid garden at Sissinghurst Castle in Kent, wrote, "For the last 40 years of my life I have broken my back, my finger nails, and sometimes my heart, in the practical pursuit of my favourite occupation."

Mrs Verey discovered what was to become her favourite occupation relatively late in life. An early fancy was to be an economist. But she abandoned university to get married and had four children. Gradually, she recalls, she was "becoming aware of the garden and its seasons". She took advice and started with common plants that are easy to grow. The garden today, though not large, less than three acres (1.2 hectares), conceals many unexpected exotics. What

is this? It is a plant from Gethsemane on the Mount of Olives. And this? From Monet's garden at Giverny. And that Greek-style temple? Her husband, an architect, had found it abandoned, dismantled it and rebuilt it in their garden.

She wrote 17 books, some of them now classics. Lecture tours followed. Potential clients lined up. What did they want? Something like Barnsley House, they said. The gardener became the businesswoman. In "Making of a Garden" Mrs Verey wrote,

When I am invited to help with the planning of a garden I like first to walk slowly around the site, taking in where the warmest corners are likely to be, where the wind comes from, the view, the existing trees, the quality of the soil ... Then it is time to go into the house and look from all the windows ... I can build up a picture in my mind of the owners' preferences ... I sometimes imagine that this is where I myself will live, so it must be a place that I will enjoy, but all the time I bear in mind that it is my clients' garden, individually designed for them, to suit their needs and their way of life.

Not everyone admired the Verey style. Even in the calming world of gardening there is what might be called landscape politics. Minimalist gardens are seen by their practitioners as reflecting modern architecture and painting. They see the simplicity of Stonehenge as a more interesting English tradition than rose hedges. Warming to their theme, they claim that minimalism is right for a world of dwindling resources. You can symbolise the universe in a few square metres.

But "every garden", said Rosemary Verey, "should have a space where you can walk and sit and feel alone with nature, a quiet and shady place, with mown paths winding between ornamental trees and shrubs, and flowers studding the grass". Well, it you put it like that ... ∎

Elizabeth Vining

Elizabeth Gray Vining, Japan's royal tutor, died on November 27th 1999, aged 97

AFTER JAPAN was defeated, one of the problems facing the victors was what to do with its royal family. General Douglas MacArthur, who became virtual ruler of Japan, decided magnanimously not to put the emperor on trial for war crimes; in any case, he felt the most important royal was the emperor's elder son, Akihito. How was he to be brought up as future head of state of the new, democratised, American-style Japan? Enter Elizabeth Vining. In 1946, when Prince Akihito was 12, she became his tutor, teaching him English and something of American ways.

Mrs Vining said in a book of her experiences, *Windows for the Crown Prince*, that it was the emperor's own idea that an American teacher should be brought into the closed circle of the imperial court. Presumably she believed that. She believed most things she was told. But little happened in Japan during the American occupation without MacArthur's approval. His was the real government within the formal government. Indeed, Mrs Vining tells of interviews with the general, "a fine looking man with an old-fashioned courtesy", when he questioned her closely about young Akihito's progress.

She seemed to be genuinely surprised that she had been chosen for the job. Among the Americans and British in Japan after the war there were dozens of linguists with teaching experience. In the emperor's court itself there were officials with a good knowledge of English and who had travelled widely. Mrs Vining had no Japanese and had never previously visited Japan. She came from an old American family of Scottish descent. She had worked for a time as a teacher, and had written a number of books for children. She was a Christian, but, as a Quaker, a moderate one. Now, in her late 40s, she was a widow and childless. The headhunters sent from Japan decided that she was the perfect American schoolmarm for Prince Akihito.

A prince called Jimmy
When Elizabeth Vining first met the prince, her reaction was, "Poor little boy." Not for him the happy home life celebrated on cereal packets in America. The prince lived apart from his parents, visiting them once a week when they had dinner together. Mrs Vining saw him as a "small boy, round faced and solemn", but "lovable looking". The future emperor did not record what he thought when he first met Mrs Vining, but it is reasonable to speculate that, for different reasons, he did feel pretty solemn.

Here was this towering foreigner who knew not a word of his language and insisted on calling him Jimmy because she found his real name difficult to pronounce. However, the tall lady and the little boy seemed soon to have achieved a common purpose. Indeed, they had little choice: two quite different people thrown together by the extraordinary circumstances of the time, and having to make the best of it.

The prince proved to be easy to teach. He was bright, and had learnt a few English words before Mrs Vining arrived. By the time she left Japan four years later he was fluent in English and was picking up French and German as well. Mrs Vining acknowledged that there were times when she felt she was the student, acquiring bits of Japanese.

If she had a worry it was how the officials of the emperor's court regarded her. They were invariably polite, but what was going on behind their imperturbable features? They must, she thought, wonder just what she was doing "to their adored prince". A lot of people today, in Japan and abroad, also wonder what influence Elizabeth Vining had, in his formative years,

on the prince, who was to become emperor on his father's death in 1989. The answer may be that she had quite a lot. Mrs Vining promoted in the prince the unJapanese idea of individualism, of making up his own mind, rather than always turning to a court official for direction: "of daring to make mistakes". Even today in Japan, government policy tends to be made by officials, with politicians simply providing their public voice. The dictates of the royal household mean that Emperor Akihito keeps his counsel, but those who know him say that his liberal-minded views are probably ahead of those of most Japanese. He and his wife (a commoner whom he met playing tennis) brought up their three children as a close family. He has sought more from life than ceremony. He is an authority on ichthyology, the study of fishes, and

has published 25 papers on the subject. Much of his worldly outlook was no doubt shaped by visits to some 40 countries, repeatedly having to handle nagging demands to atone for his father's sins. But Mrs Vining sowed the seeds of his independent thinking. After she left Japan Akihito wrote to her from time to time, and he visited her at her home in Philadelphia. She was a guest at his wedding, the only foreigner to be invited.

The Japanese government decided to present Mrs Vining with a medal, the Order of the Sacred Crown, an award given only to women and with eight degrees of merit. It was explained that the first and second degrees were reserved for princesses. Would Mrs Vining be content with the third? "*Mottai nai*," ("It's too good") she said in her best Japanese. ■

Kurt Waldheim

Kurt Waldheim, a diplomat with a selective memory, died on June 14th 2007, aged 88

ONCE, IN more glorious times, the empire of Austria stretched from Prague and Cracow to Trent, below the Dolomites, and Ragusa on the Adriatic. Vienna drew the intelligentsia of Europe. Hungarian wheat fed the Austrians, and Bohemian coal kept their economy booming. Dozens of tribes and peoples clustered under the Habsburg wing, forming Europe's first and last buffer against the Turks.

This was the Austria Kurt Waldheim pined for. It was not the one he was born into. In 1918 Austria – often "she" in Mr Waldheim's writings, like an unfortunate princess in a fairy tale – was a "defeated, ruined, truncated remnant" of what she had been. The wheatfields and the coal mines had been forfeited. Moravia, South Styria and South Tyrol had been carved off too. Yet in 1919, "to add insult to injury", Austria was obliged to pay reparations to countries ravaged by the fighting. Mr Waldheim, a man of old-fashioned gallantry, could only uphold and defend her.

Her fate was his own. He was "always hungry" as a boy, staring hopelessly at the rare cakes and biscuits he could not have, as the country was hit by periodic famine. Austria was impoverished; his family, too, had lost all their savings when the crown was devalued. "In severe psychological shock" Austria had recurrent dreams of an alliance with Germany, sometimes the rescuing hero and sometimes the overbearing, jackbooted rapist. The young Kurt, too, flirted with Hitler's Reich; but somehow, like Austria, failed to recall the details.

In 1985, preparing to run for the presidency of Austria after a distinguished career as a diplomat and ten years as secretary-general of the United Nations, he produced an autobiography, "In the Eye of the Storm". "In the course of writing this book", his introduction ran, "I have come to appreciate the frailty of memory." Indeed. In 1938, after the *Anschluss* that absorbed Austria into Nazi Germany, he remembered his father being arrested by the Gestapo and himself, an intrepid member of the Austrian *Jungvolk*, distributing pamphlets urging citizens to resist and being "quite badly beaten up for it". Journalists and researchers, who began to investigate him in 1986, found him instead in an SA horse detachment, wearing the brown shirt unabashed.

He misremembered more. In 1941, forced into the Wehrmacht as all Austrians were unless they had money or connections, he went to the Russian front; his memory told him that his unit was full of dissenters, that he read anti-Nazi pamphlets under the blankets and that when he was wounded he returned, relieved, to his law studies in Vienna. Fact, confirmed by an international commission of historians in 1988, was that by April 1942 he was back in uniform in the Balkans and that within a year he was in Army Group E, commanded by a man so brutal that he was later executed for war crimes.

"A clerk and an interpreter" was Mr Waldheim's description of his job, when confronted; too lowly to notice the long lines of Jews, a quarter of the town's population, driven out of Salonika to the death camps, or to smell the corpses of

While secretary-general of the UN from 1972–82, a post in which he hoped to "evoke the conscience of mankind", his self-delusion went undetected. It was noticed that he showed uncommon deference to the powerful, preferring quiet diplomacy and studied neutrality, as Austria now did, to ruffling feathers; but in those years, with the world frozen into Soviet and American blocks and the UN turbulent and impotent, he had little choice. Only later, as his story began to surface under the persistent digging of *Profil* journalists and the World Jewish Congress, did it seem that he might have bowed and kissed hands just a little too much in life.

partisans strung up on makeshift gallows along the roads, or to hear – though they happened some hundred yards from his office – the summary executions of captured British commandos.

Deference and neutrality

He had not known, said Mr Waldheim. Or, if he had, to know was not a crime. Nor was it a crime to fail to defy orders, though some might wish he had. At the urging of the Austrian government, "moral guilt" was removed from the report on him. He did his duty. Like Austria, he dulled his conscience and lost his identity for the duration of the war. And after it he made himself a victim, travelling home from Vienna with his wife and baby daughter in a windowless cattle-car, "refugees", like thousands of his fellow-countrymen.

Many Austrians thought it did not matter. Defiantly, they voted for him as their president in 1986 – and saw him sit for six years in the Hofburg without a state invitation, as the world turned its back on him. Ostracisation shocked both the country and the man. It also forced an examination of conscience that has not ended yet.

Mr Waldheim's last will and testament regretted "Nazi crimes", but not his own behaviour. Moral ambiguity remained, and might even save him. "When death comes to you," he wrote, "all the distinctions in life disappear. Good and bad, dark and light, merits and mistakes, stand now in front of a judge who knows the truth. I can go there with trust, because I know His justice and His mercy." ∎

Wang Li

Wang Li, Mao's orator of violence, died on October 21st 1996, aged 75

ONE WAY to think of Wang Li is as a Goebbels of China. Mr Wang was a propagandist for Mao Zedong, serving him with the same fierce dedication that Goebbels gave to Hitler. He was a fiery and persuasive orator. In Beijing in August 1967 Mr Wang spoke to a group of Red Guards, an organisation of young communist toughs, urging them, in Mao's words, "to sweep away old things". The Red Guards, whose slogan was "Destruction before construction", set to work with a will. They first turned on the bureaucrats of China's foreign ministry, taking over the building and wrecking it. They then moved into Beijing's diplomatic district, terrifying foreign envoys. On August 22nd they set fire to a building in the British embassy compound.

This was in the early days of the cultural revolution, which had started in 1966 and was, by some calculations, to continue until 1969. The cultural revolution was reactionary rather than revolutionary and certainly not cultural. But it was an artful phrase that served to conceal Mao's struggle to regain absolute power after the failure of the "great leap forward" (1958-60), an ill-thought-out attempt to match the economies of rich countries quickly, which led to widespread famine.

The cultural revolution set back the Chinese economy, which had almost recovered from the "leap forward", but from Mao's point of view it was a success. His opponents who had sought to oust him were denounced as "capitalist roaders" and "representatives of the bourgeoisie" in *Red Flag*, a party newspaper of which Mr Wang was an editor. They were "Khrushchevs" – a reference to the Soviet leader easing his country from Stalinism. The head of state, Liu Shaoqi, was purged as "a lackey of imperialism" and died in prison. Deng Xiaoping, later to become China's paramount leader, was sent to work in a tractor factory. Many thousands of teachers, writers, scholars, doctors and other workers of the brain were beaten up, lost their jobs and, in some cases, were sent to China's gulag.

The master's voice

Wang Li was born into a middle-class family and joined the Communist Party in the 1930s, when its forces were fighting the Japanese. Mao seems to have taken to him and he rose rapidly through the ranks, handling various propaganda jobs with aplomb. Mr Wang was an enthusiast for continuing the class struggle that underpinned the cultural revolution. He said later that he had been blamed for Mao's excesses. But this is one of the penalties of being an enthusiastic acolyte of a monster. Chairman Mao, as he was affectionately known by some foreign visitors, would explain that Comrade Wang had been a bit over-keen, just as Hitler, before the second world war, would publicly chide Goebbels for his vitriol, and Stalin would distance himself from Beria, Russia's jailer. Mr Wang said that the speech which had set the Red Guards afire had been approved by Mao. No doubt it was, but speeches often get their life from the way they are delivered. The Red Guards, urged on by Mr Wang,

eyes, the involvement of the military commander suggested the re-emergence of warlordism, a nightmare for a new government trying to hold China together. The Red Guards eventually prevailed, with some outside military help and the persuasion of, among others, Mr Wang (who was briefly held by the Million Heroes and had an arm broken).

Mr Wang returned to Beijing the hero of the hour. Party leaders were at the airport to applaud his victory over the "counter-revolutionaries". A few weeks later Mr Wang was arrested. He remained in prison for the next 15 years. The party accused him of causing chaos

speaking for his master, were now on the rampage throughout China, spreading alarm in local communist fiefs, bullying, and sometimes killing, officials who did not knuckle under and confess to betraying the revolution.

In 1967 in Wuhan, a major industrial town on the Yangtze, the Red Guards had come up against real opposition. The Wuhan party, supported by the local military commander, was prepared to fight it out. A coalition of "conservatives" calling itself the Million Heroes faced a Red Guard troop supported by some factory workers and students. The Red Guard mob were outnumbered. In one street battle, fought mainly with pitchforks and axes, more than 100 people died. Worse, in Mao's

throughout China, which of course he had done: that had been his task. But Mao, frightened by what had happened in Wuhan, cooled towards the Red Guards, and apparently decided to get rid of their promoter.

Mr Wang was never formally accused of a crime. Mao died in 1976, Deng Xiaoping put China on the capitalist road and, in 1982, someone remembered that Mr Wang was still in prison and let him out. From his flat in Beijing Mr Wang sent more than 100 requests to the party seeking rehabilitation. It was never granted. The party prefers to forget the cultural revolution and Mao's other mistakes. But for such errors China would almost certainly now be richer than it is. ■

Lancelot Ware

Lancelot Lionel Ware, the founder of Mensa, died on August 15th 2000, aged 85

IN THE beginning, so it is said, members of Mensa saw themselves as people of superior wisdom, to whom governments would humbly turn for guidance. Lancelot Ware later denied this, and he was far too pleasant a man to be doubted. It would have been impolite to suggest, as some mischievously claimed, that no government showed any enthusiasm for Mensa's advice.

In any case, the origins of Mensa are obscure. The generally accepted version, in Victor Serebriakoff's history of Mensa, is that Mr Ware and Roland Berrill, an Australian, were strangers on a train, in a first-class carriage, when, in an unEnglish way, the Australian sought to make conversation. He asked if the publication Mr Ware was reading was *Hansard*, a report of proceedings in Parliament.

"Obviously," said Mr Ware. "You can see it from the title."

Not a promising first encounter, but by the end of the journey the two men, both lawyers, had formed a tentative interest in each other. They discussed cleverness. The Australian thought it could be measured by studying bumps in the head. Mr Ware was a fan of intelligence tests and offered to give his new companion a test. The Australian did brilliantly well and was immensely pleased; no one had said he was clever before. Would it not be a splendid idea to bring together an aristocracy of gifted people to attend to the problems of the world? It would indeed, the two men agreed. In 1946 Mensa was born with the aim of recruiting the 600 most intelligent people in Britain. They first thought of calling it Mens, Latin for mind, but this was thought to be too close to *Men Only*, a magazine that had photographs of nude women, albeit rather prim ones. They settled for the more prosaic Mensa, a table, explaining to the puzzled that the group was like a round table where no one had precedence.

Who was first?

The question of who actually founded Mensa was for years a matter of dispute. Roland Berrill had his supporters. He put up the money to start the group and wrote the first pamphlets, but he upset some members with his preoccupation with bumps, interest in the occult and passion for bright clothes. He left the group in 1950. Mr Ware's claim to have started the organisation was also challenged. Cyril Burt, an academic, believed that he was the first to propose a legion of the elite in a broadcast on the BBC some years earlier. Others point to the writings on heredity of Francis Galton, a Victorian, but these days they seem tinged with racism, and no one in Mensa would want to have anything to do with that.

In 1967, after some 20 years of mulling over the matter, Mensa declared that Mr Ware was indeed its founder, and had run a similar group back in 1938. There is a plaque on a house in Oxford, where Mr Ware once lived, informing passing Romans that he was *fons et origo Mensae*. Founder he might be, but in the 1950s Mr Ware also quit Mensa, apparently tired of arguments among the elite. Like Roland Berrill, he had other interests, among them real tennis, which predates the Wimbledon sort and, according to addicts, is its superior. He sought to prove that the plays attributed to Shakespeare were by other hands, and he collected what he described as "useful pieces of wood".

His law career was prospering – he specialised in "intellectual property", such as copyright – and he took an interest in politics at a local level. Nevertheless, in 1961 he was easily persuaded to rejoin Mensa. He had "an easy rapport" with people of high intelligence, he said. By then Mensa had outgrown its infant waywardness. Victor Serebriakoff, who took over from Mr Ware, turned a wobbly membership of about 100, rather than the hoped-for 600, into a national, then an international, organisation.

Mensa now has about 100,000 members, almost half of them in the United States. Admission is by intelligence test. One reproduced in Mr Serebriakoff's book would probably not tax any reader of The Economist. But being intelligent, if in fact any test can measure intelligence accurately, does not guarantee wisdom. Some of Mensa's critics scoff that it is not selective enough. Mr Ware said he was disappointed that so many members spent so much time solving puzzles. "It's a form of mental masturbation," he said. "Nothing comes of it." A Mensa gathering is "a place where eggheads get laid", said a probably jealous outsider. Mensa has had many rivals, but few have lasted. Some were simply potty, like the Cinque, which aimed to consist of the world's five brightest people. Mr Serebriakoff concedes that people in Mensa "bicker a lot", but "we shall survive".

Mensans, as they call themselves, take all jibes stoically. The American Mensans see themselves as a brotherhood and sisterhood who laugh and play and "cry on each other's shoulders". They display stickers on their car bumpers, proudly announcing their membership of Mensa. The British, as might be expected, tend to be more reticent. The pioneer members wore yellow buttons, but soon discarded the practice. You could never be sure, but some stranger might try to start up a conversation in a train. ■

Pierre Werner

Pierre Werner, father of the euro, died on June 24th 2002, aged 88

IN THE end Pierre Werner was mildly surprised that Europeans had meekly abandoned their proud currencies, the franc, mark, lira and so on, and accepted the euro. Perhaps, he suggested, they were weary of arguing. He felt a bit weary himself. He had first suggested a common currency for Europe back in 1960, but had to wait for 42 years before it was launched as real notes and coin six months ago.

Mr Werner is generally accepted as the father of the euro. The euro's paternity is probably shared among the pioneers of what eventually became the European Union. A common currency for Europe is hinted at in the Union's founding treaty signed in Rome in 1957. But Mr Werner became its most public advocate; more than that, a zealot. His European colleagues, who tended to be, in public at least, less zealotish, were content that a scheme they adopted in 1971 that eventually led to the euro should be called the Werner Plan. He would get the credit and, if things went wrong, he could also get the blame.

Neither credit nor blame appeared to matter to Mr Werner. What mattered was ending Europe's terrible tribal wars. Economic problems in Germany had led to the second world war, he said. Now economics would be the peacekeeper. In a speech in 1960 he argued for a common currency called the "euror", a name soon dropped, perhaps because it sounded like "error". But Mr Werner persisted, and in his 1971 plan proposed that the economies of European states should come under the control of a central authority in perpetuity. Wouldn't

national sovereignty be sacrificed? Of course, he said. That was the idea. A federal Europe? A logical development.

The simple logic of the Werner proposals has vexed European political leaders that have nationalistic voters. None of the 12 members of the Union that have adopted the euro appears to favour a federal state, certainly not France or Germany, the master-builders of European unity. Its prospect frightens many people in Britain from even contemplating joining the euro. Best then to belittle the Werner Plan. Much had happened since it was nodded through all that time ago. Pierre Werner was a good man, but with limited authority. Did you know he was prime minister of Luxembourg for 20 years? Yes, Luxembourg, an odd country in some ways.

How very European

As a fervent European Mr Werner could not have chosen to be born in a more suitable place. Luxembourg was ruled at various times by many other European countries, among them France, Spain, Austria and even the Netherlands. Sometimes the country was sold or given away: its handy size, only 84km (51 miles) by 52km, made it easy to package as a gift to seal an alliance. Germany ignored Luxembourg's pleas of neutrality and occupied it during both world wars.

Mr Werner was brought up bilingually. His father spoke French and his mother German. He set out to be a lawyer and took a law degree in Paris. Then economics took his fancy and at the outbreak of the second

were executed; all this shaped Mr Werner's view of how Europe had to be changed for the betterment of its people (including his five children).

He went into politics, and was elected to his country's parliament in 1945. He rose swiftly and served two long stints as prime minister. But Mr Werner outgrew Luxembourg. He became close to Jean Monnet and others who were creating the Common Market, the forebear of the Union. In his memoirs Mr Werner wrote, "To awake Europeans to the weakness and division of Europe became an intellectual obligation for me."

world war he was working for a bank in the Luxembourg capital, also called Luxembourg. With memories of the first world war still fresh, many people fled to safer places. Grand Duchess Charlotte, the head of the royal family, moved to Canada. Mr Werner, newly-wedded, stayed put with his bride.

The German occupation turned out to be worse than it had been in the first world war. Many Luxembourgers were conscripted into the German army. Jews were sent to extermination camps. In 1944 Luxembourg was the setting for one of the biggest battles of the second world war when allied forces were nearly surrounded, suffered huge casualties, and came close to defeat in what became known as the battle of the Bulge. The experience of war, the ravaged land, the humiliation of the people, the revenge that followed victory when German collaborators

In those heroic days, no one seemed to question that the central aim of European unity was to prevent war. Economic gain, though useful, was a secondary consideration. Later, Mr Werner noted sadly, economic gain seemed to have become all important for the Union's members and applicants. Luxembourg itself has become immensely rich, partly as a result of being a founder member of the Union. Britain's decision on whether to adopt the euro may turn on five economic tests.

But while Europeans no longer fought each other, many other tribes around the world still did. Mr Werner said there was a road to peace: gradual economic union leading to a single currency for the world. Mondo, he said, would be a suitable name. There may be quite a long wait. ■

General William Westmoreland

William Childs Westmoreland, soldier, died on July 18th 2005, aged 91

THOUGH MANY tried to dissuade him, in 1974 William Westmoreland (General, US army, retired) ran for the governorship of South Carolina. He lost, and was not surprised. "I'm used to a structured organisation", he confessed afterwards, "and this civilian process is so doggone nebulous."

That word, for him, summed up the frustrations of a general's life in a democracy. During his years in Vietnam, as commander of American forces from 1964 to 1968, he had been fighting not only a subtle, nimble enemy hidden in villages and jungle, but a miasma of criticism, hatred and political timidity at home. He was never his own master, but the servant of Lyndon Johnson and his civilian advisers. He could not even choose where to direct the bombing of North Vietnam, since, as he growled in his memoirs, "this or that target was not

to be hit for this or that nebulous non-military reason."

General Westmoreland himself was the reverse of nebulous: tall, well-eyebrowed, jut-chinned, and with an impressive scar on his left cheek from hurtling through a windscreen as a child. His creed was "Duty, Honour, Country", as drilled into every cadet at West Point. His approach to strategy was bluntly old-fashioned, not to say heavy-handed. The South Vietnamese army had to be structured as a conventional force, ready for large-scale military operations, even though it was fighting guerrillas. America needed to hit North Vietnam "surely, swiftly, and powerfully ... with sufficient force to hurt", as at Khe Sanh, where B-52s dropped more than 100,000 tonnes of bombs over two months. And troops needed to be poured in. General Westmoreland's tactics were simple:

take the war to the enemy, and kill him faster than he could be replaced. Where possible, apply overwhelming, stunning force. "A great country", he liked to say, quoting the Duke of Wellington, "cannot wage a little war."

On General Westmoreland's watch, the numbers of Americans in South Vietnam rose from 15,000 military "advisers" in 1964 to 500,000 troops by 1968, and he wanted more. The conflict, he believed, was winnable. A combination of flawed intelligence, book-cooking, random "body-counts" and wishful thinking led to chronic underestimates of the strength of the enemy. He could win the war, he told Johnson early in 1968, if he had 206,000 extra men and if the reserves were mobilised. At this suggestion, Johnson's advisers sharply drew in breath. If this was what was needed to reach "the light at the end of the tunnel", America could not do it. Within the year, General Westmoreland had been replaced, the bombing of the North moderated, and the scene set for talks.

He was blamed for losing the war, America's only defeat in its history. In his view, however, this "noble" conflict was lost only in the public mind and in the pages of the *New York Times*. True, in April 1975 helicopters had winched the last Americans from the rooftops of Saigon as the city fell to the Vietcong; but this, in General Westmoreland's view, was a defeat for the South Vietnamese. American troops had not been bested in any engagement of significance. Instead, in 1973 the politicians had made them stop fighting, like a boxer who, with his opponent on the ropes, suddenly and inexplicably throws in the towel. They would certainly have won, the general insisted, if they had been allowed to expand operations into Laos, Cambodia and the North, disrupting chains of supply and recruitment to the Vietcong.

But Johnson, fearing to stir up Russia or China, had never allowed it.

From horses to helicopters

The chaos and complexities of Vietnam were not what General Westmoreland had been trained for. On his graduation in 1936, as an artillery officer, the big guns he encountered were Model 1897 French 75s with steel-rimmed wooden wheels, drawn by horses. His great-uncle, who had fought for the Confederacy with many other ardent South Carolinians, would have recognised this style of warfare. General Westmoreland, however, came to shape modern ways of fighting, especially with his massive use of helicopter gunships to gain mobility in battle. These, flying in assault formation, became the motif of the Vietnam war.

In a less controversial conflict, General Westmoreland might have been given more credit. He took care of his men, to the point of parachuting first from aircraft in case the wind was dangerous. He believed in keeping up morale with copious medals and commendations (his commendation of Charlie Company, after its infamous torching and massacre of the village of My Lai, being an unfortunate mistake). But he was not forgiven for his rosy forecasts of how the war would go. He became army chief of staff, but was never promoted to the joint chiefs. As the war dragged on into the Nixon years, he was rarely sought for his advice.

Reporters sometimes asked what he thought of his "counterpart" on the North Vietnamese side, Vo Nguyen Giap. He bristled at that: not because he thought him a bad soldier or a bad man, but because Giap had been a powerful member of his government, and had been able to impose his wishes on the rest. Not so General Westmoreland, defeated by a cloud. ∎

Elsie Widdowson

Elsie May Widdowson, food scientist, died on June 14th 2000, aged 93

YOU CAN, if you have to, live on a very simple diet, Elsie Widdowson said, and said it often. She worked out that bread, cabbage and potatoes contained all the nutrients for healthy survival. For three months she and a number of her companions ate nothing else, and, to test their fitness following this bleak regime, went on a rigorous course of cycling and mountain climbing.

This was in 1940 when Britain feared that, as the war pressed on and its food ships were torpedoed, it would not be able to feed its people adequately. Miss Widdowson showed that it could, using the humble produce plentifully at hand. If you could come by the occasional egg, fruit and piece of meat, lucky you, but her basic diet would keep you healthy.

The government gratefully adopted her diet and took credit for its success. She was one of Britain's bits of wartime luck, like having academics and other brainy people who found ways of breaking the enemy's military codes. As the codebreakers were, she was driven by Britain's desperate necessity to survive. The Germans ate well for most of the war, drawing on the resources of the countries they had conquered. The United States had little shortage of food.

The British remained lean for several years after the war but, as happened in the rest of the rich world, their tummies surrendered to the temptations of the supermarket. Miss Widdowson had a respectful following in the United States, where she occasionally lectured, but never claimed any practical influence on the half of the American population that is overweight. Nevertheless, she lived to see her diet praised by nutritionists as just about the healthiest Britain has known. Children especially used to eat more bread and vegetables than they do now, while most families could not afford the sugary soft drinks popular today. Miss Widdowson shared Jonathan Swift's observation that bread was the staff of life. The army once called her in, worried that young soldiers were not putting on weight. Were they getting enough red meat? Meat was not the problem, Miss Widdowson said. The soldiers were not eating enough bread, preferring cakes instead.

A meeting in the kitchen

There were two sisters, Elsie and Eva, born in south London. Both became scientists. Eva Crane, the younger sister, is a world authority or bees. Everyone who keeps a hive knows her name. But it was diet that fascinated sister Elsie, and in 1933 her researches took her to the kitchen of St Bartholomew's, a London hospital, where a young doctor, Robert McCance, was checking on the cooking. For the next 60 years, until McCance died in 1993, they worked together on food research. Anything said about Elsie Widdowson's work inevitably touches on McCance's. They were one of the great partnerships of modern science. Their book *The Composition of Foods*, first published in 1940, and regularly updated as new foods come on the market, remains a key reference work for nutritionists. Here is item number 18 in the tables: bread, white, large loaf, with its values in protein, fat, calories and chemicals, which so impressed the Widdowson-McCance couple in their quest for a reliable basic diet.

The tables were again thumbed through when the couple advised on what food could be tolerated by the victims of the war as they were nursed to health: the starving survivors of German concentration camps; the malnourished populations of the occupied countries; and German children, many of them orphans, in a now destitute country.

Miss Widdowson was made a Companion of Honour, a rare British accolade, as well as receiving numerous scientific awards. She lived most of her working life in Cambridge. At her cottage on the river Cam she grew fruit and vegetables and had cats for company, and bees provided by her sister. The laboratories of the Medical Research Council and other research organisations were her base. One is named after her. And she could study the composition of the human body in the pathology unit at Cambridge's Addenbrooke's Hospital. Miss Widdowson and her partner would sometimes experiment on themselves to judge the effect of certain substances in the body. Miss Widdowson injected herself with solutions of calcium, magnesium and iron and prepared a paper on their effects. They tackled the wartime problem of rickety children, caused by a shortage of calcium in the diet, by getting bakers to mix chalk with the flour.

Miss Widdowson sought simple solutions; and aimed for clarity in her scientific writing. She said her ideal communicator was Alistair Cooke, a broadcaster famous in Britain for his weekly "Letter from America", and still delivering his elegant prose at the age of 93. Like him, she never thought of retiring. A few years ago she was in Labrador, scrabbling about on the ice floes to study the eating habits of seals. Reporters inevitably asked her for the secret of her long and energetic life. Was it to do with diet? She said she had simply inherited good genes from her parents. Her father had lived to 96 and her mother to 107. As for her diet, she ate butter and eggs, which some said were bad for you. And bread, of course. ∎

Markus Wolf

Markus Wolf, East German spymaster, died on November 9th 2006, aged 83

FASCINATING TO his fans, odious to his enemies, Markus Wolf embodied the dilemmas and complexities of the cold war in Europe. Seen one way, he was something of a hero: not just a professional but also a patriot and an idealist. Even his ardent communism could be excused: had not his Jewish family found refuge from the Nazis in the Soviet Union? Revealed after the collapse of communism as cultivated, charming, an accomplished cook and, to some, a heart-throb, he was utterly unlike most Soviet-block spymasters – crumpled, podgy men with thick glasses and steel teeth.

There was a whiff of glamour in the way that Mr Wolf's spies outwitted their bumbling West German rivals. As head, for 34 years, of the foreign-intelligence arm of the Stasi, East Germany's Ministry of State Security, he planted agents and recruited informers all over West Germany. Some found their way into the very departments charged with defending democracy, others into the highest reaches of the state, even the chancellery. For those who believed the West to be shamefully materialist or unduly forgiving of the Nazi past, it was tempting to admire the guile of one who so often humiliated it.

"The man without a face", he was called. His identity was so well concealed that his Western counterparts are supposed to have secured a photograph of him only in 1978. In fact, the CIA had identified him as early as 1959, from photographs taken when he had attended the Nuremberg war-crimes trials as a young radio reporter. Still, many thought he must be the model for the elusive Karla, the fictional Soviet spymaster who ran rings round his Western adversaries in the works of John le Carré, a British novelist steeped in the world of espionage. (Mr le Carré says he was not.)

Mr Wolf was, if anything, even more glamorous in defeat. Spurning American offers of a deal if he would tell all, he sought political asylum in Russia. When that was denied, he returned, and eloquently defended himself against charges of treason. "Victors' justice", he called his trials; like Western spies, he was doing a dirty but necessary job, and his sins were "those of every other intelligence agency".

The brutal reality

Yet there was nothing glamorous about the communist German state of 1949–89. Mr Wolf claimed that his subtle spycraft was a world away from the regrettable mistakes made by his Stasi colleagues in charge of internal repression and fostering terrorism abroad. After retiring – for mysterious reasons – from the Stasi in 1986, he published a book, "Troika", which criticised Stalinism. Later he said he hoped that Mikhail Gorbachev's reforms would save a system nobly based on the "combination of socialism and freedom".

He did admit that East Germany had proved a "sad reality", but in truth it was far worse than that. The regime he served was a squalid dictatorship that jailed those who challenged it and shot those who tried to escape. Its secret police exploited the smallest weakness of anyone who might be useful or threatening. Husbands were coerced into spying on their wives, parents on their children. Mr Wolf's spies played a full part in a huge security system modelled closely on the Soviet Union's, and using identical tricks.

Though cleared, on appeal, of his 1993 conviction for treason, Mr Wolf was given a two-year suspended sentence in 1997 for his part in the abduction and torture of a German woman who had worked for the Americans in West Berlin. Those may be the methods of the war on terror now, but they were not part of the West's arsenal then, in a struggle won mainly by the potency of ideas, not by force or fear.

Mr Wolf said his most successful tactic was the use of sex: his "Romeo" agents seduced and suborned the lonely spinster secretaries of West German officialdom. The practice worked brilliantly, if you were prepared to overlook the attendant tragedies, such as the death of the hapless Leonore Heinz, who killed herself when she found that her husband had married her not for love but to steal secrets from the foreign ministry, where she worked.

It was all clever stuff, but Mr Wolf's chief target was an easy one. Every East German had the right to West German citizenship. That made it simple to plant sleepers, such as Günter Guillaume, an agent sent to West Germany in 1956, who ended up as a senior aide to the chancellor, Willy Brandt. He produced startling news – not just of Brandt's womanising, but also, paradoxically, that the Social Democratic chancellor genuinely accepted the post-war division of Europe, including the sovereignty of East Germany.

That may have usefully calmed Soviet nerves. But the East Germans' carelessness was their star's downfall: they sent him a coded message congratulating him on the birth of his son. When that was cracked, he was caught. Brandt resigned, and his policy of detente with the East – *Ostpolitik* – stalled. Mr Wolf admitted that this had been a blunder. Like other people, he said, he sometimes felt remorse.

Maybe he did. Other communists, though, were much quicker to see not just the practical failures but the bankruptcy of the entire creed. Mr Wolf's mild penitence fell far short of convincing contrition. ∎

Joseph Wolfson

Joseph Wolfson, master of the surf, died on February 21st 2000, aged 50

WILL JOSEPH Wolfson become an American icon, in the manner of James Dean or Buddy Holly? His age could be against him. Dean was 24 when his brief screen career (starring in three films) was snuffed out in a car accident. Holly was 22 when he and other members of his pop group were killed when their small aircraft crashed. Youth, sudden death and unfulfilled talent are the reliable ingredients of legend. Mr Wolfson was 50, not old by today's standards, but not young. All the same, as a surfing star, he was a product of America's leisure industry, which has youth as its main customer. The kids who tried to mimic Dean's cool looks and sang Holly's songs longed to master the big waves as Joe Wolfson did. "Here's a responsible adult who wants to remain a kid," he said.

He was a New Yorker whose family moved to California when he was a child. He never gave up playing on the beach. He was happy to call himself a beach bum, which, far from being a term of derision among the cognoscenti, identified him with the culture of the Californian seashore, where life is an endless sunny afternoon. "He lives by the beach and is ruled by the beach," a friend said. Still, even beach bums need to make a living. After leaving university Mr Wolfson worked for most of his life for Carson City (motto, "Future unlimited"), a few miles south of Los Angeles, managing recreational activities. Running surfing classes was one of his jobs. Surfboards endorsed by him sold well.

Surfing is not just walking on the water, he said. Like the movies and music, it has its own literature. Surfers have adopted Byron (died aged 36), who never knew the thrill of the board but seems to have had an uncanny feeling for the sport: "Once more upon the waters! yet once more! / And the waves bound beneath me as a steed / That knows his rider."

The big spin

Joe Wolfson's steed was a board known as a bodyboard, about four feet long, rather than the longer and heavier traditional Hawaiian type. Bodyboards, filled with plastic foam, were originally designed for children, and you can see them at seasides everywhere. The story goes that Mr Wolfson was lent one in the early 1970s and was hooked, and turned bodyboarding into an activity for grown-ups. It is now a worldwide sport, with its own magazines, clubs and language. They still look like slabs of plastic, but a custom-built board can cost a lot of dollars. Mr Wolfson's most famous skill was to spin full circle up to half a dozen times as he came in on a big wave, a manoeuvre logically known as a 360. No one, it seems, had done this before. It is most easily carried out lying flat on the board. Mr Wolfson made the manoeuvre more difficult by doing it sitting up. He won numerous contests in surfing centres around the Pacific. To his admirers he was Doctor 360. He liked the title and made it his car registration.

In 1998 Joseph Wolfson learnt that he had cancer. He seemed an unlikely victim. He did not smoke or drink. He was so fit that he could spend up to ten

hours in the water without feeling ill effects. Still, a scan revealed a tumour, and it was inoperable. Mr Wolfson made careful preparations to end his life before it was taken from him. He drew out about $100,000 from his savings and distributed it to friends in need.

One sum went to pay for a colleague's eye surgery, and another to help out with a nephew's university education. Gradually he gave away his possessions, including his car. In November 1998 he wrote a farewell note – "I've had a great life, and it's time to say goodbye" – with a cheque for $5,000 for a party. He swallowed some sleeping tablets, put on his wetsuit and entered the sea at Manhattan Beach, not far from his home.

He paddled out on his board to a buoy about 150 yards offshore, far enough to be in deep water, but not so far that he could be taken by a shark. He tied up to the buoy and went to sleep, believing that he would not wake up. However, about six hours later a lifeguard on the shore saw something bobbing in the water and went out to

investigate. Mr Wolfson, now comatose and probably close to death, was given a kiss of life and recovered. His story was given much attention by newspapers and television. A movie was talked of, provisionally entitled *Full Circle*.

From being famous in the specialised world of surfing, and a local hero with his picture in Uncle Bill's Pancake House, Joe Wolfson became a national celebrity. In the 15 months that remained of his life before he died in a car crash last week he was frequently asked in interviews about suicide and he tended to oblige with the conventional answer that suicide was bad.

Among the letters he had received, many were from young people he had taught to surf. "If you can ride a 20ft wave, you can ride this," one wrote. Mr Wolfson said that his wish to end his life was "the worst message in the world I could send them". But no one knows what was going through his mind when his car unaccountably left the road and crashed into a eucalyptus tree. Byron's line, perhaps, "And I have loved thee, ocean." ∎

Shoichi Yokoi

Shoichi Yokoi, a Japanese survivor, died on September 22nd 1997, aged 82

THE HIDING place on the Pacific island of Guam where Shoichi Yokoi lived for nearly 27 years was destroyed by a typhoon. Never mind, the replica that has replaced it looks just as inhospitable to the many Japanese who come to marvel how their compatriot survived. Only in January 1972, when he was 56, did Sergeant Yokoi of the Japanese Imperial Army abandon his jungle life after being spotted fishing by two local people, and, as he said, after being urged by the spirits of his dead comrades to come out of hiding.

He was taken to hospital, where the doctors wanted to x-ray him. Unfamiliar with modern medical equipment, he told them, "If you want to kill me, kill me quickly." The doctors calmed the living fossil who had adapted to the jungle, living on fruit and nuts, with fish and the odd rat or frog for protein. When his army uniform rotted away, Mr Yokoi dressed in clothes that he had woven from tree bark. It was helpful that he had been a tailor in civilian life.

He returned to Japan, 31 years after he had left, to a flag-waving welcome, but he was a reluctant hero. "I have

a gun from the emperor and I have brought it back," he said. He apologised that he could not fulfil his duties. "I am ashamed that I have come home alive."

His was the guilt of the survivor. Of the 22,000 Japanese soldiers defending Guam, some 19,000 were killed when the Americans regained the island in 1944, and 2,000 survivors fled to the jungle. Most gave up when Japan surrendered in 1945, but Mr Yokoi and a few others did not, apparently unaware that the war had ended. His two remaining colleagues died in 1964, leaving Mr Yokoi on his own for another eight years.

An oddity of history
While admiring Shoichi Yokoi's resourcefulness as a Japanese Robinson Crusoe, the post-war generations have not shown much sympathy for his grief that, by eventually returning, he had let down the army and Emperor Hirohito. Among older Japanese there may be nostalgia for the imperial days, but to most modern Japanese emperor worship is an historical oddity: fewer than half of the Japanese polled cared a cent about the ascension of Akihito, Hirohito's son, to the chrysanthemum throne in 1990 after his father's death. But to the likes of Mr Yokoi, doing the bidding of the emperor, a descendant of the Sun Goddess, was a religious duty relayed by his more worldly army superiors. As Muslims pray facing towards Mecca, so Japanese schoolchildren at that time turned towards Tokyo in morning assembly. These were the days of the kamikaze pilots who were prepared to crash into oblivion, because that was the emperor's command. In Saipan, families hurled themselves over a cliff shouting loyalty to the emperor, rather than be captured by the advancing Americans. (So-called Banzai Cliff is another place that draws astonished Japanese tourists.) Only after the war, at the behest of the Americans, who thought that emperor worship contributed to the Japanese view of themselves as superior to other races, did Hirohito renounce divinity in his "Declaration of Humanity".

Although Mr Yokoi was the most famous of the old warriors to return from the jungle, there were others who refused to believe that Japan could have been defeated. Two years after Mr Yokoi returned, Hiroo Onoda, a lieutenant, was discovered in the Philippines with two other Japanese soldiers. His rifle (unlike Mr Yokoi's) still worked and he had potted a few locals over the years. The strength of his commitment to emperor and country was, if anything, even fiercer than Mr Yokoi's. Only when his former commander was flown to the Philippines was Mr Onoda persuaded to surrender.

Mr Yokoi adapted to the hustle of modern Japan remarkably quickly. Nine months after returning he was married. He became a pacifist, wrote the first of his two books and became a television commentator on survival tactics. He even stood for election to Japan's upper house of parliament in 1974.

Yet he was unhappy with many aspects of Japan. The country was experiencing heady economic growth. What had happened to its old qualities of elegance, harmony and simplicity? "Golf courses should be turned into bean fields," wrote Mr Yokoi. The Japanese people should live simply, frugally and without waste. Mr Yokoi was, according to the slogan of his election campaign, an "endurable-life critic". His view of life contained much wartime puritanism: "Don't eat excessively. Don't wear too much. Don't be vain, use your brain." Evidently, Japanese voters preferred not to, and Mr Yokoi was not elected. Undeterred, he continued to preach the virtues of autarky.

In his later years, Mr Yokoi faded from public life. He took up pottery and calligraphy, grew organic vegetables and became ever more disenchanted with modern Japan. "I'm not happy with the present system of education, politics, religion, just about everything," he said. After several years of illness he died of a heart attack. And perhaps there was heartbreak, too, as he looked back fondly at his "natural" life in the jungle. ∎

Yasser Talal al-Zahrani

Yasser Talal al-Zahrani, a prisoner in Guantánamo, died on June 10th 2006, aged 21

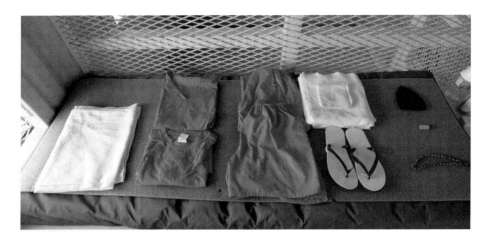

NOTHING MUCH distinguished Yasser Talal al-Zahrani from the 500 or so other prisoners held by the Americans at Guantánamo Bay, in Cuba. In his loose-fitting orange clothes and flip-flops, he spent the long days sitting or lying in his wire-mesh cell. He washed with water from one bucket, made water in another.

Five times a day, when the call to prayer came over the camp PA system (sometimes overlaid, or garbled, with announcements in English), he would spread a towel on the cement floor and pray. At least it was not hard to determine Mecca's direction. The sun blazed in through the mesh and baked the roof of corrugated iron. If he left his cage to be escorted, in leg shackles, to interrogation or the hospital, humidity quickly soaked his shirts with sweat.

In his letters home, Mr Zahrani told his father he was behaving well and had memorised the whole Koran. Guantánamo's guards, however, said he was troublesome, surly and a rule-breaker. Unlike some other prisoners, he was angry rather than depressed. He did not have a lawyer, indeed refused to have one. If there were points to be made about conditions and legalities, he would make them himself.

He was young, having come to the camp at 17. Whether he was innocent was a different question. Though born in Saudi Arabia, at 16 he was in Afghanistan: working for charities, his family said, or running guns for the Taliban, according to the Americans. After his capture, in Pakistan in 2002, he got involved in a prison riot in which a CIA agent was killed. As a dangerous element, he was flown to Guantánamo and kept there.

Like all but a handful of the detainees, he was not charged with anything. He was not, therefore, a proven criminal. But nor was he a prisoner-of-war. The conflict he had fought in had not been between states, but part of the amorphous war on terror that America had been prosecuting, against brutal but shadowy jihadist networks, since the attacks of September 11th 2001. Mr Zahrani himself had never been a soldier, wearing insignia or a uniform and carrying weapons openly; the label "unlawful enemy combatant" therefore seemed right, in American eyes. It also seemed right to them that neither the Geneva Conventions nor the usual American rules of legal process should apply to him. He was to be confined without charge indefinitely; for, if released, it was clear that he would try to kill more Americans.

Mr Zahrani's ways of getting attention were fairly limited. One was to go on hunger strike. When the plastic pouch of breakfast came round – a pastry, cream cheese, an orange – he would refuse to open it. When lunch came – cereal bars, peanuts – he would push that aside, too. Once the guards realised he was on hunger strike, they would make him sign a waiver form to show he was aware that he might die. But Mr Zahrani apparently had no interest in dying, just in being a nuisance.

Means of martyrdom

He was not alone. A hunger strike last September involved more than 100 prisoners. Most of them, like him, went back to eating fairly quickly, rather than be strapped in restraint chairs and force-fed – the usual practice in American prisons – with liquid supplements or Gatorade through tubes inserted in their noses.

Others were more determined. Mr Zahrani was in touch with Ali Abdullah Ahmed, said to be a mid- to high-level operative for al-Qaeda, who had been force-fed after eight months on hunger strike. Together with another Saudi prisoner, Mani Shaman Turki al-Habardi al-Utaybi, allegedly a member of a jihadist recruiting group, they began to consider a different way of drawing attention to the cause.

That way was suicide – forbidden under Islam, but reinterpreted, by bombers and others, as a glorious act of martyrdom. Since Guantánamo had opened, in January 2002, there had been 41 suicide attempts, most of them, according to the military authorities, "manipulative, self-injurious behaviour". In mid-May, Mr Zahrani would have heard of the "suicide attempt" that had been used to lure guards to a cell where, as they slipped on a floor slicked with excrement and soap, they were set upon by prisoners.

He himself, according to his family, was not the least suicidal. He did not wish to die, but to make a statement. Not just ideology lay behind it: a myth had taken hold in Guantánamo that if three prisoners killed themselves, they would all be released. Yet suicide was tricky. Mr Zahrani was not on medication, so he could not hoard pills for an overdose, as some others did. He was not in a cell – as in Camp 5, the new highest-security wing – where fans and electrical fittings could be fashioned into blades. But he had sheets and clothes from which, thread by thread, he could make a rope.

Since his cell could be easily seen into, discretion was essential. On June 10th, near midnight, he made his bed to look as if he was in it, wrote a suicide note, pushed a wad of cloth into his mouth, then hanged himself among the laundry drying from the ceiling. His colleagues did the same.

As he had hoped, his death led voices around the world to demand that the camp be closed. One senior American official, immovable, called his suicide "a good PR move". She may have been right; Guantánamo, alas, remains wrong. ■

Picture credits

Red Adair, Popperfoto/Getty Images; Alex the African Grey, Gerald Davies/Rex Features; Momofuku Ando, Getty Images; Brooke Astor, Sipa Press/Rex Features; Leona Helmsley, Time & Life Pictures/Getty Images; Oscar Auerbach, © CORBIS; Digby Baltzell, PA Photos; Sirimavo Bandaranaike, © CORBIS; Christiaan Barnard, PA Photos; Doak Barnett, John Hopkins University Paul H. Nitze School of Advanced International Studies; Syd Barrett, Getty Images; Jean Baudrillard, © Sophie Bassouls/Sygma/Corbis; Saul Bellow, © CORBIS; Ingmar Bergman, PA Photos; Bip, Sipa Press/Rex Features; Vere Bird, Willia Aylene/AP/PA Photos; Jean Bedel Bokassa, © CORBIS SYGMA; Joseph Bonanno, PA Photos; Habib Bourguiba, © Hulton-Deutsch Collection/CORBIS; Donald Bradman, Getty Images; Rosemary Brown, Topfoto; John Cairncross, Sipa Press/Rex Features; Jeanne Calment, © Jean-Paul Pelissier/Reuters; Alec Campbell, © Newspix/News Ltd; Marcel Carne, Ginies Michel/Rex Features; Barbara Cartland, Patrick McGuinness/Rex; Bonnie Cashin, © CORBIS; Charles Causley, © Mark Gerson/National Portrait Gallery, London; Regine Cavagnoud, Reuters; Eddie Chapman, Barratts/PA Photos; Eugenia Charles, © Della Zuana Pascal/CORBIS SYGMA; Ray Charles, Leon Morris/Redferns; Julia Child, Jon Chase/AP/PA Photos; Ion Cioaba, © CORBIS; Christopher Cockerell, Getty Images; The Columbia Seven, PA Photos; Charles Conrad, © Bettmann/CORBIS; Alistair Cooke, PA Photos; Maurice Couve de Murville, Getty Images; George Dawson, Lm Otero/AP/PA Photos; Magda Denes, Courtesy of Gregory Radomsili; Jacques Derrida, hannah@opale; The Duke of Devonshire, John Giles/PA Archive/PA Photos; Diana, Princess of Wales, Tim Graham/Getty Images; Manuel Elizalde, © CORBIS; Juan Fangio, © CORBIS; Joey Faye, AP/PA Photos; Thomas Ferebee, Courtesy of NC Museum of History; Ibrahim Ferrer, AFP/Getty Images; Virginia Fiennes, Bryn Campbell/The Observer; Bobby Fischer, Getty Images; Paul Foot, The Guardian; Gerald Ford, PA Photos; Janet Frame, Jerry Bauer photograph, Pegasus Press Collection, Canterbury Museum; Betty Friedan, Getty Images; Imre Friedmann, Dale T Andersen; Takeo Fukuda, © Bettmann/CORBIS; John Kenneth Galbraith, © Barnabas Bosshart/CORBIS; Allen Ginsberg, Getty Images; Francioise Giroud, © CORBIS; Paolo Gucci, © CORBIS; Thom Gunn, © Marc Geller; Kenneth Hale, © J D Sloan; Lionel Hampton, David Redfern/Redferns; Pamela Harriman, Barry Thumma/AP/PA Photos; George Harrison, David Magnus/Rex Features; John Harsanyi, © Blake Sell/Reuters; Sir Joshua Hassan, PA Photos; Edward Heath, © Dan Chung/Reuters; Freddy Heineken, © Amet Jean Pierre/CORBIS SYGMA; Ernest Hendon, Andy Hails/AP/PA Photos; Maria Julia Hernandez, AFP/Getty Images; Charlton Heston, Paramount/The Kobal Collection; Thor Heyerdahl, ©The Kon-Tiki Museum www.kon-tiki.no; Albert Hoffmann, Siggi Bucher/Reuters; Bob Hope, Used with permission from Stars and Stripes. © 1972, 2008 Stars and Stripes; Ulrich Inderbinen, © Bettmann/CORBIS; Steve Irwin, Getty Images; Junius Jayewardene, Getty Images; Roy Jenkins, © CORBIS; Elroy Jeppesen, Courtesy of Jeppesen Corporate Communications; John Paul II, AFP/Getty Images; Lady Bird Johnson, © Bettmann/CORBIS; Yousuf Karsh, Getty Images; Genichi Kawakami, Courtesy of Yamaha Corporation, Tokyo; Noel Keane, Howard Kaplan/AP/PA Photos; Karl Kehrle,

Sipa Press/Rex Features; Stanley Kubrick, SNAP/Rex Features; Konrad Kujau, Norbert Foersterling/AP/PA Photos; Stanley Kunitz, Getty Images; Akira Kurosawa, AFP/Getty Images; Freddie Laker, Getty Images; Alice Lakwena, AFP/Getty Images; Hedy Lamarr, PA Photos; Morris Lapidus, Getty Images; Alan de Lastic, Saurabh Das/AP/PA Photos; Estee Lauder, © CORBIS; Frank Launder, Getty Images; Laurie Lee, Getty Images; James Lees-Milne, © Theo Richmond; Roy Lichtenstein, Getty Images; Walter Lini, © CORBIS; Joan Littlewood, Jane Bown/The Observer; Christopher Lloyd, JonathanBuckley.com; Bernard Loiseau, © Rougemont Maurice/CORBIS SYGMA; Cardinal Lustiger, AFP/Getty Images; Majarishi Mahesh Yogi, Ferdinando Scianna/Magnum Photos; Norman Mailer, Mickey Brennan, Scope Features; Tommy Makem, Janet Knott/LANDOV/PA Photos; Michael Manley, Peter Marlow/Magnum Photos; Esther Manz, Getty Images; Stanley Marcus, Getty Images; Princess Margaret, Rex Features; Marie-Jose, © Hulton-Deutsch Collection/CORBIS; Albert Marshall, Rebecca Naden/PA Archive/PA Photos; Benito Martinez, AFP/Getty Images; Eugene McCarthy, Getty Images; Malcolm McLean, Getty Images; George Melly, Nigel R. Barklie/Rex Features; Erich Mielke, Elke Bruhn-Hoffmann/AP/PA Photos; Arthur Miller, Inge Morath © The Inge Morath Foundation/Magnum Photos; Theodore Monod, © Reuters/CORBIS; Akio Morita, © Bettmann/CORBIS; Kathryn Murray, Popperfoto/Getty Images; Kiharu Nakamura, Getty Images; Eric Newby, Victor Watts/Rex Features; Stavros Niarchos, Rex Features; Duke of Norfolk, Getty Images; Patrick O'Brian, Marine Pics Ltd/Rex Features; Sir Mark Oliphant, Getty Images; Harry Oppenheimer, AFP/Getty Images; Henri d'Orleans, © CORBIS; Maureen O'Sullivan, PA Photos; David Packard, Getty Images; Kerry Packer, Getty Images; Maurice Papon, © Gyori Antoine/CORBIS SYGMA; Rosa Parks, Everett Collection/Rex Features; Luciano Pavarotti, PA Photos; John Peel, Andrew Buurman/Redferns; Alejo Peralta, Reuters; Max Perutz, Gert Eggenberger/AP/PA Photos; Pham Van Dong, Getty Images; Abbe Pierre, Getty Images; Gene Pitney, Getty Images; George Plimpton, Getty Images; Anna Politkovskaya, Gueorgui Pinkhassov/Magnum Photos; Lazare Ponticelli, Francois Mori/AP/PA Photos; Anthony Powell, Jonathan Player/Rex Features; Kukrit Pramoj, Universal/The Kobal Collection; Rama Rao, Getty Images; Allen Read, Coumbia University Archives; Robert Rich, Rich Products Corporation; Bobby Riggs, © Bettmann/CORBIS; Amalia Rodrigues, Armando Franca/AP/PA Photos; Andres Rodriguez, © CORBIS; Brother Roger, © John Schults/Reuters; Mstislav Rostropovich, Getty Images; Miriam Rothschild, Time & Life Pictures/Getty Images; Tiny Rowland, Getty Images; Herbert Simon, Mike Haritan/AP/PA Photos; Frank Sinatra, Getty Images; Anna Nicole Smith, Danny Moloshok/AP/PA Photos; Marie Smith, © Nathalie Forbes/CORBIS; Reg Smythe, PA Photos; Muriel Spark, Getty Images; Stephen Spender, © National Portrait Gallery, London; Dr Spock, © Bettmann/CORBIS; Chidambaram Subramaniam, The Hindu Photo Archives; Robert Taylor, The Scotsman; Graham Thomas, © NTPL; Hunter S Thompson, Getty Images; Leonard Tose, PA Photos; Gilbert Trigano, © CORBIS; Pierre Trudeau, © Reuters/CORBIS; Galina Ulanova, Raoul Fornezza/AP/PA Photos; Leo Valiani, ANSA/Alinari Archives-Florence; Cyrus Vance, © John Schults/Reuters; Veerappan, Sipa Press/Rex Features; Rosemary Verey, © Andrew Lawson; Elizabeth Vining, © Bettmann/CORBIS; Kurt Waldheim, Ronald Zak/AP/PA Photos; Lancelot Ware, British Mensa Ltd; Pierre Werner, Sipa Press/Rex Features; General William ;   Westmoreland, PA Photos; Elsie Widdowson, Medical Research Council, Cambridge; Markus Wolf, Getty Images; Joseph Wolfson, Ricardo DeArantanha, © 1999, Los Angeles Times. Reprinted with permission; Yasser Talal al-Zahrani, Getty Images